FINANCING SOCIAL SECURITY

A Conference Sponsored by the
American Enterprise Institute for Public Policy Research

FINANCING SOCIAL SECURITY

Edited by Colin D. Campbell

American Enterprise Institute for Public Policy Research
Washington, D.C.

Library of Congress Cataloging in Publication Data

Main entry under title:
Financing social security.

(AEI symposia; 78H)
Papers presented at a conference sponsored by the
American Enterprise Institute for Public Policy Research,
held in Washington, D.C., Oct. 27 and 28, 1977.
1. Social security—United States—Finance—
Congresses.   I. Campbell, Colin Dearborn, 1917–
II. American Enterprise Institute for Public Policy
Research.   III. Series: American Enterprise Institute
for Public Policy Research.   AEI symposia; 78H.
HD7125.F56   338.4'3   78–21683
ISBN 0–8447–2140–9
ISBN 0–8447–2139–5 pbk.

AEI Symposia 78-H

Printed in the United States of America

MAJOR CONTRIBUTORS

Robert J. Barro
Professor, University of Rochester

Edwin F. Boynton
Actuary, The Wyatt Company

Edgar K. Browning
Professor, University of Virginia

James M. Buchanan
Professor, Virginia Polytechnic Institute and
State University, and Adjunct Scholar,
American Enterprise Institute

Colin D. Campbell
Professor, Dartmouth College, and Adjunct
Scholar, American Enterprise Institute

James B. Cardwell
Commissioner, Social Security Administration

Barry R. Chiswick
Professor, University of Illinois at Chicago Circle

Barber B. Conable, Jr.
U.S. Congressman, New York

Michael R. Darby
Professor, University of California, Los Angeles

Thomas C. Edwards
President, Teachers Insurance and Annuity
Association of America

Martin S. Feldstein
Professor, Harvard University, and President,
National Bureau of Economic Research

Alan N. Freiden
Economist, Social Security Administration

Lawrence H. Thompson
Office of the Secretary, Department of
Health, Education, and Welfare

Norman B. Ture
Norman B. Ture, Inc., and Adjunct
Scholar, American Enterprise Institute

Al Ullman
U.S. Congressman, Oregon

J. W. Van Gorkom
President, Trans Union Corporation

W. Allen Wallis
Chancellor, University of Rochester, and
Adjunct Scholar, American Enterprise Institute

CONTENTS

PART FIVE
THE FUTURE OF THE SOCIAL SECURITY SYSTEM

INTRODUCTION

Colin D. Campbell

A conference on financing social security, sponsored by the American Enterprise Institute for Public Policy Research, was held in Washington, D.C., on October 27 and 28, 1977. The eight papers presented, commentaries on the papers, selected portions of the discussion and questions from the floor, and a televised round table discussion held during the conference are included in this volume.

The conference was divided into four sessions. The first session, which I chaired, was on the topic "Indexing Social Security: What to Do?" The second session, "Indexing Social Security: Some Important Consequences," was chaired by C. Lowell Harriss. The third session, "The Future Financing of the Social Security System," was chaired by Thomas F. Johnson. The fourth session, chaired by Edwin B. Lancaster, was "Interaction of Social Security and Private Pensions."

Three important topics discussed at the conference were the current size of social security benefits, the nature of the alternative benefit formulas and indexing proposals, and the relative advantages and disadvantages of wage indexing as compared with price indexing.

The Size of Social Security Benefits

A major conclusion of several of the papers is that social security benefits have become very large. Alicia Munnell reports that the ratio of the average worker's social security benefit to his pre-retirement earnings (the replacement ratio) has risen from 30 percent in 1969 to 45 percent in 1977. If an average retired worker in 1977 had a wife aged sixty-five, his replacement ratio would be 67 percent. Martin Feldstein and Anthony Pellechio estimate that in 1972 future social security benefits of the average family were worth approximately $28,000, and that by 1978 this would have risen to more than $51,000 per family. Robert Kaplan calculates that the average young worker now entering the labor force will receive a real rate of return of 2 to 3 percent on the taxes he and his employer paid in if he lives to age seventy-eight or seventy-nine—the average life expectancy for someone who reaches age sixty-five. This is higher than the real rate of return that has been

1

earned in the past on tax-free municipal bonds and U.S. government securities. Dennis Logue reports that, among retired persons who have both social security and a private pension, the average social security benefit in 1975 ($1,700 a year in constant 1970 dollars) was larger than the average private pension benefit ($1,575 a year in 1970 dollars). Before the 1970s, the average private pension benefit adjusted for inflation was larger than the average social security benefit. No matter how one looks at it, social security benefits have become very large.

Munnell's data on replacement ratios are significant because they show that, for retired couples with earnings up to the average, social security alone now provides virtually all the income required to maintain the same standard of living that they had while working. Because of reduced work-related expenses, medicare, and lower taxes, retirees generally require only 65 to 80 percent of pre-retirement earnings to maintain the same living standard. Official statements almost always stress that the objective of the social security system is to provide no more than a floor of protection for retired individuals—to be supplemented by private pensions, insurance, and private savings.[1] Benefits have become so large that such statements no longer accurately describe the benefit policies of the system.

Munnell measures the adequacy of social security benefits by replacement ratios rather than by the average benefit received by retired workers. In the past, the most commonly used measure of the adequacy of social security benefits has been the data on average monthly benefits for retired workers—currently about $240 a month. Although these data are published monthly in the *Social Security Bulletin*, data on replacement ratios are not regularly available. When measured by the average monthly amount paid to retired workers, social security benefits seem to be low; when measured by replacement ratios, they appear to be high. In his paper, William Hsiao shows that, even when the adequacy of benefits is measured by the amount of the benefit, the initial benefits awarded in 1976 to retired persons exceeded the amount needed for a "modest standard of living" in all earnings categories except single persons with very low earnings ($3,790 a year). The initial benefits of single persons with low earnings were approximately the same as the amount needed for the federal government's "poverty threshhold" for the elderly.

Feldstein and Pellechio's estimates of social security wealth are

---

[1] See, for example, U.S. Congress, House of Representatives, *Reports of the Quadrennial Advisory Council on Social Security*, House Document no. 94-75, 94th Congress, 1st session, March 10, 1975, pp. 7–10; and statement by Congressman Al Ullman (Democrat, Oregon) in this volume, p. 327.

significant because they provide empirical support for Feldstein's view that the distribution of total wealth—including social security wealth—is different from the usual concept of the distribution of wealth. The value of the social security benefits that persons are entitled to is not only the most important asset of the vast majority of households, but it is also distributed very equally among households with high and low incomes. By excluding social security wealth, most studies of the distribution of wealth have exaggerated economic inequality.

The decline in the relative importance of private pensions, discussed by both Munnell and Logue, may have significant effects on saving and capital formation. While the funds accumulated by private pension systems are invested in capital, social security is financed on a pay-as-you-go basis. The empirical analysis by Munnell, which is based on data for 1930–1974, concludes that pension saving declines when anticipated social security benefits increase. This supports Logue's conclusion that the rapid rise in social security replacement ratios in the 1970s will sharply reduce the role of private pensions.

The data presented in the conference papers indicate that the amounts paid in social security benefits may have become excessive. Yet, as is explained in the papers by Hsiao and June O'Neill, before the 1977 amendments to the Social Security Act, the system had a long-run financing problem because of (1) a flaw in the way benefits were indexed to rise automatically with consumer prices, and (2) the decline in the birth rate that had its start about sixteen years ago. Although the flaw was corrected in the 1977 amendments, it is believed that eventually higher payroll taxes than those in the 1977 amendments will be necessary to offset the anticipated future decline in the number of workers per beneficiary. The future financing problems of the system could be solved by reducing benefits rather than by raising payroll taxes or resorting to financing from general revenues. Benefit levels that give many workers a higher standard of living after retirement than while they were working may not be worth the higher taxes necessary.

The Alternative Benefit Formulas and Indexing Proposals

The principal topic of the papers by Hsiao, Lawrence Thompson, Feldstein and Pellechio, Kaplan, and O'Neill is the nature of the benefit formula and the way the various types of indexing affect future replacement ratios. Three main types of indexing are discussed:

- The traditional method of adjusting benefits to inflation used prior to the 1977 amendments to the Social Security Act (in

3

technical terms, increasing the percentages allowed with no indexing of earnings histories or the formula wage brackets);

- The indexing method in the 1977 amendments (wage indexing of earnings histories and the formula wage brackets with no change in the percentages allowed); and

- The Hsiao indexing method (price indexing of earnings histories and the formula wage brackets with no change in percentages allowed).

These three types of indexing have different effects on future replacement ratios and, consequently, on the future financing needs of the social security system. The actuaries of the Social Security Administration have estimated that, if the current rate of inflation and the current rate of growth in real wages continue, the type of indexing used prior to the 1977 amendments would have caused replacement ratios to rise. According to Hsiao, the new system of indexing in the 1977 legislation will tend to cause replacement ratios to remain steady, whereas his indexing plan would cause replacement ratios to fall. The reasons why the alternative indexing systems have these different results have not been well understood.

Calculating Benefits

The procedure for calculating benefits is divided into two parts: first, the average monthly wage on which a worker's benefits are based is determined; and, second, the amount of benefits payable is calculated, based on a table of percentages that is applied to different portions of the worker's average monthly wage. Table 1 shows how a worker's average monthly wage was calculated before the 1977 amendments; it uses as examples men aged sixty-five who were entitled to the maximum monthly benefit. To receive the maximum monthly benefit, a worker must have had earnings equal to the maximum wage base throughout his averaging period. The averaging period is based on all years of covered employment from 1951 through the year prior to that in which a person attains age sixty-two, excluding the five years of lowest earnings. If a person continues to work past age sixty-two up to age sixty-five, these three years of earnings may be substituted for three earlier years of lower earnings.

As Table 1 shows, for a man retiring on January 1, 1976, the maximum possible average monthly wage was $586. For a man retiring on January 1, 1977, the maximum average monthly wage was $634. The increase to $634 was caused by substituting the new maximum

TABLE 1

CALCULATION OF AVERAGE MONTHLY WAGE OF MEN AGED SIXTY-FIVE
ENTITLED TO THE MAXIMUM MONTHLY BENEFIT, 1976–1978

(dollars)

Year or Period	Maximum Wage Base per Year	Covered Wages for Men Retiring in January		
		1976	1977	1978
1956–1958	4,200	8,400	4,200	—
1959–1965	4,800	33,600	33,600	33,600
1966–1967	6,600	13,200	13,200	13,200
1968–1971	7,800	31,200	31,200	31,200
1972	9,000	9,000	9,000	9,000
1973	10,800	10,800	10,800	10,800
1974	13,200	13,200	13,200	13,200
1975	14,100	14,100	14,100	14,100
1976	15,300	—	15,300	15,300
1977	16,500	—	—	16,500
Total covered wages		133,500	144,600	156,900
Total years covered		19	19	19
Average yearly wage		7,026	7,611	8,258
Average monthly wage		586	634	688

SOURCE: Social Security Administration, *Social Security Bulletin, Annual Statistical Supplement, 1975* (1977), pp. 7 and 32.

earnings base of $15,300 in 1976 for the low base of $4,200 in 1957. On January 1, 1978, the maximum average monthly wage rose to $688.

From 1976 to 1978, the total number of years covered for men was frozen at nineteen. This was done to eliminate the difference that previously existed in the averaging periods for men and women. Starting in 1979, the total number of years covered for men and women will increase by one each year until thirty-five years are covered.

The second step in calculating benefits prior to the 1977 amendments is shown in Table 2. The primary insurance amount (PIA) is the monthly benefit of a covered worker retiring at age sixty-five. This amount does not include benefits of a wife or other dependents. The table shows the percentage of the worker's average monthly wage payable in benefits and the wage brackets for each of the percentages. A single person with an average monthly wage of only $110 (the lowest wage bracket), for example, would receive a monthly social security

5

TABLE 2

Social Security Benefit Formula, Starting in July 1977

Percentage Allowed	Level of Average Monthly Wage (dollars)	Primary Insurance Amount (dollars)
145.90	First 110	160.49
53.06	Next 290	153.87
49.58	Next 150	74.37
58.30	Next 100	58.30
32.42	Next 38	12.32
	Total 688	459.35

Source: U.S. Congress, Senate, Committee on Finance, *Staff Data and Materials Relating to Social Security Financing*, 95th Congress, 1st session, June 1977, p. 5.

pension of $160, and a single person with an average monthly wage of $400 (the sum of the two lowest brackets) would receive a monthly pension of $314 (the sum of the two lowest primary insurance amounts). Because the maximum possible average monthly wage of a person retiring on January 1, 1978, was $688, the largest possible retirement benefit for a single person was $459 a month.

Table 3 shows the traditional indexing method that was used prior to the 1977 amendments to increase social security benefits. In 1972 and 1974, there were legislated increases in the percentages allowed. In 1975, 1976, and 1977, the percentages allowed were automatically increased in accordance with the 1972 amendments. In 1977, for example, because the consumer price index had increased 5.9 percent, the percentages allowed were increased by that amount.

The new indexing method in the 1977 legislation changes the calculation of the average monthly wage by indexing the annual wages on which the average is based. Each preceding year's wage is multiplied by the ratio of the average covered wages of all workers two years prior to that in which a worker reaches age sixty-two to average covered wages in the year the wage was earned. For example, if average covered wages doubled between 1967 and 1977, a worker's 1967 earnings of $7,000 would be multiplied by two, and the resulting $14,000 would be the amount included in the 1977 calculation of his average indexed monthly wage (AIMW). The earnings for each year of his working history (1951 and later) would be indexed in the same way. Indexed

TABLE 3

PERCENTAGE OF AVERAGE MONTHLY WAGE GIVEN IN
SOCIAL SECURITY BENEFITS, 1972–1977

Level of Average Monthly Wage	Percentage Allowed				
	1972	1974	1975	1976	1977
First $110	108.01	119.89	129.48	137.77	145.90
Next $290	39.29	43.61	47.10	50.10	53.06
Next $150	36.71	40.75	44.01	46.82	49.58
Next $100	43.15	47.90	51.73	55.05	58.30
Percent increase in benefits over preceding period	20	11	8	6.4	5.9

SOURCE: *Social Security Bulletin, Annual Statistical Supplement, 1975,* p. 19; Senate, Committee on Finance, *Staff Data and Materials Relating to Social Security Financing,* p. 5.

annual wages would then be averaged and converted to a monthly figure in the same way as unindexed wages formerly were.

Table 4 shows the new benefit formula in the 1977 amendments that replaces the benefit formula shown in Table 2. In Table 4, the percentages of the AIMW allowed are lower than the percentages of the average monthly wage in Table 2. In order to yield approximately the same level of benefits, lower percentages were necessary to offset the higher AIMWs.[2] Under this new method of calculating benefits, the future benefits of workers who are still employed will be increased in step with the rise in the average covered wages of all covered workers. Although a worker's AIMW will not change after he retires, his benefits will increase automatically in line with consumer prices, as under the 1972 amendments.

Under the new method of indexing benefits, the percentages in Table 4 will not be changed because of inflation, as they were previously (see Table 3). The formula wage brackets in Table 4 will be raised, however, as covered wages rise. If covered wages rise 10 percent, for example, the lowest bracket would be raised from $180 to $198, and the middle bracket would be raised from $905 to $996. The purpose of this adjustment is to keep rising levels of wages from pushing a higher

---

[2] For a person retiring at any time from 1979 through 1983, his starting benefit will be calculated with both the old and the new formulas, and he will be paid the higher of the two amounts.

TABLE 4

New Social Security Benefit Formula, 1977 Amendments

Percentage Allowed	Level of Average Indexed Monthly Wage (dollars)	Primary Insurance Amount (dollars)
90	First 180	162.00
32	Next 905	289.60
15	Remainder above 1,085	

Source: P.L. no. 95-216, 91 Stat. 1514–1515 (December 20, 1977).

proportion of earnings up into the higher brackets, in which the percentage allowed is smaller.

The Hsiao plan of indexing is similar to the indexing method included in the 1977 amendments except that wages in the earnings history and the wage brackets in the formula are indexed to the consumer price index rather than to the average covered wages of all covered workers.

Rising Replacement Ratios

Under the old system of indexing, the benefits of workers retiring in future years could have risen rapidly relative to their pre-retirement earnings. As shown in Table 3, when the consumer price index rose, the percentage of the average monthly wage payable in benefits was increased in like proportion. In addition, for persons not yet retired, because wages also rise when prices rise, the amount of the covered wages of most workers would rise and consequently would increase their average monthly wage used as the base for calculating their benefits. As a result, each year the benefits of the average retiree would rise by more than that year's increase in the consumer price index (but not always by more than the rise in pre-retirement earnings). The combined effect of the higher percentages allowed and the increase in the average monthly wage is referred to as overindexing or double indexing.

Before the new system of indexing was adopted in 1977, whether replacement ratios rose and got out of control depended on the relation between the rise in prices and the rise in wages. If prices rose faster than wages, as they did in 1973 and 1974, benefits would increase faster than pre-retirement earnings, and replacement ratios would rise. Even under the more normal situation in which prices rise less rapidly than wages, if the increase in prices was not much less than the rate of expansion in wages, replacement ratios would rise. As shown by Hsiao,

8

replacement ratios would rise if the rate of increase in prices were 6 percent and the rate of increase in wages were 8 percent (a rate of inflation only 25 percent less than the rate of increase in wages). The rise in a worker's average monthly wage because of the rise in wages, combined with the increase in the percentages allowed because of the rise in consumer prices, would be large enough to cause the average benefits of persons retiring each year to rise faster than their pre-retirement earnings. Replacement ratios did not rise, however, when the rate of increase in prices was 2 percent a year and the rate of increase in nominal wages was 4 percent a year (a rate of inflation half the rate of increase in wages).

Several factors kept replacement ratios from rising in spite of double indexing when rates of inflation were low. First, prices did not ordinarily rise as fast as wages. Second, because the formula wage brackets were not adjusted for inflation, the portion of a worker's average monthly wage in the higher brackets (in which the percentages applied were lower) became larger as wages rose. This tended to cause replacement ratios to decline. Third, because inflated wages were summed with previously earned, unindexed, lower wages to determine a worker's average monthly wage, the increase in the average monthly wage was not always very large.

Steady and Falling Replacement Ratios

The difference between the steady trend of replacement ratios under the new indexing system and the declining trend that would occur under the Hsiao plan is the result primarily of two factors: first, the different effects on replacement ratios of wage and price indexing resulting from the increase in the number of years that will be included in the averaging period for calculating average monthly wages (this will occur until the maximum number of years to be included is reached in 1994); and, second, indexing the formula wage brackets to wages rather than prices. Contrary to what one might expect, the difference is not the result of indexing a worker's earnings history at a higher rate under wage indexing than under price indexing. Thompson, Michael Darby, Dean Leimer, and John Palmer all agree on this point.

As Table 5 shows, the rate at which earnings histories are indexed does not affect the future trend of replacement ratios. This is illustrated with a simplified arithmetical example of wages indexed by both prices and wages for persons retiring in two successive years (Mr. A retiring in year 6 and Mr. B retiring in year 7). For both persons, five years are included in the averaging period. Table 5 shows the same results as

9

those in Darby's more complicated formulas. The example assumes a constant wage increase of 6 percent a year and a constant price increase of 4 percent a year. Column 1 shows that, because of the assumed rise in wages of 6 percent a year, the average unindexed monthly wage of Mr. B is 6 percent higher than that of Mr. A, who retired a year earlier.

Column 4 of Table 5 shows the amount of the average monthly wage of Mr. A and Mr. B when their wages are indexed to a 4 percent rise in consumer prices. Column 6 shows the amount of their average monthly wage when their wages are indexed to a 6 percent rise in wages. Whether indexed at 4 percent or 6 percent, the average indexed wage of Mr. B is 6 percent higher than that of Mr. A who retired in the previous year. The two indexing systems do not differ in their effects on replacement ratios. What determines the percentage rise in indexed wages for persons retiring in successive years is the percentage rise in their wages without indexation rather than the precentage rate at which their wages are indexed.

The correct explanation of the different predicted trends of replacement ratios for the new indexing system and the Hsiao plan has to do, in part, with the number of years included in the averaging period for determining AIMWs. Over the next sixteen years, the averaging period will increase from nineteen years (the maximum number of years averaged in 1978) to thirty-five years (the maximum legal limit for the number of years to be averaged). Because wage indexing of past earnings puts earnings in earlier years on a par with wages at the time of retirement, adding another year's wages to wages earned in earlier years does not reduce the amount of a person's AIMW. On the other hand, if past earnings are indexed to prices, as under the Hsiao plan, earnings in earlier years would not be put on a par with wages at the time of retirement because prices usually do not rise as rapidly as wages. Under such conditions, a worker's earnings would tend to rise continuously throughout the averaging period, and increasing the number of years in the averaging period would lower the amount of a person's AIMW. The lower AIMWs would cause benefits to rise less rapidly and replacement ratios to decline.

A second reason for the decline in replacement ratios in the Hsiao plan, but not in the new indexing system included in the 1977 amendments, has to do with the indexing of the formula wage brackets; this is well explained by Hsiao and Thompson. Table 4 shows that the percentages of the wage brackets paid out in benefits decline as wages get larger. Benefits are weighted in favor of the low-wage earner. An employee in the lowest wage bracket, who has an AIMW of $180, will receive a retirement benefit of $162, 90 percent of his AIMW. Employees in the middle wage bracket, with AIMWs above $180 but under $1,085, will receive in additional benefits only 32 percent of the added amount of their AIMWs. For AIMWs in the highest wage bracket, above $1,085, only 15 percent will be added in benefits.

By indexing the wage brackets to average covered wages, the new indexing system adopted in 1977 tends to maintain the progressivity of the formula. Because the wage brackets would be indexed to prices under the Hsiao plan, the boundaries of the wage brackets would not normally be raised as much as they would be under wage indexing. With the Hsiao plan, as wages rose, more of earnings would be in higher wage brackets, benefits would rise less rapidly than wages, and replacement ratios would decline.

Wage Indexing versus Price Indexing

In the 1977 amendments to the Social Security Act, the Congress rejected price indexing, which had been recommended by the Consultant Panel on Social Security appointed in 1975 by the Senate Committee on Finance and the House Committee on Ways and Means and chaired by William C. Hsiao.[3]

The principal argument in support of price indexing is that it costs less than wage indexing. Hsiao concludes that wage indexing would eventually require either substantial increases in payroll tax rates or financing from general revenues. He advocates price indexing because with this type of indexing the increase in the cost of financing the social security system starting about 2005 (as a result of a decline in the number of workers per beneficiary) could be offset completely by a decline in replacement ratios. This would be an advantage because the financing of the social security system is on a pay-as-you-go basis, and the ability of the system to meet its commitments under wage indexing is somewhat in doubt—it is not absolutely certain that future taxpayers will be willing to pay the higher taxes required. Hsiao also argues that, under wage indexing, the social security system's flexibility to adjust to future changes and conditions will be diminished because future increases in tax rates are already committed to financing the present program. In addition, he believes that some reduction in the amount payable in social security benefits would have a desirable effect on private saving.

---

[3] U.S. Congress, *Report of the Consultant Panel on Social Security to the Congressional Research Service, Prepared for the Use of the Committee on Finance of the U.S. Senate and the Committee on Ways and Means of the U.S. House of Representatives*, 94th Congress, 2nd session, August 1976.

TABLE 5

Hypothetical Example of Indexing of Earnings for Persons Retiring in Two Successive Years, Assuming a Five-Year Averaging Period

Year (t)	Annual Covered Earnings (W)[a] (dollars) (1)	Consumer Price Index (P)[b] (2)	Price-Indexing Factor[c] (3)	Price-Indexed Earnings (dollars) (4)	Wage-Indexing Factor[d] (5)	Wage-Indexed Earnings (dollars) (6)
Mr. A						
1	10,000	100.0	1.16986	11,698.60	1.26248	12,624.80
2	10,600	104.0	1.12487	11,923.62	1.19102	12,624.81
3	11,236	108.16	1.08160	12,152.86	1.12360	12,624.77
4	11,910.16	112.486	1.04000	12,386.57	1.06000	12,624.77
5	12,624.77	116.986	1.00000	12,624.77	1.00000	12,624.77
6	—•					
Sum of 5 years' earnings	56,370.93			60,786.42		
Average annual earnings	11,274.19			12,157.28		12,624.77
Average monthly earnings	939.52			1,013.11		1,052.06

Mr. B						
2	10,600	104.0	1.16986	12,400.52	1.26248	13,382.29
3	11,236	108.16	1.12486	12,638.93	1.19102	13,382.30
4	11,910.16	112.486	1.08160	12,882.03	1.12360	13,382.26
5	12,624.77	116.986	1.04000	13,129.76	1.06000	13,382.26
6	13,382.26	121.665	1.00000	13,382.26	1.00000	13,382.26
7	—e					
Sum of 5 years' earnings	59,753.19			64,433.50		
Average annual earnings	11,950.64			12,886.70		13,382.26
Average monthly earnings	995.89			1,073.89		1,115.19
Mr. B's/Mr. A's average monthly earnings	1.06			1.06		1.06

a Assumes a constant rise of 6 percent a year.
b Assumes a constant rise of 4 percent a year.
c For Mr. A $= P_5/P_t$; for Mr. B $= P_6/P_t$.
d For Mr. A $= W_5/W_t$; for Mr. B $= W_6/W_t$.
e Year of retirement.

SOURCE: Author's calculation.

The Congress chose wage indexing because this type of indexing maintains future replacement ratios at the high levels to which they were raised during the past eight years. As stated by Congressmen Al Ullman (Democrat, Oregon) and Barber Conable (Republican, New York), there was political opposition to reducing replacement ratios because it was believed that such a reduction would deliberalize social security benefits. This point of view is criticized by Kaplan. He believes that the liberality of social security benefits should be measured by the rate of return that workers receive on the taxes paid for their benefits. A higher rate of return, for example, would indicate that benefits had become more liberal. Kaplan's estimates show that the rate of return under price indexing is only slightly less than the rate of return under wage indexing.

A significant result of wage indexing is that people will be required to purchase much larger social security benefits than under price indexing, and the role of the federal government in providing for the retirement needs of persons will be larger. Under price indexing, as the standard of living rose, the percentage of real income spent for social security would decline and people would have greater opportunity to decide for themselves how they wished to spend their incomes.

Thompson supports wage indexing over price indexing primarily because wage indexing distributes benefits so that people maintain the same relative income position they had before retirement. Also, wage indexing maintains the progressivity of the benefit formula, whereas price indexing does not. Thompson believes that the different trends of replacement ratios under price and wage indexing are not of crucial importance, because the demographic changes that could raise the cost of the social security system are uncertain. He believes that, as a practical matter, the decision about how to meet such costs can probably best be made at the time costs rise—at the earliest, sometime in the twenty-first century.

Feldstein and Pellechio, as well as Edgar Browning, analyze the choice between wage and price indexing in terms of the predictable response of the government to political forces. If it is assumed that governments tend to select those policies that maximize the self-interest of the voters (as voters perceive it), Feldstein and Pellechio conclude that the Congress would be expected to support wage indexing over price indexing. They estimate that net social security wealth is larger under wage indexing than under price indexing. Net social security wealth is the value of the benefits that workers can expect to receive less the value of the taxes they must pay until they retire; it measures the amount to be transferred from future generations (who do not yet vote) to current workers (who do vote).

Browning also concludes that the Congress would reject the Hsiao plan. The Hsiao plan is, in effect, a movement away from unfunded toward funded retirement arrangements because the role of social security would decline relative to private saving. Such a shift would not be in the interests of older workers. Browning shows that, in the start-up period, pay-as-you-go financed retirement programs, such as social security, are attractive to older workers who pay in taxes for only a few years before they retire and are taxed at the relatively low rates that are sufficient to cover the costs of a pay-as-you-go program during its early years. Under these conditions, older workers receive high rates of return on the taxes they pay in, and any change, such as the Hsiao plan, that would lower their expected benefits would also lower the rate of return that they receive. Because the social security system will soon be beyond the start-up period, the Hsiao plan would have little effect on the rate of return received by young workers just entering the system—their benefits and taxes would both be reduced. Politically, however, young voters are a minority.

Browning believes that funded retirement programs benefit society much more than unfunded systems such as social security. This is because the real rate of return to society from the capital investments that could be financed by funded systems of saving for retirement is 10 to 12 percent. This gain from capital accumulation is lost by shifting from funded to unfunded arrangements for supporting people in their retirement.

Browning suggests several unusual types of reforms. The purpose of such changes would be to create a framework in which the public could more clearly understand the benefits and the costs of the various ways of providing for retirement and which would provide a political basis for effective reform of the social security system. First, he would have the Social Security Administration send each taxpayer an annual statement reporting the implicit wealth he has accumulated. This would enable taxpayers to perceive the actual return they are likely to receive on the taxes they have paid in. Second, he would eliminate the portion of the payroll tax paid by the employer and have the entire tax paid by the employee. This would make it clearer to the employee how large the tax burden is. Third, he would greatly reduce the taxation of income from capital. This would increase the return that people could realize from private saving and make them aware of the true opportunity cost of an unfunded system.

15

PART ONE

INDEXING SOCIAL SECURITY: WHAT TO DO?

An Optimal Indexing Method for Social Security

William C. Hsiao

Social security touches the life of every American.[1] It is the largest and most successful social economic institution created in the United States. Currently more than 33.3 million people receive benefits under this system.[2] The estimated annual outlay for calendar year 1977 is $87.7 billion, which represents 4.8 percent of the U.S. gross national product. Approximately 93 percent of the total American work force—84 million workers—are paying a significant portion of their earnings into the social security program.[3]

The financing of social security is largely influenced by its benefit structure. First, the benefit formula determines the equity and adequacy of the income provided to beneficiaries. Second, it determines the financial cost of the program. The appropriate design for the social security benefits is a paramount issue that goes beyond the success and stability of this program alone. It affects the patterns of savings and consumption in the United States for decades to come.

At the end of 1977, the Congress amended the social security law to correct the technical error in the social security benefit formula legislated in 1972. In that earlier legislation, the Congress had inadvertently double indexed the benefits. The new 1977 benefit formula is commonly known as the wage-indexing method. Because of its technical complexity, the wage-indexing method was the subject of little public discussion and debate before it was adopted. The general public, on

---

[1] As used in this paper, the term "social security" refers to the Old-Age Survivors and Disability Insurance (OASDI) program only. It does not include the Medicare program. The paper is largely based on U.S. Congress, *Report of the Consultant Panel on Social Security to the Congressional Research Service, Prepared for the Use of the Committee on Finance of the U.S. Senate and the Committee on Ways and Means of the U.S. House of Representatives*, 94th Congress, 2nd session, August 1976.

[2] Social Security Administration, *Monthly Benefit Statistics*, September 14, 1977, p. 1.

[3] Calculation based on the annual outlay estimated by the Board of Trustees reported in U.S. Congress, House, *1977 Annual Report of the Board of Trustees of the Federal Old-Age and Survivors Insurance and Disability Insurance Trust Funds*, House Document no. 95-150, 95th Congress, 1st session, May 10, 1977, table 20, p. 54.

19

the whole, has not examined other viable alternatives nor understood the potential impacts of the wage-indexing formula.

Almost before the ink is dry on the new law, the administration and the Congress are already discussing redesigning the benefits and financing of social security. The next section of this paper describes the benefit formula under present law and under a superior alternative indexing method. The respective impacts of these two methods on adequacy, equity, cost, and economic efficiency are compared in the final section of the paper.

Benefit Formula

Brief descriptions are given for the two benefit formulas. The formula for calculating social security benefits under the present law—that is, the 1977 amendment to the Social Security Act—employs the wage-indexing method. A superior alternative formula analyzed in this paper employs the price-indexing method.

Wage-Indexing Method: The Formula under Present Law. Social security benefits are calculated in two steps. The first step is computing the worker's average indexed monthly earnings (AIME). The second step is computing the benefit by applying a three-bracket formula to the AIME to obtain the primary insurance amount.

Average indexed monthly earnings. Starting in 1978, average monthly indexed earnings are based on a worker's covered earnings for all years of employment from 1951 through the year in which he or she attains age sixty-two. The five years in which earnings were lowest are excluded from this computation. If the worker continues to work past age sixty-two up to age sixty-five, he or she may substitute those three years of earnings for three earlier years of lower earnings. For those who attained age sixty-five in 1978, the averaging period is nineteen years. Thereafter, the averaging period will increase by one each year for all workers until it reaches a maximum value of thirty-five years in 1994.

The amount of a worker's earnings covered by social security is limited by legislation. In the earlier years of the program, the maximum amount of covered wages was quite small. In the past decade, however, the maximum taxable earnings base has risen rapidly. Under present law, the maximum base will increase to $29,700 in 1981, and thereafter it will increase automatically as wages rise. Table 1 shows the maximum taxable earnings base under social security from 1937 to 1981.

TABLE 1

MAXIMUM TAXABLE EARNINGS BASE, 1937–1981

(current dollars)

Year or Period	Maximum Taxable Earnings Base
1937–1950	3,000
1951–1954	3,600
1955–1958	4,200
1959–1965	4,800
1966–1967	6,600
1968–1971	7,800
1972	9,000
1973	10,800
1974	13,200
1975	14,100
1976	15,300
1977	16,500
1978	17,700
1979	22,900
1980	25,900
1981	29,700

SOURCE: U.S. Congress, Senate, Committee on Finance, *Summary of H.R. 9346, the Social Security Amendments of 1977 as Passed by the Congress*, 95th Congress, 1st session, December 23, 1977, p. 3.

Under present law, the initial benefit for those attaining age sixty-two after 1978 is computed from indexed wage records. The indexing procedure is to adjust the actual earnings for all years before the second year prior to attaining age sixty-two by the rate of increase in general wage level between the year the wage was earned and the second year prior to attaining age sixty-two. Wages earned after the second year before attaining age sixty-two are used unadjusted.

The average monthly indexed earnings can be expressed as:

$$\text{wage-indexed } AIME = \frac{\overline{W}_{s-2}}{T-2} \sum_{s-T-1}^{t=S-3} \frac{W_t^i}{\overline{W}_t} + W_{s-2}^i + W_{s-1}^i,$$

where W_t^i is the covered earnings of the ith individual in year t; T is the length of the averaging period; S is the year attaining age sixty-two; and $\overline{W}_t$ is the average wage under covered employment in year t.

The calculation of the average monthly indexed earnings can be made more clear by an example. For a worker attaining age sixty-two

21

in 1979, all of his covered earnings before 1977 are increased to the 1977 wage level by multiplying the actual earnings by a factor that represents how much higher the general level of wages was in 1977 as compared with what it was in the particular year the wage was earned. The covered earnings for 1977 and 1978 are used without any adjustment.

Primary insurance amount. The primary insurance amount (PIA) is the benefit that a retired worker would receive. His spouse is eligible for a spouse benefit that equals 50 percent of the primary insurance amount. The benefit table for the PIA in effect on January 1, 1979, is shown in Table 2. After that date, the weights (or percentage of AIME allowed in each of the three wage brackets)—90 percent, 32 percent, and 15 percent—will be fixed. The breakpoints—$180, $905, and $1,085—will increase in future years as average covered wages increase.

Price-Indexing Method: An Alternative. An alternative method of determining social security benefits was proposed by the Consultant Panel on Social Security. This method would index earnings histories by the consumer price index (CPI), whereas the method under present law indexes past earnings by the rate of wage increases. This alternative method, which is referred to as the price-indexing formula, can be expressed as:

$$\text{price-indexed } AIME = \frac{CPI_{S-1}}{T} \frac{\overset{t=S-1}{\underset{S-T}{\Sigma}}}{S-T} \frac{W_t^t}{CPI_t},$$

where CPI_t is the consumer price index in year t.

The benefit formula proposed by the consultant panel would also consist of three weights and three breakpoints (see Table 3). Following

---

TABLE 2

CALCULATION OF THE PRIMARY INSURANCE AMOUNT FOR A PERSON RETIRING JANUARY 1, 1979, UNDER PRESENT LAW

Percentage Allowed	Level of Average Indexed Monthly Earnings (dollars)	Primary Insurance Amount (dollars)
90	First 180	162.00
32	Next 905	289.60
15	Remainder above 1,085	

SOURCE: Author's calculation based on the benefit formula under present law.

TABLE 3

CALCULATION OF THE PRIMARY INSURANCE AMOUNT
FOR A PERSON RETIRING JANUARY 1, 1979,
UNDER PROPOSED PRICE-INDEXING FORMULA

Percentage Allowed	Level of Average Indexed Monthly Earnings (dollars)	Primary Insurance Amount (dollars)
80	First 250	200
35	Next 500	175
25	Remainder above 750	

SOURCE: Author's calculation with pricing-indexing benefit formula proposed by the Consultant Panel on Social Security.

the proposed effective date of January 1, 1979, the weights—80 percent, 35 percent, and 25 percent—would remain fixed. The breakpoints— $250, $500, and $750—would change with the rate of increase in prices.

Wage Indexing Compared with Price Indexing

Over the years, the Congress has adhered to four fundamental principles to guide its decisions about social security: (1) individual equity balanced with social adequacy, (2) controllability and long-run stability, (3) floor of protection, and (4) economic efficiency. These principles continue to be perceived as necessary to and consistent with the overriding goal of the system: to provide economic security to American workers and their families in the event of lost income because of retirement, disability, or death. This goal was stated in the original report of the President's Committee on Economic Security, and it has been widely accepted by the Congress and the general public ever since. Because the four principles are the criteria by which any new legislation is judged, they provide a frame of reference for evaluating and comparing alternative solutions.

Indexing earnings histories by wages would produce adjusted wages that reflect the relative lifetime earnings position of the worker. Indexing earnings histories by prices would produce adjusted wages that reflect the real purchasing power of previous earnings. The two methods result in different patterns of benefits for future retirees. They differ significantly in their impacts on social adequacy, equity, cost and financing, controllability and long-run stability, and economic efficiency.

23

Social Adequacy. Opinion differs on standards of adequacy. Life styles differ, costs of living differ, family structures differ. What constitutes adequacy for one might seem affluence to another and penury to a third. What constitutes an adequate level of social security benefits is a collective value judgment revealed through the political process. There is, however, general agreement that, once a benefit has been awarded, the purchasing power of the initial benefit should be maintained.

Because there is no normative standard to measure the adequacy of initial benefits, three different bench marks have been widely used. Each is rational in its limited context. Nonetheless, each provides only a narrow measurement. Advocates of a particular benefit structure sometimes select one standard that supports their proposal, and they mislead the public by insisting that it is the only way to measure adequacy. This kind of tunnel vision can confuse the public. The three widely used bench marks for measuring adequacy are: the benefit awarded now in light of the current standard of living; the initial benefits that would be awarded to persons retiring in the future compared with those to persons retiring now; and the percentage of pre-retirement earnings that the initial benefit replaces, frequently referred to as the replacement rate.

Current benefit awards and the current standard of living. The purpose of social security is to prevent financial dependency when workers find their earnings reduced because of retirement, death, or disability. Although estimates of the income required to maintain a basic adequate standard of living vary, one way to obtain an approximate indicator of the basic income needed is to ascertain the amount required to purchase various market baskets of goods. The U.S. government has attempted to define poverty levels in this manner. The collection of commodities and services necessary for a subsistence standard of living are identified. Average prices in urban areas and rural areas for each item in this market basket are obtained. The total average annual cost of this market basket is calculated by summing the products of price and quantity of all items. That represents the income needed for subsistence. An indicator of the income required for a modest standard of living is found by using the same method. The difference between the indicators for subsistence and modest standards of living is in the items and quantities included in their respective market baskets. Undoubtedly, these estimates are crude. Nevertheless, they may be used for a rough measure of the adequacy of social security benefits.

The initial benefits awarded in 1976 to workers with various lifetime earnings histories are compared with the U.S. government poverty levels in Table 4. In all cases, the initial benefits awarded to workers

24

TABLE 4

COMPARISON OF THE INITIAL ANNUAL BENEFITS AWARDED
TO PERSONS WITH DIFFERENT EARNINGS HISTORIES AND
U.S. GOVERNMENT POVERTY LEVELS, 1976

(dollars)

	Initial Social Security Benefits			U.S. Government Poverty Levels	
	Low earnings ($3,790)[a]	Median earnings ($8,870)	Maximum earnings ($15,300)	Poverty threshold for elderly[b]	Near poor but adequate for elderly[b]
Male worker retiring at age 65	2,736	3,901	4,743	2,730	3,413
Male worker retiring at age 65 with dependent spouse also age 65	4,104	5,852	7,115	3,345	4,181

[a] Represents a person who has worked steadily at slightly below the minimum wage.
[b] U.S. Bureau of Census, *Consumer Income*, ser. P-60, 107, September 1977. The near poor threshold is 125 percent of the poverty threshold. Both thresholds exclude farm workers.
SOURCE: Calculations by the author, based on the 1975 benefit awards updated by the 1976 automatic benefit increase of 6.4 percent and increase in average wages of 7.4 percent.

exceeded the income required to maintain a subsistence standard of living. The benefit for a low-income worker with a dependent spouse is approximately equal to the amount needed to maintain a modest level of living. The initial benefit awarded to a single worker with low earnings is about 25 percent less than a modest standard of living. With the exception of the single worker with low earnings histories, social security benefits appear to be providing a modest standard of living for retired persons. Workers with wage histories below the minimum wage standard—the lowest level of earnings shown in Table 4—would probably receive assistance through the Supplemental Security Income (SSI) program, the first tier of the federal government's income maintenance program.

The SSI program, enacted by the Congress in 1972, provides uniform, nationwide, means-tested income support financed from general revenues, and states may supplement SSI payments. As of July 1976, SSI guarantees income of $167.80 a month for one recipient and $251.80 a month for an eligible couple. The first $20 of additional monthly income does not affect the SSI payment. Any unearned income above the guaranteed amount reduces the SSI payment dollar for dollar.

Initial benefits awarded now and in the future. The initial benefits for future retirees may be compared with the currently prevailing level of benefits for adequacy. If current benefits are considered "adequate," then a benefit formula can be evaluated as either increasing, decreasing, or maintaining the current level of adequacy for persons retiring at the present time.

The initial benefits produced by wage and price indexing are presented in Table 5. With both wage and price indexing, the initial benefits for workers retiring in the future, measured in constant 1977 dollars,

TABLE 5

INITIAL PRIMARY INSURANCE AMOUNT FOR WORKERS WITH AVERAGE EARNINGS RETIRING AT AGE SIXTY-FIVE, SELECTED YEARS, 1979–2050

(constant 1977 dollars)

Year	Initial Primary Insurance Amount	
	Wage indexing	Price indexing
1979	4,410	4,369
1985	4,620	4,428
1990	5,046	4,515
1995	5,476	4,631
2000	5,953	4,820
2010	7,034	5,263
2020	8,311	5,855
2030	9,821	6,546
2040	11,605	7,361
2050	13,713	8,325

NOTE: Estimates are based on the long-range assumptions that the consumer price index increases at 4 percent a year while real wages increase at 1.75 percent a year.

SOURCES: U.S. Congress, Senate, Committee on Finance, *Staff Data and Materials Relating to Social Security Financing*, 95th Congress, 1st session, June 1977, pp. 50–53; and author's computation.

increase steadily over time. The standard of living for future retirees will be higher than that for retirees in the past. Nevertheless, the two indexing methods produce different rates of increase in real benefits. Because wages usually rise faster than prices, wage indexing provides a more rapid rise in real benefits than does price indexing. Over a seventy-five-year period, real benefits would increase more than 300 percent with wage indexing. By this measurement, wage indexing produces for workers retiring in the future benefits that far exceed the level of adequacy now existing.

When social security benefits for future retirees increase significantly over persons retiring in earlier years, the benefit structure creates a disparity in the adequacy of retirement income between the various generations of retirees. This is because the life styles of retirees have more similarity than those of other groups. Their life styles are similar with respect to leisure time, small family size (mostly singles or two-person families), reduced physical strength, and long years of experience. As a result, consumption patterns among retirees vary less than those of the working population.

Figure 1 presents an illustration of this disparity. With wage indexing, the annual PIA for a worker with average earnings retiring in 1979 and the annual PIA for another worker who is eleven years younger and retiring in 1990 are $4,326 and $5,169, respectively—a 20 percent increase. With price indexing the difference would be smaller: $4,369 and $4,515.

Replacement rates. Until 1974, replacement rates were not a widely used criterion for measuring the adequacy of social security benefits. A disadvantage of using replacement rates is that the majority of American workers have earnings that fluctuate widely over their working lifetime. Few workers experience a steady rise in their normal wages. Also, most workers have declining real wages just before their retirement. Very few workers have a pattern of lifetime earnings similar to the national average; therefore, relying on a single relationship between post-retirement and pre-retirement earnings can be misleading.[4]

Yet, the replacement rate is a concept that is easy to understand. Many workers are familiar with this concept because of its use in private pension programs. In private pension programs, benefits are often based on a person's salary in his final year or years of employment and on his years of service. Each year of service generates a benefit that equals a certain percent of the final salary.

---

[4] U.S. Congress, *Report of the Consultant Panel on Social Security*, pp. 41–56.

FIGURE 1
INITIAL PRIMARY INSURANCE AMOUNT FOR WORKERS, WITH AVERAGE EARNINGS, RETIRING AT AGE SIXTY-FIVE, SELECTED YEARS, 1979–2050
(constant 1977 dollars)

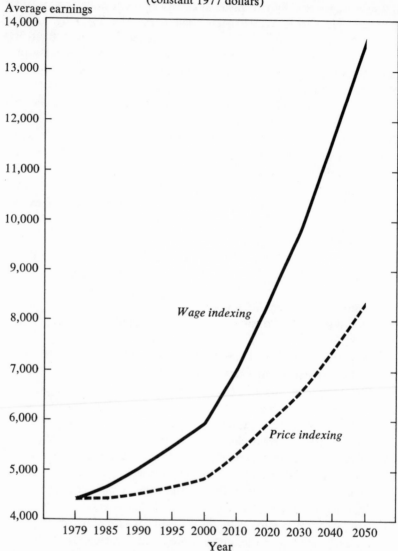

NOTE: Estimates are based on the long-range assumptions that the consumer price index increases at 4 percent a year while real wages increase at 1.75 percent a year.

SOURCES: U.S. Congress, Senate, Committee on Finance, *Staff Data and Materials Relating to Social Security Financing*, 95th Congress, 1st session, June 1977, pp. 50–53; and author's computation.

TABLE 6

REPLACEMENT RATES FOR THE WORKER WITH AVERAGE EARNINGS
WITHOUT SPOUSE, SELECTED YEARS, 1979–2050

(percent)

	Wage Indexing		Price Indexing	
Year	Replacement rate gross earnings	Replacement rate net earnings[a]	Replacement rate gross earnings	Replacement rate net earnings[a]
1979	44	57	45	59
1985	41	55	41	54
1990	41	55	38	50
1995	41	55	36	48
2000	41	55	34	45
2010	41	55	32	42
2020	41	55	30	40
2030	41	55	28	37
2040	41	55	27	36
2050	41	55	26	34

[a] Net earnings are gross earnings less social security taxes, federal and state income taxes, and work-related expenses. Tax data obtained from Alicia H. Munnell, *The Future of Social Security* (Washington, D.C.: The Brookings Institution, 1977), p. 59. Work-related expenses are assumed to be 7 percent of gross income and equal to approximately $550 a year.

SOURCES: Senate, Committee on Finance, *Staff Data and Material Relating to Social Security Financing*, pp. 50–53; and author's computation.

Estimated replacement rates for workers with average earnings are shown in Table 6. It is assumed that workers have steadily rising wage levels over their working lifetimes. The replacement rates shown are based on the workers' earnings in the year before retirement. With the wage-indexing method, the replacement rates remain constant in the future—initial benefits are a constant ratio of pre-retirement earnings. On the other hand, with the price-indexing method, the ratio of initial benefits to pre-retirement pay would decline in the future.

Equity. Equity can be of three types: individual, horizontal, and vertical.

Individual equity. The equity for each individual worker covered by social security can be measured by the rate of return on his contributions to the program. Various studies have shown that workers would receive a fair rate of return on their contributions under either wage indexing or price indexing.[5]

Horizontal equity. Horizontal equity refers to whether or not persons in similar situations are treated similarly. To calculate a worker's average monthly wage, his entire earnings history is collapsed into a single number. Wage indexing and price indexing use different weights in calculating the average wage. Since average wages tend to rise more rapidly than prices, using a wage index results in a heavier weight for earlier working years than does the use of the consumer price index. Among persons who have the same average wage, individuals who had rapid wage growth over their lives do relatively better with price indexing, whereas those who had slower wage growth do relatively better under wage indexing.

Vertical equity. Vertical equity refers to the allocation of benefits among persons with different levels of lifetime earnings. The basic needs of retirees do not vary proportionately with their earnings levels. Also, the marginal utility of income probably decreases as income increases; that is, an added dollar of income has less value to a person with a higher income than to someone with a lower income. If so, the equitable treatment of persons with various levels of lifetime earnings would demand a progressive benefit formula.

A progressive benefit formula redistributes income from persons with higher lifetime earnings to those with lower lifetime earnings. Although redistribution through the federal income tax program is based mostly on annual earnings, redistribution through the social security program is based on lifetime earnings.

The benefit formulas for both wage indexing and price indexing apply declining weights to the AIME. Initially, both benefit formulas have a similar progressiveness, which is designed to replicate the progressiveness of the initial benefits awarded under current law. The wage-indexed benefit formula maintains constant progressivity for the average worker because the breakpoint for each bracket rises according to the rate of increase in average wages. The price-indexed benefit formula, however, has a progressive benefit that slowly declines in its progressivity because the breakpoints are indexed to the CPI. When average wages rise more rapidly than prices, the increase in real wages would fall into the brackets with smaller weights. In the absence of any

---

[5] For the computation on the relative rate of return under the wage-indexing formula, see William C. Hsiao, "Social Security and Income Transfer" (Paper delivered at the annual meeting of the Southern Economic Association, New Orleans, Louisiana, November 13, 1975). For the rate of return under the price-indexing formula, see Robert S. Kaplan, *Indexing Social Security: An Analysis of the Issues* (Washington, D.C.: American Enterprise Institute, 1977).

legislative change over the next seventy-five years, a larger portion of the AIME would exceed the upper breakpoint of $750 in 1979 prices. The benefits would still be progressive, but not as progressive as in 1977.

Cost and Financing. A rationally designed benefit formula must strike a reasonable balance between benefits and the costs of providing them. Every increase in benefits must be financed by an increase in taxes— whether the funding is from payroll taxes or from general revenues.

Under the pay-as-you-go method of financing, taxes paid by each generation of workers are immediately paid out to people who have already retired. The retirement benefits of current workers are to be financed by the payroll tax contributions collected from future generations of workers. The expectations of current workers will be realized only if future generations of workers are willing to pay the required taxes. If the promised benefits are unreasonably high, the program could encounter financial difficulties.

Wage indexing and price indexing result in different future benefits, and their costs are very different (see Table 7). Wage indexing could require future generations to pay payroll taxes 70 percent higher than they are now. Price indexing results in expenditures that are relatively level as a percentage of taxable payroll.

As a percentage of gross national product (GNP), estimated expenditures with wage indexing increase steadily from 4.5 percent in 1979 to 7.8 percent in 2030. A greater portion of the nation's total resources would be channeled through social security to those receiving benefits. With price indexing, outlays remain relatively level as a percentage of GNP.

In 1977, the Carter administration proposed a system of wage indexing for social security benefits, but the long-term consequences of this proposal are so unwieldy and ominous that the administration did not include provisions for dealing with the costs. Provisions were made only for social security over the next twenty-five years, when the costs are relatively low and manageable. Decisions on the long-term financing of future social security benefits were left for future Congresses.

Some proponents of wage indexing have recommended reducing the cost by gradually increasing the eligibility age for *full* benefits from age sixty-five to age sixty-eight. This proposal would reduce benefits for future retirees, and it raises serious equity questions that have not yet been examined. The recent trend is for workers to retire earlier rather than later. Although some workers retire because they have adequate incomes for retirement from both social security and private pensions,

31

TABLE 7

COMPARISON OF OASDI LONG-RANGE COSTS UNDER WAGE INDEXING
AND PRICE INDEXING, SELECTED YEARS, 1979–2050

(percent)

Year	Expenditures as Percentage of Taxable Payroll[a]		Expenditures as Percentage of GNP	
	Wage indexing	Price indexing	Wage indexing	Price indexing
1979	10.9	10.9	4.5	4.5
1985	11.2	11.0	4.7	4.5
1990	11.6	11.0	4.9	4.5
1995	11.9	10.8	5.0	4.5
2000	12.2	10.5	5.1	4.4
2010	13.5	10.6	5.7	4.3
2020	16.4	12.0	6.9	4.3
2030	18.7	12.8	7.8	4.9
2040	18.1	11.8	7.6	5.3
2050	17.5	10.9	7.3	4.9
				4.5

[a] One percent of taxable payroll equals $8 billion in 1977. The expenditures are computed as a percentage of a taxable payroll, which is based on a maximum taxable earnings base (MTEB) of $17,700 for 1978 and automatically adjusted according to the average rate of increase in covered wages. The 1977 amendment raised the MTEB. If the estimated expenditures as a percentage of taxable payroll were computed based on the higher MTEB, they would be slightly lower.

NOTE: Cost estimates are based on the long-range assumptions that price increases at 4 percent a year while real wages increase at 1.75 percent a year. Wage-indexing and price-indexing benefit formulas used to prepare these cost estimates are based on the current law and on the proposal made by the Consultant Panel on Social Security, respectively.

SOURCES: Senate, Committee on Finance, *Staff Data and Material Relating to Social Security Financing*, pp. 50–53; and author's computation.

information collected from surveys shows that many workers retire early because of poor health. Whether this is true and whether it is a socially acceptable excuse for retiring for other reasons is not certain.

Controllability and Long-Run Stability. Most workers contribute to social security for more than forty years before they are eligible for benefits. Moreover, the economic welfare of most of the participants depends largely on the long-run integrity of the program. Thus, the social security program depends greatly on public confidence in its long-term stability.

Furthermore, any successful social insurance program must be flexible in its design and must have a financial margin of safety in order to adapt to changes. Thus, the social security program should keep pace with changes in economic, social, political, and demographic conditions. Indeed, some pressures for change have already surfaced, and many others can be expected to evolve in the future. For example, one possible modification of the social security program has to do with spouse's benefits. The issue goes beyond simply providing more equitable treatment between one- and two-worker families. It is also related to the treatment of women who labor as housewives. Greater frequency of divorce in the U.S. society has increased the number of individuals of retirement age who have not had substantial earnings records and are not eligible for spouse or survivor benefits. The major point is that social security cannot be a static program. It must be able to change in response to alterations in the nation's socioeconomic environment.

Wage indexing and price indexing result in different levels of benefits for workers retiring in the future. Price indexing guarantees a moderate benefit that compares favorably with the benefits of workers who have retired previously. The benefits would also exceed the income levels that have been accepted by the government as the amounts required to maintain a modest standard of living. Price indexing would also guarantee a benefit that is protected against inflation. Moreover, the benefits of future retirees would tend to increase even without future congressional action because of the rise in workers' productivity. The estimated expenditures under price indexing are relatively level as a percentage of the taxable payroll and as a percentage of the GNP. Therefore, it provides a margin of safety for the nation to raise the benefits or to make necessary modifications to social security in light of prevailing economic, social, and demographic conditions at that time. The price-indexing method, furthermore, preserves the flexibility for the social security program to adapt to changing environments, thus assuring a needed stability for this long-term program.

The wage-indexing method, on the other hand, would make benefit levels fully automatic. These automatic adjustments provide benefits at a level high enough to require an increasing percentage of taxable payroll to finance them. Also, a greater share of the gross national product would automatically go to social security benefits. Future voters would have less financial flexibility to deal successfully with changes.

Advocates of wage indexing argue that price indexing, in the absence of congressional action, represents a deliberalization of the benefits because it results in declining replacement rates. Their political judgment was that the Congress would continue to improve the program

33

regardless of whether the benefit formula used was based on wage indexing or price indexing.[6] If their prophesy comes true, then the need for financial margin in the program design is even greater.

Economic Efficiency. Social security affects economic behavior in two principal ways. First, retirement benefits and the earnings test influence the labor supply. Second, provisions for retirement income through social security reduce private saving. In addition, social security has two secondary economic impacts: higher payroll taxes increase prices, at least in the short run; and the portion of the payroll tax that is not shifted back to labor increases the relative price of labor and thus reduces total employment.

Social security provides a certain amount of income to the worker at age sixty-five or an actuarially reduced income at age sixty-two. Purely because of the availability of this income, older workers are encouraged to choose leisure instead of work. Moreover, retirement income payable under most private pension plans is integrated with social security. Therefore, employees and employers are conditioned to accept the age that a worker becomes eligible for social security retirement benefits as the normal retirement age. Another effect of social security on the labor supply is the earnings test. Currently, a beneficiary below age seventy-two whose earnings exceed $3,240 a year has his benefit reduced by 50 cents on every dollar earned in excess of that amount; that is equivalent to an income tax surcharge at a 50 percent rate. The incentive for older workers to stay in the labor force may be greatly reduced by this high marginal tax rate. Very few empirical analyses have been performed on the question of social security and retirement decisions. A number of current economic research studies are under way, however.[7]

People save for various reasons. One important reason for saving is to have adequate income when earnings are reduced because of retirement. Social security guarantees workers retirement benefits based on their lifetime earnings. To the extent that workers think of their social security contributions as saving for their own retirement, they will tend to save less in other ways. Under a pay-as-you-go financing system, contributions collected by the program are paid out immediately

---

[6] Alicia H. Munnell, *The Future of Social Security* (Washington, D.C.: The Brookings Institution, 1977), p. 145.

[7] Among those who are currently studying this important question are Michael Boskin, Anthony Pellechio, and Joseph Quinn. See Michael Boskin, "Social Security and Retirement Decisions," *Economic Inquiry*, vol. 15 (January 1977), pp. 1–25.

as benefits. No sizable fund is accumulated. As a result, the possible reduction in private saving is not offset by public saving; consequently, less capital is accumulated.

On the other hand, the social security program may have a positive impact on saving through its retirement effect. If social security encourages voluntary and earlier retirement, people may save more because of the shortening in working years and the lengthening in retirement years.

Recent empirical studies have shown that the net impact of social security reduces aggregate private savings. These studies, however, differ widely on the magnitude of the reduction. The study by Alicia Munnell estimated that the reduction in saving in 1969 was $3.6 billion.[8] The study by Martin Feldstein concluded that the reduction in saving for the same year was $38.2 billion.[9] An important factor that was not included in the study by Feldstein is the retirement effect. This may account for some of the difference. Although there is no agreement on the degree that social security has reduced capital accumulation, the decline in the age of retirement has slowed and this may cause the social security program to have a greater negative impact in the future on saving.

Since the two indexing methods guarantee different levels of retirement benefits, their effects on private saving would be different. Even without a complete model on saving for consumption, one can still provide a partial analysis of their respective effects on saving by examining the replacement ratios yielded by each indexing method. When social security benefits replace a greater portion of the pre-retirement income, there would be less need and less incentive to supplement the benefits by private pensions and personal saving.

If a worker makes rational choices on his lifetime consumption patterns and uses replacement rates as his guide, he would save and plan for his retirement an amount of income that is consistent with his pre-retirement disposable income, not his pre-retirement gross income. Earned income is subject to the social security payroll taxes and federal and state income taxes. Social security benefits are not subject to any payroll or income taxes. In addition, a worker incurs certain additional expenses directly related to work, such as travel expenses, uniforms or clothing for work, lunches and coffee, and contributions to office parties and gifts. Upon retirement, work-related expenses cease. An analysis

---

[8] Munnell, *The Future of Social Security*, p. 117.

[9] Martin S. Feldstein, "Social Security, Induced Retirement, and Aggregate Capital Accumulation," *Journal of Political Economy*, vol. 82 (September–October 1974), pp. 905–26.

TABLE 8

REPLACEMENT RATES BASED ON 1977 DISPOSABLE INCOME FOR VARIOUS HYPOTHETICAL
WORKERS WITH DIFFERENT EARNINGS HISTORIES, SELECTED YEARS, 1979–2050

(percent)

	Wage Indexing			Price Indexing		
Year	Low earnings ($4,600)	Average earnings ($10,152)	Maximum earnings ($16,500)	Low earnings ($4,600)	Average earnings ($10,152)	Maximum earnings ($16,500)
For a single worker						
1979	69	57	46	73	59	44
1990	67	55	45	62	50	38
2000	67	55	45	55	45	37
2010	67	55	45	52	42	37
2020	67	55	45	49	40	36
2030	67	55	45	46	37	34
2040	67	55	45	43	36	33
2050	67	55	45	39	34	32

For a worker with spouse

Year						
1979	100	83	67	106	87	63
1990	98	81	65	90	74	55
2000	98	81	65	81	66	53
2010	98	81	65	76	62	53
2020	98	81	65	72	58	51
2030	98	81	65	67	54	50
2040	98	81	65	63	52	48
2050	98	81	65	58	50	46

NOTE: Disposable income is the gross income less social security payroll taxes, federal and state income taxes, and work-related expenses. Work-related expenses are assumed to be $400, $550, and $600 for workers with earnings in the low, average, and maximum categories, respectively. No deduction is made from gross income for employee's contributions toward pensions and health insurance.

SOURCES: Tax data obtained from Munnell, *The Future of Social Security*, p. 59. Information on replacement rates for gross income obtained from Senate, Committee on Finance, *Staff Data and Material Relating to Social Security Financing*, pp. 50–53; and author's computations.

that employs replacement rates as a tool should use disposable income as its base.

An examination of replacement rates based on disposable income is shown in Table 8. Wage indexing maintains replacement rates at the same level for workers retiring in the future, whereas price indexing results in initial benefits for future workers that decline relative to pre-retirement disposable income.

For workers with spouses, wage indexing provides benefits to those who had low earnings that equal their standard of living before they retired. Beginning in 1990, this indexing method also replaces 81 percent and 65 percent of the disposable income for those who had average earnings and earnings at the maximum taxable base, respectively. As for the single workers whose needs are reduced because of being a one-person family, the wage-indexing method provides benefits that replace 67 percent, 55 percent, and 45 percent of the disposable income for workers who had low, average, and "maximum" earnings histories, respectively.

Low and average income workers will have little need to supplement their social security retirement benefits with private pensions and personal savings because social security provides retirement benefits that replace all or a large part of their pre-retirement disposable income. It is reasonable to expect that such high replacement rates will reduce capital accumulation.

On the other hand, in the absence of congressional actions to raise benefits, price indexing would provide adequate retirement income and still leave some incentive for private saving.

Summary

Social security provides retirement income based on earnings over a worker's lifetime. The benefit calculation collapses the lifetime earnings history into one average monthly wage. Earnings for a given year must be indexed in order that the wages of one year can be realistically averaged with another. The question becomes, then, what is the most appropriate index to use? Two separate indexes have been suggested: wage and price. In order to decide which one is better, each must be examined in light of the goals that the social security program is designed to achieve. Five principles have guided the program since its inception. They are the criteria by which any indexing method is judged. These principles are: social adequacy, equity, cost and financing, flexibility and stability, and economic efficiency.

Adequacy has been commonly measured in three ways. First, benefits are measured against some reasonable but arbitrary national standard such as the poverty and near-poor thresholds. Both wage indexing and price indexing produce benefits that, in general, exceed the income needed for a modest standard of living. Second, initial benefits for persons retiring in the future are measured against the current prevailing level of benefits. Both indexing methods provide increasing initial benefits over current level, although the wage-indexing method increases the initial benefits much more rapidly. Third, initial benefits are measured against the pre-retirement earnings—the replacement rate. The initial benefits computed based on the wage-indexing method have constant levels of replacement rates, whereas the initial benefits computed based on the price-indexing method have declining levels of replacement rates.

The two indexing methods differ significantly with respect to costs. Wage indexing guarantees higher future benefits and thus costs more. The total payroll tax rates will have to be raised to 17 to 18 percent in the next century to finance the wage-indexing formula as compared with the 10.1 percent rate in 1978. On the other hand, the price-indexing formula guarantees a moderate benefit that can be financed without any significant increase in payroll taxes. Correspondingly, wage indexing automatically gives a larger share of the gross national product to social security benefits. Price indexing would keep that share constant.

The nation's social, economic, and demographic conditions will change. The social security program needs flexibility and a margin of safety in its benefit structure to adapt to changes. The wage-indexing method makes the benefit levels fully automatic. It leaves no margin for future voters to make any necessary modifications to the program and to decide how the increase in benefits should be divided among different classes of beneficiaries, reflecting the social needs of the time. On the contrary, the price-indexing method embraces a moderate automatic approach and leaves a financial margin and flexibility for future voters, thus providing the social security program with greater stability.

Economic behavior is affected by the social security benefits, by the cost of the program, and by its method of financing. Recent studies have consistently concluded that the social security program has reduced the aggregate saving. The wage-indexing method maintains replacement rates that provide sufficient retirement income to almost half the covered population. It leaves very little need for those workers to save. Meanwhile, the price-indexing method would produce initial benefits that decline as a percentage of the pre-retirement disposable income. It gives greater incentive for private saving to supplement the social security benefits.

In conclusion, price indexing is the far superior method for calculating social security benefits. It provides equitable benefits yet, in contrast to wage indexing, does not tend to provide benefits that become overly adequate. The cost for the price-indexing formula is manageable, whereas the cost for the wage-indexing formula becomes ominous. Moreover, price indexing gives a margin of safety to the social security program and thus provides greater stability. Also the price-indexing formula promotes greater incentive for private saving. Apparently, wage indexing is superior in only one area. It produces a constant replacement rate, whereas price indexing produces declining replacement rates.

Indexing Social Security: The Options

Lawrence H. Thompson

The current debate over "decoupling" the social security system is essentially a debate over how the system should be indexed.[1] The debate began with the spreading realization that the particular method of indexation that was introduced by the 1972 amendments to the Social Security Act contained serious flaws. It has continued because of differences in opinion about the most equitable distribution of a fixed sum among the members of a retirement cohort (the group of persons retiring in a given year), the role that social security should play in supplying retirement income to future generations, and the degree to which indexing decisions made now will or should determine that role.

This paper outlines the technical and philosophical issues that are involved in this debate. It examines:

- the points in the procedure for computing social security benefits at which indexing would be desirable, and

NOTE: Any views expressed in this paper are those of the author alone; they do not necessarily reflect the views of the U.S. Department of Health, Education, and Welfare. Computational assistance was provided by Elizabeth Peters. Paul Van de Water provided helpful comments on an earlier draft, and he, Jane Ross, Ron Davis, and a number of others have helped me crystalize my thinking. Of course, none of these people necessarily share all of my views. Throughout the paper, "present law" refers to the provisions of the Social Security Act as of September 30, 1977.

[1] The social security system is said to be "coupled" because, since 1972, the same formula has been used for indexing the benefits of those who are already retired and for indexing the potential future benefits of those who are still working. The word "decoupling" has come to be used to refer to all proposals designed to correct this flaw.

Of necessity, this paper presents only a brief discussion of the decoupling options and their various implications. The reader interested in an excellent, comprehensive analysis of the equity issues involved in constructing an alternative social security indexing procedure is referred to Dean R. Leimer, Ronald Hoffman, and Alan Freiden, "A Framework for Analyzing the Equity of the Social Security Benefit Structure," *Studies in Income Distribution No. 6*, Social Security Administration, Office of Research and Statistics (January 1978); and Dean R. Leimer and Ronald Hoffman, "Designing an Equitable Intertemporal Social Security Benefit Structure," mimeographed, Social Security Administration, Office of Research and Statistics (November 1976).

- the various economic and demographic considerations and the philosophical viewpoints that influence one's perspective on the desirability of particular approaches.

Background

The Socal Security Benefit Computation Process. Social security benefits are computed in a three-step procedure. The first step is to compute the worker's average monthly wage (AMW), a measure of the average level of pre-retirement earnings on which the worker paid social security taxes.[2] The AMW of a worker reaching age sixty-two in 1977 is computed by averaging the worker's annual taxable earnings for the highest twenty-one years between 1951 and the year immediately preceding his retirement and then converting that result to a monthly rate. The number of years included in the AMW calculation increases by one for each successive birth cohort until 1991. Those who reach age sixty-two in 1991 and their successors will use the highest thirty-five years of taxable earnings in computing their AMWs.

The second step is to compute the worker's primary insurance amount (PIA), the basic building block upon which all social security benefits are based. PIAs are derived by multiplying the AMW by a benefit formula that is structured according to several wage brackets.[3] The formula is progressive so that, as a worker's AMW increases, his PIA increases at a decreasing marginal rate.

The third step is to compute the benefit due to the worker or his dependent. The benefit is computed by multiplying the wage earner's PIA by an arithmetic factor that adjusts for the age of the individual at the time benefits were first drawn and the relationship between the individual drawing the benefits and the wage earner. The benefit awarded a retiree who is sixty-five years of age equals his PIA; most other benefits are some fraction of the PIA.

Indexation in Social Security at the Present Time. From the inception of the social security program in 1935 until the time of the 1972 amend-

---

[2] For consistency, the abbreviation AMW is used throughout the paper. This abbreviation has traditionally been used in the statute, even though average monthly *earnings* (AME) became a more accurate description when the self-employed were also covered. With the enactment of a decoupling bill, the statute will probably be changed so that henceforth this figure will be referred to as the average indexed monthly earnings (AIME).

[3] Under present law, benefits are actually derived from a table for which the multibracket benefit formula is only an approximation.

ments, no part of the program was explicitly indexed. Over the years, however, a series of ad hoc adjustments was made: in benefit levels, in the maximum amount of earnings subject to the tax (the taxable maximum), and in the amount a retiree could earn without reducing his social security benefits (the retirement test exempt amount). Benefit increases were always granted by increasing the percentage of the AMW allowed (that is, the marginal rate) in each wage bracket of the benefit formula, so that the benefit associated with every AMW level rose by the desired percentage amount. Whenever the taxable maximum was raised, the benefit formula was expanded by the addition of a new wage bracket (containing a marginal benefit rate of about 20 percent) in order to accommodate the higher AMWs thereby made possible. No other changes were made in the structure of the benefit formula.

The result of these periodic adjustments can be seen in Tables 1 and 2. Between 1953 and 1970, both the replacement rates (the ratio of the initial benefit to the worker's pre-retirement wage) for newly retired workers and the fraction of covered wages and salaries subject to the social security tax remained roughly constant. During that same period, benefit amounts after retirement rose somewhat faster than prices were rising.

In 1971, benefits were increased by 10 percent and, in 1972, they were increased by 20 percent. This caused a sharp increase both in the replacement rate of workers retiring after the increases and in the cumulative benefits since retirement of those who retired before them. The increases were financed, in part, by increasing the taxable maximum enough to capture roughly 85 percent of the earnings in employment covered by social security.[4]

In the 1972 act, several features of the program were indexed so that future adjustments would be made automatically, using the same procedures that had been used previously on an ad hoc basis. Benefit increases were tied to the consumer price index, which meant that the future rate of growth of benefits after retirement would be slowed in relation to the rate of increase during the 1950s and 1960s, and especially in relation to the early 1970s. Extensions of the benefit formula and increases in both the taxable maximum and the retirement-test exempt amounts were tied to changes in average earnings levels. In effect, this froze the relative position in the earnings distribution of both the taxable maximum and the exempt amount.

---

[4] At present, the taxable maximum includes about 67 percent of self-employed earnings and about 87 percent of wages and salaries. See Social Security Administration, *Social Security Bulletin, Annual Statistical Supplement, 1975*, tables 36 and 37, pp. 69–70.

TABLE 1

REPLACEMENT RATES FOR REPRESENTATIVE MALE WORKERS
AND TAXABLE EARNINGS IN EMPLOYMENT COVERED BY
SOCIAL SECURITY, 1953–1976
(percent)

| Year | Replacement Rates[a] | | | Percent of Covered Earnings Taxed |
	Low earner	Average earner	Earner at maximum	
1953	53.5	30.7	28.3	78.5
1954	51.9	29.3	28.3	77.7
1955	54.8	34.3	32.8	80.3
1956	53.8	33.5	29.6	78.8
1957	52.3	32.5	31.0	77.5
1958	50.8	31.9	31.0	76.4
1959	52.7	33.5	33.1	79.3
1960	51.8	32.8	29.8	78.1
1961	49.6	31.7	30.0	77.4
1962	48.8	31.3	30.2	75.4
1963	46.8	30.3	30.5	74.6
1964	46.4	29.8	30.8	72.8
1965	48.9	31.5	32.9	71.3
1966	48.1	31.3	33.2	80.0
1967	52.1	34.2	27.9	78.1
1968	49.7	32.4	28.4	81.7
1969	47.1	30.8	24.7	80.1
1970	52.2	34.3	29.2	78.2
1971	51.5	36.4	32.8	76.3
1972	52.3	34.9	33.2	78.3
1973	58.4	39.4	35.5	81.7
1974	56.3	38.3	30.5	85.1
1975	59.7	40.7	28.8	84.5
1976	60.6	42.4	31.0	n.a.

n.a.: Not available.

[a] These replacement rates are the initial primary insurance amount of a man retiring at the beginning of each year divided by the earnings in the year before retirement. The average earner in each year earned the annualized first-quarter average wage; the low earner's wage grows at the same rate as the average earner's and is $3,200 in 1974.

SOURCE: The replacement rates are from Robert J. Myers, "Summary of the Provisions of the Old-Age, Survivors, and Disability Insurance System, the Hospital Insurance System, and the Supplementary Medical Insurance System," privately mimeographed, June 1977. The fraction of earnings that was taxable is from Social Security Administration, Social Security Bulletin, Annual Statistical Supplement, 1975, table 36, p. 69.

TABLE 2

CUMULATIVE PERCENTAGE INCREASE IN PRICES AND IN BENEFITS
AFTER RETIREMENT, BY YEAR OF RETIREMENT, 1953–1974
(percent)

Year of Retirement	Increases to July 1970		Increases to July 1975	
	Prices	Benefits	Prices	Benefits
1953	45.2	68.1	101.2	166.0
1954	44.7	68.1	100.2	166.0
1955	45.0	48.8	101.0	135.4
1956	42.9	48.8	98.0	135.4
1957	38.0	48.8	91.2	135.4
1958	34.3	48.8	86.1	135.4
1959	33.2	39.0	84.7	120.3
1960	31.1	39.0	81.7	120.3
1961	29.8	39.0	79.9	120.3
1962	28.4	39.0	77.9	120.3
1963	26.8	39.0	75.8	120.3
1964	25.2	39.0	73.5	120.3
1965	23.1	30.0	70.6	105.6
1966	19.7	30.0	65.8	105.6
1967	16.3	30.0	61.2	105.6
1968	11.6	15.0	54.7	82.0
1969	5.9	15.0	46.8	58.2
1970			38.6	58.2
1971			32.9	58.2
1972			28.7	43.9
1973			21.1	19.9
1974			9.1	8.0

SOURCE: Price increases are cumulative percentage change in the annual average consumer price index, *Economic Report of the President 1977*, table B-47, p. 241. Benefit increases are cumulative average percentage change from July to July, Social Security Administration, *Social Security Bulletin, Annual Statistical Supplement, 1974*, pp. 18–19.

The procedure used to index the taxable maximum and the retirement-test exempt amounts has worked as intended. Subsequent analysis has shown that the method chosen to index benefit levels is seriously flawed, however. Although the method appeared to produce a desirable result in the 1950s and 1960s, it will not necessarily produce that result in future years. It is likely that the present adjustment mechanism will produce higher replacement rates for future retirees and higher tax rates for future workers than was originally intended.[5]

Indexing Options and Consequences

In the debate over how to restructure the procedure for computing the social security benefits, the basic question is: What is the most desirable way to index three major elements in the procedure in order to construct an alternative automatic adjustment mechanism? The three elements are: the computation of the worker's AMW, the adjustment of the formula used to compute initial benefit amounts, and the level of benefits after retirement.[6] The debate is not solely over how to correct the overadjustment resulting from the 1972 amendments; that flaw could be eliminated by repealing the provisions inserted that year. Unfortunately, the debate has tended to focus on only one aspect of the indexing question—namely, the long-term change in the average replacement rate—and to ignore other aspects of the indexing question.

Indexing Earnings Histories. The calculation of the AMW plays two roles in the benefit computation procedure.[7] First, it collapses all of the information in an individual's earnings record into a one-dimensional descriptor that serves to rank that individual in relation to the other persons retiring in the same year (intracohort ranking). The higher the AMW of a particular worker is relative to the mean AMW of his cohort, the higher his benefit is relative to the mean benefit of the cohort. Second, it serves to position persons retiring in a given year relative to persons retiring in other years (intertemporal positioning). If other changes in the benefit computation process are disregarded, the higher the mean AMW of one retirement cohort is relative to that of another,

---

[5] This problem and its causes have been documented in several different places. See, for example, Colin D. Campbell, *Over-Indexed Benefits: The Decoupling Proposals for Social Security* (Washington, D.C.: American Enterprise Institute, 1976); and Lawrence H. Thompson, "Toward the Rational Adjustment of Social Security Benefit Levels," *Policy Analysis*, vol. 3 (Fall 1977), pp. 485–508.

[6] In addition, a case could be made for indexing the measure used to determine calendar quarters of coverage and the substantial gainful activity measure used in disability insurance. In fact, under the provisions of H.R. 9346 (the Social Security Financing Amendments of 1977) as passed by the House of Representatives, the quarter-of-coverage measure would be indexed in the future. These indexing questions are not dealt with in this paper.

[7] This discussion assumes no changes in the present rules governing the number of years that a given birth cohort includes in its AMW computation or the period of time from which those years are to be selected. Changing these rules involves issues that lie well outside the scope of a discussion of indexing.

the higher the mean benefit of that cohort will be relative to the mean benefit of another.[8]

Intracohort ranking. In the U.S. economy, price and wage levels change over time and different workers have different earnings at different ages—that is, they display strikingly different age-earnings profiles. In this situation, indexing earnings histories can produce significant differences in the distribution of benefits among persons retiring in a given year. There are essentially three approaches to indexing earnings records: not indexing at all (the current practice), indexing each prior year's earnings by the change in prices occurring since that year, and indexing each year's earnings by the change in average wage levels.[9]

In theory, the choice of the most desirable index could be made through either a philosophical judgment or an examination of the kind of people who win or lose when one procedure is substituted for another. In practice, the latter strategy is the less fruitful because it requires a priori specification of who ought to win and who ought to lose, and it suffers from the fact that knowledge about individual earnings records is rather limited.

Conceptually, indexing by prices amounts to counting each prior year's earnings at the current value of the goods and services the earnings would then have purchased. The intracohort ranking thereby produced is a ranking according to relative lifetime purchasing power. Indexing by wages amounts to counting each prior year's earnings at the current value of the relative wage those earnings then represented. The intracohort ranking thereby produced is a ranking according to relative average lifetime earnings.[10] There appears to be no conceptual framework that would imply that earnings records should not be indexed.

As compared with the present practice, indexing of earnings records by either wages or prices would give relatively higher benefits to those whose earnings tended to peak early in their careers and relatively lower

---

[8] The introduction of indexing of earnings records will change the value of every individual's AMW. This discussion assumes that an offsetting adjustment in the benefit formula will be made at the same time that indexing is instituted, so that taken together the two changes leave the average level of benefits unchanged. What is at issue, then, is how the two changes taken together affect individual retirees or entire retirement cohorts.

[9] This discussion of wage indexing implicitly assumes that the index will be constructed from an economy-wide average wage. In theory, one could also use either a cohort-specific wage index or the wage of a particular "representative worker" as the wage index.

[10] To the extent that the average rate of increase in money wages is roughly equivalent to the riskless rate of interest, wage indexing of earnings records can also be viewed as converting all earnings into their present value at the time of retirement.

47

benefits to those whose earnings peaked late. Therefore, indexing should help less-educated, blue-collar workers relative to better-educated, white-collar workers.

Intertemporal positioning. Regardless of whether earnings histories are indexed and, if they are indexed, regardless of the index used, the mean AMW of one retirement cohort will always exceed the mean AMW of the previous retirement cohort by exactly the same percentage as the average increase in money wage levels, provided that three conditions are met:

- that wage and price levels have grown by the same constant percentage in each year over which the average is computed,
- that the number of years included in the averaging period is held constant from one cohort to the next, and
- that the members of successive cohorts have identical age-earnings and age-participation profiles.

Since none of these conditions actually holds, the decision to index and the choice of an index does affect the intertemporal positioning of the members of successive cohorts.

1. Changing wage and price levels: The percentage change in price and money wage levels varies erratically from one year to the next. Other things being equal, when earnings records are not indexed, the mean AMW of one cohort exceeds the mean AMW of another by roughly the average rate of change in money wage levels over the entire averaging period. Thus, in periods of relatively high inflation, the mean AMWs of successive cohorts do not rise as rapidly as money wage levels in the economy are rising; in periods of relatively low inflation, the mean AMWs of successive cohorts rise more rapidly than money wage levels in the economy are rising.

Indexing by prices removes all of the effect of erratic price behavior. If the other conditions hold, the mean price-indexed AMW of one cohort will exceed the mean price-indexed AMW of its predecessor by (1) the average increase in real (that is, adjusted for inflation) wages over the averaging period and (2) the increase in price levels between the retirement dates of the two cohorts.

Indexing by wages treats all prior year's earnings as if they were earned in the year of retirement. Other things being equal, the mean wage-indexed AMW of one cohort will exceed the mean wage-indexed AMW of its predecessor by the amount that the base value of the wage index used to compute its AMWs—presumably average wage levels in a particular year prior to retirement—exceeds the base value of the wage index used to compute its predecessor's AMWs. If real wages fall between those two points in time, the real value of the mean AMW will also fall; if real wages rise, the real value of the mean AMW will rise.[11]

Judged solely on its ability to produce a rational, predictable pattern of intertemporal adjustments among different cohorts, price indexing is the superior option when the averaging period and the cohort earnings profiles are constant. Price indexing adjusts correctly for any inflation occurring between the retirement date of one cohort and that of another, and it advances each cohort's mean real AMW by the rate of growth in real wage levels.

2. Changing averaging period: With respect to the vast majority of participating workers, the social security system will not be fully mature until about the year 2000. At that time, all new retirees will compute their AMWs by averaging the highest thirty-five years of taxable earnings selected from any period in their working lives. Until that time, earnings from early in a person's career (before 1951) cannot be used, and the number of years over which the average is computed is the number of years elapsing between 1955 and the year the individual turns sixty-two.[12]

The practical effect of these rules is that, between now and the year 1994, the portion of an individual's lifetime earnings that is available for inclusion and the number of years included in the AMW computation increases by one year for each successive cohort of retirees. With no indexing or with price indexing, the inclusion of this additional year would depress the rate at which the average AMW of successive cohorts would grow since both money and real wage levels would have grown over the working lives of cohort members. The effect of lengthening the averaging period under wage indexing depends on the particular shape of the age-earnings profile of cohort members and the location of the incremental year in that age-earnings profile. In general, though, the effect is far less significant.

Table 3 shows estimates of the actual effect this lengthening of the

---

[11] A more extensive discussion of the behavior of AMWs computed in different ways can be found in Lawrence H. Thompson, "An Analysis of the Issues Involved in Security Constant Replacement Rates in the Social Security OASDI Program," Technical Analysis Paper no. 5, U.S. Department of Health, Education, and Welfare, Office of the Assistant Secretary for Planning and Evaluation, Office of Income Security Policy (May 1975).

[12] Under present law, earnings from before 1950 can be used but only in an "old-start" calculation, which follows a somewhat different procedure than that described here. Fewer than 10 percent of new retirees find old-start calculations advantageous. There is a popular misconception that earnings from before age twenty-one can never be used. This is not true. Earnings from any year after 1950 can be used, regardless of the individual's age at the time.

TABLE 3

ESTIMATED EFFECT OF LENGTHENING THE AVERAGING PERIOD:
EFFECT IF APPLIED RETROSPECTIVELY TO THE COHORT
REACHING AGE SIXTY-FIVE IN 1978

Averaging Rule	Age 65 Cohort to Which Rule Will Apply	Percentage Decline in Mean AMW		
		No indexing	Price indexing	Wage indexing
High 19 of previous 27	1978	—	—	—
High 20 of previous 28	1979	2.4	1.4	0.4
High 25 of previous 33	1984	13.0	8.0	2.1
High 30 of previous 38	1989	22.3	13.7	3.8
High 35 of previous 43	1994	30.5	20.1	6.9
High 35 of previous 46	1997	30.2	19.2	4.7

NOTE: The table shows the percentage decline in the mean AMW from the mean produced by the rules actually in effect under current law for those turning sixty-five in 1978.

SOURCE: These estimates are based on an analysis of the constructed wage histories that are discussed in Lawrence Thompson, Paul Van de Water, and Jane Ross, "Wage Averaging Rules and the Distribution of Social Security Benefits" (Paper delivered at the annual meeting of the Southern Economic Association, New Orleans, Louisiana, November 13, 1975).

averaging period can have by comparing the effect of applying different averaging rules to the retirement cohort reaching age sixty-five in 1978. Over the range in which the number of years available for inclusion and the number of years required to be included are increasing equally, the mean AMW for the cohort falls. As compared with the high nineteen years of the previous twenty-seven (the computation rules actually applicable to the cohort reaching age sixty-five in 1978), inclusion of the high thirty-five of the previous forty-three would cause a reduction of 30.5 percent in the mean unindexed AMW, a reduction of 19.2 percent in the mean price-indexed AMW, and a reduction of 6.9 percent in the mean wage-indexed AMW of the cohort. Other things being equal, each 4 percent reduction in the cohort's average AMW translates into a reduction of about 1 percentage point in the mean replacement rate awarded cohort members.[13]

---

[13] Because of the progressive structure of the formula, a 4 percent decline in the average AMW would produce a decline in the average PIA of a little over 2 percent. A 2 percent decline in benefits would lead, in turn, to a decline of 2 percent or about 1 percentage point in replacement rates.

The percentage reduction from the computation based on the present law is somewhat less for the last computation rule—the high thirty-five of the previous forty-six—because of the addition of three more years from which wages can be selected without a corresponding increase in the number of years that must be included. (Since these three years represent the earnings at ages nineteen through twenty-one, the effect of adding them is greatest under wage indexing.)

3. Changing age-earnings profiles: As lifetime participation patterns of cohort members change, the mean AMW of successive cohorts will also change, unless the computation is specifically designed to adjust. Whether or not this is desirable is a philosophical question more closely related to the discussion of intracohort ranking than to the discussion of intertemporal adjustment. If one favors the intracohort ranking produced by price indexing, these intertemporal changes should not present a problem. They merely reflect differences in mean lifetime living standards among different cohorts. If one favors wage indexing, the intertemporal changes produced by differences in cohort age-earnings profiles may or may not be a problem. They are a problem if the desired intracohort ranking is to be the individual's wage relative to a specified representative worker's wage or relative to a cohort average. They should not be a problem if the desired ranking is to be based on the individual's wage relative to the economy-wide average wage.

Indexing the Benefit Formula Used for New Retirees. The benefit formula is a multiple-bracket formula through which a worker's primary insurance amount (PIA) is determined once his AMW has been computed. The formula has two attributes that control the average level and the relative distribution of benefits: the wage bracket widths (also called bracket boundaries or bend points) and the marginal replacement rates (also called benefit rates or benefit factors). Depending on the objective sought, either or both can be indexed.

The procedure for computing a PIA is similar to that used for computing income tax liability. An individual whose AMW is high enough to be in the third wage bracket receives a PIA that is the sum of the marginal rates in the first two brackets multiplied by the widths of these brackets and the marginal rate in the third bracket multiplied by the amount by which his AMW exceeds the lower boundary of the third bracket.

In essence, the brackets serve to differentiate beneficiaries by AMW level, allowing variation among beneficiaries in both marginal and average replacement rates. The structure and level of benefits, however, is determined by the interaction of the whole structure of marginal

51

replacement rates and wage bracket widths since the benefit paid to workers in higher brackets depends in part on the widths of and the marginal replacement rates in the lower brackets.

Indexing the bracket widths. The only reason for the multi-bracket benefit formula is the desire to have a progressive benefit structure. Therefore, the primary reason for indexing the brackets in the formula is the desire to achieve some particular pattern over time in the progressivity produced by the formula.

Over time, rising average money wage levels lead to increases in the nominal value of all workers' AMWs. Other things being equal, when the bracket boundaries are not indexed, rising AMW levels lead to an ever increasing fraction of retirees landing in the top bracket of the benefit formula. The lower wage brackets of the formula gradually become less effective in differentiating among retirees, so that the structure of new benefit awards gradually becomes less progressive. (Although the bracket boundaries are not indexed under present law, the progressivity of the benefit structure is not necessarily reduced over time because of the offsetting influences of the indexing of the marginal replacement rates and the periodic addition of new brackets.)

As long as the relative distribution of AMWs remains roughly constant, the effect of rising nominal AMW levels can be offset by indexing the bracket boundaries. If the brackets are indexed by the rate of change from one cohort to the next in the average AMW, the relative structure of the formula is preserved; the distribution of retirees by formula bracket will remain roughly constant over the years. (Those seeking this result usually advocate indexing the bracket boundaries by changes in the average wage level, assuming that this is a reasonable proxy for changes in the mean AMW of successive cohorts.[14])

If the bracket boundaries are indexed by the rate of change in prices, the real absolute structure of the formula is preserved; the place in the formula that is occupied by a given average real earnings level remains constant through the years.

Because real wages rise over time, the critical difference between price indexing and wage indexing of the bracket boundaries is found in the frame of reference used to evaluate the progressivity of the formula. Price indexing preserves the real absolute progressivity of the formula, whereas wage indexing preserves the relative progressivity of the formula.

Indexing marginal replacement rates. The simple, direct way of causing an equal proportionate change in the benefits of a cohort of

---

[14] This proxy may not work all that well in any given year, although it should work fairly well over a period of, say, five or more years.

newly retiring workers is to make a proportionate adjustment in the marginal replacement rates. Under present law, this occurs whenever a cost-of-living increase is granted to those who have already retired, and it provides the source of the overindexing of future benefit awards. Under an alternative system of computing benefits, such an adjustment could be used to provide for across-the-board increases or decreases in the benefit levels of successive cohorts.

Indexing Benefits after Retirement. The basic purpose of the 1972 amendments was to index to the consumer price index the benefits of those people who had already retired; that objective was achieved. The difficulty is that, with inflation rates at recent or currently projected levels, the indexing method selected had unintended effects on the benefits to be paid persons retiring in the future.

The method. The problem with present law is that the same benefit formula that is used to compute the benefits of newly retired workers is also used to compute the benefits of current retirees. As a result, the system is said to be "coupled." Any benefit increase given to one group is also automatically given to the other.

The most straightforward method of continuing to index the benefits of those who are already retired without introducing unintended adjustments in the benefits of those not yet retired is to "decouple" the computation process. Benefit increases after retirement would be granted by direct adjustment of the worker's primary insurance amount and would not cause any change in the formula used for newly retired workers.

The index. The present practice is to index the benefits of retirees to the general consumer price index. Two obvious alternatives are to index to a special retired person's price index and to index to changes in average wage levels.

1. Price indexing: Conceptually, price indexing of benefits after retirement (whichever price index is employed) amounts to maintaining the purchasing power of the retirement benefit at its initial level. When real earnings levels are rising, a price-indexed benefit will not increase as rapidly as average earnings levels. To the extent that their social security benefit is their primary source of income, the living standards of retirees will gradually fall relative to those of workers. On the other hand, when real wage levels decline (in years like 1975 and 1976), the present policy causes the living standards of retirees to rise relative to those of workers.

One common suggestion is to index social security benefits to a specially constructed consumer price index that more accurately reflects

53

the prices of the goods and services consumed by the elderly. Although this idea deserves some further consideration, it appears at this time that such a change in policy may not be worth the effort.

First, about one out of every four social security beneficiaries is not aged. They are younger families dependent on a worker who has died or become disabled. If there were significant differences between the movements in the general CPI and those in a retired workers' CPI, it may be that the former would better represent the effect of inflation on these younger beneficiaries than would the latter.

Second, one should not be surprised to find that movements in a retired workers' CPI are not enough different from movements in the general CPI to justify the breaking of the connection between social security benefit adjustments and the generally publicized index of inflation. This is the result found recently in one study that examined the need for a special poor persons' price index.[15]

2. Wage indexing: Although price indexing of retirement benefits is far more common among social security systems in developed nations, several major systems—including those in France, West Germany, and Austria—index retirees' benefits by wages.[16] To the extent that retirees depend on social security for their retirement income, indexing of their benefits by wages preserves their relative living standards after retirement.

One obvious difficulty in indexing by wages is its cost. It is estimated that, other things being equal, the adoption of such a policy would increase the long-range cost of the U.S. system by about 14 percent.[17] Indexing benefits after retirement by wages would require either that the combined payroll tax rate be increased by about 2 per-

---

[15] John L. Palmer, Michael C. Barth, and others, "The Impacts of Inflation and Higher Unemployment: With Emphasis on the Lower Income Population," Technical Analysis Paper no. 2, U.S. Department of Health, Education, and Welfare, Office of Income Security Policy (October 1974). Cumulative increases over the 1967–1976 period in the poor persons' price index totaled 73.6 percent, as compared with cumulative increases of 70.5 percent in the general consumer price index.

[16] Social Security Administration, *Social Security Programs throughout the World, 1975*, Research Report no. 48 (1976).

[17] Social Security Administration, Office of the Actuary. Under the Alternative II set of assumptions contained in the 1977 Trustees Report, the change would increase the long-range (seventy-five-year) average cost of the Carter administration's proposal (H.R. 8218) from 14.07 percent of taxable payroll to 15.99 percent of taxable payroll. In these assumptions, real average social security earnings grow at 1.68 percent a year. If the growth rate of real earnings is more rapid, the cost of wage indexing benefits after retirement would be greater; if the growth of real earnings is slower, the cost would be less.

centage points or that initial benefit levels be reduced by about 12 percent.

Summary of the Effects of Indexing in a Decoupled System. To the extent that they are not altered by subsequent legislative action, the various indexing decisions discussed in this section interact to determine the aggregate level and relative distribution of the social security benefits paid future retirees.

Given a level of aggregate expenditures to be made over the lifetime of a particular retirement cohort, the distribution of initial benefit amounts is controlled by (1) the intracohort ranking produced by the AMW computation and (2) the structure (progressivity) of the benefit formula. The time pattern in the receipt of benefits (their distribution by beneficiary life expectancy) is controlled by the method used to index benefits after the initial entitlement.

Given the relative distribution of benefits among the members of the cohort and the index to be used for post-retirement adjustments, the aggregate amount of the expenditure to be made is controlled by the level of initial replacement rates. In turn, these are determined by (1) the intertemporal pattern produced by the way AMWs are indexed, (2) the pattern of adjustments in marginal replacement rates (if any), and (3) the procedure used to index the wage brackets in the benefit formula.

Note that two indexing decisions—the one involving the AMW computation and the other involving the benefit formula brackets—affect both the level and the distribution of the lifetime benefit stream accorded a given retirement cohort.

Considerations

Before the indexing choices of this paper are specified, the philosophical views upon which those choices are based will be set out. These views concern the proper way to adjust incomes derived in different years in order to evaluate the adequacy of benefit levels and distribution, the role that social security should play in supporting the income of future retirees, and the trade-offs that must be made in order to adjust to a changing age structure of the population. The choices are also based upon an assumption about the most likely result when future legislative action is combined with the automatic adjustment provision written into the law.

Relative versus Real Absolute Income Comparisons. One thread that runs through the whole discussion of indexing options is the choice between wage indexing a particular aspect of the benefit computation and price indexing that aspect. This dichotomy is found in choosing how to index earnings in the computation of the AMW, in selecting a frame of reference to evaluate changes over time in the progressivity of the benefit formula, in determining how to index benefits after retirement, and in evaluating the adequacy of the average social security benefit of future retirement cohorts. Typically, the wage-indexing option corresponds to the view that the proper approach is to compare relative income levels, whereas the price-indexing option corresponds to the view that the proper approach is to compare the purchasing power of income. A reasonable case can be made for either approach. The evidence, however, suggests that, as individuals and as a society, Americans tend to adopt the relative standard rather than the real absolute standard.

As real incomes rise, the fraction of income that is consumed in the aggregate remains roughly constant. As a group, consumers behave as if their desired consumption level were a function of their relative income and not of their real absolute income. It follows that desired retirement consumption for any given individual should also be a function of the individual's pre-retirement earnings. In other words, in the eyes of retirees, the standard with which the adequacy of retirement income is judged will be a relative standard.

Analysts also adopt the relative income framework when they examine income distribution trends. A comparison of changes over time in the distribution of income or in the progressivity of taxation invariably is a comparison against a relative standard rather than an absolute standard.

The major U.S. public assistance program—Aid to Families with Dependent Children (AFDC)—makes implicit use of a relative standard. Between 1953 and 1974, the average real benefit per AFDC recipient grew at an annual rate of 1.83 percent.[18] By comparison, real per capita disposable income grew at an average annual rate of 2.24 percent, and median real annual earnings of men working for four quarters in employment covered by social security grew at an annual rate of 1.6 percent.

Estimates of social security replacement rates over the 1953–1974 period were shown above in Table 1. Essentially, those data suggest that replacement rates for workers at a given relative position in the earnings distribution were kept surprisingly constant between the early 1950s and the late 1960s. Replacement rates show an upward trend only in the last seven or eight years.

---

[18] *Social Security Bulletin, Annual Statistical Supplement, 1974*, table 17, p. 50.

Public and Private Sector Roles. Although social security benefits represent the major source of retirement income controlled by the federal government, the level and distribution of total retirement income is also influenced by private sources, including private pensions. A relative decline in the role of social security could be entirely offset by a relative expansion in the role of private pensions.

Even though the social security system and the present private pension system share the same objective—the provision of retirement income—they should not be viewed as substitutes for each other. The two institutions are quite different, each with its own particular strengths and weaknesses.

Social security is fundamentally a mandatory, universal (or very nearly so), vested, and fully portable pension system. If wage histories are indexed, social security benefit computations will automatically update the value of earnings derived in a job that ended a number of years before retirement age was reached. Because of these attributes, absolute reliance can be placed on the actual receipt of a social security pension at the end of all but the briefest work careers. Earnings from a job left in mid-career will produce a pension of reasonable size, and the benefit formula can be calibrated to accomplish whatever redistribution society desires. At the same time, however, the terms and conditions governing the receipt of social security benefits and the computation of the amount due must be uniform throughout the society and can leave no room for voluntary alteration by individuals, employers, or employee organizations.

The social security system is also current-cost financed; for all intents and purposes, a given year's benefit payments are financed from that year's taxes. Current-cost financing of a pension program has the inherent advantage of allowing benefits to be indexed after retirement. The changes in price or wage levels that trigger an increase in retirement benefits will simultaneously produce the income necessary to finance those increases. Current-cost financing has the inherent disadvantage of making the relationship between revenues needed from each worker and benefit payments paid to each recipient dependent on the relative size of each group.

The present private pension system is (more or less) voluntary. Subject to limitations such as those imposed by the Employment Retirement Income Security Act of 1974 (ERISA), benefit amounts, retirement ages, and other attributes are tailored to the needs and preferences of individual employers and employee groups (and, to a far lesser extent, individual participants). Pension coverage is far from universal; at present, just under half of the jobs in the private economy are covered

57

by a pension plan.[19] Prospects for further extensions of private pension coverage are uncertain, and those for near universal coverage are nil.

Recent reforms assure that workers covered by a private sector pension plan will accrue vested rights to a pension if they stay with the same employer or employee group long enough and that such vested obligations will be met. There is, however, no assurance of pension portability; no assurance that an individual who changes jobs frequently will acquire vested pension rights, even if all his jobs have pension plans; and no requirement that earnings credits based on a job that ended in mid-career will be updated before retirement benefits are computed.

The private pension system is being forced to move gradually to full reserve financing. This will have the advantage of further assuring that benefit obligations will be met. It will also insulate private pension financing from the effects of shifting employment patterns, and will generate additional funds to finance new capital formation. It will have the disadvantages of significantly increasing the short-run cost of providing a given level of pension benefits and, in the longer run, of making it virtually impossible to index private pension benefit amounts after retirement.

The current differences between private pensions and social security are probably inherent in the respective institutions. An attempt to mandate universal coverage, portability, or some minimum degree of redistribution in private pensions would undoubtedly involve such extensive government specification of the required attributes of the plan that any advantage of a voluntary, private system would be all but eliminated. If private pension benefits were allowed to be indexed through, say, the government's issuing purchasing power bonds, there would be a risk of merely introducing current-cost public financing of a portion of private sector pension benefits. Similarly, an attempt to expand social security by allowing voluntary supplementation of benefits would probably accomplish nothing that could not be accomplished more directly by expanding the availability of Individual Retirement Accounts (IRAs).

A change in the relative size of the social security system un-

---

[19] The most recent estimate is that 44 percent of private wage and salary workers are covered by pensions; see Walter W. Kolodrubetz, "Employee-Benefit Plans, 1972," *Social Security Bulletin*, vol. 37 (May 1974), pp. 15–21. This does not mean that 44 percent of workers reaching retirement age will have pensions. Some of the 44 percent in jobs now covered by pensions will not remain in their jobs long enough to be vested, while some in the 56 percent of the jobs not covered by pensions will have pension coverage from a different job at the time they retire.

doubtedly would cause an offsetting change in the relative size of the private pension system. In view of the inherent differences between these two institutions, the important issue is whether the interests of the U.S. society are better served by the relative expansion of one and the relative contraction of the other.

Changing Population Structure. If the recent low fertility rates continue into the future, and if immigration policies are not changed, the age structure of the U.S. population will shift dramatically. Between 1977 and 1990, the youth dependency ratio—the ratio of people under the age of twenty to those aged twenty through sixty-four—will decline; beginning in about the year 2010, the aged dependency ratio—the ratio of those aged sixty-five and older to those aged twenty through sixty-four—will rise sharply. This pattern emerges in the central set of population projections used in the 1977 report of the social security trustees; it is shown in Table 4.

Unfortunately, under these population projections, the decline in the youth dependency ratio will probably not be sufficient to offset the increase in the aged dependency ratio. For one thing, current public

TABLE 4

PROJECTED DEPENDENCY RATIOS FOR THE AGED
AND YOUTH, 1975–2050

Year	Aged Ratio[a]	Youth Ratio[b]
1975	0.189	0.640
1980	0.192	0.550
1990	0.203	0.475
2000	0.203	0.476
2010	0.209	0.453
2020	0.268	0.463
2030	0.336	0.491
2040	0.328	0.484
2050	0.306	0.484

[a] Aged dependency ratio is the ratio of the population aged sixty-five and older to the population aged twenty through sixty-four.
[b] Youth dependency ratio is the ratio of the population under the age of twenty to the population aged twenty through sixty-four.
SOURCE: U.S. Congress, House, *1977 Annual Report of the Board of Trustees of the Federal Old-Age and Survivors Insurance and Disability Insurance Trust Funds*, House Document no. 95-150, 95th Congress, 1st session, May 10, 1977, Appendix table B, p. 63.

TABLE 5

FUTURE REPLACEMENT RATES AND COSTS UNDER FOUR DIFFERENT AUTOMATIC ADJUSTMENT PROVISIONS
(percent)

Plan[a]	Average 75-Year Cost	Year 2000		Year 2030	
		Replacement rate	Average cost	Replacement rate	Average cost
A	15.3	45	12.7	45	19.3
B	13.7	40	11.3	40	16.9
C	12.6	40	11.9	31	14.3
D	11.3	34	10.5	28	12.8

[a] Plan A is the Carter administration's proposal, in which replacement rates are held constant at their projected 1979 levels. Plan B is replacement rates held constant at a level roughly 10 percent below projected 1979 levels. Plan C is a combination plan, in which replacement rates are held constant at projected 1979 levels through 1988 and allowed to decline between 1988 and 2030. Plan D is the House-Senate consultant's proposal, commonly called the Hsiao proposal, in which replacement rates begin to decline immediately.

SOURCE: U.S. Congress, Senate, Committee on Finance, *Staff Data and Materials on Social Security Financing Proposals*, 95th Congress, 1st session, September 1977, pp. 23–29.

expenditures per person under age twenty are less than half the current level of public expenditures per person over age sixty-five. Other things being equal, the youth dependency ratio must fall by more than two percentage points to offset an increase of one percentage point in the aged dependency ratio. For another thing, most of the gain from the decline in the youth dependency ratio is realized some twenty years before the increase in the aged dependency ratio begins. If plans are not made for the future, the U.S. society could become acclimated to the public expenditure levels implied by the lower youth dependency ratio long before the increase in aged dependency occurs.[20]

If the shift in the population structure implied by these projections actually occurs, the United States will face a choice between higher tax rates and lower replacement rates early in the next century. The trade-off is illustrated in Table 5 by a comparison of present projections of future tax and replacement rates under four different indexing plans

[20] Once the magnitude of the problem is a little better known, one way to plan ahead is to begin accumulating larger trust fund reserves so that they can be drawn down during the 2025–2035 period when aged dependency peaks.

considered by the Senate Finance Committee. The replacement rates shown are for a worker retiring in a given year after having always earned the average social security wage. Average cost is, in effect, the combined (employer and employee) tax rate that would have to be instituted today in order to finance each plan for the next seventy-five years with a level tax rate. In effect, the cost in a given year is the combined tax rate that year if a pure current-cost financing policy is employed. Average cost in 1979 is projected at 10.9 percent of taxable payroll and the scheduled 1979 combined tax rate is 9.9 percent.[21]

The assumption in the central set of population projections in the 1977 trustee's report is that total fertility will gradually increase to an average of 2.1 children per woman by the first decade of the twenty-first century. Thereafter, total fertility is assumed to be constant. Although this assumption appears perfectly reasonable now, it may not appear so reasonable in ten or fifteen years.

Few economic or demographic measures have displayed as wide a variation over the last forty-five years as has the total fertility rate. Between 1926 and 1936, the rate fell from 2.91 children per woman to 2.15 children per woman. Over the next twenty-four years, the rate rose steadily, reaching 3.64 in 1960. Thereafter, it declined steadily, to 2.43 in 1970 and to an estimated 1.72 in 1976.[22]

If fertility rates begin to increase in the next few years, the aged dependency ratios in the twenty-first century could be significantly lower than those shown in Table 4. Moreover, even if total fertility stabilizes in the future at today's level of 1.7 children per woman, the aged dependency ratio will not rise above 21 percent for at least the next thirty years.[23]

Cutting back on social security benefit payments now does not seem necessary if the only motivation is the anticipation of a structural shift in the population. If the structural shift now being forecast does materialize, however, sometime in the mid-1990s the United States will be faced with the choice between reducing benefit payments and increasing taxes early in the twenty-first century.

---

[21] In this context, cost is defined as total expenses as a percent of taxable payroll. It is the combined payroll tax rate that would raise just enough money to cover that year's expenditures. Trust fund balances would increase by the amount of the interest that was earned on them.

[22] Social Security Administration, Office of the Actuary. The fertility rates are adjusted for underenumeration of the population and underregistration of births.

[23] See the Alternative III projections in U.S. Congress, House, *1977 Annual Report of the Board of Trustees of the Federal Old-Age and Survivors Insurance and Disability Insurance Trust Funds*, House Document no. 95-150, 95th Congress, 1st session, May 10, 1977, Appendix table B, p. 63.

Future Legislative Action. The long-range cost estimates associated with each particular indexing approach are based on the assumption that no further changes will be made in the law. The future scope of the social security system will be determined, however, by the automatic adjustment provisions incorporated at the time of decoupling in combination with the legislative changes made over the years after the new indexing scheme is adopted. If one assumes that the law will undergo no major changes in the future, then these estimates represent today's best guess of future costs. On the other hand, if one assumes that the plan adopted today will be repeatedly modified by future Congresses, then today's best guess of the future cost of the program must incorporate the cost of the expected modifications.

Many of the differences in opinion about the desirability of particular indexing approaches arise because of differences in opinion about the likelihood that the Congress will modify the law. Some assume that whatever is enacted today will serve only as a baseline from which future Congresses will inevitably make liberalizations. Others believe that future Congresses and future administrations will want, and should be given, the freedom to liberalize the program periodically. Those holding either of these views believe that the automatic adjustment provisions should produce a relative decline in the scope of social security so that future statutory liberalizations are anticipated. Some assume that the future statutory liberalizations will offset entirely the effect of the automatic adjustment provisions, leaving the system with constant replacement rates. Others hope that replacement rates actually will decline.

Some argue that, when the effect of future legislative activity is included, a plan that produces declining average replacement rates may actually lead to a larger social security system than would be produced by an indexing scheme that produces constant average replacement rates. They believe that declining average replacement rates will simply legitimize periodic liberalizations, which will more than offset the automatic reductions.

Finally, still others believe that the Congress will either liberalize or deliberalize the program in response to future conditions. Their view is that the indexing procedure that is most appropriate for the next ten or fifteen years should be adopted today because the legislative process will produce whatever changes are required in that procedure as the environment in the twenty-first century becomes clearer.

A Strategy for This Round

During most of 1977, the administration and the Congress worked together to develop a new method for indexing the social security benefit computation procedure. In the process, projections have been made of the effect that each option would have over the next seventy-five years, provided that all the current long-range economic and demographic assumptions prove to be correct and no other changes are made in the law. Although such projections are useful, they have many limitations.

In the first place, any seventy-five-year population projection contains major uncertainties, especially regarding future fertility rates. In the second place, it would be a remarkable departure from past practice if the social security system were not changed significantly over twenty years, to say nothing of seventy-five years. The program that was set up in 1935 was substantially modified in 1939, in 1950, in 1956, and again in 1965. Another substantial modification occurred in 1977 and yet another will probably occur in the next three or four years.

Neither the administration nor the Congress views the 1977 legislation as the last adjustment that will occur in the social security program in the foreseeable future. Both see the need for a continuing review of the program, with particular emphasis on the way in which the disability program is working and the way in which the retirement program treats different types of households.

In view of the uncertainties about future economic and demographic trends and the interest in making other, substantial alterations in the social security program, it does not seem necessary to solve at this time all of the problems that may or may not arise in the next fifty years. Rather, a reasonable strategy would be to concentrate now on creating a new, decoupled process for computing benefits. The concentration should be on removing the unintended overadjustment in future benefits and on instituting a new adjustment process that (1) makes sense for the next ten to fifteen years, (2) sets the social security program on a desirable future course, and (3) does not foreclose options for dealing with the problems that may develop in the next century.

The discussion that follows offers my personal view of how this can be done.

Indexing Earnings Records. As noted above, the AMW computation plays two roles: an intracohort role, whereby each member of a particular retirement cohort is ranked, and an intertemporal role, whereby the members of the whole cohort are ranked relative to members of previous and subsequent cohorts. On balance, it appears that wage indexing of earnings records is the best way to handle both of these functions.

Although a reasonable philosophical case can be made for the intracohort ranking produced by either wage indexing or price indexing, I know of none that can be made for not indexing at all. Between the two indexing approaches, wage indexing appears to be more sensible when combined with a thirty-five-year averaging period.

Price indexing focuses on average pre-retirement living standards. It would provide a reasonable method for determining an intracohort ranking if AMWs were being computed over a relatively small number of years immediately preceding retirement.[24] It has less philosophical appeal, however, when earnings from age eighteen are being used to compute benefits. Earnings that far removed from the date of retirement are hardly what one usually thinks of as "pre-retirement earnings." With a long averaging period, the philosophical choice is between a lifetime average purchasing power and a lifetime average relative wage. I prefer the latter.

The crucial difference between wage and price indexing of earnings records, however, involves the intertemporal role of the AMW computation. Because of the scheduled lengthening of the averaging period, price indexing of earnings records would introduce a significant, though hidden, decline in average replacement rates. For all intents and purposes, wage indexing would not. If a decline in replacement rates is going to be engineered, it should be done in the open and in a manner that allows control over the timing and pattern of the decline. It should not be the byproduct of the maturation of the AMW computation.

Indexing the Benefit Formula. The method chosen to index the bracket boundaries and marginal replacement rates in the benefit formula is probably the most controversial aspect of the decoupling debate because the method provides the key to controlling the average level and structure of future replacement rates. In discussing the merits of the various options available, it is useful first to examine the alternatives in a world in which the age structure of the population is forever constant and then to examine how adjustments can be made to the projected shift in that age structure.

If the age structure of the population remained constant, the cost of supporting a given average replacement rate would remain constant through the years. The issue of how the benefit formula should be indexed would then turn on considerations of the desired future relative

---

[24] As the system now operates, social security benefits could not be based only on wages earned in the ten or fifteen years immediately preceding retirement because not all retirees even worked in those years. Individuals qualify for benefits as soon as they have worked forty quarters, or ten full years. An individual who worked only from age eighteen through age twenty-seven is entitled to benefits just as is an individual who worked only from age fifty-five through age sixty-four.

roles of the public and private retirement income systems, the most appropriate manner in which to evaluate the progressivity of the benefit formula, and the desired role to be given future legislation in determining the scope of social security. In such a world, I believe that a constant relative structure of replacement rates—wage indexing of the wage brackets and constant marginal replacement rates—makes the most sense.

As has been noted, private pensions and social security are two quite different institutions. Although today's private pension system may be a reasonably effective device for many people to use in supplementing social security, its coverage is not now and probably never will be universal, and the actual receipt of a private pension benefit by every person who works in employment covered by a pension plan is not now and probably never will be assured. For the great bulk of workers, private pensions are simply not an adequate substitute for social security. Consequently, reducing the relative role that social security plays in supporting the incomes of future retirees would necessarily reduce the incomes of many—probably the majority of—future retirees relative to the incomes of future workers.

The frame of reference that most individuals use to evaluate their own status is a relative one. Accordingly, one's view of what constitutes an adequate retirement income should focus on relative incomes of retirees—their retirement incomes relative to their pre-retirement incomes or their retirement incomes relative to the earnings of their counterparts who are still working. Because I do not believe that an expansion of private pensions would provide an adequate offset to any contraction in the relative role played by social security, I conclude that the provision of adequate retirement incomes to future retirees requires that social security average replacement rates be held constant.

The framework in which the progressivity of virtually all activities in the public sector are evaluated invariably focuses on relative incomes, and this is the same framework that should be applied to evaluating the progressivity of the social security program. It may well be that, with the advent of the Supplemental Security Income program and a comprehensive reformed welfare program, the social security program could be relieved of some of the transfer functions that are now handled through the progressive benefit formula. That is a separate question, however, that can be addressed by adjusting the structure of the benefit formula explicitly and directly. Once again, those adjustments need not be hidden in the level and structure of social security benefits that are believed to be appropriate, and this particular problem need not be solved as a part of decoupling.

Finally, I sense that neither the Congress, nor the last administration, nor the present administration is terribly concerned about any limitation on future freedom of action that might result from legislating constant average replacement rates. On the contrary, I believe that they would prefer—to the extent that future events will allow—to review and modify the way that other facets of the program work without having to worry every few years about recent trends in replacement rate levels.

The major argument against the maintenance of constant replacement rates is the costs that will result in the twenty-first century if the projected shift in the age structure of the population occurs. Essentially, it is the concern that the United States simply cannot afford social security benefits at the level implied by the maintenance of constant average replacement rates.

As was discussed earlier, if the shift in the age structure occurs as projected, the Congress will be faced with a choice between levying higher taxes to support today's replacement rate levels and cutting replacement rates in order to avoid major tax increases. One way to look at this choice is to ask whether the burden of increased aged dependency should be borne entirely by future workers, entirely by future retirees, or by both proportionately.

It is interesting to compute the kind of adjustment that would be required if future workers and future retirees were to bear the burden proportionately; the computation suggests that the benefit adjustments required under such an accommodation would not be difficult to institute. If it is assumed that employers fully shift their share of the social security tax to their employees, today's system costs workers 10.3 percent of what their (taxable) wage would be in the absence of social security. If the payroll tax reached a combined rate of 17 percent, workers would be paying 16.1 percent of that same (taxable) wage. Their income after social security taxes would have fallen by 6.5 percent.[25]

The imposition of a similar 6.5 percent reduction in social security benefit levels would have the effect of reducing the replacement rate

---

[25] The 1979 current cost of social security is 10.9 percent of taxable payroll. Assuming that the employee's wages are lowered by the amount that his employer pays in social security taxes, the employee is actually paying 10.3 percent (10.9 divided by 105.45) of the wage he would have had in the absence of social security. A 17 percent combined rate imposes a tax at the effective rate of 16.1 percent of the pre–social security wage (17 divided by 105.45). Before the tax increase, the individual received 89.7 percent of the wage he would have gotten in the absence of social security. After the tax increases, he receives 83.9 percent of the same wage. The reduction in after-tax earnings is the reduction from 89.7 percent of the pre–social security wage to 83.9 percent of the same wage, a 6.5 percent decline.

for an average worker from the level of a little more than 45 percent that both the Ford and Carter administrations proposed to 42.4 percent. If this is the adjustment procedure adopted, a benefit reduction of this size could likely be instituted in some future year without a great deal of trauma. Moreover, social security taxes in some countries—for example, West Germany—are already at 18 percent of payroll; thus, a 17 percent combined rate in the United States is not beyond the realm of possibility.

It must be remembered, however, that this division between future workers and future retirees is an artificial one, for the future workers are also the future retirees. In the last analysis, the question of how to adjust to a shifting age structure will be answered by the workers themselves as they decide whether to pay higher taxes during their working years in order to receive higher social security benefits in their retirement years. Essentially, that is a decision that workers must make through the political process, and it is one to which there is no right or wrong answer.

Indexing Benefits after Retirement. Although action on this is not a necessary part of decoupling, I think there should be more discussion of benefit adjustments after retirement. The present practice freezes the real value of social security benefits at their initial level. As economic growth allows others to enjoy higher standards of living, the income of those who have been on the social security benefit rolls for a long time gradually falls in relation to the rest of society.

One option worth exploring would be to index benefits to wages and make an offsetting reduction in initial replacement rate levels. Another option, which might prove more acceptable, would be to have a schedule of periodic increases to be received after a beneficiary has been on the rolls for, say, ten consecutive years. This latter strategy could serve to insure that those on the rolls a long time receive some of the benefit of the long-run growth of the economy without also entailing excessive costs for the social security system.

Commentaries

John L. Palmer

Two discussion topics are suggested by the papers of William Hsiao and Lawrence Thompson. The first is the behavior of replacement rates over time that will be implicit in whatever changes are made in the social security law when decoupling occurs. The second is the method chosen to index earnings in the computation of workers' average monthly wages (AMWs). I am going to shortchange the first topic for several reasons, the foremost of which is that it now appears to be only an academic issue.

I found the second set of issues, dealing with the indexing of earnings in the AMW calculation, to be most provocatively, but less than adequately, explored in Thompson's paper. Clearly they have not yet received the attention they merit, although Thompson's paper represents a major step toward remedying that lack. Because Thompson's presentation, though lucid, deals with such a complex set of interrelationships, let me state in my own terms what I understand to be his main points.

First, when decoupling occurs, indexing will enter into the calculation of benefits in two distinct and important ways—in collapsing lifetime earnings histories into AMWs and in adjusting the wage brackets in the formula by which primary insurance amounts (PIAs) are derived from AMWs.

Second, a strong conceptual case can be made for desiring the effects of either price or wage indexing on the distribution of benefits among workers retiring in a given year (the intracohort effect).

Third, in a properly defined "equilibrium," both price and wage indexing will yield the same pattern of average AMWs among successive retirement cohorts. This pattern probably would be unanimously agreed upon as the desirable one: the mean indexed AMW of a cohort will exceed the mean indexed AMW of its predecessor by the average increase in real wages over the averaging period plus the increase in price levels between the retirement dates of the two cohorts. Because certain

NOTE: The views expressed in these comments are the author's own, and they do not necessarily reflect those of other staff, the officers, or trustees of the Brookings Institution.

equilibrium conditions are not met, however, neither price nor wage indexing yields exactly the desired result. In particular, the lengthening of the averaging period results in a serious decline (relative to the desired pattern) in the values of average price-indexed AMWs for successive cohorts and a lesser decline in wage-indexed AMWs, and the year-to-year fluctuations in average real wage changes will be reflected in corresponding fluctuations in the real value of mean wage-indexed AMWs for successive cohorts.

After elegantly establishing those points, Thompson proceeds to introduce his own (explicitly acknowledged) value judgments and argues persuasively that, on balance, wage indexing provides the most satisfying outcome for the remainder of the century with respect to all three critical effects: the intracohort distribution of benefits; the intertemporal pattern of average AMWs among successive cohorts; and the behavior of average replacement rates over time, as determined by the indexing of the wage brackets in the benefit formula. In doing so, however, I believe that Thompson (as well as Hsiao) gives the impression that the range of options open for indexing is somewhat narrower than is the case. Specifically, I think his paper would have benefited from some discussion of the following topics.

First, it should be explicitly pointed out that there is no reason, other than simplicity, why the same type of indexing must be employed in determining the consequences for each of the three areas indicated above. Thompson has not made this clear in his paper. For example, if one preferred that intracohort rankings be based on the average purchasing power of lifetime earnings, but that average replacement rates should be held roughly constant over time, price indexing to calculate AMWs could be combined with wage indexing of the wage brackets in the benefit formula. Or, even less obviously, the indexing of AMWs could be done so that it would yield, on the one hand, the intracohort effects of price indexing and, on the other hand, the intertemporal patterning of mean indexed AMWs resulting from wage indexing.

Second, from the perspective of intracohort positioning, there appears to be a strong conceptual basis for preferring the effects of either price or wage indexing, but no other variant; this is not the case, however, for the indexing of the wage brackets and the consequent effects on average replacement rates among successive cohorts over time. As both Thompson and Hsiao make clear, this latter judgment depends crucially upon such things as notions of adequacy and willingness to bear commensurate tax burdens, and the desired role of social security as compared with private saving. Depending upon prevailing public attitudes about these issues, almost any pattern of replacement rates over time that is not capriciously affected by economic or demographic variables might be desired. Straight price or wage indexing of the bracket widths yield just two, relatively extreme, results from among the infinite number that could be sensibly defended.

Furthermore, if a decline in replacement rates is desired, it may be preferable to accomplish this through adjusting the percentages applied to the wage brackets in the benefit formula while still wage indexing the bracket widths. The degree of progressivity desired in the benefit structure is an issue that can be separated from that of the behavior of the average replacement rates over time among successive cohorts, and it should be approached as such.

Third, I think Thompson takes too lightly the deviation produced by wage indexing from the desired intertemporal pattern of average AMWs. Should the Congress decide upon across-the-board wage indexing, it undoubtedly will be done in the belief that this will produce stable average replacement rates. Yet, as Thompson explains, the effect of the lengthening of the averaging period now in the law is to produce a generally downward trend in average replacement rates over the next two decades that will reduce benefits by an average of about 4 percent (relative to a regime of stable replacement rates). Moreover, the use of a pre-retirement year base for wage indexing will produce year-to-year fluctuations in average indexed AMWs equivalent to year-to-year fluctuations in average real wage growth. At the onset of a recession, this could easily result in a cohort of retirees receiving lower real benefits than the one that preceded it.

Clearly, neither of these problems is as severe as the irrationality created by the coupling problem, but they will result in significant deviations of benefit levels from what the Congress intends and thinks it will be getting. I also suspect that these will be viewed as inequitable and undesirable. Once they are widely recognized, I can picture the lead-in to newspaper articles that will be written sometime in the 1980s:

> Because of a flaw in the indexing procedures adopted in the 1977 social security amendments when the overadjustment for inflation was eliminated, the lengthening of the averaging period and the erratic real wage growth performance of the economy have combined to produce an unintended effect on the initial benefit levels.

Steps could be taken to replace or eliminate these possible effects of wage indexing. For example, the averaging period could be fixed at twenty years, and the base for the wage index could be constructed from the average of several years just before retirement. (If the base were constructed from the entire averaging period, the wage index would have the same effects as a price index, other things being equal.) Some discussion of these types of possibilities and their pros and cons would be desirable.

These issues are indicative of an even larger number that lurk behind the various choices for indexing the social security system. It is hoped that all the issues will receive the attention they deserve in the near future. They have not to date, in part because of their complexity, and in part because of the overriding focus on the behavior of average replacement rates over time. Specific resolutions of the issues will fall out of the decisions about decoupling, which will be made largely on the basis of concern about the behavior of replacement rates over time; but the consequences of these resolutions will not have been subject to appropriate public scrutiny. Fortunately, there will be ample opportunities in the future to refine and modify the automatic indexing procedures in light of more informed judgments on these issues, while still preserving the desired future behavior of average replacement rates.

Dean R. Leimer

Most of the comments that I will make are based on work that I have done with Ronald Hoffman and Alan Freiden. Several papers detailing the results of this work are available for the asking.[1]

The papers presented by Lawrence Thompson and William Hsiao argue the relative merits of the two most widely discussed "decoupling" options. I will refer to these as the price-indexing and the wage-indexing options. Although both papers are good presentations of the considerations involved in the choice of alternative benefit structures, neither gives sufficient attention to some of the equity implications of these two decoupling options.

In addition, I agree with John Palmer that the list of options that has been presented is too limited. One possible reason for this may be that the appropriate functions of the various components of the benefit structure have not received enough attention in the decoupling debate.

---

[1] See Dean R. Leimer and Ronald Hoffman, "Designing an Equitable Intertemporal Social Security Benefit Structure," mimeographed, Social Security Administration, Office of Research and Statistics (November 1976); Dean R. Leimer, Ronald Hoffman, and Alan Freiden, "A Framework for Analyzing the Equity of the Social Security Benefit Structure," *Studies in Income Distribution No. 6*, Social Security Administration, Office of Research and Statistics (forthcoming); and Dean R. Leimer, "An Empirical Analysis of Alternative Social Security Benefit Structures," *Studies in Income Distribution No. 9*, Social Security Administration, Office of Research and Statistics (forthcoming).

An examination of the functions of those components leads one to consider other indexing alternatives besides the two major proposals presented here.

Consequently, my comments are structured around what I believe to be the appropriate functions of the major components of the benefit structure—the benefit base, the benefit base bracket adjustment and the marginal benefit rate adjustment. In my comments, I refer to both intra-cohort and intercohort effects, with "cohort" being defined as the group of workers retiring in a given year.

The benefit base under the present system is the AME (average monthly earnings). Under the proposed price-indexing and wage-indexing options, the benefit base is denoted as the AIME (average indexed monthly earnings). The benefit base is the measure of each worker's prior earnings which, in conjunction with the benefit formula, determines the amount of the worker's initial benefit. As such, the benefit base is part of the index of equality in the social security system—it positions workers within each cohort relative to the progressivity that is embedded in the benefit formula. Together, the benefit base and the benefit formula determine the distribution of initial benefits and replacement rates among workers retiring in a given year.

In a social security system aimed at replacing earnings, the benefit base should reflect the measure of prior earnings that one wants to replace. Consequently, the index used to compute the benefit base should be chosen on the basis of what is believed to be the appropriate measure of each worker's earnings position relative to other workers retiring in the same year. As both papers point out, the conceptually appropriate choice of this index is not obvious and involves a value judgment. A price index does not adjust for increases in productivity over time, and some people might think that is an important omission. An average earnings index is sensitive to changes in the composition of the reference group of workers. Other alternatives might also be considered. For example, the index for each group of workers retiring in a given year might be based on the prior average earnings experience of only workers belonging to that cohort; alternatively, the benefit base might be specified as the sum of each worker's prior earnings accumulated over time using some interest rate series.[2] The essential point is that the decision about which index to use to adjust prior earnings should be based primarily on how that index positions workers within their retirement group.

I was glad that Thompson emphasized the importance of the

---

[2] For a fuller discussion of the equity implications of these and other alternative specifications of the benefit base, see the papers cited above, note 1.

benefit base index on the relative intracohort positions of workers. Nevertheless, he argues that "the crucial difference between wage and price indexing of earnings records . . . involves the intertemporal role of the AMW computation." As Palmer pointed out, this might be the case if the index used to adjust the benefit base brackets over time is the same as that used to index each worker's earnings record; but there is no conceptual reason to impose this restriction a priori. These two adjustments may involve quite different criteria of equity. There are alternative ways to adjust for shifts in the distribution of the benefit base between cohorts as wages rise without distorting the essential role of the benefit base as a device for positioning within the cohort.

The adjustment of the benefit base brackets is also part of the index of equality, and, in this case, the adjustment is between successive cohorts. The adjustment of the benefit base brackets repositions the benefit formula across the distribution of the benefit base for a given cohort, thereby determining the degree of effective progressivity. Unless the brackets are adjusted to reflect shifts in the distribution of the benefit base between successive cohorts as a result of higher wages, the effective progressivity can be expected to change over time.

This is the case under either the price-indexing or the wage-indexing options. Under the price-indexing option, the distribution of the benefit base will tend to shift into successively higher brackets of the benefit formula, causing the replacement rates of workers at the low end of the distribution to fall more rapidly than those of workers at the high end. This is not a trivial effect. Using the projected replacement rates in Table 6 of Hsiao's paper, it can be seen that the replacement rates of the low earner are projected to decline by 47 percent between 1979 and 2050, whereas the decline is only 27 percent for the maximum earner. This constitutes a potentially serious criticism of the price-indexing option, particularly when it is recognized that the stated advantages of this option—including the use of the purchasing power standard and the declining replacement rates—can be achieved by other alternatives without producing this dramatic change in effective progressivity.

The direction of the changes in effective progressivity under the wage-indexing option is not certain because changes in the index of average earnings depend on various types of compositional effects. Previous empirical work suggests, however, that important changes in the effective progressivity can occur over time under either type of indexing.[3] Changes in progressivity also affect the predictability of future program costs.

---

[3] Leimer, "An Empirical Analysis of Alternative Social Security Benefit Structures."

Effective progressivity in the benefit formula might be maintained over time in several ways, if that is desired. One way would be to adjust the benefit base brackets over time by the percentage change in the average benefit base between successive cohorts. This adjustment might also be coupled with periodic adjustments to reflect changes in the shape of the distribution of the benefit base. This adjustment procedure might not be practical, either because of administrative difficulties or because of a lack of public understanding of the program. A more practical alternative might be: first, to adjust the benefit base brackets on a year-to-year basis using an average earnings series (as is done under the wage-indexing option); and, second, to monitor actual changes in the distribution of the benefit base between cohorts and periodically adjust the benefit base brackets in the benefit formula to take account of differences between shifts in the distribution of the benefit base and changes in the average earnings index. The monitoring process in the second part might take the form of computing the average benefit base for each successive cohort, or analyzing changes in the entire distribution.

Finally, the bracket adjustment need not be chosen on the basis of the intertemporal pattern of projected program costs or replacement rates. As indicated earlier, the bracket adjustment can be chosen on the basis of the changes desired in the effective progressivity on the benefit formula over time. Once the brackets are determined for each future cohort, the absolute amounts of initial benefits and replacement rates can be set at any desired level (without altering the effective progressivity of the formula) by uniform changes in the marginal benefit rates. In this way, the stated goals of the price-indexing option could be achieved without producing dramatic changes in the effective progressivity of the formula over time.

That brings us to strategies for current reform. It is unrealistic and probably undesirable to legislate an "automatic" benefit structure with the expectation that it will remain unchanged for all time. Whatever benefit structure is enacted, there will undoubtedly be a need for periodic ad hoc revisions to reflect changing social and economic conditions. Nevertheless, any major reform of the social security system that is perceived as permanent will form the basis of life-cycle decisions. The great uncertainty associated with long-run projections suggests that it would be prudent to allow some margin for error on the conservative side in the automatic nature of the system.

Unfortunately, only a small number of options have received serious consideration in the current policy debate. A wide variety of alternatives should also be considered. Some of these alternatives might be viewed as combining the best features of the price-indexing and wage-indexing options. In addition, both the price-indexing and wage-indexing options have equity implications that have not been adequately explored. I believe that more study is required before the Congress should legislate a major change in the social security system.

Michael R. Darby

The discussions of the impending problems posed by the baby bust remind me of the sales manager for Gerber baby foods who urged his sales force to go out and create a demand. But I will concentrate on alternative means of financing social security.

The papers by William Hsiao and Lawrence Thompson adequately present the implications for benefits and taxes of the two main alternative proposals for indexing earnings histories of social security recipients: wage indexing and price indexing. These provide alternative means of "decoupling" the adjustment of benefits of new retirees from indexing of benefits of previous retirees. I would like to go one step further and decouple the discussion of whether implied replacement ratios should decline from the discussion of which indexing method should be used.

To do so, I refer to two formulas for computing the average indexed monthly wage (AIMW) under the proposals considered in the two papers. The price-indexed AIMW for individual i is:

$$PAIMW_i \equiv \frac{P_{S-1}}{T} \sum_{t=S-T}^{S-1} \frac{W_t^i}{P_t}$$

$$= P_{S-1} \sum_{t=S-T}^{S-1} \frac{1}{T} w_t^i , \qquad (1)$$

where S is the retirement year, T the averaging period, P_t the price index in year t, W_t^i the nominal wage of i in year t, and w_t^i the real (or deflated) wage of i in year t. The wage-indexed AIMW for i is:

$$WAIMW_i \equiv \frac{\overline{W}_{S-1}}{T} \sum_{t=S-T}^{S-1} \frac{W_t^i}{\overline{W}_t} = \frac{\overline{W}_{S-1} P_{S-1}}{T} \sum_{t=S-T}^{S-1} \frac{w_t^i}{\overline{W}_t} \qquad (2)$$

$$= P_{S-1} \sum_{t=S-T}^{S-1} \left[\frac{1}{T} \frac{\overline{W}_{S-1}}{\overline{W}_t} \right] w_t^i , \qquad (3)$$

75

where $\overline{W}_t$ is the average nominal wage in year t, and $\overline{w}_t$ is the average real wage in year t.

Comparing the rewritten formulas (1) and (3) makes three points obvious. First, price and wage indexing by themselves[1] do not differ in the rate at which the mean AIMW grows from one cohort to the next. Both proposals are simply the price index in the last pre-retirement year times a weighted average of real wages. Therefore, each grows from one cohort to the next by the sum of the growth rate of the price level from one pre-retirement year to the next and the trend growth rate of real wages.[2] Second, the PAIMW formula weights all real wages equally, whereas the WAIMW weights early real wages more heavily. Third, the sum of real-wage weights in the PAIMW is unity, whereas the sum of the real-wage weights in the WAIMW exceeds unity and is a function of both the trend growth rate of real wages g and the averaging period T. This latter sum is:

$$WSUM \equiv \sum_{t=S-T}^{S-1} \frac{1}{T} \frac{\overline{w}_{S-1}}{\overline{w}_t} \approx \frac{1}{T} \frac{(1+g)\,T - 1}{g}. \qquad (4)$$

The approximation holds exactly only if the year-to-year growth in real wages is always at the trend rate g, although deviations would be trivial in view of the long averaging period.

Most of the arguments presented by Hsiao for the PAIMW method and by Thompson for the WAIMW method turn on the effect of lengthening the averaging period T from twenty-one to thirty-five years over the next decade and a half. Increasing the averaging period for a constant sum of the weights (as in the PAIMW method) reduces the cohort's average AIMW relative to its average pre-retirement wage, since earlier below-average earning years are being added. This amounts to a covert reduction in benefits. If the WAIMW formula were used, the sum of weights would increase as the averaging period was lengthened, and this would offset nearly all of the reduction in benefits. Using the historical trend value of 1.8 percent a year for g, the approximation in equation (4) implies that the sum of the weights is increased by 14.5 percent when the averaging period is lengthened from twenty-one to thirty-five years.[3] This is precisely the difference Thompson calculates for constructed wage histories in his Table 3.

Hsiao recommends taking advantage of the ability to offer an

---

[1] That is, for a given length of the averaging period T, as explained below.

[2] The weighted average of real wages is centered one year later for each succeeding cohort.

[3] The sum of the weights increases from 1.20229 to 1.37638.

apparently constant real benefit structure in terms of the PAIMW and using the covert effect of the lengthening averaging period to provide a reserve for the coming demographic bulge. Thompson would prefer to act openly, decreasing benefits or increasing taxes if the bulge eventuates, and he argues that it is premature to do either now.

But this issue has virtually nothing to do with wage indexing versus price indexing; it is concerned only with the sum of the weights for a constant real benefit schedule or, equivalently, with the appropriate increase in the real benefit schedule to offset the effect on the AIMW caused by lengthening the averaging period. In steady-state equilibrium with appropriate settings, the two proposals would not differ with respect to replacement rates or progressivity so long as the brackets for computing the primary insurance amount (PIA) were adjusted to each cohort's average AIMW.

Thus, it seems inappropriate to me to choose between price indexing and wage indexing on the basis of cost or progressivity. Cost depends on a separate issue—namely, how to offset the effects of increasing the averaging period. Effects on progressivity are eliminated by tying the wage brackets to the cohort's average AIMW.

The question of which type of indexing to choose thus really turns on what weights to apply to real wages. If A_s is the desired sum of weights at time S, the general formula for AIMW is:

$$GAIMW_i = \frac{P_{s-1}}{T} A_s \sum_{t=S-T}^{S-1} v_t w_t^i \,, \tag{5}$$

where

$$\frac{\sum_{t=S-T}^{S-1} v_t}{T} = 1.$$

What relative weighting of early versus late real wages is desirable? One criterion is horizontal equity, which requires that benefits be proportional to the value of contributions except for the progressivity implicit in going from the AIMW to the PIA. In a mature system with constant tax rates, this would imply that the weights on early contributions should be much higher than on later contributions because the actuarial cost of benefits rises with age. One could debate whether this would or should be offset for previously lower tax rates during the start-up phase, but it would seem that equity does imply that the weights should move toward heavier earlier weights. On this basis, wage indexing is preferred, though it may go too far or not far enough.

Although I believe that, if a young person is to be fully taxed, he should receive full credit, it certainly seems to me that the weighting issue should be clearly separated from the issue of level of benefits.

By the way of anticlimax, I must object to the way both papers analyze the effect of social security on aggregate saving. In steady-state equilibrium, even if the saving of workers were reduced dollar-for-dollar by the amount of social security taxes, this would not be reflected in aggregate saving. The reason is that retired workers would dissave less from accumulated wealth because of the social security benefits. The net effect of social security—as of private saving for retirement—on aggregate saving occurs only because workers are more numerous and have higher lifetime earnings than the retired. The proportionate effect on aggregate saving in the steady state is approximately the trend growth rate of real income multiplied by the proportionate decrease in the capital stock because of social security. Plausible values of this effect vary between nil and a 20 percent decrease.

Robert J. Myers

The papers by Lawrence Thompson and William Hsiao are interesting and thought-provoking. Of course, it should be realized that the decision about what method to use in computing social security benefits has already been made. Both congressional committees concerned with social security have deliberated fully on the matter of decoupling, and the Congress will pass a bill using the wage-indexing approach. All major organizations—business, labor, and senior citizen groups—as well as both the present administration and the previous one endorsed wage indexing.

Thompson has given a scholarly treatment of the alternatives and of their pros and cons. In fact, it was difficult for some time to see which alternative he ultimately would recommend. He concluded that the best course of action is wage indexing of the earnings record and price indexing of benefits in course of payment. Those are my views, too. Thompson, however, was not clear about whether the replacement rates, as measured for steady workers, should be at the level that would result in 1979 under current law (as both the Ford and Carter administrations proposed), or at a somewhat lower level (as I have advocated for several years). Both congressional committees have adopted the latter approach—with the replacement rates being lowered somewhat more than 5 percent in each case.

Thompson's position on wage indexing of earnings is, in my opinion, quite soundly based on his following statements: "Price indexing preserves the real absolute progressivity of the formula, whereas wage indexing preserves the relative progressivity of the formula"; and "a constant *relative* structure of replacement rates . . . makes the most sense" (emphasis added).

As to the proper treatment of benefits in course of payment, I strongly favor maintaining only purchasing power—which means price indexing. I would, however, have one exception—namely, in the unlikely event that prices increase more rapidly than wages over an extended period of years, benefits should not rise more than wages. I see no reason why the living standard of retirees should rise in the same way as that of active workers. There are those who believe that the benefits of retirees need not increase as rapidly as the cost of living—let alone as rapidly as the living standards of active workers—on the ground that they have relatively fewer needs as they grow older. This viewpoint, based on a limited sample of Canadians, is brought out by Geoffrey N. Calvert in his book, *Pensions and Survival*.[1] I do not agree with this view; rather, I believe that, in all equity, pensioners should have the real value of their pension maintained from the time of retirement for the rest of their lives.

Thompson states that the indexing of pensions in the course of payment cannot be done by private pension plans because they are necessarily financed under actuarial reserve principles. That is not correct. It is quite possible to adopt such indexing and to develop proper actuarial methods for reserve financing. In brief, one needs only to use a valuation interest rate of relatively low size—such as the "real" rate of about 3 percent, assuming no price inflation. On this basis, excess interest earnings (because of high rates caused by inflation) can be utilized to finance the indexing.

Thompson is quite properly concerned about the high costs of OASDI resulting from future demographic conditions. He does not, however, mention the possibility—in my view, the desirability—of gradually increasing the minimum retirement age for full benefits, beginning in about two decades and phasing in gradually over the next one. Such a change is desirable from the demographic and cost aspects, but it can also be viewed as a "keeping up to date." In three decades, the life expectancy at age sixty-five will probably be at least three years greater than it now is, and certainly than it was when the program established age sixty-five as the minimum retirement age.

I have quite the opposite view from Hsiao about the course of action that should be taken. I am not at all convinced by Hsiao's argu-

---

[1] Geoffrey N. Calvert, *Pensions and Survival* (Toronto: Maclean-Hunter, Ltd., 1977).

ments about the wage-indexing approach treating different generations of retirees unfairly because I think that what is important to individuals is the maintenance of their *own* relative financial situation and purchasing power. Nor am I convinced about his point that analyses of benefits should not be based primarily on steady workers. Admittedly, many persons do not fall in this category, although I have some doubts about the data in the study by the Consultant Panel on Social Security. In any event, I think that proper pension planning—whether for a private plan or for a social insurance program—should be based on what will occur for the steady worker; for persons with other work patterns, let the results occur as they will.

I believe that the price-indexing approach is undesirable for a number of reasons. First, it does not represent proper pension planning because relative benefits will be lower for the longest-term contributors. Certainly, such an approach of declining relative benefits has never been considered suitable in private plans. The younger generation can logically argue that such a policy is a "rip-off"; as compared with the current older generation, they would pay longer and at higher tax rates (expressed as percentages of pay) and yet would receive lower relative benefits. Some proponents of the price-indexing approach argue that the Congress will, and should, change the situation in the future so that such declining relative benefits will never really occur—and thus the vaunted savings of the price-indexing approach over the wage-indexing approach will not occur either! It seems to me that it would be poor legislative development to institute a plan that is known to be defective and known to need changing.

Hsiao falls into the common trap of referring to the present coupled procedure as involving double indexing and as resulting in a significant overadjustment for inflation. He uses the former term, although he recognizes that one factor—namely, the weighted nature of the benefit formula—operates in the opposite direction. For some period of years, another factor—namely, the lengthening averaging period for the AMW—also operates in the opposite direction. The author does not recognize that these various elements can be counterbalancing under certain economic conditions (as his Table 1 shows), and, in fact, benefits could be overadjusted downward under certain unlikely economic conditions.

Neither author has recognized two important elements of any indexing procedure that can have quite significant effects on the resulting benefits. The first of these factors is the extent of the lag between the indexing year and what might be termed the initial year of benefit payment (or potential benefit payment). For administrative reasons, because of the annual (instead of quarterly) reporting of wages that will go into effect next year, this lag will probably have to be two years rather than one year. This can be compensated for by higher benefit percentages in the formula, although whether such compensation will be adequate depends upon the trend of wage increases.

The other factor involved in analyzing the results of indexing enters in only with regard to retirement cases. Such indexing can be done based either on the year of first benefit receipt (technically referred to as "entitlement") or on the year of first eligibility for benefits (that is, age sixty-two). It has been appealing to those who do not fully understand the operations of OASDI—and who want to "consider only broad policy implications and not be bothered with details"—to use the entitlement basis as being the most reasonable approach, because this would appear to encourage individuals to defer retirement. What such persons do not realize is that retirement is not a discrete matter like death, and many individuals move in and out of retirement, or else do not know precisely the best moment to retire from the standpoint of maximizing their OASDI benefit. The entitlement basis would be an administrative nightmare and would result in all sorts of inequities between beneficiaries, especially for the vast majority who do not understand all the intricacies of the system.

On the other hand, the eligibility basis of indexing depends solely on demographic conditions, so that people cannot be affected by haphazard conditions or by poor or uninformed choices. I have favored the eligibility approach ever since the decoupling matter has been under discussion. It is interesting to note that both the Ford and the Carter administrations proposed the entitlement basis (despite, I understand, contrary views of the experienced technicians within the Social Security Administration), and that nonetheless both congresional committees have adopted the eligibility approach.

One final matter that should be considered with regard to the technical aspects of indexing the earnings record in a decoupling process is that using the eligibility basis results in lower replacement rates for those first drawing benefits after age sixty-two. For this reason, the Senate Finance Committee's stated reduction in replacement rates of 2.5 percent below those that would result under present law in 1979 is an understatement on the average, because of the effect for retirees beyond age sixty-two. For the same reason, the House Ways and Means Committee's approach, which is stated to be a reduction of 5 percent in replacement rates, is really more than that, even though it adds the offsetting feature of an additional 2 percent annual deferred retirement increment, beginning at age sixty-five.

Discussion

PROFESSOR HSIAO: I would like to make a few points about Thompson's paper. If it is desirable to design a program that is not too costly, then a political analysis of the program should be integrated with an economic analysis. The political reality is that it is always easier to increase benefits than to decrease them.

Although Thompson said that Congress decreased benefits in the 1977 amendments, Congress did not really do that. In 1972, Congress enacted a benefit structure that could be financed by a particular tax rate, which they thought was the portion of the U.S. resources that was being allocated to retirees. Congress did not select that benefit structure without looking at how much it would cost. Nevertheless, Congress later discovered that the cost was going to be much higher, and thus they are now willing to modify the benefit structure. The important question is how much financing has been provided and what portion of U.S. resources has been allocated to pay for retirement benefits? In the new bill Congress is allocating even more resources to future retirees.

We need to recognize that it is much easier for the decision makers to increase benefits than to reduce them. People plan for their retirement over a lifetime. If Congress has to make changes, such as reducing the benefits, that will seriously hurt some people in their planning for retirement.

Also, I would like to point out that the discussion about indexing wages can be separated from the discussion about indexing the bracket widths. The Consultant Panel on Social Security examined this question and found that, if different indexes are used to index the wage history than those used to index the wage brackets, some odd results are obtained. The reason is that the relationship between wages and prices can fluctuate from year to year. In the long run, there is a relatively steady relationship between nominal wages and prices. In the short run, however, that relationship fluctuates with economic conditions.

Thompson stated that in the past Congress provided, on an ad hoc basis, for a roughly constant replacement ratio for retirees. It should be pointed out that this was done during a period of relatively stable eco-

82

nomic and demographic conditions. In those years, more workers were coming into the labor market than were leaving it to retire. Also, Congress did not make the stabilization of replacement ratios automatic. Congress legislated each change and based it on prevailing social and economic conditions. Now it is being proposed that Congress make this process automatic, regardless of future conditions. I think that is a major difference.

DR. THOMPSON: At the end of his comment, Myers compares indexing to entitlement with indexing to eligibility. I would call this the issue of indexing to age sixty-two as compared with indexing to the date of retirement, because the terms "entitlement" and "eligibility" are confusing. It is not a trivial question. It has to do with the incentives to continue working and with the certainty of the amount of benefits one is going to get. If a person retires at age sixty-six, for example, should his wages be indexed up to age sixty-two, his first year of eligibility, or through age sixty-five?

Indexing earnings histories significantly reduces the incentive to keep working—more so under wage indexing than under price indexing. When earnings are not indexed, a person who works another year may substitute that year's wages of, say, $16,500, for wages of $4,200 in an earlier year. In an averaging period of twenty-one years, this has a substantial effect on the size of a person's PIA. In addition, if a person between age sixty-two and age sixty-five works another year, his PIA will be larger because the actuarial reduction in his benefit will be smaller. When wages are indexed, the year replaced is no longer a lot lower than the year added, and the impact on a person's benefit is much smaller.

Under wage indexing, indexing to retirement also makes uncertain the real value of a person's retirement benefit. I believe that indexing to retirement is a mistake, largely because of the unpredictability of wages in any given year. If past wages are indexed to a person's retirement date, he cannot be sure that working an additional year will actually result in higher benefits. His benefit may, in fact, decline if his indexing point is a year in which real wages declined.

The comments about the somewhat sloppy behavior of replacement rates over time were correct. Wage indexing is not going to produce absolutely constant replacement rates from year to year. This is because the age-participation profiles for cohorts change. The replacement rates could be made more nearly constant over time by means of a number of complex refinements in the benefit computation process. But there is a trade-off between reaching this objective and maintaining the understandability of the program. Making things so complicated has its cost. Also, it is politically impossible to get congressional approval for policies that are too complicated to explain.

Moreover, some refinements have bizarre results. For instance, in one scheme, the wage index actually indexes down the final five or six years' earnings, and this effect is offset in the formula. It all works out mathematically. Nobody gets hurt. But you cannot envision somebody sitting in a social security district office with an auto worker saying: "Now, your last wage is not posted yet, so the computer printout that we got from Baltimore is not right. We are going to have to do a hand computation. Let me explain how we do this: We take what you earned last year and we knock 10 percent off." There is a price to pay for introducing that sort of complexity.

Palmer raised the question of the length of the averaging period. Someone else asked, "When you decide to analyze the effect of making one change, how do you decide what to hold constant?" With social security as with other programs, one change affects everything else. If it is decided that lengthening the averaging period is causing a problem, the lengthening process can be stopped. It can be fixed at twenty years. But the length of the averaging period affects a whole other set of issues that have not yet been discussed. Does twenty years make more sense than thirty-five, or forty, or ten? Even though there are many ramifications about who is helped and who is hurt, it is necessary to stop the discussion at some arbitrary point and say, "We are going to take a certain set of provisions in this program as fixed, and we are going to play only with what is remaining." I did the same thing in my paper.

My last comment is on politics. I am not sure that anybody is in a position to predict the responses of future Congresses; I certainly am not. I would like to note, however, that in addition to their decisions about decoupling, both the House Ways and Means Committee and the Senate Finance Committee adopted a series of minor provisions; some of these provisions liberalize benefits, but some of them deliberalize benefits. On balance, the Senate may well have reduced benefits on the rolls. This is the result of changes in the retirement test and in the way cost-of-living adjustments are calculated for people who retire early.

When special interest groups come up with ideas for liberalizing benefits, the first question the congressional committees ask is, "What is the long-run cost?" The long-run cost is presented as a percentage of taxable payroll averaged over seventy-five years. The only way the actuary can make that projection is to assume that what is in the law today will stay in the law for the next seventy-five years, because he obviously cannot make projections of new laws. He adds this one item and finds out what it does to the total cost. The congressional committees then accept and reject proposals based upon 0.1 percent of payroll being too high, but 0.05 percent being an acceptable cost.

If declining replacement rates are enacted, the long-run cost of each of these small liberalizations will be lowered. Each will appear less expensive because of the way it is costed out. If declining replacement rates are enacted even though it is expected that periodic changes will produce constant replacement rates, the long-run cost estimates of each liberalization will be understated.

I believe that, if the Congress feels it can expand benefits periodically and if the costing mechanism understates the long-run cost of benefits, there will be overcompensation for the automatic decline. It is my own personal opinion—and I am an economist, not a political scientist—that declining replacement rates may, in the end, lead to a bigger program.

PROFESSOR JAMES SCHULZ, Brandeis University: In his paper, Thompson gave a commonly quoted figure for private pension coverage of 44 percent. That is the Social Security Administration's estimate. The 44 percent figure is statistically unreliable, however, as the people who made the estimate would admit. Moreover, the figure is used without reference to the fact that it includes not just private pension plans but also profit-sharing plans. Yet, we know even less about profit sharing than we do about private pensions. I have done some work that indicates the 44 percent figure would drop at least to 40 percent if workers who are covered solely by profit-sharing plans were excluded. The distinction is important because profit sharing differs significantly from private pensions in many ways, especially with respect to the certainty of benefits.

Our understanding of the role of private pensions is further complicated by the fact that people who are not covered by private pensions are a very heterogeneous group and we do not know much about them. We should divide people at least into primary and secondary wage earners, or part-time and full-time workers; then we will be able to see who is not covered by a private pension, and whether or not private pension coverage really is as limited as it appears to be.

PROFESSOR MICHAEL BOSKIN, Stanford University: I have four questions or comments that are all related to the conceptual basis of what has been discussed.

First, there was no discussion of whether the consumer price index is a reasonable price index to use to maintain the living standards of the elderly after retirement. In my opinion, it is a very poor index to use for the elderly. Their "consumption bundle" is quite different from that used to generate the consumer price index.

Second, I object to the notion that we have lots of years to worry about the demographic bulge. The reason we do not have lots of years to worry about the bulge and its implications on taxes and benefits is that people have to decide now on their savings plans for the future: what pension plan to go into, how much to put aside in a variety of ways. Because of the uncertainty, people have to try to outguess what the government is going to do. They have to wonder, for instance, whether Congress will legislate a 60 percent increase in tax rates on the next generation so that this generation's retirement benefits will be assured.

Third, in making long-run comparisons of OASDI costs with wage and price indexing, expenditures are expressed as a percentage of taxable payroll or as a percentage of gross national product (GNP). It should be pointed out that, even if the people who make these estimates have a good idea of the numerator of that ratio, the way they estimate the denominator is, by an economist's standards, abominable. They ignore a number of significant factors: the growth in the labor force participation rate for women, the continued increase in the number of early retirees, the changes in the relative wages of younger and older workers, the question of whether workers with different experience are imperfect substitutes in production, and the potentially large increase in the relative wages and tax rates of those born in the last few years who will be supporting my generation when we retire. Consequently, these numbers—particularly the denominator of the ratio, but also the numerator—may be far off the mark.

Finally, I would like to offer my own proposal for indexing, though I have not worked it out in detail. First, I would write down some utility function over a lifetime for individuals. That utility function may well depend on people's relative consumption as well as their absolute consumption. Second, I would try to estimate the parameters of that utility function by estimating a system of demand equations. Third, using the well-developed economic theory for looking at constant utility index numbers, I would solve for the level of social security benefits that would keep people on the same level of lifetime utility for perturbations in incomes and prices.

DR. THOMPSON: I do not know exactly how the costing is done. The social security actuaries do make projections of changing labor force participation. I do not know how well those projections enter into the numerator, but they do enter into the denominator. Many other errors in projection affect both the numerator and the denominator in a roughly equal way.

PROFESSOR BOSKIN: The actuaries make mechanical extrapolations, and there is no model of labor supply. When tax rates double to finance social security benefits, the world will look very different. But these factors are left out.

PROFESSOR HSIAO: You are right. There is no complete general equilibrium model for forecasting. But assumptions are made and sensitivity analyses are done to show what will happen if the marketplace changes. An estimate has been made, for example, of what the system would look like if the female labor force participation rate rose to 95 percent. The cost projection models are not so bad as you say.

DR. PALMER: I would like to return to Boskin's first point about the different price indexes—the consumer price index and a price index for the elderly. What is relevant is not whether, at some given point, the levels of those indexes are different, but how they vary over time, in terms of adjustment. I think that the deviations would not be that significant over an extended period of time; certainly, they would not be enough to warrant the additional problems of collecting and constructing a separate index for the elderly. Furthermore, although it may be desirable from a political point of view to advance benefits somewhat faster than the CPI if the price index for the aged went up faster, I think it would be difficult to defend advancing it slower in periods when it went up somewhat less.

PROFESSOR BOSKIN: My concern is not about what happens in periods of moderate inflation. But, if price indexing according to the CPI is embodied in the law, and if we then experience a very different inflation history and a very different change in relative prices, substantial deviations could occur. I do not claim that, if we index with the CPI now, major deviations will occur in each of the next three years, or anything of that sort.

PROFESSOR DARBY: I would expect that the higher the rate of inflation is, the more accurate the CPI would be in relative terms. You are just adding a constant error.

Also, Hsiao said that it hurts people if they save too little and then benefits are reduced relative to expectations. Well, it also hurts people if they save too much and then benefits are raised relative to expectations. They would have given up consumption when it had a higher value. It seems to me that there is no a priori way of saying which hurts more. I would guess they are roughly equal.

MR. BERT SEIDMAN, AFL-CIO: Except for some of Thompson's concluding comments, I get the feeling that the discussion is all in terms of a constant benefit structure, which I find to be very unrealistic. The focus this year—except for the deliberalization involving decoupling—has been entirely on the financial aspects of the program rather than on benefits. But, as everybody knows, there are some strong candidates for changes in benefits.

Some benefit changes will have an impact on replacement rates, whereas other changes will not. For example, if occupational disability benefits are introduced, that may have some slight impact on replacement rates. On the other hand, if it is decided that people over age seventy-five should get a different level of benefits than people under age seventy-five, that will likely have a substantial impact on replacement rates. In my opinion, however, these decisions will not be made on the basis of their effect on replacement rates, assuming that there is no further major deliberalization of replacement rates. Rather, as Thompson stated, Congress will look at what each change means over a seventy-five-year period as a percentage of taxable payroll, and at whether or not there is a politically acceptable source of financing for whatever the change is, regardless of whether it will have an impact on the replacement rates.

PART
TWO

INDEXING SOCIAL SECURITY:
SOME IMPORTANT
CONSEQUENCES

Social Security Wealth: The Impact of Alternative Inflation Adjustments

Martin S. Feldstein and Anthony Pellechio

The distribution of wealth is one of the most important and least studied features of our economic life. A lack of good data on household wealth is the primary reason for the inadequate attention to this subject. Moreover, the evidence that is available from household surveys and estate records excludes the most important asset of the vast majority of households: the value of future social security benefits.[1] The purpose of the current paper is to present evidence on the distribution of social security wealth and to use these estimates to analyze the impact of alternative methods of adjusting future benefits for changes in the price level.

Social security wealth is defined as the actuarial present value of the social security benefits to which an individual becomes entitled at age sixty-five.[2] The sum of ordinary (fungible) wealth and social security wealth is equal to the value of the retirement annuity that an individual could buy at any time. This sum is equivalent to the present value of the consumption in the retirement years after age sixty-five that would be possible if the individual did no future saving.[3] For the current paper, we are interested in social security wealth as part of an accurate description of an individual's total wealth, and we will not explore any of the implications of social security wealth for savings behavior. One plausible implication that we have examined elsewhere is that social security wealth induces households to reduce their accumulation of other

NOTE: This study is part of the research program on social insurance by the National Bureau of Economic Research (NBER). The authors are grateful to the National Science Foundation for financial support and to Michael Boskin, Michael Darby, and William Hsiao for useful comments. The paper has not been reviewed by the Board of Directors of the NBER.

[1] For several recent contributions to the study of the distribution of wealth, see J. D. Smith, ed., *The Personal Distribution of Income and Wealth*, National Bureau of Economic Research, Studies in Income and Wealth (New York: Columbia University Press, 1975), part 4.

[2] The idea of social security wealth was introduced in Martin Feldstein, "Social Security, Induced Retirement, and Aggregate Capital Accumulation," *Journal of Political Economy*, vol. 82 (September/October 1974), pp. 905–26.

[3] We do not subtract future social security taxes. The current measure of social security wealth plus ordinary fungible wealth plus human capital (based on labor income net of tax) represents the lifetime budget constraint.

wealth by an equal amount;[4] if this is correct, the total wealth distribution that could be estimated by adding fungible wealth and social security wealth is also the distribution of ordinary fungible wealth that would have existed in the absense of social security.[5]

The present study is an extension of earlier research by Feldstein on the distribution of social security wealth.[6] That earlier study was based on the 1962–1963 Federal Reserve Board *Survey of Consumer Finances*, which provided survey data on the income and fungible assets of approximately 2,000 households with a heavy oversampling of high-income households.[7] Although these data probably provide the best information on the distribution of fungible wealth, the basis for estimating social security wealth was very limited.[8] In contrast, the current study uses a new source of data that permits a very accurate calculation of social security wealth; the precise nature of the data and the estimation method are described in the next section.

The focus of this paper is exclusively on social security wealth. Studies of the wealth distribution could, of course, be extended in a number of other ways. Some of these, such as including the value of private pensions and of other social insurance benefits, would be useful, but they are much smaller than social security wealth. Other extensions to include human capital, anticipated taxes, and anticipated intergenerational transfers might be useful in some contexts, but they would blur

---

[4] Martin Feldstein and Anthony Pellechio, "Social Security and Household Wealth Accumulation: New Microeconomic Evidence," *Review of Economics and Statistics* (forthcoming).

[5] The extent to which social security wealth displaces ordinary wealth is a controversial issue; for recent evidence and discussions of earlier evidence, see Robert J. Barro, *The Impact of Social Security on Private Saving—Evidence from the U.S. Time Series* (Washington, D.C.: American Enterprise Institute, 1978); Michael R. Darby, *The Effects of Social Security on Income and the Capital Stock* (Washington, D.C.: American Enterprise Institute, forthcoming); Martin Feldstein, "Social Security and Saving: The Extended Life Cycle Theory," *American Economic Review*, vol. 66 (May 1976), pp. 77–86; Laurence J. Kotlikoff, "Essays on Capital Formation and Social Security, Bequest Formation, and Long Run Tax Incidence" (Ph.D. diss., Harvard University, 1977); and Alicia H. Munnell, "Private Pensions and Saving: New Evidence," *Journal of Political Economy*, vol. 84 (October 1976), pp. 1013–32.

[6] Martin Feldstein, "Social Security and the Distribution of Wealth," *Journal of the American Statistical Association*, vol. 71 (December 1976), pp. 800–807.

[7] Dorothy S. Projector and Gertrude S. Weiss, *Survey of Financial Characteristics of Consumers* (Washington, D.C.: Board of Governors of the Federal Reserve System, August 1966).

[8] Social security wealth was estimated on the basis of current earnings, age, and marital status; no information on the earnings history was available. The assumption about future benefits was also quite crude. The method is described in detail in Feldstein, "Social Security and the Distribution of Wealth."

the basic distinction between wealth and income that makes the study of wealth a subject of independent value.

It is now widely argued that the current social security law (as of October 1977) contains a serious technical error that requires legislative correction. More specifically, the current law adjusts benefits and taxable wages in response to inflation in a way that is accurately described as "overindexed": an increase in the price level causes a more than proportionate increase in social security benefits.[9] In 1976, the Ford administration proposed a method of price adjustment that has become known as wage indexing; according to this proposal, the tax and benefit schedules are adjusted for changes in the average level of nominal wages. This method has the effect of keeping the ratio of benefits to previous earnings unchanged at each relative earnings level. The wage-indexing method has since been proposed by the Carter administration and by the key Senate and House committees. The analysis of this paper therefore focuses on social security wealth under the assumption that the method of wage indexing is adopted.

An alternative method of adjusting was proposed by a panel of consultants appointed by the Congress and chaired by William Hsiao.[10] The Hsiao proposal calls for adjusting the tax and benefit schedules on the basis of changes in the price level and is therefore known as price indexing. The price-indexing method would have substantial long-run advantages for the economy.[11] It is therefore worthwhile to analyze the implication of this major alternative for the total value and the distribution of social security wealth. Our analysis of price indexing suggests the reason it lacks the political support that it deserves on long-run economic grounds.

Data and Method of Estimation

The data used in this study are a unique combination of household survey information and Social Security Administration (SSA) records for the same individuals.[12] The file is based on the March 1973 Current

---

[9] For a clear description of this problem, see Congressional Budget Office, *Financing Social Security: Issues for the Short and Long Term* (July 1977).

[10] U.S. Congress, *Report of the Consultant Panel on Social Security to the Congressional Research Service, Prepared for the Use of the Committee on Finance of the U.S. Senate and the Committee on Ways and Means of the U.S. House of Representatives*, 94th Congress, 2nd session, August 1976.

[11] These advantages are discussed in Martin Feldstein, "Facing the Social Security Crisis," *The Public Interest*, no. 47 (Spring 1977); Congressional Budget Office, *Financing Social Security*; and U.S. Congress, *Report of the Consultant Panel on Social Security*.

[12] See F. J. Scheuren et al., *1973 CPS-SER Exact Match Codebook*, Social Security Administration (1975).

Population Survey (CPS). The Social Security Administration has matched summary information from its records with the survey information.

Our sample contains all such persons aged twenty-five and older whose CPS and SSA records are properly matched and who are covered by the social security program. There are 61,327 persons, consisting of 23,529 married couples and 14,269 single individuals. We treat couples and single individuals as units of analysis; the sample thus contains 37,798 potential household observations. To reduce computation costs, we have used a sample of 10,000 observations. The sampling weights permit the extrapolation of our results to the entire population.

Our analysis estimates the social security wealth as of the end of 1972 for each household (that is, couple or single individual) in the sample. Recall that this social security wealth is the value of the benefits for which the couple or individual will be eligible at age sixty-five. These benefits are calculated on the assumption that the current (October 1977) method of double-indexing benefits for inflation will be replaced by the wage-indexing method proposed by the Carter and Ford administrations.

A number of assumptions make our estimates an understatement of the total value of future social security benefits. We focus exclusively on the retirement benefits of the worker and, when appropriate, on the dependent or survivor benefits of his spouse. We exclude completely the value of benefits going to surviving children and the value of disability benefits; these now amount to 30 percent of the retirement and survivor benefits that are included. We ignore the opportunity for early retirement; although there is in principle an actuarial reduction of benefits, the opportunity for self-selection conveys an advantage. We also do not consider the benefits provided under the Supplemental Security Income program. Finally, we ignore workers under the age of twenty-five because of the difficulty of estimating their future incomes.

The calculations assume that the consumer price level rises in the future at 4 percent a year. Because of growth in productivity, real wages rise at 1.75 percent. Future benefits are discounted to the present with a real discount rate of 3 percent; this is equivalent to assuming a 7 percent after-tax rate of return when the inflation rate is 4 percent.[13] Because the double indexing is assumed to be removed, the choice of a 4 percent inflation rate is of little consequence; the real growth of bene-

---

[13] This real rate of interest is higher than households have obtained for the past twenty-five years. This again causes our estimate of social security wealth to be an underestimate. The appendix to this paper presents estimates based on a real discount rate of 1 percent.

fits and the real social security wealth are essentially unchanged if a different inflation rate is assumed.

An example will illustrate the logic of our calculation of social security wealth. Readers who are not interested in the precise method may skip to the beginning of the next section without loss of continuity.

Consider a single working man who was less than sixty-five years old at the end of 1972. The social security administrative record indicates his average monthly covered earnings between 1951 and 1972, together with information about the years in which he did not have covered earnings. The first step in our calculation is to estimate covered earnings in each previous year subject to his given overall average and to the maximums given by the social security law. The basic assumption of the interpolation used to obtain the individual earnings is that wages grow at an exponential rate. Each individual's growth rate is determined to satisfy the known 1972 earnings and the average for the period. The individual's earnings are then extrapolated into the future by the assumption that his 1972 wage will grow at the same rate as all other wages (that is, 5.75 percent).

This provides the earnings record for all of the relevant years of his working life—say, W_{it} for individual i in year t. This is converted into an indexed wage by dividing each W_{it} by the overall average covered monthly earnings in that year (W_{ot}); individual i's indexed wage is thus W_{it}/W_{ot}. A simple average over the relevant number of working years provides a normalized averaged monthly earnings (NAME), which is the basis of the benefit calculation.

The NAME for a worker who has always had the average earnings will be one. The principle of wage indexing makes the ratio of the retiree's benefit at age sixty-five to average covered earnings in that year a function of his NAME. A specific table indicates the benefit ratio for each NAME.[14] Our calculation uses the NAME to calculate this benefit ratio and thus the dollar benefit at the time of retirement. Benefits after retirement are increased at the rate of consumer price inflation.[15]

This procedure yields the stream of benefits that the individual will collect at each age after sixty-five if he is alive. We find the actuarial discounted value of these benefits as of 1972 by using the 1970 Census

[14] For values of NAME up to 0.28, the benefit ratio is 0.80; for the next amount of earnings between NAME = 0.28 and NAME = 0.84, the marginal benefit ratio is 0.35; above that value of NAME, the marginal benefit ratio is 0.25. This implies, for example, that a retiree with a NAME of 0.84 receives initial benefits of 50 percent of the product of NAME and the average earnings in the year of his retirement.

[15] This method of describing the benefit calculation may appear different from the legislative proposal, but it is actually computationally equivalent.

Bureau Actuarial Tables to calculate the probability of survival and then discounting future benefits at a nominal rate of 7 percent.

For married couples, the calculation is more complex because: (1) an extra benefit is available if the retiree has a dependent spouse; (2) a surviving spouse is entitled to a benefit; but (3) if the wife has an earnings record, she may choose to receive her own benefits as a retired worker. Our computer program makes all of the correct choices for the family on the assumption that, if there is a working wife, she will choose to retire when her husband reaches age sixty-five.

We recognize that these calculations might be significantly improved as more information becomes available. We nevertheless believe that the current information can provide a useful basis for analysis.

Basic Estimates of Social Security Wealth

Our method of estimation implies that the social security wealth of the population in 1972 was $1.85 trillion, approximately twice the 1972 national income of $952 billion. Social security wealth was nearly as large as the 1972 total financial net worth of the household sector, $2.4 trillion. Even the most inclusive traditional measure of household sector wealth was $4.0 trillion, about twice the size of our estimate of social security wealth.[16] By any standard, the value of social security wealth is of major significance in describing the total wealth of the population.

Although our detailed evidence is only available for 1972, it is useful to have even a rough estimate of a more current value. We have made such an estimate on the conservative assumption that social security wealth grew at the same rate as national income. On that assumption, social security wealth will reach $3.4 trillion by the end of fiscal year 1978.

As we emphasized above, even these astoundingly large figures are likely to be a substantial understatement of social security wealth. Our estimates deal only with the population over age twenty-five, thus omitting a substantial fraction of the current and future labor force. Our benefits exclude payments for disability and dependent children, which together account for more than 30 percent of the basic benefits for retirees and surviving spouses. At every point in our calculation, we have chosen the assumption that would understate rather than overstate social security wealth.

Table 1 shows the distribution of the 1972 social security wealth by income and age. Each couple or single individual is classified by

---

[16] This total net worth includes the value of consumer durables and the assets of nonprofit organizations.

TABLE 1

DISTRIBUTION OF SOCIAL SECURITY WEALTH, BY AGE AND INCOME
(percentages of total social security wealth)

| | Age of Household Head | | | | | | |
Income	25–34	35–44	45–54	55–64	65 and older	All	35–64
Less than $3,000	0.6	0.7	1.1	3.4	17.7	23.4	8.8
$3,000–$6,000	0.8	0.7	1.2	1.5	1.4	5.7	5.8
$6,000–$9,000	2.4	1.8	2.2	2.8	1.0	10.1	11.4
$9,000–$12,000	4.0	3.2	4.3	4.1	1.0	16.6	19.7
$12,000–$15,000	3.6	3.1	3.4	2.9	0.5	13.6	15.9
$15,000–$25,000	4.9	5.8	6.0	4.5	0.9	22.2	27.7
More than $25,000	1.0	1.6	2.5	2.2	0.9	8.3	10.8
All	17.4	17.0	20.7	21.5	23.3	100.0	100.0

NOTE: All figures relate to the distribution of total 1972 social security wealth of $1.847 trillion.

SOURCE: The calculations in all tables were done by the authors.

total income in 1972 (excluding social security benefits) and by the age of the individual or, in the case of couples, by the age of the man.

The most interesting feature of Table 1 is the very small fraction of the social security wealth that is accounted for by higher income families.[17] Only 8.3 percent of total social security wealth belongs to families with incomes over $25,000. Approximately half of social security wealth is accounted for by families with incomes over the 1972 median of $11,000.

Since the incomes of retirees and of young workers are misleading as indicators of their lifetime income positions, it is useful to look at families in which the head is between the ages of thirty-five and sixty-four. A summary for this age group is presented in the final column of Table 1. Even for this restricted group, only 11 percent of social security wealth is accounted for by the families with incomes over $25,000 and 39 percent by families with incomes over $15,000.

This contrasts sharply with the well-documented concentration of ordinary fungible wealth. Although exact data on the wealth distribution for 1973 are not available, some useful inferences can be made on the basis of the 1962–1963 Federal Reserve Board *Survey of Consumer*

---

[17] The term "family" refers to both couples and single individuals except when something else is explicitly stated.

Finances.[18] In a 1976 study, Feldstein estimated that, among households in which the head was between thirty-five and sixty-four years old, 63 percent of fungible wealth belonged to households with incomes over $10,000 and 44 percent to households with incomes over $15,000.[19] Since per capita personal incomes increased by slightly less than 100 percent between 1962 and 1972, it is reasonable to assume that by 1973, families with incomes over $25,000 had between 44 and 63 percent of the wealth of their age cohort. This compares with the mere 11 percent of social security wealth shown in the last column of Table 1. To state the same thing in a different way, the income group that has only about 50 percent of fungible wealth has more than 90 percent of social security wealth.[20]

The distribution of social security wealth can be examined in a different way by studying the average dollar value of social security wealth at each age and income level. The basic figures for this analysis are presented in Table 2. The average individual or couple had $28,093 of social security wealth at the end of 1972. The most important feature of the distribution is that benefits rise so little with income. This is best seen by focusing on the group aged thirty-five to sixty-four to avoid the distortion caused by the high wealth and low income of the aged. For this group, social security wealth per household shows almost no increase for those with incomes more than $9,000. Even those with incomes less than $3,000 have social security wealth of nearly $18,000, or more than half the social security wealth of those with incomes over $25,000.

Separate figures are shown for each age group. A common feature is that, in each age group, there is little effect of income over $9,000 on social security wealth. It is interesting also that, in the group up to age fifty-four, the highest income class actually has slightly lower social security wealth than the group with incomes between $15,000 and $25,000.

Social Security Wealth Net of Future Taxes

Social security wealth is the actuarial present value of the benefits to which individuals are entitled at age sixty-five. The sum of an individual's

---

[18] Projector and Weiss, *Survey of Financial Characteristics of Consumers.*

[19] Feldstein, "Social Security and the Distribution of Wealth."

[20] Similarly, the 1962 data indicate that families with 1962 incomes less than $7,500 had 25 percent of fungible wealth. If we therefore infer that by 1972 families with incomes less than $15,000 had 24 percent of fungible wealth, this can be compared with the 65 percent of social security wealth shown in the last column of Table 1.

TABLE 2

SOCIAL SECURITY WEALTH PER FAMILY, BY AGE AND INCOME
(dollars)

Income	Age of Household Head						
	25–34	35–44	45–54	55–64	65 and older	All	35–64
Less than $3,000	8,610	11,762	13,017	23,498	28,693	24,159	18,075
$3,000–$6,000	12,262	14,301	18,541	23,909	33,657	19,695	19,266
$6,000–$9,000	18,156	20,357	23,800	32,643	38,105	23,983	25,520
$9,000–$12,000	23,824	27,276	32,129	39,251	43,610	30,291	32,604
$12,000–$15,000	25,886	28,287	33,584	42,907	44,143	31,478	33,763
$15,000–$25,000	26,830	32,011	35,822	42,649	44,830	33,658	35,876
More than $25,000	25,097	29,468	35,403	43,141	45,462	34,830	35,803
All	21,726	25,691	28,978	34,403	30,823	28,093	29,585

NOTES: All dollar amounts refer to 1972. See text for definition and methods. Families are either couples or single individuals.

99

social security wealth and his ordinary fungible wealth is thus the present value of the total resources that would be available for retirement consumption if the individual did no further saving out of other income.[21] The social security wealth analyzed in the previous section is therefore the relevant variable to compare with the distribution of fungible wealth.

There is, however, a different concept of social security wealth—net of future social security taxes—that may be relevant for discussing other issues. For a person who has reached age sixty-five and is ready to retire, there is no difference between gross social security wealth and net social security wealth. For a younger individual, net social security wealth can be considerably less than the gross value.

The tax rates that will be levied in future years are the subject of substantial debate. Our strategy is to assume that the maximum taxable wage level will rise at the same rate as the average wage and that the tax rate will then be set in each year to make the year's total tax revenue equal the year's total benefit outlay.[22] The resulting tax rate rises from 10.7 percent in 1980 to 12.4 percent in 2000 and 14.9 percent in 2015.

The net social security value—that is, the value of social security wealth net of the present value of the individual's future social security tax—measures the value to the individual of the continued existence of the social security program. If the program were abolished, he would lose the future benefits but would also avoid the future taxes. Although eliminating social security is not a relevant policy option, the estimates of net social security wealth show who gains and who loses from the continuation of the current program and from the adoption of alternative benefit and tax rules.[23]

An individual's net social security wealth does not measure the lifetime subsidy that he receives from the social security program. It is equal instead to that subsidy plus the value of the taxes that he has already paid. For the entire population over age twenty-five, the net social security wealth represents the present value of the net intergenerational transfer to it that is yet to take place. In different words, the total net social security wealth of the cohort over age twenty-five is the value

---

[21] That is, if the individual's saving in each future year until age sixty-five equaled the income from his fungible wealth.

[22] The calculations used to derive this tax rate assume fertility rates of 1.6 in 1980, 1.8 in 1990, 1.9 in 2000, and 2.1 in 2025 and thereafter. A different assumption about the maximum taxable earnings is developed in the next section when price indexing is discussed.

[23] There are, of course, the further gains and losses that arise to the extent that social security reduces the capital stock and thus changes factor incomes. These are ignored in the current calculations.

of the transfers that they will receive from those who are currently less than twenty-five or yet unborn.

At the end of 1972, the total value of this net social security wealth was $1.06 trillion, or 57 percent of the gross social security wealth. By the same extrapolation as before, this implies a net social security wealth of $2.0 trillion by the end of fiscal year 1978. The distribution of net social security wealth is shown in Table 3.

The striking feature about Table 3 is that net social security wealth is actually negative for families aged twenty-five to thirty-four. These individuals and couples can expect to pay more in social security taxes than they receive in benefits (when both are discounted to their present value). This is true at every income level over $6,000. Since these individuals have already paid considerable taxes, this represents a substantial understatement of their net lifetime loss because of the social security program.

The negative net social security wealth of young families has an important implication about the future social security program. If the current relation between benefits and taxes were to remain unchanged, each new generation would find that its initial net social security wealth was negative. That is, each generation would pay taxes with a greater present value than the benefits it received. Moreover, the demographic developments over the next fifty years will make the situation even worse than Table 3 suggests. Because the number of retirees will grow more rapidly than the number of workers, the ratio of taxes to wages must rise relative to the ratio of benefits to wages. This in turn means that the net social security wealth of each new generation will be even more negative.

The net social security wealth has potentially important political implications for the social security program. Anyone with a negative net social security wealth could gain from a contraction of the social security program. There are now some 150 million adults of voting age in the United States. Of these, approximately 50 million have negative net social security wealth.[24] The older groups have positive net social security wealth because they are closer to receiving benefits and have fewer taxpaying years left. Although each generation may lose over its lifetime because of the social security program, the distribution of net social security wealth is currently capable of maintaining and expanding the social security program. The changing demographic structure, however, will increase the fraction of the population with negative net social security wealth and could thereby weaken the political support of the

---

[24] Included in this figure are those aged eighteen to twenty-four who are not reflected in Table 3.

TABLE 3

Social Security Wealth Net of Future Taxes per Family, by Age and Income
(dollars)

Income	Age of Household Head							
	25–34	35–44	45–54	55–64	65 and older	All	35–64
Less than $3,000	1,299	6,549	9,357	22,197	28,608	22,778	15,298
$3,000–$6,000	1,153	5,512	13,487	22,299	33,633	14,043	14,387
$6,000–$9,000	−1,066	6,122	15,320	29,965	37,987	12,643	17,030
$9,000–$12,000	−2,784	6,676	20,692	34,906	43,373	13,935	20,194
$12,000–$15,000	−3,373	5,966	20,250	37,879	43,563	12,319	18,918
$15,000–$25,000	−4,421	5,834	20,468	36,898	44,431	12,931	18,404
More than $25,000	−2,470	6,819	20,566	37,654	45,072	19,292	21,247
All	−2,280	6,164	17,889	30,867	30,713	16,175	18,061

NOTES: All dollar amounts refer to 1972. See text for definition and methods. Families are either couples or single individuals.

program. If, for example, net social security wealth only became positive at age forty-five, a majority of the voting-age population would have negative net social security wealth. The changing demography and the resulting deterioration of the ratio of benefits to taxes therefore poses a serious threat to the ability of the program to go on paying the promised benefits in the future.[25]

A Price-Indexed Program for Social Security

Until now, we have assumed that the "overindexing" of the existing law will be remedied by adopting a system known as wage indexing. The basic characteristic of wage indexing is that it makes the retiree's replacement rate (that is, the ratio of benefits to the pre-retirement wage level) depend on his relative income. For example, a retiree in 1976 who has always had median earnings received a basic benefit equal to 43 percent of his immediate pre-retirement earnings; with wage indexing, workers with median earnings would continue to have a 43 percent replacement rate when they retire.

The method of wage indexing has several unfortunate implications.[26] The first and most obvious of these is the substantial increase in the tax rate that would be required as the ratio of retirees to workers rises. According to official estimates of the Social Security Administration, the current social security payroll tax of 9.9 percent (excluding hospital insurance) would have to rise under wage indexing to 12.4 percent in the year 2000 and to 18.8 percent in the year 2050. Adding such high payroll tax rates to existing income taxes could produce substantial distortions in labor supply.

Second, wage indexing based on the current schedule of replacement rates produces some extremely high replacement rates, distorting retirement decisions and depressing saving. For example, a single worker with median earnings now gets 43 percent of his immediate pre-retirement wage; if he is married, however, he can get 150 percent of this basic benefit. The married retiree with median earnings thus receives 65 percent of his pre-retirement income. Since this benefit is untaxed, it is really equivalent to a replacement of 80 percent or more of net earnings. A worker who is not far below the median can thus obtain an effective replacement rate of more than 100 percent. Such high replacement rates

---

[25] A more detailed analysis of who would gain and who would lose under alternative assumptions about the future could make the ideas of this paragraph more precise and operational.

[26] These adverse effects are discussed more extensively in Feldstein, "Facing the Social Security Crisis." See also Congressional Budget Office, *Financing Social Security*.

are a strong incentive to retire at age sixty-five or earlier. They also eliminate the reason for substantial retirement saving, either directly or through private saving.

These problems with the wage-indexing method prompted the Consultant Panel on Social Security, directed by William Hsiao, to propose an alternative method that is commonly referred to as price indexing. The distinguishing characteristic of the performance of price indexing is that it makes the individual's replacement rate depend on his real income rather than his relative income. As real incomes rise over time, the average replacement rate would fall; social security benefits would grow with time, but less rapidly than income. This reduced rate of growth of social security benefits would permit a slower rate of growth of taxes. The tax rate required to finance the benefits implied by the Hsiao proposal would be only 10 percent in the year 2000 and 11.3 percent in the year 2050. The lower replacement rates would also reduce the adverse distortions in retirement and saving behavior.

Table 4 shows the tax rates and maximum taxable earnings under price indexing and wage indexing for selected years. The total tax reve-

TABLE 4

TAX RATES AND MAXIMUM TAXABLE WAGES UNDER WAGE AND PRICE INDEXING, SELECTED YEARS, 1980–2045

Year	Tax Rate (percent)		Maximum Taxable Wages[a] (dollars)	
	Wage index	Price index	Wage index	Price index
1980	10.7	10.6	19,513	18,560
1985	11.2	10.5	25,806	22,581
1990	11.8	10.5	34,129	27,474
1995	12.0	10.0	45,137	33,426
2000	12.4	10.0	59,694	40,668
2005	12.9	10.0	78,946	48,478
2010	13.4	10.0	104,408	60,198
2015	14.9	10.7	138,081	73,240
2025	17.7	12.0	241,511	108,413
2035	18.9	12.2	422,415	160,477
2045	18.9	11.6	738,827	237,545

[a] Dollar amounts are in the prices of each year; an inflation of 4 percent is assumed.

nue in future years is lower under price indexing because of both the lower tax rate and the lower maximum taxable earnings.[27]

It is clear from the difference between the required tax rates—19 percent for wage indexing and 11 percent for price indexing—that price indexing would be substantially better for the welfare of the population that reaches maturity in the next century and beyond. Moreover, the analysis presented below shows that the choice between the two indexing mechanisms has relatively little effect on the social security wealth of the current population over age twenty-five. This is true of both the gross social security wealth and the net social security wealth. Unfortunately, our analysis also shows why wage indexing is likely to be chosen by the political process: at every age and income level, the net social security wealth is higher with wage indexing than with price indexing. This difference reflects the fact that wage indexing is designed to achieve a greater transfer from the next generation than price indexing.

Table 5 compares the gross social security wealth per family (that is, couple or single individual) under the two methods of indexing. The average wealth of $28,093 under wage indexing is reduced by less than one-fifth, to $22,965, under price indexing. The extent of the reduction varies by age group, with the greatest differences for the young. But even for this group, the present value of benefits under price indexing is about one-third less than under wage indexing. Although we cannot now produce a full analysis of this issue, we believe that the loss in benefits associated with using price indexing would be small relative to the permanent gains for all future generations that would thereby be achieved.

Table 6 shows why price indexing is nevertheless unlikely to be adopted: for every age and income group, the use of price indexing rather than wage indexing reduces the implied transfer from the next generation and therefore decreases net social security wealth. These decreases are small but the fact that they are decreases implies that, on selfish grounds, there is no reason for the current voters to favor price indexing over wage indexing.

The analysis for the youngest group of families may be surprising. Before the calculations were done, we anticipated that this group might have a higher net social security wealth under price indexing than under

---

[27] The basic mechanics of price indexing are similar to those of the wage-indexing system described earlier, but a price index rather than a wage index is used. Thus, the maximum taxable earnings grow each year at the rate of inflation instead of at the (generally higher) rate of nominal wage increase. Similarly, the tax payments are converted to dollars of the retirement year by a price index and the replacement rate table is increased for the growth of prices. The nonlinearity of the benefit schedule causes this to lower the average replacement rate.

TABLE 5

EFFECT OF PRICE INDEXING ON SOCIAL SECURITY WEALTH PER FAMILY, BY AGE AND INCOME
(dollars)

Income	Age of Household Head						
	25–34	35–44	45–54	55–64	65 and older	All	35–64
Less than $3,000							
Wage indexing	8,610	11,762	13,017	23,498	28,693	24,159	18,075
Price indexing	6,148	8,717	10,426	20,309	26,701	21,010	15,091
$3,000–$6,000							
Wage indexing	12,262	14,301	18,541	23,909	33,657	19,695	19,266
Price indexing	8,243	10,432	14,829	21,779	32,528	16,610	16,080
$6,000–$9,000							
Wage indexing	18,156	20,357	23,800	32,643	38,105	23,983	25,520
Price indexing	12,142	14,726	19,055	29,511	36,217	19,159	21,005
$9,000–$12,000							
Wage indexing	23,824	27,276	32,129	39,251	43,610	30,291	32,604
Price indexing	15,862	19,861	25,856	34,975	42,331	23,819	26,538

$12,000–$15,000							
Wage indexing	25,886	28,287	33,584	42,907	44,143	31,478	33,763
Price indexing	17,199	20,655	26,902	38,423	42,709	24,388	27,240
$15,000–$25,000							
Wage indexing	26,830	32,011	35,822	42,649	44,830	33,658	35,876
Price indexing	17,869	23,265	28,629	38,397	43,791	26,216	28,743
More than $25,000							
Wage indexing	25,097	29,468	35,403	43,141	45,462	34,830	35,803
Price indexing	16,632	21,441	28,307	38,681	44,524	28,379	29,185
All							
Wage indexing	21,726	25,691	28,978	34,403	30,823	28,093	29,585
Price indexing	14,509	18,707	23,213	30,724	28,965	22,965	24,068

NOTES: All dollar amounts refer to 1972. See text for definition and methods. Families are either couples or single individuals.

TABLE 6

EFFECT OF PRICE INDEXING ON SOCIAL SECURITY WEALTH NET OF FUTURE TAXES PER FAMILY, BY AGE AND INCOME

(dollars)

Income	Age of Household Head						
	25–34	35–44	45–54	55–64	65 and older	All	35–64
Less than $3,000							
Wage indexing	1,299	6,549	9,357	22,197	28,608	22,778	15,298
Price indexing	−346	3,877	6,893	19,039	26,618	20,555	12,441
$3,000–$6,000							
Wage indexing	1,153	5,512	13,487	22,299	33,633	14,043	14,387
Price indexing	−1,679	2,291	9,933	20,176	32,505	11,390	11,444
$6,000–$9,000							
Wage indexing	−1,066	6,122	15,320	29,965	37,987	12,643	17,030
Price indexing	−5,002	1,562	10,849	26,842	36,100	8,750	12,963
$9,000–$12,000							
Wage indexing	−2,784	6,676	20,692	34,906	43,373	13,935	20,194
Price indexing	−7,602	833	14,773	30,656	43,098	8,869	14,792

$12,000–$15,000							
Wage indexing	−3,373	5,966	20,250	37,879	43,563	12,319	18,918
Price indexing	−8,499	107	14,063	33,453	42,143	6,967	13,285
$15,000–$25,000							
Wage indexing	−4,421	5,834	20,468	36,898	44,431	12,931	18,404
Price indexing	−9,592	−765	13,866	32,704	43,403	7,289	12,363
More than $25,000							
Wage indexing	−2,470	6,819	20,566	37,654	45,072	19,292	21,247
Price indexing	−7,510	589	14,069	33,263	44,139	14,027	15,450
All							
Wage indexing	−2,280	6,164	17,889	30,867	30,713	16,175	18,061
Price indexing	−6,662	721	12,519	27,223	28,856	12,062	13,207

NOTES: All dollar amounts refer to 1972. See text for definition and methods. Families are either couples or single individuals.

wage indexing. We based this anticipation on the much lower tax rate that they would eventually pay under price indexing. As Table 4 shows, the tax rates do not differ very much during the next decade but begin to differ quite substantially when the current group of young families approaches retirement in 2000 to 2015. These tax savings are not enough, however, to compensate for the lower benefits that price indexing entails. The much greater difference in tax rates during their actual period of retirement represents the greater intergeneration transfer entailed in wage indexing.

The political preference for wage indexing may offer a useful insight into the nature of the social security program and its historic growth. Wage indexing was explicitly compared with price indexing and then chosen by the Ford administration, the Carter administration, the Senate Finance Committee, and the House Committee on Ways and Means. These decisions can be regarded as an indication of a widespread political preference by today's voters to transfer income to themselves from the next generation of workers. Seen in this way, the rapid historic growth of social security is very different from the growth of other government programs. Social security has grown because voters are prepared to tax themselves because they expect that they will actually benefit by receiving more from the next generation.

This interpretation of the political support for social security expansion also sheds light on one aspect of the debate about the effect of social security on private saving. Robert Barro has ingeniously argued that social security need not depress private saving if the current workers save in order to increase their bequests to offset the greater tax burden that the social security program imposes on their children.[28] This argument regards social security as a policy imposed on the population "by the government" rather than as a policy chosen by the voters themselves. It seems more appropriate to regard the generation of worker-voters as voting to transfer income from future generations to themselves and therefore as having no desire to offset this transfer by increased bequests. The nature of the political support for social security thus implies that it does in fact reduce private saving.

Summary

An individual's social security wealth is the actuarial present value of the benefits that he will be eligible to receive at age sixty-five. Unlike most other forms of wealth, social security wealth is not backed by physi-

---

[28] Robert Barro, "Are Government Bonds Net Wealth?" *Journal of Political Economy*, vol. 82 (November/December 1974), pp. 1095–1117.

cal capital in the form of structures and equipment. Nevertheless, these claims on future taxpayers are the most important asset for the majority of U.S. families.

In this paper we have used an important new body of data to estimate the social security wealth of a representative sample of 38,000 households. Because the data for each household include the actual administrative records of the Social Security Administration, our calculations of social security wealth are substantially more accurate than any previous estimates. The sample was chosen in a way that permits estimating social security wealth for the entire population and for groups classified by income and age.

In our analysis of these data, we have emphasized five salient results:

1. The social security wealth is very large. At the end of fiscal year 1978, the social security wealth of the population over age twenty-five will exceed $3.4 trillion.

2. Social security wealth is distributed very equally. Households with incomes of $25,000 or more account for only 10 percent of social security wealth but more than 50 percent of ordinary fungible wealth. The distribution of total wealth, including social security wealth, is therefore much less concentrated than the distribution of ordinary wealth.

3. Net social security wealth, that is, net of future social security taxes, will be $2.0 trillion by the end of fiscal year 1978. This represents the transfer to persons now over twenty-five that will be made by those who are younger or not yet born. This implicit claim on future transfers provides strong political support for social security.

4. The net social security wealth of individuals aged twenty-five to thirty-four is negative: the present value of the taxes that they will pay exceeds the present value of the benefits for which they will be eligible. The fraction of the population with negative net social security wealth will grow with time, reducing the political support for high social security taxes.

5. The calculation of social security wealth is useful for comparing the price-indexing method of adjusting future benefits with the wage-indexing method that has been proposed by both the Ford administration and the Carter administration. Price indexing would limit the eventual rise in the payroll tax to 12 percent instead of the 19 percent or more required by wage indexing. Price indexing would also have long-run advantages for the supply of both capital and skilled labor. Our analysis shows that the total social security benefits of current workers would be little affected by the choice of indexing methods; the difference

in social security wealth between the two methods is less than 10 percent. Nevertheless, wage indexing promises current workers a greater net transfer from future generations; the net social security wealth is greater under wage indexing for every age group. This may explain its political support. The growing fraction of the population with negative net social security wealth should serve as a warning: the choice of wage indexing may not only be bad economics, but also a bad bet on the generosity of future taxpayers.

Appendix: Social Security Wealth Estimates Based on a 1 Percent Real Discount Rate

This appendix presents Tables 7, 8, 9, and 10, which are analogous to Tables 1, 2, 3, and 6 in the text but are based on a real discount rate of 1 percent. This is close to the real net rate of interest available over the past twenty-five years on long-term debt.

Discounting at this lower rate substantially raises the estimates of social security wealth. The aggregate gross social security wealth is increased from $1.85 trillion at the end of 1972 based on a 3 percent real discount rate to $3.02 trillion with a 1 percent real discount rate. The

TABLE 7

DISTRIBUTION OF SOCIAL SECURITY WEALTH, BY AGE AND INCOME,
BASED ON 1 PERCENT REAL DISCOUNT RATE
(percentages of total social security wealth)

Income	Age of Household Head						
	25–34	35–44	45–54	55–64	65 and older	All	35–64
Less than $3,000	0.8	0.8	1.1	2.7	12.6	18.0	7.8
$3,000–$6,000	1.2	0.9	1.1	1.2	1.0	5.5	5.7
$6,000–$9,000	3.5	2.1	2.2	2.3	0.7	10.7	11.1
$9,000–$12,000	5.8	3.9	4.2	3.4	0.7	17.9	19.7
$12,000–$15,000	5.2	3.7	3.4	2.4	0.4	15.1	16.3
$15,000–$25,000	7.0	7.0	6.0	3.8	0.7	24.4	28.6
More than $25,000	1.4	1.9	2.5	1.9	0.7	8.3	10.8
All	24.9	20.3	20.4	17.7	16.7	100.0	100.0

NOTE: All figures relate to the distribution of 1972 social security wealth of $1.847 trillion.

TABLE 8

SOCIAL SECURITY WEALTH PER FAMILY, BY AGE AND INCOME, BASED ON 1 PERCENT DISCOUNT RATE
(dollars)

Income	Age of Household Head						
	25–34	35–44	45–54	55–64	65 and older	All	35–64
Less than $3,000	20,116	22,446	20,911	30,486	33,323	30,262	26,072
$3,000–$6,000	28,991	27,613	29,544	31,475	39,399	30,936	29,689
$6,000–$9,000	42,827	39,841	38,221	43,354	45,132	41,446	40,397
$9,000–$12,000	55,725	53,080	51,523	53,095	51,579	53,462	52,506
$12,000–$15,000	60,342	55,060	54,673	58,326	53,940	57,165	55,707
$15,000–$25,000	62,223	62,157	58,204	57,844	54,454	60,226	59,709
More than $25,000	58,769	56,708	57,439	58,751	54,460	57,529	57,593
All	50,745	49,876	46,826	36,023	48,296	45,888	47,618

NOTES: All dollar amounts refer to 1972. See text for definition and methods. Families are either couples or single individuals.

113

TABLE 9

Social Security Wealth Net of Future Taxes per Family, by Age and Income, Based on 1 Percent Discount Rate
(dollars)

Income	Age of Household Head						
	25–34	35–44	45–54	55–64	65 and older	All	35–64
Less than $3,000	9,708	15,667	16,528	28,987	33,228	28,473	22,668
$3,000–$6,000	13,131	16,113	23,530	29,714	39,375	23,434	23,641
$6,000–$9,000	15,422	21,149	21,113	40,441	45,005	26,230	29,806
$9,000–$12,000	17,954	26,097	37,935	48,321	51,313	31,650	37,038
$12,000–$15,000	18,846	25,814	38,652	52,717	53,268	31,538	37,025
$15,000–$25,000	17,931	27,816	39,743	51,450	53,992	32,734	37,670
More than $25,000	19,573	27,093	39,569	52,600	54,023	37,370	39,461
All	16,662	24,290	33,536	42,197	35,898	30,055	33,180

Notes: All dollar amounts refer to 1972. See text for definition and methods. Families are either couples or single individuals.

114

TABLE 10

EFFECT OF PRICE INDEXING ON SOCIAL SECURITY WEALTH NET OF FUTURE TAXES PER FAMILY, BY AGE AND INCOME, BASED ON 1 PERCENT DISCOUNT RATE

(dollars)

Income	Age of Household Head						
	25–34	35–44	45–54	55–64	65 and older	All	35–64
Less than $3,000							
Wage indexing	9,708	15,667	16,528	28,987	33,228	28,473	22,668
Price indexing	5,283	10,376	12,494	24,873	30,927	25,426	18,341
$3,000–$6,000							
Wage indexing	13,131	16,113	23,530	29,714	39,375	23,434	23,641
Price indexing	5,565	9,578	17,770	26,869	38,056	18,402	18,711
$6,000–$9,000							
Wage indexing	15,422	21,149	21,113	40,441	45,005	26,230	29,806
Price indexing	4,630	11,669	20,807	36,206	42,794	18,318	22,779
$9,000–$12,000							
Wage indexing	17,954	26,097	37,935	48,321	51,313	31,650	37,038
Price indexing	4,490	13,948	28,239	42,464	49,775	21,297	27,652

Table 10 continues next page.

115

TABLE 10 (continued)

Income	Age of Household Head						
	25–34	35–44	45–54	55–64	65 and older	All	35–64
$12,000–$15,000							
Wage indexing	18,846	25,814	38,652	52,717	53,268	31,538	37,025
Price indexing	4,410	13,490	28,248	46,607	51,504	20,240	26,907
$15,000–$25,000							
Wage indexing	17,931	27,816	39,743	51,450	53,992	32,734	37,670
Price indexing	3,331	13,937	28,717	45,557	52,704	21,068	26,689
More than $25,000							
Wage indexing	19,573	27,093	39,569	52,600	54,023	37,370	39,461
Price indexing	5,322	14,239	28,717	46,427	52,844	27,316	29,350
All							
Wage indexing	16,662	24,290	33,536	42,197	35,898	30,055	33,180
Price indexing	4,434	12,951	24,643	37,217	33,741	22,068	24,700

NOTES: All dollar amounts refer to 1972. See text for definition and methods. Families are either couples or single individuals.

corresponding aggregate net social security wealth is increased from $1.06 trillion to $1.99 trillion.

The basic distributional features of these revised social security estimates are very similar to the results presented in the text. The only important difference is that net social security wealth is no longer negative for any age-income groups. The conclusion that the net social security wealth is higher for everyone with wage indexing is unchanged.

A Comparison of Rates of Return to Social Security Retirees under Wage and Price Indexing

Robert S. Kaplan

It is widely acknowledged that the Congress made a serious error when it provided for the automatic indexing of social security benefits in the 1972 amendments to the Social Security Act.[1] The problem has been well known for several years, and various proposals for eliminating the error have been made. Apparently, there is a virtual consensus about the procedure for achieving a reasonable indexing scheme for social security. Under the current system, past covered earnings are averaged (on an unadjusted basis) to compute a worker's average monthly wage (AMW);[2] in contrast, under the reform proposals, past earnings would be multiplied by a suitable index before an average lifetime wage is computed so that they would be more comparable with current earnings. Thus, a worker's benefit would be based on an averaged indexed monthly wage (AIMW). The benefit formula to produce a primary insurance amount (PIA) would consist of a sequence of declining marginal percentages applied to the AIMW as follows:

X_1 percent of the first Y_1 of AIMW,

X_2 percent of the next Y_2 of AIMW,

X_3 percent of AIMW in excess of $(Y_1 + Y_2)$,

---

[1] This error has been noted and discussed in numerous places, including U.S. Congress, House of Representatives, *Reports of the Quadrennial Advisory Council on Social Security*, House Document no. 94-75, 94th Congress, 1st session, March 10, 1975, pp. 14–16, 105–106; U.S. Congress, Senate, *Report of the Panel on Social Security Financing to the Committee on Finance, United States Senate*, 94th Congress, 1st session, February 1975; Colin D. Campbell, *Over-Indexed Benefits: The Decoupling Proposals for Social Security* (Washington, D.C.: American Enterprise Institute, 1976); U.S. Congress, *Report of the Consultant Panel on Society Security to the Congressional Research Service, Prepared for the Use of the Committee on Finance of the U.S. Senate and the Committee on Ways and Means of the U.S. House of Representatives*, 94th Congress, 2nd session, August 1976; and Alicia H. Munnell, *The Future of Social Security* (Washington, D.C.: The Brookings Institution, 1977).

[2] The average monthly wage (AMW) is the basis of the initial benefit computation when individuals become entitled to social security benefits.

[3] The proposed benefit formula is illustrated with only three regions. In practice, a formula with more regions could be considered but such a formula has not been proposed.

with $X_1 > X_2 > X_3$.[3] The marginal benefit percentages—X_1, X_2, and X_3 —are assumed to remain constant over time, but the formula bracket limits—Y_1 and Y_2—will be indexed each year to keep abreast of the increasing AIMW.[4] The initial benefit, based on the primary insurance amount, will then be increased in each subsequent year proportional to increases in the consumer price index (CPI). This post-entitlement benefit adjustment would be identical to the provision under current law.

Although it is generally agreed that the above procedure would achieve a properly indexed social security system, a considerable debate has developed regarding the index that should be used to update the past earnings records of workers for computing an AIMW and the benefit formula bracket limits (Y_1 and Y_2 in the example). The 1974 Advisory Council on Social Security and the Ford administration in H.R. 14430 recommended that a wage index be used to compute the AIMW and to adjust the formula bracket limits.[5] Two consultant panels to the Congress, both under the chairmanship of William Hsiao, advocated that a price index (specifically, the consumer price index) be used for these purposes.[6] Although the choice of the specific index to use for computing AIMWs and for updating benefit formula bracket limits would seem to be a technical issue of no great consequence, the choice actually has substantive implications for the future costs and benefits of the social security system.

Wage versus Price Indexing

The debate between advocates of either wage or price indexing usually focuses on three dimensions: equity within and between different retirement groups, replacement ratios, and future cost.[7]

---

[4] The proposed formula with an indexed benefit base (AIMW), constant benefit percentages (X_i) and indexed bracket limits (Y_i) is exactly the opposite of the current double-indexed formula, which uses an unindexed benefit base, indexed benefit percentages, and constant bracket limits.

[5] House of Representatives, *Reports of the Quadrennial Advisory Council on Social Security*; and U.S. Congress, House of Representatives, Subcommittee on Social Security of the Committee on Ways and Means, *Decoupling the Social Security Benefit Structure*, 94th Congress, 2nd session, June 18, July 23, and 26, 1976.

[6] Senate, *Report of the Panel on Social Security Financing*; and U.S. Congress, *Report of the Consultant Panel on Social Security*.

[7] A fourth dimension—the reliability and validity of wage indexes as compared with price indexes—is discussed in Robert S. Kaplan, *Indexing Social Security: An Analysis of the Issues* (Washington, D.C.: American Enterprise Institute, 1977).

Equity. The arguments about equity involve many subtle considerations;[8] ultimately, however, they require subjective value judgments about what constitutes "fair" treatment under social security. Reasonable people can disagree about what constitutes fair treatment. For example, should individuals retiring at different times who had the same relative standing in the distribution of earnings have equal ratios of initial benefits to indexed lifetime earnings (as they would under wage indexing)? Or, should retirees with the same real earnings history have the same real retirement benefits (as they would under price indexing)? Among individuals with the same average lifetime wage, those with rapid wage growth over their lives would do relatively better under price indexing, whereas those with slower wage growth would do relatively better under wage indexing. It is not clear to me how one can make a choice based on these intertemporal equity considerations.

Within a group of workers retiring at the same time, wage indexing would maintain the tilted benefit structure under which individuals with lower incomes would receive relatively higher social security benefits than individuals with higher incomes. This tilting is a consequence of the declining marginal benefit percentages as the AIMW increases. Under price indexing, the distribution of AIMWs would increase faster than the indexed formula brackets would rise (assuming that the historic pattern, whereby wages increase faster than prices, is maintained), so that eventually almost all individuals would have AIMWs in the upper bracket of the benefit formula in which the marginal benefit percentage is lowest. Although some tilting of the benefit structure toward lower-income individuals would still exist, the amount of redistribution would be much less than if the present benefit distribution is maintained, as it would be under wage indexing. Thus, advocates of wage indexing can argue that price indexing reduces the "social adequacy" role of social security by severely reducing the current tilted benefit structure toward lower-income individuals. Advocates of price indexing can respond by showing that, with wages increasing faster than prices over long periods of time, lower-income individuals in the future would have real purchasing power comparable to that of today's middle- and upper-income individuals, so that the justification for a tilted benefit structure is weakened. Only a rigid commitment to the definition of some bottom

---

[8] These arguments are well developed in Dean R. Leimer and Ronald Hoffman, "Designing an Equitable Intertemporal Social Security Benefit Structure," mimeographed, Social Security Administration, Office of Research and Statistics (November 1976); and Dean R. Leimer, Ronald Hoffman, and Alan Freiden, "A Framework for Analyzing the Equity of the Social Security Benefit Structure," *Studies in Income Distribution No. 6*, Social Security Administration, Office of Research and Statistics (forthcoming).

fraction of the income distribution as poor, independent of the purchasing power of these individuals, would generate a defense of maintaining the current redistributive nature of the benefit formula indefinitely into the future. In any case, the equity argument fails to give a clear signal in favor of wage or price indexing because of difficulties in defining what constitutes equity or fairness.

Replacement Ratios. The impact of wage and price indexing on replacement ratios constitutes the second dimension of the debate. The replacement ratio for a worker is defined as the ratio of his initial social security benefit to his gross covered earnings in the year before entitlement. This ratio has come to represent the most important summary statistic of the adequacy of current and proposed benefit formulas. Under the current law, a worker retiring without any dependents at age sixty-five in January 1977 will have replacement ratios ranging upwards from 0.33 for a high-income worker (at the maximum earnings base), to 0.46 for a median-income worker, and finally to 0.58 for a low-income worker (at the federal minimum wage level).[9] The increases in replacement ratios for lower-income workers is a consequence of the tilted benefit structure previously discussed. With the indexing error in the current law, these replacement ratios could rise in the future to 0.48, 0.70, and 1.06 respectively, representing a substantial and unintended across-the-board expansion of social security benefits.[10] Wage-indexing proposals are designed to stabilize the distribution of replacement ratios at about the current levels, independent of the actual rate of inflation that occurs in the future.[11] The price-indexing proposal, however, results in declining replacement ratios. For example, the replacement ratio for a median-income worker retiring at age sixty-two would decline from a level of 0.42 in 1978 to 0.40 in 1980, 0.35 in 1990, and 0.30 in 2000.[12]

---

[9] These replacement ratios apply to a single worker. They increase by 50 percent if the worker has an eligible dependent spouse. Further, social security benefits are tax free, whereas the earnings before retirement are subject to both income and payroll taxes. Finally, retired individuals avoid many work-related expenses and receive extensive medical benefits through the Medicare program. Thus, a replacement ratio of 50 percent can easily result in a standard of living from social security benefits comparable to what was enjoyed before retirement.

[10] U.S. Congress, House of Representatives, *1977 Annual Report of the Board of Trustees of the Federal Old-Age and Survivors Insurance and Disability Insurance Trust Funds*, House Document no. 95-150, 95th Congress, 1st session, May 10, 1977, table 26, p. 46.

[11] A minor exception to this has been advocated by Robert Myers who proposes a wage-indexing scheme but with a reduction in replacement ratios by about 10 percent to levels prevailing in 1972.

[12] House of Representatives, *Decoupling the Social Security Benefit Structure*, p. 69. Note that these replacement ratios are for workers retiring at age sixty-two, not for those retiring at age sixty-five, as previously cited.

The decline in replacement ratios under price indexing has been the cause of virtually all the criticism directed at this proposal. Critics use these declining ratios as self-evident proof that social security benefits have been substantially "de-liberalized," and they consider that to be clearly unacceptable. An exclusive emphasis on replacement ratios seems misplaced, however, for at least three reasons. First, replacement ratios are not well defined because of the erratic behavior of earnings in the ten years before retirement. The Consultant Panel on Social Security studied this phenomenon extensively and devised a modified definition of replacement ratio (based on the middle seven out of the final ten years of earnings) to obtain a measure that would be broadly representative of the widely dispersed patterns of pre-retirement earnings.[13]

Second, if replacement ratios are to be the most important measure of the merits of alternative benefit functions, then it seems foolish to have a benefit base that may not be representative of pre-retirement earnings. With a properly indexed thirty-five-year earnings history, the effect of pre-retirement earnings is relatively small. Logically, those who argue for achieving certain replacement ratios should also advocate reducing the averaging period for the benefit base to five or seven representative years of pre-retirement earnings. Only if the benefit base is defined in such a way, can we be sure of achieving desired replacement ratios for almost all workers. Once one grants that benefits should be a function of lifetime earnings rather than pre-retirement earnings, a more proper measure to evaluate the adequacy of various benefit functions is the rate of return various classes of workers can expect by receiving retirement benefits based on the lifetime pattern of social security taxes they paid.

Third, the emphasis on replacement ratios probably derives from the social adequacy role of social security. Here again, however, critics of price indexing are fixating on the wrong issue if they claim that only a constant pattern of replacement ratios will fulfill the social adequacy objective. In the most recent comprehensive review of the role of social security, the 1974 Advisory Council on Social Security stressed that social security should provide a floor of protection for retired individuals, to be supplemented by private pension, insurance, and savings programs.[14] Thus, social security is supposed to provide a minimal level of

---

[13] U.S. Congress, *Report of the Consultant Panel on Social Security*, pp. 15, 19, 23–26.

[14] House of Representatives, *Reports of the Quadrennial Advisory Council on Social Security*, pp. 7–10. This point is also developed in Munnell, *The Future of Social Security*, chapter II.

retirement income, and individuals should expect to supplement this guaranteed benefit through personal savings or through an employer-sponsored plan to achieve their desired level of retirement income. As the economy grows and all individuals become wealthier (this is implied by wages rising faster than prices), there is more opportunity for individual initiative in planning for retirement. That is, social security will likely fulfill its social adequacy role by assuring that the market basket of goods and services it provides to retirees does not shrink over time. There appears to be no compelling reason why social security needs to provide a steadily increasing real level of benefits in order to fulfill its social adequacy function.

Table 1 shows how the real benefit to a median worker increases over time under both the wage-indexing and the price-indexing proposals. Under wage indexing, the worker retiring in 1981 will receive 19 percent more in purchasing power (measured in constant terms) than the worker retiring just five years earlier, whereas the worker retiring in 1991 will receive 50 percent more in purchasing power than the 1976 retiree. The price-indexing proposal also shows a rise in the purchasing power of the initial benefit, but the increase is much less. It is not clear what social adequacy role is promoted by having real benefits

TABLE 1

MONTHLY RETIREMENT BENEFIT FOR MEDIAN EARNER RETIRING AT AGE SIXTY-FIVE, 1976, 1981, 1991

Year of Retirement	Administration Wage-Indexing Proposal		Hsiao Panel Price-Indexing Proposal	
	Benefit amount (1976 dollars)	Ratio of initial benefit award to 1976 retiree's benefit	Benefit amount (1976 dollars)	Ratio of initial benefit award to 1976 retiree's benefit
1976	347	1.00	341	1.00
1981	413	1.19	366	1.07
1991	521	1.50	414	1.21

SOURCE: U.S. Congress, *Report of the Consultant Panel on Social Security to the Congressional Research Service, Prepared for the Use of the Committee on Finance of the U.S. Senate and the Committee on Ways and Means of the U.S. House of Representatives,* 94th Congress, 2nd session, August 1976, p. 9.

rise by 50 percent in the next fifteen-year period. Also, one can hardly consider the price-indexing proposal as reducing the role of social security when real benefits continue to rise for all workers.

Costs. Wage indexing is significantly more expensive than price indexing because of the difference between the future replacement ratios and the benefits under the two indexing methods. Both proposals reduce considerably the massive deficit now being forecast for social security by eliminating the error of double indexing future benefits for inflation. Wage indexing reduces the long-term deficit by about 50 percent, whereas price indexing reduces the deficit to near zero. With wage indexing, the deficit will average about 2 percent of taxable payroll in the twenty-five years from 1977 to 2001; 4.3 percent of taxable payroll in the following twenty-five years, 2002 to 2026; and 7.0 percent in the next twenty-five years, 2027 to 2051. (Those figures already assume a scheduled increase in the combined payroll tax rate from the present 9.9 percent level to 11.9 percent in 2010.)[15] Over the next seventy-five years, the deficit averages more than 4 percent of taxable payroll; this implies that the payroll tax rate would need to rise by an additional 2 percentage points for both employees and employers in order to meet the projected future commitments. Naturally, these estimates are a function of projected birth and mortality rates and the growth of real wages, but, unlike the present system, are scarcely affected by the level of inflation.

In contrast to the large deficit still remaining under wage indexing, the future deficit is virtually eliminated under price indexing. Data from the Consultant Panel on Social Security suggest that expenditures for the next forty to fifty years can be met with a relatively small immediate increase in the maximum taxable earnings base (from $16,500 to $18,900) and about a 0.6 percent increase in the payroll tax rate (0.3 percent for both employee and employer) to a combined rate of 10.5 percent.[16] Since this increase is already necessary just to remedy the short-term deficit position of social security,[17] such an increase coupled with adoption of price indexing would have the salutary effect of eliminating serious social security deficits in both the short and the long run. Although this is certainly a pleasant prospect, especially in view of the

---

[15] House of Representatives, *1977 Annual Report of the Board of Trustees of the OASDI Trust Funds*, table 36, p. 59.

[16] U.S. Congress, *Report of the Consultant Panel on Social Security*, table 1, p. 6. The panel actually recommended an increase to a combined rate of only 10.3 percent because it was more optimistic about future fertility rates and growth in real wages.

[17] House of Representatives, *1977 Annual Report of the Board of Trustees of the OASDI Trust Funds*, table 14, p. 28.

large deficits that have been forecast for social security, an obvious question is whether future beneficiaries will be shortchanged under price indexing. Are the large savings to future taxpayers achieved at the expense of future retirees?

Under price indexing, the real benefits to future retirees would continue to increase, even though replacement ratios would decline. Thus, future retirees would be better off than current retirees under price indexing. The more serious consideration is to determine whether these increased real benefits are reasonable when related to the lifetime taxes paid into the system by workers. An important feature of social security has always been a minimal level of individual equity for all workers. That is, benefits even for high-income workers should represent a reasonable or fair rate of return on lifetime tax payments. Just what constitutes a reasonable return or even how to measure the effective social security tax rate are not trivial questions, and they will be discussed shortly. For now, it is important to point out that looking only at benefits (future replacement ratios) or at costs (future tax rates) gives a one-sided and hence incomplete picture of the consequences of alternative indexing proposals. Computing the rate of return integrates both costs and benefits in a single evaluation. Also, by comparing social security rates of return with comparable investment opportunities in capital markets, we get an objective standard of evaluation and do not have to appeal to vague notions of social adequacy, fairness, or equity.

Rates of Return: Conceptual and Measurement Issues

The complexity of the social security benefit structure makes the computation of rates of return a difficult task. The extensive array of dependent's and survivor's benefits causes the rate of return to be a function of family size, family composition, and time and cause of initial entitlement. Also, payment into the system is a function of wage levels and length of service in the labor force. Rather than dealing with the system in all its complexity, we will focus only on the original and still most important function of social security: benefits to retired individuals. Our analysis assumes an individual who is continuously employed once he enters the labor force.

Effective Tax Rate. One problem common to all studies on rates of return to social security taxes is to determine the effective tax rate for the retirement annuity. Three issues are involved. First, we need to determine the appropriate nominal payroll tax rate that workers will encounter in the future. Clearly, the present basic rate of 4.95 percent (excluding the 0.9 percent devoted to Medicare) is inadequate both for the short term and the long run, even with the substantial cost saving realized by using price indexing. Based on the previously cited cost figures, we will use 5.25 percent as the basic payroll tax rate for the price-indexing proposal.

For wage indexing, the situation is less clear because the cost of the system increases in each future twenty-five-year period. The average cost for the next fifty years is about 13.75 percent of taxable payroll.[18] This implies a basic tax rate of about 6.9 percent. Unlike the price-indexing proposal, this rate is estimated to be inadequate for the subsequent twenty-five-year period (starting fifty years from now), when the cost of a wage-indexed system is estimated to be almost 19 percent of taxable payroll. Therefore, we are being somewhat conservative in estimating the long-range cost of a wage-indexed scheme to be around 13.75 percent of taxable payroll when the average seventy-five-year cost is 15.45 percent of taxable payroll.[19]

The second issue in determining the effective payroll tax rate is to eliminate the effects of disability, dependency, and survivorship benefits so that we may concentrate solely on the worker retirement program. Of the present basic payroll tax rate of 4.95 percent, 0.60 percent goes to disability. The disability program is currently in deficit, however, and the percentage devoted to this program is scheduled to increase to 0.65 percent in 1981 and to 0.70 percent in 1986. Computations based on data in the 1977 OASDI Trustees Report suggest that the long-run cost of the disability program will be an even higher percentage of the basic payroll tax rate than these anticipated tax rates would indicate. Data on either the segmented costs of the OASI and DI programs or the expected number of beneficiaries in each category in the future indicate that the disability program will absorb 18 percent of the payroll tax rate, leaving 82 percent for the retirement, dependency, and survivorship programs.[20] Thus, under price indexing, the payroll tax necessary to finance the OASI program is $0.82 \times 5.25 = 4.30$ percent. Under wage indexing, the OASI payroll tax rate is $0.82 \times 6.9 = 5.65$ percent.

For a single individual without dependents, these are the appropriate rates because such an individual receives no value from the

---

[18] This figure is obtained by averaging the average deficits in the next two twenty-five-year periods; see ibid., table 35, p. 58. The 13.75 percent cost for wage indexing is not precisely comparable to the 10.5 percent estimated cost for price indexing because of slightly different demographic and economic assumptions and also because the wage-indexing estimate did not assume an immediate jump in the maximum earnings base to $18,900.

[19] House of Representatives, *1977 Annual Report of the Board of Trustees of the OASDI Trust Funds*, table 35, p. 58.

[20] Ibid., table 28, p. 50, and Appendix tables C and D, pp. 67 and 69.

extensive program of benefits to dependents and survivors. Workers with dependents, however, receive these additional benefits over and above their own retirement benefits. For these workers, the effective tax to pay solely for retirement benefits is less than 4.3 or 5.65 percent. At present, about 65 percent of benefits from the OASI program are paid directly to retired workers (the principal other recipients are survivors of deceased workers who receive 27 percent).[21] The 65 percent figure roughly corresponds to the percentage of all beneficiaries who are retired old-age workers.[22] In future years, the percentage of retired workers is expected to increase; thus, to be conservative, we will assume that 25 percent of future OASI payroll taxes will go to dependents and survivors and that 75 percent can be counted as contributing directly to benefits for retired workers. The effective tax rate solely for retirement benefits for individuals with dependents and potential survivors is thus $0.75 \times 4.3 = 3.25$ percent under price indexing and $0.75 \times 5.65 = 4.25$ percent under wage indexing.

The third issue in computing the effective tax rate on social security contributions is deciding who pays the employer's share of the payroll tax. In some circles it is popular to believe that taxing a corporation has no impact on employees or consumers—for example, the Carter administration proposed to remove the maximum earnings limitation for the employer's share, but not the employee's share, of the payroll tax. Most economists, however, agree that the employer's share of the tax is shifted to the employee in the form of lower wages.[23] Other studies of the rate of return to social security taxes have also assumed that the employer's share of the payroll tax is fully shifted to the employee.[24] An alternative

---

[21] These percentages are taken from tables in the annual trustees reports for the past five years.

[22] House of Representatives, *1977 Annual Report of the Board of Trustees of the OASDI Trust Funds*, Appendix table C, p. 67.

[23] Munnell, *The Future of Social Security*, pp. 86–88, and John A. Brittain, *The Payroll Tax for Social Security* (Washington, D.C.: The Brookings Institution, 1972), pp. 60–81.

[24] Other studies on the rate of return to social security recipients include Colin D. Campbell and Rosemary G. Campbell, "Cost-Benefit Ratios under the Federal Old-Age Insurance Program," and John Brittain, "The Real Rate of Interest on Lifetime Contributions toward Retirement under Social Security," both in *Old-Age Income Assurance*, Part 3, *Public Programs: A Compendium of Papers on Problems and Policy Issues in the Public and Private Pension System*, 90th Congress, 1st session, 1967, pp. 72–84 and 109–132; Yung-Ping Chen and K. W. Chu, "Tax-Benefit Ratios and Rates of Return under OASI: 1974 Retirees and Entrants," *Journal of Risk and Insurance*, vol. 41 (June 1974), pp. 189–206; and Alan Freiden, Dean R. Leimer, and Ronald Hoffman, "Internal Rates of Return to Retired, Worker-Only Beneficiaries Under Social Security, 1967–70," in *Studies in Income Distribution No. 5*, Social Security Administration, Office of Research and Statistics (October 1976).

view is that, although part of the employer's share of the payroll tax is shifted to the employee, part is a tax on capital or is shifted forward to consumers, not all of whom are subject to the payroll tax. This view receives some support from the policy of taxing self-employed individuals at 150 percent of the employee tax rate rather than at 200 percent, which would be appropriate if it were obvious to everyone that the employee bore the full share of the employer's tax. Thus, we will consider two assumptions on the shifting of the employer's tax: first, that it is fully shifted so that the true tax on employees is twice the nominal rate; and, second, that it is only partially shifted so that the true employee tax is one-and-a-half times the basic rate.

The combination of workers with and without dependents and two assumptions of shifting of the employer's tax produces three basic tax rates, which are summarized in Table 2. Rates of return for the two indexing proposals will be computed for each of the three basic tax rates shown in Table 2.

Lifetime Earnings History. Workers differ not only according to the number of dependents they have, but also according to their level and pattern of lifetime earnings. Because of the tilted benefit formula, low-income workers receive higher rates of return on their social security taxes than high-income workers. A further complication is introduced because an individual's wages naturally tend to increase as he gets older. He does not stay in the same percentile of the income distribution over

TABLE 2

EFFECTIVE FUTURE TAX RATES TO FINANCE RETIREMENT
BENEFITS UNDER PRICE AND WAGE INDEXING
(percent)

Assumptions	Price Indexing	Wage Indexing
Worker with no dependents, full shifting of employer tax	8.6	11.3
Worker with no dependents, 50 percent shift of employer tax; also worker with dependents, full shifting of employer tax	6.5	8.5
Worker with dependents, 50 percent shift of employer tax	4.85	6.35

SOURCE: Author's calculations.

TABLE 3

RATIO OF WAGE-INDEXED EARNINGS AT A PARTICULAR YEAR TO EARNINGS AT AGE FIFTY

Age	Ratio
20	0.273
25	0.589
30	0.783
35	0.886
40	0.961
45	0.994
50	1.000
55	0.978
60	0.954
61	0.921
62	0.947
63	0.933
64	0.926

SOURCE: U.S. Congress, *Report of the Consultant Panel on Social Security*, Appendix B, table 2, p. 90.

his working lifetime.[25] The Hsiao panel found that the average worker's relative salary peaks when he is fifty years old. This paper adopts the Hsiao panel's profile of a typical lifetime path of wage-indexed earnings in calculating earnings histories and tax contributions for representative wage earners.[26] This lifetime profile is shown in Table 3.

Furthermore, four different income classes of workers will be distinguished, as measured by their peak (at age fifty) salaries in 1977 dollars: low income ($4,000), median income ($10,000), maximum earnings base ($16,500), and high income ($25,000). These salaries are increased each year by the assumed increase in average wages in the economy. The salary for a particular worker in a year is obtained by multiplying the wage-indexed peak salary by the factor appropriate for the worker's age obtained by interpolation in Table 3.

Another assumption necessary to compute the lifetime tax payments and indexed wage of a worker is the age of entry into the labor force and retirement from it. A basic pattern of entry at age twenty and retirement at age sixty-five is assumed, but alternative patterns of entry

---

[25] This point was studied and emphasized at considerable length in U.S. Congress, *Report of the Consultant Panel on Social Security*, pp. 41–55 and 62–119.

[26] Ibid., figure 1, p. 89, and Appendix B, table 2, p. 90.

at ages twenty-five and thirty are also considered. A thirty-five-year averaging period is used and, for continuously employed workers, this implies counting wages earned from age thirty through age sixty-four. This again is a conservative assumption with respect to rates of return because workers who are not employed continuously will have lower indexed wages and hence will be in a portion of the benefit formula that generates higher relative benefits. The lowest rates of return accrue to workers who enter the labor force early and remain in it continuously until retirement. The assumption of retirement at age sixty-five is traditional and avoids complications associated with computing reduced benefits for early retirement.

Economic and Mortality Assumptions. In order to compute the benefit base and subsequent benefit payments for workers under the alternative indexing procedures, assumptions must be made about increases in wages and prices. The central assumption will correspond to that used in the 1977 Trustees Report of a 4.0 percent annual increase in prices and a 5.75 percent annual increase in wages (implying real growth in wages of 1.75 percent). To obtain the sensitivity of the various approaches to the real wage assumption, annual wage growths of 6.25 percent and 5.25 percent coupled with a 4.0 percent increase in prices, will also be investigated. The impact of higher rates of inflation will be studied by assuming annual price increases of 6 percent and wage growth of 7.75 percent.

Once a worker has accumulated a lifetime earnings history, paid the associated social security taxes, and retired at age sixty-five, the principal remaining uncertainty is how many years the worker lives to collect his social security benefits. Obviously, retired workers who die at age sixty-seven have received a much lower rate of return from their social security taxes than those who live to be eighty-seven. This is the nature of a retirement annuity program in which individual risks are pooled to produce an overall payout schedule that is adequate for the entire collection of retired workers. Some researchers have based rate-of-return computations on the expected additional lifetime of workers who have already reached age sixty-five. For male workers, this conditional expected lifetime is about thirteen years. This procedure, however, is theoretically incorrect because it computes a nonlinear function (rate of return) of an expected value rather than the expected value of the function (the sum of the present value of benefits for each possible lifetime weighted by the probability of achieving each lifetime).

Instead of computing the expected rates of return, this paper will present results showing the number of years a worker would have to live in order to achieve a given rate of return on his social security taxes. That is, tables will be presented that show—for various income classes of workers, tax rates, price and wage rate assumptions, benefit bases, and benefit formulas—how quickly a worker will be able to get a "fair" return on his social security contributions. Of particular interest will be the rate of return associated with workers aged seventy-eight or seventy-nine, which corresponds to the expected lifetime as well as the median lifetime for males who have reached age sixty-five. That is, about half the retired male workers will exceed the rate of return of retirees aged seventy-eight and half will not achieve this rate of return.

Fair Rates of Return. The final consideration before the results are presented is a judgment on what constitutes a fair rate of return on taxes paid into the social security system. The financial instrument most comparable to the system of social security taxes and subsequent benefits is a high quality (default-free) municipal bond. Both are paid for with after-tax dollars, and their benefits or receipts are tax free. Although published series on the rates of return from holding municipal bonds are not available, it is likely that the real rate of return from holding these bonds is less than 1 percent. For example, the inflation rate from 1968 to 1973 was between 4 and 6 percent, whereas high-quality municipal bonds rarely yielded more than 5 percent. In recent years, the yield on municipal bonds has been below the rate of inflation. Therefore, with an assumed inflation rate of 4 percent, it appears that a fair rate of return on social security tax payments would be 5 percent, or a real rate of 1 percent.

Further support for assuming a real interest rate of 1 percent comes from studies on the long-run average real rate of return on long-term government bonds and U.S. Treasury bills. Table 4 is extracted from a comprehensive study of the rates of return from buying and holding representative portfolios of common stocks, long-term government bonds, and U.S. Treasury bills for holding periods during the past fifty years.[27] In the postwar period, the average return on both government bonds and Treasury bills has been below the rate of price increases.

In addition, holders of default-free government bonds and high-grade municipal bonds incur a substantial risk of unexpected inflation (a risk made abundantly clear by the numbers in Table 4). Social security benefits are not only guaranteed by the government but they are also shielded from the risk of inflation (at least they should be in a

---

[27] Roger G. Ibbotson and Rex A. Sinquefield, *Stocks, Bonds, Bills, and Inflation: The Past (1926–1976) and the Future (1977–2000)* (Charlottesville, Va.: Financial Analysts Research Foundation, 1977).

TABLE 4

REAL RATES OF RETURN OF COMMON STOCKS, LONG-TERM
GOVERNMENT BONDS, AND TREASURY BILLS DURING
SELECTED HOLDING PERIODS
(percent per year)

Holding Period	Common Stocks	Long-Term Government Bonds	U.S. Treasury Bills
Through World War II			
1927–1931	−1.4	6.1	6.8
1932–1936	23.5	8.5	1.1
1937–1941	−9.3	1.6	−2.0
1942–1946	10.2	−3.1	−6.2
1927–1946	5.0	3.2	−0.2
Post–World War II			
1947–1951	11.9	−3.6	−3.2
1952–1956	19.2	0.1	0.8
1957–1961	10.9	0.8	0.8
1962–1966	3.8	1.3	1.7
1967–1971	3.7	−2.7	0.8
1972–1976	−2.3	−0.4	−1.2
1947–1976	7.6	−0.8	−0.1
1927–1976	6.6	0.8	−0.1

SOURCE: Roger B. Ibbotson and Rex A. Sinquefield, *Stocks, Bonds, Bills, and Inflation: The Past (1926–1976) and the Future (1977–2000)* (Charlottesville, Va.: Financial Analysts Research Foundation, 1977).

properly indexed system). Investors might therefore accept an even lower rate of return for such an investment opportunity. Because Treasury bills are of short duration, they are hardly subject to the risk of unexpected inflation, and these bills rarely yield more than 1 percent above the inflation rate (and usually much less than this when measured over long periods of time).

The conclusion from these data is that a real rate of return of 1 percent on social security contributions is certainly competitive with the rate of return on alternative securities involving a fixed commitment and low default risk, especially since the return from social security is not subject to the risk of unexpected inflation.

Rates of Return with Wage and Price Indexing

Price Indexing. The replacement ratios and the age at which recipients break even are displayed in Table 5 as a function of income level, assumed tax rate, and implicit interest rate under price indexing of both the benefit base and the formula brackets. The reduction in replacement ratios and the unweighting of the benefit formula are apparent when it is observed that the replacement ratio for the median-income worker is 0.29 (below the current replacement ratio for high-income workers) and the ratio for a high-income worker is only slightly lower at about 0.25. These ratios correspond to those forecast in the Hsiao panel's report.[28]

The entries for a zero interest rate indicate that even under pessimistic conditions (high-income worker and high implicit tax rate), workers receive back their nominal taxes (without interest) within five years of retirement. The more interesting computation, however, is how long workers must wait to get a reasonable return on their social security taxes.

High-income individuals at the maximum tax rate of 0.086 obtain a 5 percent tax-free return on their social security taxes if they live to age seventy-nine. When the perhaps more representative tax rate of 0.065 is used, high-income workers get a 6 percent return by living to the expected age of seventy-eight. These figures are pessimistic because they assume that these high-income workers start contributing to the system at age twenty. With the assumption of entry in the labor force at age twenty-five, the payback years are reduced by about one year at an interest rate of 6 percent. With entry at age thirty, high-income individuals receive a 6 percent return before they reach age eighty, even at the maximum assumed tax rate of 8.6 percent.

The median-wage worker receives a 6 percent return by age seventy-five with an assumed tax rate of 6.5 percent, and he breaks even with a 6 percent cost of money during the middle of his seventy-ninth year with the maximum assumed tax rate of 8.6 percent. Workers who live for the median number of years during retirement get a rate of return somewhat better than they could have earned investing in tax-free municipals or U.S. government bonds, and they are also shielded from the unexpected inflation risk that holders of these other investments must bear. Thus, despite the reduction in replacement ratios under the price-indexing proposal, the rate of return to social security beneficiaries is still fair relative to comparable alternative investments. The real return of 2 percent (in excess of the assumed inflation rate) for the median worker living the median number of years supports the estimate made by Martin Feldstein that the rate of return participants can earn in a fully mature social security system is limited to the growth rate of real

---

[28] U.S. Congress, *Report of the Consultant Panel on Social Security*, p. 18.

TABLE 5

Age for Repayment of Social Security Taxes under the Price-Indexing Proposal

Earnings at Age 50 (1977 wage levels)	Replace-ment Ratio	Tax Rate	Age for Repayment with Rate of Return of:					
			0 percent	4 percent	5 percent	6 percent	7 percent
$4,000	0.42	0.0485	65.9	67.6	68.5	69.6	71.1
		0.065	66.5	68.9	70.0	71.6	73.9
		0.086	67.3	70.5	72.0	74.3	77.8
$10,000	0.29	0.0485	66.7	69.2	70.5	72.2	74.7
		0.065	67.6	71.0	72.7	75.3	79.2
		0.086	68.6	73.3	75.7	79.5	86.0
$16,500	0.25	0.0485	67.1	70.0	71.5	73.5	76.6
		0.065	68.1	72.1	74.1	77.2	82.2
		0.086	69.3	74.7	77.6	82.2	90.9
$25,000	0.24	0.0485	67.2	70.4	72.0	74.4	78.1
		0.065	68.2	72.6	74.9	78.4	84.5
		0.086	69.4	75.3	78.6	84.0	94.9

NOTE: Assumes price increases of 4 percent and wage increases of 5.75 percent.

wages (assumed to be 1.75 percent).[29] Workers facing an effective tax rate of 4.85 percent receive an excellent rate of return on their social security taxes. Median-income workers receive a 4 percent real rate of return if they live to age seventy-nine, and high-income workers receive a real rate of return in excess of 3 percent by age seventy-nine.

When a higher rate of inflation (6 percent) and a corresponding higher rate of wage increases (7.75 percent) are assumed, the length of time required to achieve a given real rate of return is virtually identical to that shown in Table 5. That is, at a tax rate of 0.086, the median-income worker gets an 8 percent rate of return by age seventy-nine and a half. The extra rate of return (from 6 percent in Table 5 to 8 percent) is just enough to compensate the worker for the extra 2 percent assumed in the inflation rate. Thus, by adding 2 percent to the column headings in Table 5, one obtains the correct table for the higher assumptions (6 percent and 7.75 percent). This computation demonstrates that the proposed system correctly compensates for inflation.

The age for repayment in Table 5 is also scarcely affected by varying the assumption of real wage growth. Assuming real wage growth of 2.25 percent (nominal growth of 6.25 percent) increases the age for repayment by 0.2 years or less. Reducing the real wage growth to 1.25 percent (nominal growth of 5.25 percent) decreases the age for repayment by 0.2 or less. Thus, the rates of return implicit in the price-indexing proposal are relatively unaffected by specific assumptions on the increase in prices and wages.

Wage Indexing. The procedure for analyzing the rates of return under wage indexing is identical to that followed for the price-indexing proposal with one exception: the Ford administration's proposal that earnings from age sixty-two to sixty-four be included on an unindexed basis with indexed earnings up to age sixty-two has been followed literally. The specific implementation suggestion of computing benefits using indexes one or two years prior to retirement is ignored. Table 6 presents payback years on a basis comparable to those given in Table 5, with no increase in assumed tax rates.

It is immediately evident that the replacement ratios in Table 6 are much higher than those obtained from the pure price-indexing proposal (see Table 5). That is expected because the wage-indexing proposal is designed to maintain the current level and distribution of replacement ratios. It is also apparent that the rates of return under the wage-indexing proposal are from 1 to 2 percent higher than those under

---

[29] Martin Feldstein, "Facing the Social Security Crisis," *The Public Interest*, no. 47 (Spring 1977), p. 92.

TABLE 6

Age for Repayment of Social Security Taxes under the Ford Administration Wage-Indexing Proposal

Earnings at Age 50 (1977 wage levels)	Replace-ment Ratio	Tax Rate	Age for Repayment with Rate of Return of:					
			0 percent	4 percent	5 percent	6 percent	7 percent
$4,000	0.61	0.0485	65.3	66.5	67.1	67.8	68.7
		0.065	65.8	67.4	68.1	69.1	70.5
		0.086	66.3	68.5	69.5	70.9	72.9
$10,000	0.42	0.0485	65.9	67.7	68.5	69.6	71.2
		0.065	66.6	68.9	70.1	71.7	74.0
		0.086	67.3	70.5	72.1	74.4	77.9
$16,500	0.36	0.0485	66.3	68.3	69.3	70.6	72.6
		0.065	67.0	69.8	71.1	73.1	76.0
		0.086	67.9	71.7	73.6	76.4	81.0
$25,000	0.33	0.0485	66.4	68.7	69.9	71.5	73.9
		0.065	67.2	70.4	72.0	74.3	78.0
		0.086	68.1	72.4	74.7	78.1	84.0

NOTE: Assumes price increases of 4 percent, wage increases of 5.75 percent, and tax rates identical to the price-indexing proposal.

price indexing. For example, the median-income worker with an effective tax rate of 6.5 percent obtains a 6 percent rate of return by age 71.7 under wage indexing, but has only a 4 percent rate of return by age 71 under price indexing. The high-income worker ($25,000) with a 6.5 percent tax rate has a 6 percent rate of return by age 74.3 under wage indexing, but he has only about a 4.8 percent rate of return by this age under wage indexing. Even the high-income worker with a high tax rate (8.6 percent) has achieved a 2 percent real rate of return by age 78 under wage indexing.

This is not the complete story, however. Even with the assumed increase in the payroll tax rate of 5.25 percent, wage indexing still leaves the social security system with very large future deficits. The tax rates needed to support the wage-indexing proposal for just the next fifty years are considerably higher than those shown in Table 6. Table 7 presents the payback years under wage indexing using the more appropriate set of tax rates for this plan (see Table 2). Now, the differences in rates of return between wage and price indexing essentially disappear. The number of years to achieve a given rate of return under price indexing is within one year of the number under wage indexing. For any given lifetime, the difference in the rate of return between wage and price indexing is within tenths of a percentage point, well within the range of variation in the assumptions used to generate the long-range costs of the two proposals. The slight edge that wage indexing achieves must also be tempered with the realization of the large deficit—even with the assumed higher tax rates—that is projected to remain after 2025.

No substantial difference in real rates of return exists between price indexing and wage indexing. Although replacement ratios and benefits levels appear higher under wage indexing, these higher benefits require a substantial increase in tax rates. Once these tax effects are included, the two systems offer about the same rates of return. If it were desirable to increase benefit levels under price indexing to those under wage indexing, both the payroll tax rate and the percentages used in the price-indexed benefit formula could be increased to the levels desired.

The wage-indexed system is more sensitive to variations in price and wage growth. With 6 percent inflation and 7.75 percent wage growth, the time required to achieve the same real rate of return increased somewhat (by up to 0.5 years) with the wage-indexed system, whereas there was virtually no increase with the price-indexed system. Also, varying the assumption about real wage growth changed the payback period by a year or more either way. For example, a worker at the maximum earnings base ($16,500) receives a 6 percent rate of return by age 76.2

TABLE 7

Age for Repayment of Social Security Taxes under the Wage-Indexing Proposal with Self-Financing Tax Rates

Earnings at Age 50 (1977 wage levels)	Replacement Ratio	Tax Rate	Age for Repayment with Rate of Return of:					
			0 percent	4 percent	5 percent	6 percent	7 percent
$4,000	0.61	0.0635	65.7	67.3	68.0	69.0	70.3
		0.085	66.3	68.4	69.4	70.8	72.8
		0.113	67.0	69.9	71.3	73.2	76.2
$10,000	0.42	0.0635	66.5	68.8	69.9	71.5	73.7
		0.085	67.3	70.5	72.0	74.3	77.7
		0.113	68.3	72.6	74.8	78.1	83.8
$16,500	0.36	0.0635	66.9	69.7	71.0	72.9	75.7
		0.085	67.8	71.6	73.5	76.2	80.7
		0.113	69.0	74.1	76.8	81.0	88.6
$25,000	0.33	0.0635	67.1	70.2	71.8	74.0	77.6
		0.085	68.1	72.3	74.5	77.9	83.7
		0.113	69.3	75.0	78.2	83.4	93.7

NOTE: Assumes price increases of 4 percent and wage increases of 5.75 percent.

assuming a tax rate of 8.5 percent and real wage growth of 1.75 percent (see Table 7). If real wages grow by 2.25 percent, he receives a 6 percent rate of return at age 75.1; if real wages grow by only 1.25 percent, however, he must wait until age 77.6 to receive a 6 percent rate of return. Thus, another disadvantage of wage indexing is the increased sensitivity of the rates of return to both the level of inflation and the growth in real wages.

A final analysis reveals another reason why calculating rates of return rather than replacement ratios is a superior means of evaluating proposed changes in social security benefits. One proposal for ameliorating the long-term financial deficit in social security is to increase the retirement age gradually to sixty-eight. In this way, the ratio of working to retired persons can be increased, thereby reducing the cost per worker of financing social security benefits. The increased retirement age is considered reasonable in light of the general increase in health of the population since retirement at age sixty-five was first initiated in social security.

Whatever the merits of the above arguments, an increased retirement age is unquestionably a substantial deliberalization of benefits. People must pay taxes into the system for three more years and receive benefits for three fewer years. Moreover, the three years from ages sixty-five to sixty-eight are the years when the greatest number of elderly people would receive their benefits. If it is assumed that the proposed wage-indexing formula is maintained when the increased retirement age occurs and that the only adjustment is to extend the indexing period for three years, there will be virtually no effect on replacement ratios for typical workers despite the substantial deliberalization of the system. This again shows the serious inadequacies in using replacement ratios as the measure for evaluating proposed benefit structures in social security.

The rate-of-return calculation vividly reveals the deliberalization that will occur when the retirement age is increased. Paying taxes for three more years and receiving benefits for three fewer years, especially the three years for which elderly persons are most likely to survive, substantially increases the payback age—that is, the age to which someone must live before achieving a given rate of return on social security taxes. Table 8 presents the age for achieving a given rate of return under wage indexing with retirement at age sixty-eight. The tax rates are the same as those for the price-indexing proposal; those rates, however, are inadequate to finance a wage-indexed system even with the extended retirement age. Thus, the rates of return in Table 8 overestimate the rates of return that can be achieved in a self-financed system. Nevertheless, comparing Table 8 with Table 7 reveals that, up until age eighty, the wage-indexed system with retirement at age sixty-eight is less desirable than a self-financed wage-indexed system with retirement at age sixty-five. That is, even with the much higher tax rates required for the self-financed system, workers are still better off (have higher rates of return up until age eighty) than if lower tax rates are maintained but the retirement age is extended three more years. Thus, the rate-of-return computation clearly reveals the deliberalization of benefits implicit in an increase in the retirement age. That deliberalization is completely hidden when replacement ratios are used to evaluate such changes in the benefit structure.

Summary

Ultimately it must be determined whether price indexing is too drastic a deliberalization of social security to be politically acceptable. Would future benefits be too low relative to payments made into the system? To answer this question, a series of rate-of-return computations was made. Rates of return under wage indexing appear to be much higher, but only if one ignores the increased taxes necessary to finance the deficit. Once the effective tax rate is raised to cover the deficit, the rates of return for price and wage indexing appear almost identical.

Overall, the effect of wage indexing is not much different from the effect of price indexing other than in the size of the social security program implied by the two proposals. Support of wage or price indexing will probably depend primarily on a person's attitude toward the growth of the central government. Those who prefer to see an increasing share of the nation's output funneled through the government for reallocation and redistribution among its citizens will support wage indexing. These people will be distrustful of the ability of workers to supplement their current real level of benefits from social security with increased private saving or increased private retirement benefits. They will wish the government-run and government-controlled program to maintain and perhaps increase its present share of a worker's retirement income, and they will be less concerned with the associated increased costs of the program and the increased government redistribution of income.

On the other hand, those who wish to contain at the present level the share of the nation's output that is allocated through the government will probably support price indexing. They will argue for the greater responsibility of individuals to plan for their retirement, and they will claim that, since price indexing continues to increase the real level of social security benefits, it can hardly be considered niggardly. As the

141

TABLE 8

AGE FOR REPAYMENT OF SOCIAL SECURITY TAXES UNDER THE WAGE-INDEXING PROPOSAL BUT WITH RETIREMENT AT AGE SIXTY-EIGHT

Earnings at Age 50 (1977 wage levels)	Replacement Ratio	Tax Rate	Age for Repayment with Rate of Return of:					
			0 percent	4 percent	5 percent	6 percent	7 percent
$4,000	0.61	0.0485	68.4	69.6	70.2	71.1	72.2
		0.065	68.8	70.5	71.4	72.5	74.2
		0.086	69.4	71.7	72.8	74.4	76.9
$10,000	0.42	0.0485	69.0	70.9	71.8	73.1	74.9
		0.065	69.6	72.2	73.5	75.3	78.1
		0.086	70.4	73.9	75.6	78.3	82.6
$16,500	0.35	0.0485	69.3	71.5	72.6	74.2	76.5
		0.065	70.0	73.1	74.6	76.9	80.4
		0.086	70.9	75.0	77.2	80.5	86.1
$25,000	0.33	0.0485	69.4	72.0	73.2	75.1	77.9
		0.065	70.2	73.7	75.5	78.1	82.6
		0.086	71.2	75.8	78.3	82.3	89.6

NOTE: Assumes price increases of 4 percent, wage increases of 5.75 percent, and tax rates identical to the price-indexing proposal.

standard of living rose because of the real growth of the economy, individuals would have a greater opportunity to decide for themselves how they wished to distribute consumption between their working and their retirement years. There appears to be little justification for using a compulsory government program to force people to retire with high tax-free income. This is especially true when the high retirement income must be financed by high payroll tax rates during the working lifetime of individuals. Martin Feldstein has eloquently stated this position:

> High replacement ratios are . . . inappropriate for middle- and higher-income couples. . . . These high replacement ratios mean that the typical retiree receives from social security alone more than he was able to earn in his thirties, forties, and fifties—when he had children to support, a mortgage to pay, and other expenses. It is ironic and sad that social security forces many families to cut their spending even when their income is low and their responsibilities are great in order to have more to spend during retirement when their income is already as high as it has ever been.[30]

Feldstein also believes that the role of social security should be kept at about its current level to avoid adverse economic consequences. Because of the unfunded nature of social security, private capital formation in the economy will be significantly reduced as social security taxes and benefits are expanded.

> Because individuals substitute social security for . . . private saving, total private saving and private capital formation is reduced. . . . There is no real investment of social security benefits to offset the planned reduction in private savings and investment. The result is a fall in our nation's rate of saving and in our capital stock. . . . With less capital there is a lower level of productivity, lower wages and fewer good jobs. By reducing private saving through social security, we deny ourselves the opportunity to invest with a rate of return to the nation of 15 percent and limit ourselves to the implicit return of only 2 percent that social security will provide in the future.[31]

---

30 Ibid., p. 93.

31 Martin Feldstein in U.S. Congress, Joint Economic Committee, *The Social Security System*, 94th Congress, 2nd session, May 26 and 27, 1976, p. 119. This viewpoint was developed in greater detail in Martin Feldstein, "Social Security, Induced Retirement and Aggregate Capital Accumulation," *Journal of Political Economy*, vol. 82 (September-October 1974), pp. 905–26; it was criticized and discussed in Munnell, *The Future of Social Security*, chapter 6.

This argument suggests that the growth in real wages, for which we have assumed a median value of 1.75 percent, is not independent of the method of financing and indexing the social security system. That is, rather than to compare price and wage indexing with a median real earnings growth rate of 1.75 percent, it might be more appropriate to compare, for example, wage indexing with a real growth rate of 1.6 percent and price indexing with a real growth rate of 1.9 percent. Such exercises would be highly speculative because the magnitude of the reduced growth rate caused by increased social security benefits is so uncertain; nevertheless, they would emphasize that, with a program as large and complex as social security, many subtle and perhaps unexpected consequences can result from seemingly innocuous decisions.

Feldstein's statement raises another argument for limiting the size of the social security program. Although the real rate of return on social security taxes of 2 percent is reasonable as compared with other default-free fixed-income investments, it is much less than what individuals, their unions, or their employers could earn through investments in private projects. Even including the poor performance of the stock market in the past ten years, the long-term rate of return on equity investments has averaged more than 6 or 7 percentage points above the rate of inflation. Thus, as individuals are forced to provide more of their retirement income from social security, they are also forced to invest in a program whose real rate of return is far below what could be earned through a private retirement program.

Price indexing limits the growth of the social security program to its originally intended purpose of providing a floor of protection for retirement. Giving individuals the option to supplement this floor through private saving and retirement plans enables them to choose between higher incomes when working or when retired and also to choose investments with rates of return that will likely be much higher than what is available from social security. Society benefits if more savings are directed toward the projects with a higher rate of return that are available in the private sector.

Commentaries

Robert J. Barro

The paper by Martin Feldstein and Anthony Pellechio focuses on the implications of the social security program for the distribution of total wealth—which includes "social security wealth" along with the usual "fungible wealth." This analysis is a useful contribution—notably, the concept of social security wealth is likely to be more important in terms of how wealth is distributed than in terms of aggregate wealth.

One issue is whether social security wealth should be measured in a gross sense, considering only the benefit side, or in a net sense, subtracting the present value of taxes. From the standpoint of the impact of the social security program on individuals' lifetime budget constraints, it seems that the net concept is more relevant. The serious issue is how far to go in counting liabilities. Feldstein and Pellechio measure net social security wealth by including only the social security taxes that will impinge on current generations (of various present ages). This procedure omits any consideration of future liabilities (and benefits) to later generations. These generations should be weighed in the calculation of social security wealth because an expansion of the social security program would tend to reduce voluntary private transfers from children to aged parents and would also tend to increase the transfers from parents to children at various stages of the life cycle (with bequests probably playing only a minor role here). In these situations, the calculation of effective net social security wealth would have to consider the benefit and liability position of descendants. In fact, if all individuals are connected to future generations via a network of private intergenerational transfers, the correct aggregate value of net social security wealth is easy to determine—namely, zero. (This calculation does not consider any negative income effects that would result from aspects of the social security program that distort labor supply decisions.)

This modification need not drastically alter the distributional pattern of net social security wealth—at least by income, although the calculations by age would seem to be less robust. More of the entries in Table 3 in their paper would clearly become negative, so that there would be correspondingly less overall support for the social security program. It would be interesting to examine whether Feldstein and

145

Pellechio's main policy implication—that two-year-olds be allowed to vote so that they can oppose social security—would come through unscathed.

In general, it is an excellent idea to use the distributional wealth aspects of social security to analyze the sources of political support for the program. One limitation of the type of invariance argument that I have applied to social security and public debt (that adjustments of private transfers operate to undo the effects of the public program) is that it does not account for the existence of the public program. This observation does not invalidate the invariance argument as a first-order proposition, but it does suggest that something additional must be involved. The distributional aspects stressed by Feldstein and Pellechio seem to be a reasonable place to look for this something additional with respect to the social security program.

Nevertheless, it is not a fair inference from the observed political support for social security—which is presumed to be more intense among aged persons—that the program must significantly affect aggregate private saving and capital accumulation. The principal evidence on the saving issue is obtained from a direct examination of saving behavior; such an examination was pioneered in the context of social security by Feldstein in his 1974 article in the *Journal of Political Economy* and was subsequently performed by myself and others. My reading of this direct evidence is that there is no support—from either time series or cross-sectional data—for the hypothesis that social security depresses private saving. Perhaps Feldstein and Pellechio have now gone to indirect evidence because they are in accord with this assessment.

The inverse effect of social security on private saving depends on individuals' viewing social security wealth—as defined by Feldstein and Pellechio to omit consideration of future generations—as net wealth of a similar order of magnitude. Political support for social security by the aged would follow even if their perceived net wealth were a small fraction of the calculated social security wealth variable. The inverse saving effect is unlikely to follow in this situation, because a small effect on wealth could easily be offset by the early retirement aspect of social security.

A principal issue addressed in both the paper by Robert Kaplan and that by Feldstein and Pellechio is whether the benefit base should be indexed according to wages or prices. The first question is whether this issue can be examined without considering the effects on the expected total cost of the program. It could be if the benefit formula rates on average indexed monthly wages (AIMW) were regarded as adjustable, and it could not be if these rates were fixed. Under the latter assumption, which is made in the Feldstein-Pellechio paper and in the main analysis of the Kaplan paper, the choice between wage and price indexing amounts mostly to the choice between a larger or a smaller social security program. If it is assumed that real wages will grow on average at a positive rate—which is not at all an obvious proposition for an extended horizon—the choice of wage indexing amounts mostly to the choice of a larger program.

If one could abstract from the cost issue, there is a minor argument that favors wage indexing. From the viewpoint of the rate of return, the natural way to index contributions would be according to their accumulation at an alternative nominal rate of return (possibly adjusted to take account of life expectancy). To the extent that the growth rate of real wages corresponds to the real rate of return (which is theoretically possible but not inevitable), wage indexing would correspond to this accumulation concept. Indexing by prices after retirement then seems reasonable because it amounts to withdrawing real income in a uniform manner out of accumulated assets.

Kaplan seems to err in analyzing the incidence of the employer and employee parts of social security "contributions." The employer part of the tax may or may not be fully shifted to the workers (depending upon, among other things, the real wage elasticity of labor supply). The incidence of the employer and employee parts must be exactly the same, however, if one holds constant the workers' other income tax payments. The relevant economic consideration is the total wedge between the gross payout of the firm and the net receipt to the workers. This wedge depends on the sum of the employer and employee tax rates—hence, it is only this sum that can matter for workers' net earnings, employment, and so on. The labeling of one portion as employer and one as employee is not relevant for economic outcomes. Therefore, Kaplan's procedure of allocating 100 percent of the employee tax to workers and less than 100 percent of the employer tax seems incorrect. The same fraction (possibly less than 100 percent) should be applied to both parts.

One amendment to the above point is necessary if workers' income tax payments are not held constant when there is a shift in labeling between employer and employee parts of the social security tax. The employee part of social security contributions is counted as a part of workers' taxable income, whereas the employer part is not. Therefore, if workers' income tax rates (rather than tax payments) are held fixed when the fraction of contributions labeled as employer is raised, the workers' income tax payments would decline. An analysis of incidence

147

then requires a specification of the adjustments in the government budget in response to this reduction in workers' income tax payments.

It seems unreasonable to compare the rate of return from social security with that available from bonds. Bonds are far superior in terms of liquidity. It seems more appropriate to compare (as Kaplan does later in his paper) social security payments with contributions to a private pension fund. For example, retirement annuities seem comparable to social security except that the private firms enjoy a tax-deferral advantage. Some recently available instruments that also permit early liquidation would have a further advantage over social security.

Kaplan's treatment of risk differentials is also not convincing. Bonds are subject to risk from inflation, but the relevant consideration is the contribution of this asset to the risk contained in an individual's overall portfolio. For example, if the real returns on bonds are counter-cyclical, the contribution to overall risk could be negative because of a negative correlation with returns to human capital. In any case, it seems appropriate to add on the other side the important political risk associated with determining future real social security benefits.

Barry R. Chiswick

The papers by Martin Feldstein and Anthony Pellechio and by Robert Kaplan treat the effects on wealth distribution of the schemes proposed to end the double indexing of social security benefits inadvertently introduced by the 1972 amendments to the Social Security Act. The social security system has become a massive Ponzi game (chain letter) in which purchasing power is transferred from workers to the aged. The game has worked well over the past thirty years, largely because younger retirement cohorts (the whole group of those retiring in a given year) have been larger than older cohorts. In the past, each cohort received benefits in excess of its contribution; as the two papers show, however, this need not be true in the future. Because of demographic factors, the ratio of beneficiaries to contributors will be growing rapidly in the coming decades. If the social security system continues its current level of generosity relative to wages, the tax burden will necessarily rise sharply and younger cohorts may someday wish to alter sharply the "rules of the game."

I will first make several specific comments on the papers and will then discuss some additional issues on the difference between wage and price indexing. Whether wage indexing or price indexing is to be preferred cannot be determined in isolation; rather, the issue requires an assessment of the role of social security in the entire pension and retirement income system, and of the probable size of the social security population relative to the working population.

The two papers use simulation analysis to estimate the effects on wealth of wage and price indexing of the social security system. Feldstein and Pellechio estimate the social security wealth of households in 1972 as the present value of the benefits they will be eligible for at age sixty-five, using a 3 percent real discount rate. This is "gross social security wealth" because social security taxes have not been removed. They stress that the distribution of gross social security wealth is much less unequal than the distribution of net "fungible wealth." This is not surprising because gross social security wealth is, to a first approximation, roughly proportional to earnings. As shown in Table 1, the distribution of gross social security wealth for households with a head aged thirty-five to sixty-four is remarkably similar to the distribution of income by families. The distribution of other assets that "workers" invest in, including their own and their children's human capital (schooling), savings accounts, pension plans, equity in owner-occupied housing, and other consumer durables are also more equally distributed than fungible wealth. Most studies of wealth focus exclusively on those components of wealth that are most highly concentrated, thereby giving the impression of a greater inequality of wealth than actually exists.

Feldstein and Pellechio do not provide a frequency distribution of

TABLE 1

DISTRIBUTION OF GROSS SOCIAL SECURITY WEALTH AND FAMILY INCOME, 1972

(percent)

Income	Social Security Wealth	Family Income
Less than $3,000	8.8	7.2
$3,000 to $14,999	52.8	62.5
$15,000 or more	38.5	30.3
Total	100.0	100.0

SOURCE: Martin Feldstein and Anthony Pellechio, "Social Security Wealth: The Impact of Alternative Inflation Adjustments," in this volume, table 1, p. 97, for families with a head aged thirty-five to sixty-four. U.S. Bureau of the Census, *Money Income in 1972 of Families and Persons in the U.S.* (1973), table 9, p. 34.

net social security wealth by income group. This is unfortunate because net social security wealth is a more appropriate measure of the effect of the social security system on the redistribution of wealth.

Feldstein and Pellechio estimate that net present value of social security benefits for several income and age groups using a 3 percent real discount rate. Yet, the appropriate discount rate depends on the purpose of computing net wealth. And even for the same purpose, economists differ about the level of the discount rate. The pattern of gainers and losers depends in part on the discount rate because the magnitude of the taxes and benefits under social security varies by age and income. It would have been helpful if they had presented estimates of the net present value of wealth for several discount rates, or if they had computed implicit rates of return (the discount rate that sets the net present value equal to zero).[1] An advantage of the implicit rate of return is that it provides a useful summary statistic of the profitability of social security investments that each reader can compare with his own favorite discount rate.

Table 6 of the Feldstein-Pellechio paper shows the distribution by age and income class of the net social security wealth under wage and price indexing. Those who will gain the most from either indexing procedure are households headed by workers aged thirty-five to fifty-four in 1972. The biggest losers are nonpoor households headed by workers aged twenty-five to thirty-four; under either scheme, their net wealth is negative. Unfortunately, we do not learn whether the estimated unfavorable effects on net wealth represent a life-cycle phenomenon or a cohort effect. Those aged twenty-five to thirty-four in 1972 will be paying taxes and receiving no benefits for another twenty years when they are aged forty-five to fifty-four. What would their net social security wealth look like if the computations were made relative to 1992 rather than 1972?

Kaplan estimates the number of years a worker who enters the labor force today at age twenty needs to receive social security benefits after retiring at age sixty-five in order to "break even" with the system. Although he presents the estimates for several real discount rates, ranging from minus 4 percent to plus 3 percent, one would have to be familiar with estimated life expectancy to know which workers gain and which lose. Here too, presenting implicit rates of return as a descriptive summary statistic would make the interpretation easier.

The two papers offer the same qualitative conclusion about the set of estimates on which they overlap—young workers and a 3 percent

---

[1] See, for example, June O'Neill, "Rates of Return from Social Security" (Paper presented at the American Economics Association Annual Meeting, Atlantic City, New Jersey, September 1976).

real discount rate.[2] Low-income workers gain under both wage and price indexing, but middle- and high-income workers incur a loss. This similarity of findings strengthens my confidence in the estimates of both papers.

Feldstein and Pellechio find a very small difference between the net wealth under wage indexing and that under price indexing, although in their computations it is always larger under wage indexing. It would be misleading, however, to conclude that the indexing procedure does not matter. The difference in benefits (and, hence, also in taxes) under wage and price indexing is trivial in the 1980s, but it becomes larger in each successive decade. Dollars expended or received far off in the future have a relatively small present value under a 3 percent real discount rate. Hence, the authors' procedures result in a relatively small difference in net wealth for those currently working. The net wealth procedure effectively masks the dramatic differences in the social security system in the future under the two methods of indexing.

It would have been helpful if the two papers reported the net social security wealth at age thirty of workers who will be age thirty in the years 2000 and 2030. If a substantial proportion of the electorate in 2000 or 2030 find a much larger negative effect on wealth under wage indexing, there may be substantial pressures at that time to alter the social security system sharply.

The use of net wealth and the number of years to recoup one's taxes mask the much more massive redistribution of income over the life cycle implicit in wage indexing. Wage indexing implies greater taxes on workers and greater benefits for the aged. Even if there is little net effect over the life cycle, the higher taxes and benefits under wage indexing are likely to affect work effort (by both the young and the aged) and private saving adversely, thereby slowing economic growth. These aspects are easier to articulate when future replacement rates and tax rates under the two indexing schemes are examined.

In the controversy over wage indexing or price indexing, the "politicians" seem to favor the former whereas the "advisers" (actuaries and economists) seem to favor the latter. The papers indicate why politicians prefer wage indexing. Kaplan notes that the critics of price indexing point to a declining ratio of benefits to pre-retirement earnings, even though the real level of benefits for future retirees would be rising.[3]

---

[2] Both papers assume a 4 percent annual rate of inflation and a 1.75 percent annual rate of increase in real wages.

[3] See AEI Round Table, pp. 325–352, in this volume. Congressmen Al Ullman and Barber B. Conable, Jr., emphasized their opposition to legislation that would gradually lower the replacement rate for future retirees until it reached its historic level.

Feldstein and Pellechio note that wage indexing is designated to achieve a greater transfer from the next generation than price indexing. This will work only if the next generation will play the game by the rules that are set down by the current generation of workers/voters. The advisers, on the other hand, tend to focus on the tax rates and replacement rates inherent in the two systems.

An important statistic in the controversy over the two indexing methods is the replacement rate, the ratio of benefits at retirement to the pre-tax earnings of workers in covered employment in the previous year (adjusted for changes in the price level between the two years). For workers retiring at age sixty-five, this ratio is currently about 44 percent. Under wage indexing, the replacement rate would be frozen into the social security benefit structure. As average wages rise, the benefit structure would increase at the same rate, so that for all future retirees the replacement rate would be about 44 percent. Under price indexing, average replacement rates would decline over time because average wages would rise more rapidly than the price index (assuming a growth in real wages) and because the benefit schedule would rise at the same rate as the price index. That is, the replacement rate would be constant for a given level of real wages, but, because real wages increase and workers move higher up in the benefit schedule, real benefits increase while the average replacement rate declines.

The current replacement rate was not etched in stone on Mount Sinai, nor was it handed down by the Founding Fathers. From 1953 to 1970, the replacement rate for a sixty-five-year-old male retiree (who had earned the median wage) averaged 31 percent.[4] It fluctuated between 29 percent and 35 percent (it was 35 percent only one year, 1959), and there was no trend because the fluctuations were caused mainly by the discontinuous nature of increases in social security benefits. From 1970 to 1976, the replacement rate increased nearly continuously from 31 percent to 43 percent.

Developments during the 1970s, however, suggest that social security could become less important as an income replacement for the aged.[5] Federalizing the state assistance programs for the poor who are aged, blind, and disabled (ABD programs) with the enactment of Supplemental Security Income in 1972 increased both the coverage and the

---

[4] Congressional Budget Office, *Financing Social Security: Issues for the Short and Long Term* (July 1977), table 4, p. 16.

[5] For a description and analysis of the government transfer programs, see Barry R. Chiswick, "The Income Transfer System: Impact, Viability and Proposals for Reform," in *Contemporary Economic Problems 1977*, ed. William Fellner (Washington, D.C.: American Enterprise Institute, 1977), pp. 347–428.

real benefit levels for the aged poor. The food subsidy programs for the poor (food stamps and the Food Distribution Program) grew rapidly in the 1970s, particularly with the spread of the food stamp program to all the counties of the country as of July 1974. Medicare for all the aged and Medicaid for the aged poor have increased the assurance of the availability of medical care regardless of the income of retirees. Current welfare reform proposals suggest a further extension of coverage and increased benefit levels for aged persons who are poor or near-poor.

The Pension Reform Act of 1974 stipulated for the first time that private firms that maintain pension plans must meet minimum federal standards regarding the vesting of benefits in workers and the investing of the plans' assets. The objective of the legislation was to provide greater assurance that a promised private pension will, in fact, be there at retirement. Special tax advantages have been introduced to encourage saving for retirement by the self-employed and employees without company retirement plans. And even the certainty of the real value of the social security benefit during retirement has been increased since it is now indexed to the consumer price index.

The economic circumstances of the aged in the future will be far better than in 1935 when social security was enacted, or during the 1950s and 1960s. The broader coverage and higher benefit levels of the welfare system and private pensions, as well as the greater real level of other forms of private wealth, mean that social security is less essential to the economic well-being of the aged.

The Congressional Budget Office has estimated the replacement rate from 1976 to 2050 under the wage-indexing and price-indexing formulas.[6] Under wage indexing, it would remain at the current level of 44 percent. Under price indexing, the average replacement rate would decline to 34 percent in 1990, 31 percent (the average for the period 1953 to 1970) in the year 2000, 25 percent in 2030, and 23 percent in 2050. The decline in the replacement rate under price indexing gets smaller over time as increases in real wages place an ever-increasing proportion of workers in the top benefit category.

Hence, in terms of the replacement rate, price indexing has two distinct advantages over wage indexing. First, under price indexing the social security system would gradually return to its historic (post–World War II) replacement rate. Second, since the political incentives are for legislators to increase rather than decrease social security benefits, price indexing gives Congress the flexibility to increase the replacement rate periodically if a higher rate is socially desirable.

---

[6] Congressional Budget Office, *Financing Social Security*, table 11, p. 46.

The Advisory Council on Social Security reported that there were about 6 beneficiaries for every 100 workers in 1950, about 30 beneficiaries for every 100 workers in 1975, and (projecting on the basis of the likely demographic composition of the population and the likely labor force participation rates) a peak of about 45 beneficiaries for each 100 workers in the economy by 2030.[7] The rise in the ratio of beneficiaries to workers from 1959 to 1975 was partly the result of expansion in the sectors of activity covered by the system and partly the result of the maturation of the program; even in 1950 many aged persons had insufficient work experience in covered employment to qualify for benefits. The system has now matured, and coverage has been widespread for many years. The rise in the ratio of beneficiaries to workers over the next half-century will result primarily from the aging of the post–World War II baby boom population and from the lower fertility rates since the late 1950s. Other things being equal, this demographic change would necessitate more than a 50 percent increase in the payroll tax rate.

Expenditures as a percentage of taxable income (as defined in current law) would rise under wage indexing because of the constant replacement rate and the rise in the ratio of beneficiaries to workers.[8] Expenditures were 10.9 percent of taxable earnings in 1976, but they would rise to 12.4 percent in 2000 and to a peak of 18.9 percent in 2030.[9] Effective social security tax rates would have to be increased substantially. Under price indexing, the declining replacement rate would offset most of the effect of the increase in the ratio of beneficiaries to workers. Expenditures as a percentage of taxable earnings would be 10.0 percent in 2000 and 12.5 percent in 2030.

In the summer of 1977, the secretary of commerce suggested that the social security retirement age could be gradually increased from age sixty-five to age sixty-eight. Although the proposal was hastily withdrawn, it does have much merit, particularly since the minimum mandatory retirement age for the private sector has been increased from sixty-five to seventy years. Workers of today between the ages of sixty-five and

---

[7] U.S. Congress, House of Representatives, *Reports of the Quadrennial Advisory Council on Social Security*, House Document no. 94-75, 94th Congress, 1st session, March 10, 1975, p. 47. The advisory council assumed that the fertility rate would rise from the current 1.9 births per woman to 2.1 and remain at that level (zero population growth) indefinitely.

[8] Under current (October 1977) law, the first $16,500 of a worker's earnings are taxable, and the taxable earnings base is to rise each year at the same rate as average wages in covered employment.

[9] For the proportions by ten-year intervals from 1980 to 2050, see Congressional Budget Office, *Financing Social Security*, table 12, p. 50.

sixty-eight are in better general health than their counterparts in 1935, and a much smaller proportion are in physically demanding jobs. The 1974 advisory council estimated the saving that would result from increasing the retirement age by two months per year starting in 2005 and ending in 2023, so that by 2023 the retirement age would be sixty-eight and early retirement at reduced benefits would be at sixty-five.[10] This would give current workers sufficient time to adjust to the later receipt of benefits. In 2030, benefits as a percentage of taxable earnings (as defined in current law) were estimated to be lowered by 9.3 percent.

If the age at retirement were gradually increased by three years in this manner, the social security tax in 2030 would be about 17 percent under wage indexing, and 11 percent under price indexing. A tax rate of 11 percent in 2030 is not very different from the current cost of the system (10.9 percent in 1976) or the current tax rate of 9.9 percent (scheduled to rise to 11.9 percent in 2011) and would not represent a substantially increased burden on the payroll tax system.

Rudolph G. Penner

In the first part of their paper, Martin Feldstein and Anthony Pellechio provide an estimate of gross social security wealth, and they argue that such wealth is highly significant and is distributed quite differently from private wealth. To avoid overstating their case, they base their estimates on extremely conservative assumptions. Although this approach is appropriate in the first part of the paper, I question whether the same assumptions are appropriate later in the paper when the more meaningful concept of net social security wealth is treated.

In particular, the authors place some importance on the finding that net social security wealth is negative for younger generations, and they predict growing hostility toward the social security system. This result may not hold up with less conservative assumptions. It seems inevitable, however, that net social security wealth will eventually become negative for younger generations, and the hostility toward the system predicted by the authors may be only a little later in coming than their numbers suggest.

Barry Chiswick suggested that it is remarkable that the papers by Feldstein and Pellechio and by Robert Kaplan came to similar conclusions in view of the large number of assumptions that have to be made in such analyses. Although the two papers do have the same qualitative

---

[10] House of Representatives, *Reports of the Quadrennial Advisory Council on Social Security*, pp. 62–63.

conclusions, they differ in tone, particularly in their treatment of the difference between the two sets of estimates associated with the wage and price indexing of benefits. Kaplan concludes that there is no real difference between the rates of return implied by wage indexing and price indexing, whereas Feldstein and Pellechio state that net wealth is lower with price indexing.

Actually, the difference in the net wealth implied by the two indexing methods is very small in the Feldstein-Pellechio paper and might be eliminated or reversed by using slightly different assumptions. In particular, the two papers make different assumptions regarding the time profile of the social security tax burden. Feldstein and Pellechio assume that the system is financed on a pay-as-you-go basis, which causes tax rates to rise in the future. Kaplan assumes that tax rates are steady through time. Because of the difference in the pattern of costs, the comparison of the results of the two papers is likely to be sensitive to small changes in the choice of a discount rate.

As Chiswick noted, the Kaplan paper does provide a useful analysis of the sensitivity of the conclusions to changing assumptions. Like Chiswick, however, I have difficulty evaluating Kaplan's measure of the rate of return. He asks how long one has to live to achieve a particular rate of return. This is not very useful unless one possesses an actuarial table, and I appreciate the fact that Feldstein and Pellechio provided computations based on actuarial expectations.

Feldstein and Pellechio conclude that wage indexing may be politically more popular than price indexing because it implies a higher net wealth. I have questioned the assumptions that lead to this result; for the sake of argument, however, let us assume that voters accept all of the authors' assumptions, including a real discount rate of 3 percent.

Will the voters really base their choice between the two systems on estimates of net wealth? Once the political system chooses a method of indexing, that method is imposed on all those covered by social security. Price indexing may provide less net wealth, but it also provides a lower tax burden, thus giving people more freedom to spend a larger share of their income in any way they please. Unless it is assumed that individuals could gain the same freedom under wage indexing by borrowing against the higher benefits at a real rate of return equal to or less than 3 percent, wage indexing may provide less utility even though it provides more net wealth. Of course, it may not; or, put another way, people may willingly choose to use the extra after-tax dollars associated with price indexing to buy the extra benefits associated with a wage-indexed system at a 3 percent real rate of return.

The above argument assumes that individual voters are very

sophisticated about the relative benefits of wage and price indexing. In discussing the issue both on Capitol Hill and within the executive branch, I have been impressed with the difficulty of explaining the implications of the two indexing methods. Busy policymakers seem to have an aversion to complicated arithmetic. As a result, I would bet that less than 10 percent of all members of Congress could pass an exam on the differences between the two systems. Even the two expert authors of this paper expressed some surprise at the implications of their estimates for younger voters.

Consequently, estimates of net wealth may be irrelevant to the politics of the issue. The individual who knows that his one vote is unlikely to be crucial may remain "rationally ignorant" because he does not find it worthwhile to learn about the intricacies of indexing.

In conclusion, it is important to repeat a point made earlier in the discussion. Both of these papers assume that, once a system of indexing is chosen, it will remain in place forever. That is unlikely. Each person has to make a forecast about the future evolution of the system. Since these forecasts must be made under conditions of great uncertainty, it may not make sense to evaluate different indexing methods using riskless rates of return.

Discussion

PROFESSOR FELDSTEIN: The most fundamental question that has been raised about our paper is: What is the appropriate definition of social security wealth? What kind of adjustments to our figure would be appropriate? We estimated that the current figure for social security wealth is about $3.5 trillion. Kaplan suggested that using a 3 percent discount rather than zero or 1 percent was probably too conservative, and that, if we used zero or 1 percent, the $3.5 trillion would increase considerably. In an earlier paper for the American Statistical Association, we calculated gross social security wealth using a zero discount rate, and it essentially doubled social security wealth. Thus, the discount rate assumption is important. I agree that 3 percent, as a net real lending rate, is probably on the conservative side.

Barro suggested that, instead of underestimating social security wealth by roughly 100 percent, we probably overestimated it by 100 percent, and that, by one definition of the correct measure of social security wealth, there really is no wealth at all. But that measurement requires thinking in terms of overlapping generations, so that the wealth of one's family is to be interpreted as the present value of all the wealth of one's children and one's children's children, unto eternity. There might be some problems in which that is an interesting way to think about the world but, somehow, it does not move me in the current context. I am much more traditional and look at wealth in terms of the current generation in isolation.

On the more practical question of whether we should look at gross or net social security wealth, I still prefer gross wealth. Let me reiterate the reason given in the paper. The question is: What is the present value of retirement consumption that could be financed without doing any more saving out of income from labor? The answer is that it is a household's fungible wealth—the value of their bank account and stocks—plus their gross social security wealth. The budget constraint of the household is the value of the household's wealth plus their human capital—the present value of the members' earnings. If the earnings are defined net of taxes, including net of social security taxes, then the appropriate present value of the household's total wealth is ordinary fungible wealth plus gross social security wealth plus human capital. You would use net social security wealth only if you were defining human capital net of personal income taxes but gross of the payroll tax, and I do not see any particular reason to do that. We are concerned about defining the lifetime budget constraint; when you divide that into human and nonhuman capital, it is gross rather than net social security wealth that ought to be included.

I would rather avoid the temptation of talking about the effect of social security on capital accumulation. I would say only two things. First, my reading of the evidence differs from Barro's.[1] Second, it is not fair to infer that, because we cite as one piece of evidence the implications of net social security wealth on political choice, that is the only evidence in favor of our proposition. The material on political choice is simply one more bit of evidence that the traditional view of savings, rather than Barro's intergenerational view, is the correct one. I certainly would not rest the entire case that social security replaces a substantial amount of savings on this bit of amateur political science.

Chiswick commented that the distribution of gross social security wealth is similar to the distribution of family income. It is true that the distribution of gross social security wealth is more like the distribution of income than the distribution of total wealth, but the distribution of gross social security wealth is even more equal than that of income because above about $9,000 there is virtually no increase in gross social security wealth.

Internal rates of return are useful, and thus Kaplan's analysis is very informative. For our purposes, though, a comparison of present values is more useful. I know what it means to talk about an internal rate of return for a new person coming into the system. On the other hand, comparing internal rates of return at different ages means, essentially, comparing internal rates of return on investments of different sizes. That is a peculiar kind of comparison. Moreover, the retired are receiving benefits and paying nothing. To them, the internal rate of return is either infinite or undefined. Even though internal rates of return are not useful in our context, I think they can be in Kaplan's framework. I agree with Penner, however, that it would be helpful if Kaplan gave an overall internal rate of return rather than the returns conditional on reaching age sixty-five.

Chiswick raised the question about whether the negative social

---

[1] Some flavor of that comes through in *The Impact of Social Security on Private Saving: Evidence from the U.S. Times Series*, a paper by Robert J. Barro with a reply by Martin Feldstein (Washington, D.C.: American Enterprise Institute, 1978).

security wealth for those around age thirty is simply a cohort effect or a life-cycle effect that would persist. If we look far enough back in time, social security wealth would be positive for everyone; but if we look ahead, given the demographic changes in the country and the maturity of the social security system, social security wealth for new entrants will continue to be negative. Whether it is a cohort effect or a life-cycle effect depends on whether you are looking back or looking ahead.

Penner raised a good question about the conservativeness of our estimates and their appropriateness for estimating net social security wealth. Since we have underestimated benefits, we may have underestimated net social security wealth, and therefore net social security wealth may be positive rather than negative. The main omission, however, is disability benefits. We use only the OASI portion of the tax. Although we do understate gross social security wealth, we also understate the taxes. I think that they even out. We leave out other minor things, such as the benefits available for children, but I doubt that our conservatism is a major factor except with respect to the interest rate.

On the issue that social security wealth might be less under wage indexing than under price indexing if discounted at a different interest rate, we have not done that analysis, so I do not know the answer. Because of the interest in the discount rate, we will add an appendix to the paper in which we present comparable tables at zero or 1 percent.

The political model that we used is simplistic. The assumption is that voters choose those things with the highest cash value to themselves. The assumption of an informed voter is, of course, similar to the assumption that a consumer exercises rational choice; in both cases, these are characterizations and even caricatures of the truth. If the model produced different results—that is, if I found that people voted for a smaller program even though it appeared to be against their self-interest to do so—then I would scratch my head and start thinking about Barro's altruism and Penner's preference for smaller programs that preserve individual freedom. But, when I find that people choose the thing that delivers the greatest net dollar to them, I am not terribly surprised and I do not feel the need to add much sophistication to the political model.

Finally, Kaplan talked about social security being a better deal than other kinds of investments. That is true, but only because our economic system, which imposes high taxes on capital income and fails to adjust those taxes for inflation, perversely gives negative real rates of return to investors even though the return to society in the form of additional capital accumulation is very high. I am sure Kaplan would

160

agree with me that—in terms of what is a good investment—we should compare social security not with market rates of return but with the real rate of return on physical investment, which is very much higher than any of the social security rates of return.

PROFESSOR KAPLAN: I want to review what I think is the main message of my paper: namely, the age that a person must reach in order to break even on the payroll taxes he has paid is virtually the same under both price indexing (Table 5) and wage indexing (Table 7). This is true for various interest rates and for various tax rates. We can quibble about which tax rate is right. It was not my purpose to offer any further insights about what the appropriate tax rate is because I do not know; I did attempt to address the question of what is a fair rate of return. Whatever progressivity is found under wage indexing, is also found under price indexing. Consequently, I do not understand the debate over the two systems because they are essentially the same.

One point I did not make is that common stocks do have a real rate of return of about 6 or 7 percent, which is much higher than what is available in default-free investments or social security.

An advantage of price indexing is that it enables people to supplement social security with investments in the private sector—through employer-sponsored plans, Individual Retirement Accounts (IRAs), Keogh accounts, or common stock investing on their own. Wage indexing makes social security so large that it takes care of substantially all retirement needs. People do not invest at the higher rates of return in the private sector because they are forced to invest at the much lower rates of return available in social security.

I do not like the concept of the internal rate of return. In the classroom, I spend at least half of my introductory lecture on capital budgeting explaining why the internal rate of return is misleading and why it has to be adjusted before it will agree with net present value. And that is for well-determined investment projects. In the case of uncertain projects, there is no justification for computing an expected real internal rate of return. There is no theory that suggests that it is the appropriate computation to make. There is theory, however, that suggests that the expected net present value should be estimated. In order to obtain such a number, I was forced to compute something that looks like an internal rate of return. Rather than give a single rate, however, I chose to display the various break-even ages and to allow the reader to assume his own probability distribution.

Nevertheless, to find a single number to summarize the rate of return of the system, look at the rate of return for the median age of whatever lifetime probability distribution is of interest. Half the people will get a rate of return below that, and half the people will get a rate of return above that. Thus, if it is assumed that the median age, conditional on reaching age sixty-five, is seventy-nine, then the rate of return for those who live to seventy-nine is a reasonable expected return on social security taxes.

I advocate price indexing, and I go further than William Hsiao, the originator of the method. I think that he tries to make the program acceptable by saying that it will give the government the opportunity to improve the benefits periodically. If people have to worry about when the government is going to increase benefits, more uncertainty is introduced into the system and private planning becomes more difficult. I do not believe that price indexing should be sold on the basis that in the future we can count on erratic and ad hoc government intervention.

There have been comments about how difficult it is to explain to members of Congress or their staffs indexing in general, and price indexing versus wage indexing in particular. I am both unimpressed and appalled by this. We now have a Congress that is spending $2 million on each congressman. What is that $2 million a congressman being used for, if not to get some expertise on programs like this?

PROFESSOR CHISWICK: In view of all the problems that Kaplan has with the internal rate of return, I am surprised he does not see the same problems, if not more, in his own procedure that the commentators have noted.

PROFESSOR KAPLAN: I had to come up with a single number. I tried to play it down as much as I could by presenting the tabular display. I would like to make one more point. In my paper, I did not intend to introduce a political philosophy into voters' utility functions. I was just suggesting that, insofar as social security is a compulsory retirement plan, a smaller program that would allow individuals greater freedom to spend a higher proportion of their income might have a higher utility value than a larger program that allows less freedom but has higher cash value.

PROFESSOR BARRO: I think that Feldstein's defense of the concept of gross social security wealth is completely untenable on economic grounds. Feldstein says that, if you look at the lifetime budget constraint of the household and hold gross social security wealth fixed, and if you also hold disposable income aside from social security benefits fixed, then it is gross social security wealth that you want to look at.

But this is not a productive way to consider a change in the scope of the social security program. You would not want to hold disposable income fixed because it does not include social security benefits, although it does include social security taxes. Obviously, you would want to allow those taxes to go up; as a result, according to his concept, disposable income would fall. You would then want to look at the present value of this disposable income and compare that with the present value of the benefits, which is in the gross social security wealth measure. But this comparison amounts to looking at a net social security wealth concept. In what sense, then, is gross social security wealth an interesting measure?

PROFESSOR FELDSTEIN: I half agree with that. I think that Table 6, which compares net social security wealth under wage and price indexing, is the relevant way to compare the two indexing methods; that is, both the benefits and the taxes are taken into account in looking at what the indexing method does to each individual. For that purpose, you do want to take both benefits and taxes into account. But, for the purpose of looking at the total distribution of wealth at a given point in time, I think it is appropriate to distinguish between human capital and non-human capital and to define human capital "net of tax," including the social security tax. Therefore, the other part of total wealth—nonhuman capital—includes gross social security wealth.

PROFESSOR BARRO: You are saying that an increase in the rate of the social security tax reduces the stock of human capital.

PROFESSOR FELDSTEIN: It reduces the net value to the households of the human capital that they own.

PROFESSOR BARRO: I agree with that, but some of the increase in taxes is buying social security benefits in the future. You subtract the social security taxes out of human capital wealth and put them into social security wealth.

PROFESSOR FELDSTEIN: I think that is what you should do if you want to treat social security taxes like all other taxes.

PROFESSOR BOSKIN: If that is so, I think it would be appropriate to look at the distribution of total wealth, not just social security wealth plus other financial wealth, leaving out human capital which is three-quarters of all wealth.

163

PROFESSOR FELDSTEIN: I am sympathetic to that, but then one may ask, as Barro does, "Well, what about my children, as assets?" And then the list of additions begins to grow.

For a long time, people have thought it interesting to comment on the fact that the distribution of wealth is different from the distribution of income. There may still be a case for saying, "Let's not talk about the distribution of material wealth, as opposed to human capital; let's add them together." If those two are split and total wealth is said to have two parts, then within the part designated as nonhuman wealth we should include private pensions and social security wealth, as well as the ordinary assets. When that is done, the wealth that persons may bequeath or use to support retirement is very different from the highly unequal picture of wealth that is normally perceived by focusing solely on fungible wealth. It would be all the more so if human capital were added in.

DR. THOMPSON: I think the problem with Feldstein's procedure is that he separates wealth into three components, and he assigns taxes to only two of them; there is no reason to do that. It would be better to assign the taxes on fungible capital to fungible capital, assign income taxes to the returns of human capital, and assign social security taxes to social security.

PROFESSOR FELDSTEIN: Yes, that would be another interesting calculation. It would say that the distribution of current wealth is misleading because it is not a distribution of current wealth but a distribution of after-tax wealth.

DR. THOMPSON: If you want to cut wealth up into three shares, however, doing it your way gives a much larger share to social security than doing it my way.

PROFESSOR FELDSTEIN: But, if I subtracted the taxes that were implicit in ordinary wealth, I would reduce that as well.

DR. THOMPSON: The question is: Is there one way to separate this total into two parts? And the answer is no.

PROFESSOR FELDSTEIN: I agree that the two-way separation of taxes is arbitrary. What I am defending is that this is a reasonable way to separate them. I think it is reasonable to say that, from this point of view, there is no difference between one kind of tax on income and another kind of tax on income, and that we ought to subtract both of them in a calculation of human capital, since they are dependent not upon the future benefits but upon the earnings that you have along the way. But, however taxes are treated, the results come out equally well. There is $3.5 trillion in gross social security wealth or $2 trillion in net social security wealth. The coefficient of the statistical estimates of their effects on savings changes in inverse proportion to the scale of the wealth variable. The implications about savings do not look very different.

PROFESSOR DARBY: I have a couple of points regarding the Feldstein-Pellechio paper. First, the taxes are already subtracted out of wealth because wealth is valued at a tax-inclusive interest rate. Second, the net social security wealth Feldstein is using as a measure of the value of the existence of the social security program to various income groups is inconsistent with his earlier work which suggested that there is a decrease in the capital stock. Adding this reduction to the effects on the labor force might produce a reduction in real income of 3 percent of annual GNP which, at his discount rate, would have a present value equal to GNP. For many people, this may well change net social security wealth to a negative number, and it may be worthwhile to buy out. If there is a net loss of GNP, maybe social security should be terminated.

With respect to Kaplan's paper, calculating the rate of return at age sixty-five struck me as a peculiar thing to do. You would certainly want to compute net present value at entry or the expected rate of return at entry. To examine returns for those who live to age sixty-five, you should divide each previous year's taxes by the probability when they were paid that the person would live to age sixty-five. That would be the relevant amount in computing whether or not you have a fair return as compared with private plans. I expect that, if this were done, it would be difficult to come up with a 1 percent real return before about age 90, 95, or 100.

PROFESSOR KAPLAN: That is certainly a reasonable point. If someone, who does not have dependents or survivors, pays taxes from age twenty or twenty-five to age sixty and then dies, not only is he dead, but he has received a very bad rate of return on those taxes. The reason for my method of calculating is that I want to be optimistic and say, "All right, after I pay in all this money over my lifetime, is there any hope that I can get a reasonable rate of return on it?" I thought it was interesting to ask whether I will get a 1 or 2 percent real rate of return if I live to seventy-nine. I know that if I die before sixty-five, and if I do not have any dependents or survivors, I am going to lose out. But then there is survivors insurance, which I have eliminated. You are right. My figures imply real rates of return in excess of 2 percent. This return is higher than the assumed real earnings growth of 1.75 percent. The excess could arise from workers who die young and do not receive any benefits.

DR. MUNNELL: I am surprised that Feldstein gets negative values for people so low on the income scale. The Social Security Administration did some rate-of-return calculations on the effects of wage indexing for people throughout the income scale, and they got low rates of return for high-income people but quite substantial rates for low-income people. The calculations were for people entering the labor force sometime before November 1977.

The other point I want to mention is that social security wealth is very different from pension wealth. Pension wealth is benefits earned today, whereas social security wealth has benefits that are going to be earned in the future as well as benefits earned up to this point.

PROFESSOR BUCHANAN: I would like to follow up on Darby's point. I think he made the right point, although there might be some confusion about it. In one sense, the net social security wealth that exists is negative, and I think Feldstein would agree with that. I think his argument with Barro and my argument with Barro is about whether or not the debt is included. In a sense, to call this "wealth" is slightly misleading.

I would like to make two minor points. First, Kaplan remarked that, depending on what Congress does, some high-income people may in fact have negative returns; he then talked about differentials between the high and low returns. I think we should recognize that all of us have been playing games about what will happen "down the road a piece" in, say, 2030. If we recognize that something is going to happen "down the road a piece," we also have to recognize that, to the extent that differential rates of return are built into the social security system, there will be feedback adjustments, depending on the elasticities in the supply of labor. People will adjust to the system, and high and low wage rates will be driven further apart.

The second point concerns something Barro said with which I think Kaplan would agree: namely, it would have been better to compare the rate of return on social security with that on a retirement annuity. Barro then corrected the statement and said that, whereas annuities are tax free, wages are taxed before social security taxes are paid. In fact, retirement annuities are taxed at the end, so there is a counterbalancing. It may come out not too far apart.

PROFESSOR BARRO: I should have said the tax on annuities is deferred.

PROFESSOR BUCHANAN: The annuity tax is deferred, but you pay it back at the end, whereas you pay the social security tax at the front, so maybe they balance.

PROFESSOR BARRO: I do not see how they could balance. Unless you had much higher marginal tax rates at the end than at the beginning, the tax deferral would be an advantage.

PROFESSOR BUCHANAN: Yes, you would need a much higher tax rate at the end because you have this tax-free loan all the way along that is earning a rate of return.

PROFESSOR HSIAO: I would like to comment on Kaplan's calculations. They are based on a set of steady-state assumptions, whereas the tax rate is based on the anticipated impact from the demographic bulge and also from the very rapid change in the benefit structure during the past decade. To make his calculations relevant, he needs to simulate a steady-state condition in which there is no demographic bulge as well as a benefit structure that has remained unchanged for workers over their working lifetime.

Second, Kaplan stated that there is no significant difference between the two ways of indexing. We need to remind ourselves that these comparisons are based on people retiring at age sixty-five. If you subtract age sixty-five from his Tables 5, 6, and 7, you will find that the differences are in the magnitude of 10 to 15 percent. They are not large; but, on the other hand, they are not insignificant.

PROFESSOR KAPLAN: Let me clarify your first remark. Would you suggest that I use higher tax rates for wage indexing so that it is self-financing over the seventy-five-year period rather than the fifty-year period?

PROFESSOR HSIAO: Social security is currently being affected by two forces. One is the demographic phenomenon; the other is the rapid increase in the benefits legislated by Congress. I think both of those adjustments have to be incorporated in your calculations.

PROFESSOR KAPLAN: I did not want to load the results too heavily in favor of showing equality. I took the self-financing fifty-year tax rate. That leads to differences which I call small, but which you found to be

167

higher than small. I explained those away by noting that wage indexing still has a remaining deficit that must be financed.

The alternative to subtracting age sixty-five is to figure the difference in the rate of return. One might be 6 percent, the other might be 6.3 percent, and you could say that difference is either big or small. Then, you could look at real rates of return and subtract 4 percent from both figures, so that the percentage difference is much higher. I do not want to get involved in quibbling about that. I think the difference is on the order of tenths of a percentage point, 6.0 percent as compared with 6.1 or 6.2 percent. In view of all the assumptions made and the fact that the demographic and economic assumptions for the two schemes may be somewhat different because they have been prepared by different persons, I felt it was not useful to attempt to pin down precisely whether that difference in rates of return of one- or two-tenths of a percentage point was really a significant difference between the two schemes.

PROFESSOR PAUL GRIMALDI, Seton Hall University: I have some difficulty with Kaplan's rates of return for low-income persons. His estimates seem to overstate their return because many poor people receive Supplemental Security Income (SSI) and therefore they receive very little for their social security taxes, perhaps to the point of almost a zero rate of return.

PROFESSOR KAPLAN: That is a reasonable point. What you are saying is that, if they did not get social security benefits, we would bail them out through all these other programs that are designed to supplement social security. You are turning the system on its end.

PROFESSOR GRIMALDI: I would go one step further. For many people, social security is an albatross because it prevents them from qualifying for SSI and, consequently, for other transfer programs.

PROFESSOR KAPLAN: It is hard for me to believe that anybody who is currently retired and who is receiving social security benefits at the current level has gotten a raw deal from social security over his lifetime.

PROFESSOR GRIMALDI: To give a case in point, in California the SSI standard for a couple with no other income is $557 a month. If a couple with no other income was entitled to a monthly social security benefit of $510, they would also have been eligible for SSI. What return did they get for their social security contributions?

PROFESSOR KAPLAN: I suspect that your question deserves a long answer that I have not carefully thought out. The imposition of certain other welfare programs could make the rate of return on the social security program worthless. I could be optimistic and hope that in fifty years, because of the 1.75 percent real earnings growth, there will be less need for all these supplementary programs.

DR. LEIMER: I would like to comment on Kaplan's statement about the rate of return as the most important criterion in judging the performance of either the wage-indexing or the price-indexing system, and on his not being able to understand the controversy over the effects on intercohort and intracohort equity. The pattern of replacement rates within and between cohorts reflects what the system in its present form is trying to do. The system is not trying to guarantee a particular distribution of rates of return according to people's contributions to the system. It does replace earnings lost as a result of retirement, disability, or death. The benefit base provides the measure of the earnings that are replaced.

If the rate of return were the most important criterion, the system in its present form would make absolutely no sense. In that case, what we ought to be concerned with is basing people's retirement benefits on some accumulated value of their prior tax payments, not on their earnings. We could introduce some sort of distributive effect by giving people at the low end of the income scale an annuity with a higher rate of return, and vice versa for persons with high incomes. It is important to consider the pattern of benefits and average benefit rates across the distribution of the benefit base for a given cohort, as well as to look at changes in this pattern over time, because this concern reflects the outcome of the political process regarding the appropriate nature of the system.

I would also like to comment about Kaplan's findings that the distribution of rates of return seems very similar under both price and wage indexing. I have done some similar work that shows substantial declines in progressivity for future workers implied by price indexing as opposed to wage indexing.

PART THREE

THE FUTURE FINANCING OF THE SOCIAL SECURITY SYSTEM

Alternatives for Financing
a Mature Social Security System

June A. O'Neill

The social security system as established by the original legislation of 1935 was essentially a simple retirement program for workers in commerce and industry. Benefits could be paid to retired workers at the age of sixty-five years or older, and they were to be based on cumulative wages. The system was to be funded by a tax of 2 percent on the first $3,000 of a worker's earnings; this tax was to be shared equally by the employer and the employee. These tax payments were expected to exceed benefit payments in the early years, with the surpluses accumulating into a large fund. The original plan was, therefore, to establish something close to a self-financing, earnings-related, retirement program.

Even before the first benefit was paid out, however, legislation was passed in 1939 that changed important aspects of the program. The strict contributory requirements of the program gave way to a stronger welfare orientation as benefits were provided for survivors and dependents, and the benefit formula was skewed to be made more progressive. As a result, instead of accumulating in a fund, the surplus tax contributions went to finance benefits for which no explicit contribution had been made. Thus, the pattern was set for the current pay-as-you-go system. In subsequent decades, benefit amounts were raised, eligibility for benefits was liberalized, and different types of benefits were added. Coverage was also expanded to include almost all nonfederal workers.

Up until the early 1970s, increases in benefits were legislated on an ad hoc basis. They were funded by drawing down the surpluses in the trust funds and by raising both the tax rate and the taxable earnings base. While benefits awarded to new retirees increased on average at roughly the same rate as average wages, they did not do so automatically on an annual basis. The option was therefore reserved to meet temporary financing difficulties by restraining benefits as well as by raising taxes.

As a result of the 1972 amendments to the Social Security Act, benefit increases for those already retired were made automatic and were tied to increases in the consumer price index (CPI). At the same time, the legislation provided for an indexing mechanism that inadvertently created the now well-known "flaw" that can lead to an automatic overindexing of benefits for new retirees during periods of inflation. To

173

start the process off, benefits were raised by 20 percent in 1972, following a substantial increase in 1971. The cumulative effect of these increases was to raise the replacement rate—the ratio of benefits to past wages.[1] By 1975 the replacement ratio had risen 27 percent above the level that had prevailed over the twenty years preceding 1972.[2] (As a result of the 1977 amendments, the replacement rate will be held roughly constant at about the 1975 level.)

In a pay-as-you-go system in which benefit increases are automatic, great demands are placed on forecasting in order to plan the financing of the system. Although the 1972 amendments provided for automatic increases in the taxable earnings base tied to wage increases, tax rates were set in the law and were scheduled to rise by what was projected to be enough to cover future outlays. The forecast did not materialize, however. Starting in 1973, inflation increased by much more than anticipated and wages by less. The recession of 1974–1975 served to reduce still more sharply the growth in the tax base. At the same time, while real income was falling for the working population, real benefits were rising for new retirees. And the number of beneficiaries increased more rapidly than expected. The deficits in the old-age, survivors, and disability programs and the dwindling trust fund balances of the mid-1970s are the culmination of this unfortunate sequence.

Social security is not, of course, in danger of bankruptcy in the usual sense. The government is morally committed to finance benefit payments and can do so through its command over taxes and the general funds. In a more fundamental way, however, social security is at a critical stage. The current financing crisis has served to accelerate recognition of the longer-term difficulties that lie ahead.

Demography and the Long-Term Problem under the Current Pay-as-You-Go System

Perhaps the greatest problem for the long term is the dramatic change in the age distribution of the population that is expected to occur after the turn of the century, when the huge population born during the baby boom following World War II reaches retirement age. The birth rate has dropped sharply since the mid-1960s and, if current projections are realized, the working population will grow only about half as fast

---

[1] "Replacement rate" is used here as a shorthand for the ratio of the benefit awarded to a hypothetical man who had always earned the median wage to the median wage in the preceding year. This replacement rate is unlikely to be the same as the ratio of the average retiree's actual benefit to his last wage before retirement.

[2] See Congressional Budget Office, *Financing Social Security: Issues for the Short and Long Term* (July 1977), p. 14, and table 4, p. 15.

as the beneficiary population over the next fifty years. As a result, the number of beneficiaries per 100 workers would increase from about 31 per 100 to about 50 per 100 by the year 2025.

This 60 percent increase in the ratio of beneficiaries to workers has a direct bearing on the relation between benefits and taxes in a pay-as-you-go system. As the relative size of the tax-paying population falls, the tax rate must rise to compensate, if the average benefit is to rise as fast as the average wage. Under these circumstances and given current projections, an increase of 60 percent in the tax rate would be required by the year 2025. Alternatively, if the tax rate per worker is to remain constant, then the average benefit must rise proportionately less than the average wage.

Effect on Rates of Return. One important consequence of this demographically induced change is that the rate of return to an individual in the social security system will fall—that is, the rate of return implicit in his stream of tax payments and benefit receipts. Of course, a decline in the rate of return is not necessarily a cause for concern. Indeed, the implicit rate of return has undoubtedly fallen throughout the history of the program, but from a very high level.

In the early days of the program, benefits were paid out to workers who had made contributions for only a short period, and these benefits must have reflected an enormously high rate of return. As workers retired after having contributed for a greater number of years, the rate of return was bound to fall. Because of constantly expanding coverage, however, some workers are still retiring with less than a full work life of tax payments. For this reason and also because of the sharp increase in the level of benefits since 1970, individuals retiring during this decade are likely to continue to realize high rates of return since they will have paid taxes at relatively lower rates during most of their working lives. Estimates of the real internal rate of return for a sample of actual individuals retiring in 1970 show returns averaging around 10 percent for males sixty-five years of age and older.[3] Thus, although the implicit rate of return may be lower than it was in the early days of the program, it is still likely to be fairly high compared with returns realized on private savings.

---

[3] The returns presented refer only to persons surviving to age sixty-five. The rate of return would be lower if calculated for all persons entering the labor force because some will not survive to collect any benefits. See the study by Alan Freiden, Dean R. Leimer, and Ronald Hoffman, "Internal Rates of Return to Retired Worker-Only Beneficiaries under Social Security, 1967–70," *Studies in Income Distribution No. 5*, Social Security Administration, Office of Research and Statistics (October 1976).

The cohorts retiring in succeeding decades will be less fortunate. They will have paid taxes over their entire working lives and will face the limits on the implicit rate of return imposed by a mature pay-as-you-go system. Moreover, the demographic changes described earlier will lower their returns even further.

The limits on the implicit rate of return in a mature pay-as-you-go system are ultimately determined by the rate of increase in the average wage and the rate of increase in the population. With a stable population, the ratio of the size of the beneficiary group to the size of the tax-paying group would be constant and, if the share of wages transferred to social security beneficiaries did not change, the rate of return would be just about equal to the rate of increase in the real wage. If the population is growing in such a way that the working population is growing faster than the beneficiary population, then the rate of return could exceed the increase in the real wage rate. Conversely, when the population growth rate slows down, so that the working population is growing more slowly than the beneficiary population, then the implicit rate of return would fall below the increase in the real wage rate, unless a rising share of wages were transferred to beneficiaries. This last case best describes the situation into which we seem to be moving.

Several studies have calculated implicit rates of return to social security tax payments for hypothetical individuals and married couples retiring in the future. The calculations simulate the lifetime patterns of earnings, tax payments, and benefits for these "representative" cases, based on assumptions about the rate of increase of earnings, survival probabilities, and other important factors.

Based on the perhaps optimistic assumptions of a growth rate in the real wage of 2 percent a year and a fertility rate of 2.1 percent, I have estimated real rates of return under a price-indexed system for the cohort reaching age sixty-five in the year 2021. The rates of return ranged from about 1 percent to 2.2 percent for married couples. The lower bound refers to two-earner couples, in which both husband and wife have made substantial social security contributions. The higher bound refers to a couple, in which the wife has not made any social security contributions but is entitled to a spouse benefit or a widow's benefit. The rates of return for single men were estimated to be slightly negative. The rates for single women varied from 2 to 6 percent, with the high rate attributable only to those single women with extremely short contribution periods.[4]

---

[4] See June O'Neill, "Returns to Social Security" (Paper presented at the American Economics Association Annual Meeting, Atlantic City, New Jersey, September 1976).

Dean Leimer has found very low to negative real rates of return for members of the cohort that would reach age sixty-five in the year 2030.[5] These estimates are based on the more pessimistic assumptions of a 1.75 percent rate of increase in the real wage and a fertility rate of 1.9 births per woman. Leimer's results show somewhat higher (but still predominantly negative) rates of return under the coupled system that was in effect prior to the 1977 amendments than under either a wage-indexed or a price-indexed system. If the analysis were extended into the future beyond 2030, however, the sharply higher tax rates required by the pre-1977 system would eventually reduce the rate of return.

Reviewing the Assumptions. Of course, the gloomy outlook for sharply falling rates of return over the next seventy-five years depends on key assumptions about long-term trends in the population and the economy, and these assumptions are more speculative than scientific. The middle-path fertility assumption underlying the 1977 report of the trustees of the social security trust funds is that the fertility rate will rise from the present low of 1.7 births per woman to 2.1, which is the so-called replacement level fertility rate—that is, the rate needed to maintain a stationary population (assuming no net immigration). The historical pattern indicates a long-term decline in the fertility rate in the United States. From fertility rates of 5.4 births per woman in the mid-nineteenth century, there was a fairly steady decline, reaching 3.6 in 1900, 3.0 in 1925, and 2.2 in 1940. Against this long-term decline, the high fertility rates of the postwar baby boom, which lasted from the late 1940s well into the 1960s, appear as an aberration. During the height of the baby boom, fertility rates were as high as they had been at the beginning of the century. Because of the many changes in labor force participation rates, divorce rates, and the general reorganization of family life, it is most commonly assumed that fertility rates will not rise much above the 2.1 level in the future. In order to have a strong positive impact on social security finances, however, the fertility rate would have to rise considerably above that level.

The mortality assumptions of the 1978 trustees' report would result in a life expectancy at birth for men of 70.3 years by the year 2000 and 71.7 years by the year 2050. For women, these life expectancies are assumed to be 78.0 and 80.4 years, respectively. These assumptions, particularly for men, may be too conservative. Several countries have

[5] See Dean R. Leimer, "Rates of Return to Future Social Security Retirees under Alternative Benefit Structures" (Paper presented at the Western Economics Association meeting, June 1977).

already achieved life expectancies for men that exceed the projections of the trustees' report for the year 2050. One would expect that improvements in health care would have more significant effects on longevity than are now being assumed. An adjustment that reduced future mortality rates among the aged would increase the size of the beneficiary population by more than the working population and so would in itself weaken the future financial outlook for social security.

An increase in the rate of real wage growth would improve the outlook. The 1976, 1977, and 1978 trustees' reports assumed that the growth in real wages would average 1.75 percent over the long run. Although this would be above the average rate of increase since the late 1960s, a period of unusually low rates of economic growth, it is below the growth rates of earlier periods. Long-term rates of economic growth are difficult to predict because they depend on factors such as technological change and patterns of saving and investment about which very little is known. There are, however, some factors that may operate to raise the earnings growth rate. Since the relative size of the working population is expected to fall, the ratio of capital to labor would rise and, other things being the same, the productivity of labor, and hence of earnings, would rise. Moreover, one might expect that families with fewer children would invest more resources in each child (for example, providing higher quality education), and this would also increase labor productivity. Another consideration is that the labor force will be increasingly composed of workers with more experience (and, therefore, higher productivity) as the proportion of teenagers declines and as women acquire a more permanent place in the labor force. Thus, increases in real wage growth could offset, to some extent, the slowdown in population growth and thereby raise the rate of return. But, even under these highly optimistic conditions, the rate of return could probably not go much higher than 2 percent.

The rate of inflation has a direct effect on outlays, and under the overindexed system (prior to the 1977 amendments) it also had a direct effect on the tax rate needed to fund the system. The rate of inflation does not, however, affect the tax rate in a wage-indexed system and it does not, in any case, affect the real rate of return.

Financing Alternatives

The current pay-as-you-go system has been criticized for several reasons, some of which were indicated in the preceding discussion. One objection is that the implicit rates of return to individuals are low once the system matures. Moreover, this rate of return can fluctuate from generation to generation because of swings in the rate of growth of the population or of real wages. In addition, a pay-as-you-go system is highly sensitive to year-to-year changes in the economy, and this places great demands on forecasting for the planning of tax rates, even in the short run. Another objection to the current financing system is that the payroll tax is regressive.

This section of the paper will review several broad options for changing the way social security is financed. One option is to substitute a funded or partially funded system for the pay-as-you-go mechanism. Another is to allow private savings to substitute for some social security savings, either directly or indirectly by reducing the scale of the program. Finally, pay-as-you-go could be retained but general revenues could be substituted for the payroll tax. Because the role of social security is strongly influenced by the way it is financed, a discussion of alternative funding mechanisms is likely to introduce programs with different objectives.

Building a Social Security Fund. In the past few years, the idea of building up a large trust fund has been proposed as a way to increase saving in the economy. The argument is that social security substitutes for private saving because the guarantee of a retirement benefit eliminates the major reason for saving. Social security differs from a private pension plan, however, because the annual contributions are not invested and accumulated to provide for the guaranteed benefit. Instead, contributions are immediately transferred to current beneficiaries.

As explained above, there is an implicit real return to social security contributions, but this is roughly equal to the increase in average wages plus the rate of population growth. In a mature system, this implicit return is likely to range between 1 and 3 percent, and it would therefore represent a much lower return than the real pre-tax return on physical capital in the economy. Thus, society would gain from accumulating tax contributions in a fund that could be invested at the higher rate of interest, thereby providing a higher future level of income.

Both the importance of the effect of social security on saving and the idea of accumulating a large publicly held fund have been controversial. It has been argued that, in the absence of mandatory social security transfers, voluntary transfers from younger workers to their parents would occur to some extent. Another argument is that saving is partly motivated by the desire to leave a bequest to one's children and this motivation is not eliminated by social security. Moreover, it has been pointed out that provision of a social security pension can have the effect of actually increasing saving. This offsetting effect can

179

occur because social security induces early retirement, and the need for additional income in the longer retirement period results in an increase in saving during the working years. The net outcome of these opposing effects cannot be readily determined a priori.

Several studies have established the existence of both the savings-reducing effect of the social security benefit and the savings-increasing effect of the longer retirement period.[6] The studies do not agree on the relative magnitudes of the two effects, although it would appear that the balance of evidence favors a net savings-reducing effect.

Even among those who believe that social security will, on balance, decrease saving, support for a funded system is hardly unanimous. One problem is that it is enormously difficult to build up a fund once a retirement system has matured. To do so would require that current workers be taxed two times: once to pay the benefits of current retirees and again to contribute to the fund that will pay their own retirement benefits in the future. Despite the promise of an ultimately higher retirement income with the new funded system, taxes in the present may make the scheme unworkable.

Another objection to a public fund, assuming it could be achieved, is that it would require federal control over a huge amount of assets. A fund of more than $800 billion would be required to pay interest sufficient to cover a year's OASI outlays, assuming an annual interest yield of 10 percent. (The current social security trust fund holds U.S. government securities yielding interest at an average rate of only about 7.0 percent.) Moreover, a federal fund of such a size would be large enough to hold a substantial portion of the combined governmental and private market debt and could, therefore, hamper the conduct of monetary policy as well as be a destabilizing force in private markets.

Partial funding at a much smaller scale has been advocated as a way of equalizing rates of return between generations. As was discussed earlier, the implicit return will fluctuate over time in response to changes in the rate of increase of real wages and of population. If tax rates were set to balance outlays over, say, a fifty- to seventy-five-year period, the effects of these fluctuations would be shared by different cohorts; this would avoid bestowing benefits on some cohorts and losses on others.

Perhaps the largest obstacle to a funded system, however, is that, once the fund was started, a crisis or a worthy cause would come along

---

[6] See, for example, Martin Feldstein, "Social Security, Induced Retirement and Aggregate Capital Accumulation," *Journal of Political Economics*, vol. 82 (September-October 1974), pp. 905–26; and Alicia H. Munnell, *The Effect of Social Security on Personal Saving* (Cambridge, Mass.: Ballinger Publishing Co., 1974).

and the fund would represent too tempting a source of financing to be left untouched. The original social security system was designed to be funded until it seemed more attractive to pay out more in benefits.

Increasing the Private Share of Savings. Since 1970, the entire scale of the social security program has undergone an enormous expansion, with cash benefits increasing by more than 150 percent. Much of this can be attributed to an increase in the number of beneficiaries and to inflation. A considerable share of the expansion, however, is the result of a large increase in the entire level of benefits.

As a result of a series of legislated benefit increases in the early 1970s and the automatic indexing begun in 1975, the replacement rate for new retirees has risen rapidly. In 1970, the replacement rate for the hypothetical man retiring at age sixty-five who had always earned the median wage was 31 percent. By 1976, this rate had increased to 43 percent.

It has now been recognized that the way indexing was implemented in the 1972 amendments resulted in an upward spiral in replacement rates during periods of rapid increases in the consumer price index (CPI). This mechanical flaw was corrected by the 1977 amendments, which "decoupled" the system by establishing separate procedures for indexing the benefits of those who are already retired and for indexing the benefits of those who are coming up for retirement. For existing retirees, benefits will be increased each year according to increases in the CPI. For those coming up for retirement, the formula for determining benefits will be indexed (by a wage index) so that the average benefit will rise at about the same rate as average wages. Under the 1977 legislation, however, the relation of benefits to wages is to be maintained at about 1975 levels; thus, a new and very much larger share of income will be devoted to social security as a result of the expansion of the early 1970s. Under this new wage-indexed, decoupled system, the average benefit is expected to rise to about $10,000 by the year 2030, while the average wage will rise to about $24,000. (These figures are expressed in constant, present-day dollars, and they assume average annual increases in the real wage of 1.75 percent.) If the fertility rate is at the replacement level, such a system would require taxes of about 17 percent of payroll in the year 2030 under pay-as-you-go financing.

One argument against maintaining social security at the new and higher level relates to the effect this would have on the rate of return to savings. As was discussed earlier, the implicit rate of return to individuals from their social security tax payments is expected to fall below

2 percent in real terms for workers retiring over the next seventy-five years. In the long run, roughly the same return is expected under either price indexing or wage indexing. In a pay-as-you-go system, higher benefits mean higher taxes, and it is the relation between benefits and taxes that determines the implicit rate of return. If the return available in private markets will be substantially higher than the implicit return in social security, then individuals covered by social security will, in effect, be required to save a larger proportion of their income at an inferior rate, thereby lowering their future income.

Those who are concerned about this prospect have proposed various ways of expanding the role of private saving and investment. One approach would be to allow individuals to opt out of social security provided they accumulated funds for retirement in another way.[7] The difficulty with such a plan is that the option to invest elsewhere is likely to be taken by those with the highest earnings and the lowest rates of return in social security. Rates of return tend to fall at higher earnings levels because tax payments are a constant proportion of taxable income, but the benefit table is highly progressive with respect to lifetime earnings.

Leimer has shown that the implicit rate of return is lower for those with more education and, hence, higher earnings.[8] For example, projections for the cohort born in 1965 and reaching age sixty-five in the year 2030 indicate an implicit rate of return in real terms of about −1.0 percent for white married couples at the college graduate level. The rate rises slightly as the couple's education level falls, reaching zero at the level of nine to eleven years of schooling. These results assume a wage-indexed system. (Under a price-indexed system, the rate for college graduates is about the same, but it is slightly lower for couples with a lower level of education.)

If those with the highest earnings and tax payments left the system, it would be all the more difficult to finance the benefits of current retirees. General revenues would likely be required during the transition. Moreover, administrative problems could make the scheme impractical.

Another approach to expanding private savings is by simply lowering the level of benefits and taxes. This effect, for example, would be achieved gradually by the price-indexing scheme identified with William

---

[7] A proposal for permitting the option of purchasing U.S. Treasury bonds instead of participating in social security is discussed in James M. Buchanan, "Social Insurance in a Growing Economy: A Proposal for Radical Reform," *National Tax Journal*, vol. 21 (December 1968), pp. 386–95.

[8] Leimer, "Rates of Return to Future Social Security Retirees under Alternative Benefit Structures."

Hsiao.[9] Under the Hsiao scheme, the same average lifetime earnings would always produce the same benefit at retirement. Since the benefit formula is progressive, increases in the level of real earnings in the economy would result in a benefit level that declined as a percentage of earnings as more and more workers moved into the higher earnings brackets with lower replacement rates. With an increase in real earnings of 2 percent a year in the future the annual benefit of the hypothetical worker who always earned the median wage would rise to about $6,000 for those retiring in the year 2030, and this would represent a replacement rate of 25 percent. Because benefits do not rise as fast under the price-indexed formula as under a wage-indexed formula that maintained replacement rates at current levels, smaller tax payments would be required. Therefore, individuals would have more disposable income to put into private saving. In this way, retirees would continue to have a guaranteed retirement income from social security, although it might reflect a low, possibly negative, return on their tax payments. They would also, however, have a retirement income from private saving, probably at a higher rate. If the two are combined, the average rate of return would then be greater than under the current wage-indexed system.

Opponents of a reduction in the role of social security argue, first, that individuals, particularly those with low to middle incomes, will not save unless it is mandatory and, second, that high rates of return on capital will not be accessible to the average person. These issues will perhaps be better resolved when more is known about the effect of social security on private saving and about the effect of rising levels of education and income on the amount of saving and on the sophistication of behavior connected with saving.

General Revenue Funding. The recent projections of the growing social security burden in the future have given rise to serious consideration of using funds from general revenues to help finance social security. Proponents of funding from general revenues cite the tax and transfer aspects of social security. They argue that much of the social security benefit structure is closer to a welfare program than to a contributory retirement plan. For example, benefits to dependents and the minimum benefit reflect transfers that are not really based on contributions. Therefore, it would be more appropriate to fund much of social security with general revenues derived from the more progressive income tax rather than by the current tax on earnings and payroll.

Those who oppose funding from general revenues point out that

---

[9] See the discussion in Congressional Budget Office, *Financing Social Security*.

it would be difficult to use general revenues to pay higher benefits to higher-income people. Spouse benefits, for example, rise with the earnings of the wage-earning spouse. How then could one justify paying these benefits without applying a means test? And if a means test were applied, the essential character of the program would change. Logical consistency would in fact argue that the contributory parts of the program be strengthened and that the aspects of the program that are more welfare oriented be handled through the many other programs that have been developed for these purposes (such as Supplemental Security Income and food stamps).

The extent to which the payroll tax should be regarded as regressive has also been challenged. If one views the tax as a contribution to a guaranteed retirement benefit, then the progressivity should be measured in terms of the implicit rate of return. As mentioned above, estimates of the rate of return suggest that it tends to fall with income so that the ultimate redistributive effects would be progressive.

Even if it were viewed just as a tax, however, the extent of regressivity of the payroll tax is less than is commonly believed. The tax does take a constant proportion of a worker's earnings up to the set maximum. As earnings rise above that point, the tax becomes a decreasing proportion of the worker's total wages. The distributional effects of the tax, however, are perhaps better evaluated in terms of the burden on family income. The covered earnings of any one worker are not necessarily indicative of his other sources of income or the income of his family. When social security taxes are measured against family income from all sources, the tax rises somewhat as a percentage of family income up through the fourth income quintile (that is, for 80 percent of all families) before declining slightly.[10] This pattern is explained by the tendency for families in the lowest quintile to depend more on transfers than on taxable earnings. Moreover, families with higher incomes tend to have multiple earners, so that the total earnings of many families remain taxable considerably beyond the income level corresponding to the taxable maximum for an individual. Thus, although the payroll tax is regressive compared with the progressive income tax, it is not fair to describe it as falling most heavily on the poor.

It should also be noted that the introduction of the earned-income tax credit helps relieve the burden of the social security tax for many families with taxable earnings in the lowest income group. The credit was introduced by the Tax Reduction Act of 1976. It is equal to 10 percent of the first $4,000 of earned income, and it is then reduced by

---

[10] Ibid., pp. 9–12.

10 percent of adjusted gross income exceeding $4,000. The credit, however, is limited to families with dependent children.

The payroll tax may have other undesirable distributional effects, however, with respect to labor markets. Roughly half the tax is paid by employers at the time of collection, although many analysts believe that the employer's share is eventually shifted to the worker in the form of lower wage increases than otherwise would have occurred. A difficulty arises, however, when a worker is paid the minimum wage. In this case, a tax increase cannot legally be shifted to the worker. A payroll tax increase acts then like an increase in the minimum wage and would be expected to reduce employment opportunities for low-wage workers.

A contributory system need not use a payroll tax. One alternative would be to use an earmarked income tax. The tax could be based on a constant or graduated proportion of income up to a selected ceiling. This could avoid the misallocation of resources that may be induced by a payroll tax and would permit more thoughtful consideration of the effects on income distribution. From a political standpoint, the transition to such a tax would undoubtedly be difficult to implement because individuals would immediately bear the full burden of the tax. Wages might well rise (or prices fall) as employees reacted to their reduced social security taxes. But the change in wages and prices would be much more uncertain than the increase in an individual's tax payments.

One important advantage cited for an earmarked tax over funding from general revenues is that a certain amount of fiscal restraint is always imposed by the need to match benefits with taxes. Reliance on transfers from general revenues could make it more difficult to keep program expansion within bounds.

The Politics of Social
Security Reform

Edgar K. Browning

Public choice theory is the study of the processes through which government policies are determined and implemented. It is thus a study of the way politi al factors influence the development and design of policy. As I hope to show in this paper, the social security system can be fruitfully examined from this perspective. Although a number of conclusions emerge from this analysis, it should be stressed at the outset that they are tentative. Public choice economics is of comparatively recent origin, and it does not yet possess a fully developed and tested general model. Nonetheless, I believe that a number of important insights are provided by applying the elementary propositions of the theory as it now stands. At the very least, it raises questions of obvious significance.

The view of government provided by public choice theory differs sharply from the implicit conception contained in much economic analysis. Until recently most analysts seemed to believe that, once the "truth" was ascertained by applying the appropriate theoretical and empirical tools, government officials would proceed to act in a way that furthers the public interest. An invisible hand was thought to exist in government that served the public interest, subject only to the uncertainty about the actual consequences of policies. Public choice theory has shattered this naive conception of government. Government is instead viewed as a process that responds to political forces which can sometimes lead it to behave counterproductively. According to this view, there is such a thing as "government failure," which is quite analogous to the "market failure" that occasionally arises in the private sector. A major thesis of this paper is that the provision of retirement benefits is a type of government policy in which government failure can be predicted to occur because of perverse political forces.

An attempt to demonstrate government failure can proceed in two ways. The first approach is to assert certain goals for policy and then to show that the policy fails to achieve them. This is the welfare-economics framework of most economic analysis, which emphasizes economic efficiency and equity as goals. It is subject to the drawback that the goals of members of the public may differ from those assumed

187

by the analyst. A second approach, that of public choice theory, is to examine the political process to see if it will cater effectively to the goals of the public, whatever those goals may happen to be. Both approaches are useful, and they should be viewed as complementary. Although the emphasis in this paper will be on the public choice approach, the following section will briefly evaluate social security within the conventional welfare-economics framework. The reason for beginning in this way is to suggest that no convincing rationale for social security has been developed even within the welfare-economics framework; if this conclusion is true, it should serve to strengthen the suspicion that the political process is not functioning well in the area of social security.

Economic Rationale for Social Security

Any justification for social security as it has emerged in the United States must provide reasons for at least two (potentially) separate elements in the system: first, the requirement that all persons save a certain portion of their income for retirement purposes; second, the government's pay-as-you-go mechanism for providing retirement benefits. Each of these will be considered in turn.

Forced Saving. Why is it in the interest of the public to require that everyone save for their own retirement? Probably the strongest argument is based on the self-interest of those who would save even in the absence of compulsion. If some people failed to provide for their retirement, society would virtually be compelled to provide transfers to these persons when they became elderly, since the general public would obviously not allow the elderly who have no means of self-support to starve. Thus, persons who do not save can impose costs on those who do. To prevent this, the nation may simply require everyone to save at least certain minimal amounts.[1] An essentially similar argument starts from the premise of an existing income-tested transfer program for the aged poor and argues that forced saving will offset the disincentive to save which is contained in such a program. Both arguments are logically identical to the case for work requirements in welfare programs: people who can support themselves should not be allowed to behave irresponsibly and to impose costs on others.

Although this argument clearly stresses a legitimate concern, it is

---

[1] This argument has been developed in some detail in Richard Musgrave, "The Role of Social Insurance in an Overall Program for Social Welfare," in *The American System of Social Insurance*, ed. William G. Bowen and others (New York: McGraw Hill, 1968), pp. 23–40.

pertinent to inquire how quantitatively important the issue is. An implicit assumption in the argument seems to be that, if people do not save for retirement, society must support them when they reach age sixty-five. Yet people have another method of supporting themselves after age sixty-five even if they have not saved: they can continue working. It is only for those who are physically unable to work that this argument has much validity. Perhaps only 15 percent of the elderly fall into this category.[2] The relevant question is thus how many people will both be unable to work and have insufficient accumulated savings upon reaching retirement age. This combination of circumstances may be rare. If 10 percent of the public does not save for retirement, and if these persons are as likely as others to become disabled, then only 1.5 percent of the elderly will be both disabled and without savings.

Despite the arbitrary nature of those figures, it seems likely that very few elderly persons will be in a position in which society must support them with transfers. One way of dealing with this problem is to require 100 percent of the public to save to avoid the cost of supporting the 1.5 percent who would otherwise require assistance. In view of the magnitudes involved, however, it seems likely that an asset-tested transfer program for the disabled elderly would impose smaller costs than a program requiring everyone to save specified amounts. In any event, the quantitative significance of this argument for forced saving is open to serious question.

Two other reasons for requiring people to save are sometimes given.[3] One stresses that it is difficult and costly for individuals to make the complex economic decisions required to provide for their retirement. But, by using a compulsory program designed in line with people's needs, the high cost of reaching individual decisions can be reduced.[4] A second reason emphasizes that people, when young, may systemat-

---

[2] A survey indicating that 16.4 percent of males and 8.5 percent of females over sixty years of age give disability or ill health as a reason for being outside the labor force is cited in W. Kip Viscusi and Richard Zeckhauser, "The Role of Social Security in Income Maintenance," in *The Crisis in Social Security*, ed. Michael J. Boskin (San Francisco: Institute for Contemporary Studies, 1977), p. 54.

[3] These arguments are discussed briefly in Martin Feldstein, "Social Insurance," in *Income Redistribution*, ed. Colin D. Campbell (Washington, D.C.: American Enterprise Institute, 1977), pp. 78–81.

[4] It is not necessarily true that the costs of private decision making will be reduced, at least so long as social security does not completely replace private saving for retirement. As long as people supplement social security, it is possible that decision-making costs may actually rise, because in this situation people must understand both public and private mechanisms for retirement provisions in order to plan rationally. In addition, the increase in the costs of public decision making may not be negligible.

ically underestimate their needs when old and therefore save too little. Myopic individual behavior can, however, be offset by appropriate government rules.

Discussing these last two arguments for forced saving, especially the second one, is difficult because they are so vague. They may contain an element of truth but, to my knowledge, no one has ever bothered to develop the arguments carefully enough to permit an appraisal. As they have been stated, they argue just as strongly for government regulation of other aspects of our lives. On exactly the same grounds, one could argue that government should: choose the food people eat; force them to exercise; select their jobs, their spouses, their religion; and determine the number of children they may have. All these examples involve decisions that have much in common with providing for retirement; an individual making a decision confronts complex issues, with potentially high costs if mistakes are made, and decisions are, to a degree, irreversible. High costs and myopic behavior probably characterize all these decisions. Yet few people would seriously favor having government make decisions in these and similar matters. The surprising thing is that, when applied to saving for retirement, such arguments are not only taken seriously but are generally accepted, even in the absence of evidence.

Pay-as-You-Go Social Security. Even if the argument that people should be required to save for retirement is accepted, a further step must be taken to justify the social security system: it must be shown that a pay-as-you-go, or unfunded, system of retirement benefits has advantages over both a funded governmental system and a compulsory private program.

An unfunded government system, such as the current one, could conceivably be a better method of providing for retirement than the existing alternatives. Under an unfunded government system, the taxes collected from today's workers are not invested on their behalf; instead, they are immediately paid out to those now retired. What today's workers receive is an implicit promise that, when they retire, the government will tax future workers to provide them with retirement benefits. Although there is no real investment under such a pay-as-you-go system, it is nonetheless possible for every retiree to receive in retirement benefits an amount greater than the taxes he paid while younger. This possibility arises because of the real growth of the economy over time. For example, if the government levies a flat tax rate on wage income, and real wage income grows over time, then tax revenue will also grow. A retired person will be supported by higher absolute per capita taxes than he paid during his working years, since wage income was then lower; thus, it is possible for his benefits to be greater than the taxes paid. This is true for all retired persons as long as the economy continues to grow.

The argument that retired persons can receive benefits in excess of taxes paid is not sufficient to justify social security because this is true of any system that provides a positive rate of return. The relevant question is whether pay-as-you-go social security provides a better rate of return than existing alternatives. In the long run, the real rate of return of unfunded social security is linked to the rate of growth of the economy—more precisely, to the rate of growth of the tax base used to finance the transfers. If the economy grows at a real rate of 3 percent, then all persons could possibly receive retirement benefits that represent a real rate of return of 3 percent on their tax payments. (The temporary effects when the system is first begun are ignored here; these are considered below.)

It is frequently held that a real rate of return equal to the growth rate of the economy is an attractive bargain for the public, representing a return as good as or better than they could achieve by saving privately (or by utilizing a funded social security system). To a limited extent, this is so; nonetheless, it remains true that an unfunded system yields a rate of return substantially below existing alternatives. Although the return an individual receives on his private saving may be quite low and hence comparable to the rate of economic growth, this is not relevant. The rate of growth of the economy—which is the implicit rate of return of unfunded social security—should not be compared with interest rates that reflect after-tax rates of return on private investment in real capital. What is relevant is not the after-tax yield of investments in, say, corporate capital, but the before-tax yield. If corporate capital yields a real return of 10 percent, while individuals can realize a return of only 3 percent because of taxes (such as the corporation income tax and property taxes), it is the before-tax return that should be compared with the rate of growth of the economy. The reason is simple: society realizes the before-tax return, partly through expanded tax collections. In economic terms, the opportunity cost of providing a rate of return equal to the rate of growth of the economy is the sacrificed before-tax returns that could otherwise have been generated by investing in real capital.

The following sketch will perhaps clarify this issue and indicate the magnitudes involved. The real growth rate of the economy is expected to be no more than 3 percent a year in the foreseeable future, and it may well be around 2 percent. By contrast, Martin Feldstein and Lawrence Summers have estimated that the real net return on capital invested in the corporate sector has averaged more than 12 percent over the 1946–1975 period.[5] This probably overstates the average real return on capital accumulation because approximately half of the economy's capital stock is in the noncorporate sector, which yields lower returns. Nonetheless, an average return of 10 percent is quite plausible. This means that, if the approximately $3 trillion in unfunded "wealth" in social security had been invested in real capital, the annual yield would be about $300 billion.[6] Instead, society realizes from unfunded social security a real return of only about 3 percent, or $90 billion on an annual basis. Thus, society loses $210 billion a year in real income by relying on an unfunded social security system as a method of providing retirement income.

These rough figures make it clear that an unfunded social security system is inefficient as an ongoing means of providing retirement income, and that a system producing an accumulation of real capital could provide a significantly higher return. This conclusion does not depend on whether social security has reduced private saving below the level that would have occurred had the system never begun. Because of the attention now being focused on the impact of social security on private saving, this last point will be treated in greater detail.

The least implausible reason why an unfunded social security system might not depress private saving is that it may substitute for voluntary intergenerational transfers among family members. People may provide for their retirement not by saving, but by having children and by receiving assistance from them after retirement. In this setting, the introduction of an unfunded social security system simply nationalizes a system of voluntary transfers to the retired. Younger workers respond not by curtailing saving, but by reducing transfers they would have made to their parents. No reduction in the national saving rate need occur. But an unfunded social security system introduced in this setting is still inefficient because the opportunity cost of an unfunded system is the 10 percent yield on real capital accumulation. The important point here is that an unfunded social security system and voluntary intergenerational transfers are both inefficient as compared with invest-

---

[5] Martin S. Feldstein and Lawrence Summers, "The Rate of Profit: Falling or Cyclical," cited as forthcoming in Martin S. Feldstein, "National Saving in the United States," in *Capital for Productivity and Jobs*, ed. E. Shapiro and W. White (Englewood Cliffs, N.J.: Prentice-Hall, 1977), pp. 124–54.

[6] Of course, the marginal productivity of capital would decline with an increase of $3 trillion in the capital stock, but under plausible assumptions about the production function the decline would not be large enough to affect significantly the comparison being made here.

ment in real capital. As long as the yield on capital exceeds the growth rate of the economy, any pay-as-you-go system, including voluntary intergenerational transfers, generates a smaller return than capital accumulation. What happens to the savings rate when social security is introduced is not relevant.

Up to this point, the unfunded social security system has been considered from a long-run perspective: how the system affects persons who pay taxes at a given rate over their entire working lives and receive benefits in retirement. People who receive retirement benefits without paying taxes over their entire lifetimes, however, fare much better. This can be seen by examining how such a system affects those who are older when the system begins. Suppose the system, with a 10 percent tax on wage income, begins this year. Since it is a pay-as-you-go system, the tax revenues are transferred to those currently retired, even though those persons paid no taxes in earlier years. They clearly secure great benefits. Those nearing retirement age also receive large benefits. For example, a person who is one year from the retirement age pays taxes for only one year, but he secures the same retirement benefits he would have gotten had the 10 percent tax rate been in effect over his entire lifetime. In general, the closer one is to retirement when the system begins, the greater his benefit—that is, the higher the real rate of return realized on his tax payments. Persons who are older when the system begins receive a return above the growth rate of the economy. Only those who are young, and all subsequent generations, receive a return that, on average, equals the economy's growth rate.

This "start up" phenomenon means that a major redistribution of income in favor of relatively older individuals occurs when the pay-as-you-go system begins. Although later generations receive only the low return provided by the economy's growth, early generations do much better. This net benefit to retirees in early generations can provide the basis for an argument favoring an unfunded system. Since the early generations have lower lifetime incomes (because of the economy's growth over time), the redistribution is from those with higher incomes (later generations) to those with lower incomes. Thus, an unfunded system produces greater equality in the distribution of lifetime incomes between early retirees and later generations.[7]

It is surprising that this argument is not used more often in sup-

---

[7] This redistribution would not occur (and hence this argument would not be valid) if social security simply substituted for voluntary intergenerational transfers among family members. In this case, early retirees are no better off because their social security benefits are offset by reductions in transfers from their children.

port of an unfunded social security system, since a funded system does not involve this type of redistribution.[8] The argument does have some problems, however. It raises troublesome ethical questions concerning why early retirees should be benefited indiscriminately (since some early retirees who benefit are not poor), and why the retired should be helped rather than the poor generally. More important, a desire to redistribute income in favor of the currently older generation does not call for an ongoing unfunded system. A "one-shot" redistribution from young to old would achieve this goal without locking all subsequent generations into a system in which they receive retirement benefits representing a very low rate of return. Thus, even the redistribution achieved by the start-up phase is not an adequate justification for a system of pay-as-you-go social security.

Conclusions. These brief observations do not deal exhaustively with all of the arguments that can be made in support of an unfunded social security system.[9] Nonetheless, the major arguments have been considered. The conclusions of this discussion are that the case for compulsory saving is not very convincing, and that the case for providing retirement benefits through an unfunded social security system is even less so. Although these conclusions may require some qualifications, it appears fair to say that the social security system has not been shown to be a corrective for a massive "market failure." On the contrary, a case can be made that it is a good example of "government failure." The remainder of this paper is concerned with why such a system is the predictable outcome of democratic political institutions, and what the public choice approach implies for reform of the system.

The Political Appeal of Unfunded Social Security

Social security is frequently referred to as "the most successful social program enacted by the U.S. government."[10] If success is equated with broad public support, this is perhaps true. At least until quite recently,

---

[8] This argument is developed in Kenneth V. Greene, "Overexpansion in the Social Insurance Budget and the Constitutional Perspective," *Economic Inquiry*, vol. 15 (July 1977), pp. 449–54. For a response, see Edgar K. Browning, "Social Insurance: The Constitutional Perspective," in the same issue.

[9] Two other arguments sometimes made concern the fact that annuities are not available on actuarially fair terms in private markets, and that social security should be viewed in part as a welfare program to help the elderly poor. Neither of these arguments is very convincing. This paper largely neglects the redistribution among retired groups that results from a benefit formula that gives higher rates of return on their taxes to poor retirees than to wealthy retirees.

[10] Joseph A. Pechman, "The Social Security System: An Overview," in *The Crisis in Social Security*, ed. Michael J. Boskin.

the system enjoyed a degree of public support unmatched by other domestic programs. Yet the analysis above suggests that social security is an inefficient method of providing retirement benefits. Why, then, is it so popular? This section addresses that question and suggests that the political appeal of an unfunded social security system stems largely from two factors. First, the distributional effects associated with the start-up phase of the program make it very attractive to older members of the population. Second, the public misunderstands the operation of the system.

Start-up Phase. Unfunded social security is a peculiar tax-expenditure program. Consider what happens to workers and retirees when social security taxes are increased. Because the system is on a pay-as-you-go basis, retired persons receive an immediate increase in their retirement benefits. They will gain from an expansion in the system and can be expected to support politically any move to increase the size of the system. At the same time, the workers whose higher taxes finance those benefits may perceive no net burden associated with an enlarged system. Although they pay higher taxes now, they will receive greater benefits after retirement. The tax burden is not a net burden for workers; rather, it is a sacrifice of current income in exchange for future benefits. Therefore, higher taxes may impose no net costs on taxpayers and confer obvious benefits on retired persons.

A program that appears to have benefits and no costs is a politician's dream. In fact, an unfunded social security system is identical in all relevant respects to deficit financing of retirement benefits. Government, in effect, borrows from workers with the promise of repaying the loan when they retire, and then uses the proceeds to finance current benefits to retirees. Insofar as it is a concealed form of deficit finance, an unfunded social security system is subject to much the same political pressures James Buchanan and Richard Wagner discuss with respect to more overt uses of this method of finance.[11]

It might be helpful to examine somewhat more carefully how a change in the scale of an unfunded social security program affects various age groups differentially. Assume that total wage income is growing at a rate of 3 percent a year, and that the government introduces a social security system, financing benefits with a flat tax rate of 10 percent on wage income. As mentioned earlier, persons who spend their entire lifetimes under such a system can receive retirement benefits that represent a 3 percent rate of return on their taxes. Persons

---

[11] James M. Buchanan and Richard E. Wagner, *Democracy in Deficit* (New York: Academic Press, 1977).

195

who are already working or retired receive a return that depends largely on their age when the system begins.

The net benefit is greater the older a person is when the system is introduced. Persons already retired receive the greatest gain because they receive benefits but paid no taxes. If the retirement age is sixty-five, a person of age fifty-five can receive retirement benefits after paying taxes for only ten years. The fifty-five-year-old can receive a real rate of return of 30 percent a year on his taxes—clearly, an attractive investment. For a forty-five-year-old, the return is 10 percent a year on the taxes he will pay for twenty years. For a person just entering the labor force, the return is only 3 percent a year.

In general, older persons have a strong incentive to support an unfunded social security system. Moreover, exactly the same incentives operate with respect to changes in the scale of the program. At any point in time, an increase in social security taxes yields a fifty-five-year-old a marginal return of 30 percent on the additional taxes he pays, whereas a reduction in taxes causes him to sacrifice a return of 30 percent. Not surprisingly, the political pressure to enlarge the system, or to oppose any reduction in it, will be most intense among older age groups.

It should be clear that an unfunded social security system is very attractive politically in large part because of the benefits it promises for older persons. This remains true even if the long-run return of 3 percent received by younger workers and subsequent generations is exceedingly low relative to alternative investments.

Because the return for younger persons is so low, it would seem likely that they would reject the system when they become older. It is important to understand why they do not. If the tax rate financing the program remains 10 percent, a young person when retired will receive benefits representing a 3 percent return. This is an average return over his entire lifetime. Once retired, however, he will be better off if the system is then expanded and worse off it if is contracted. Similarly, a young person who pays taxes of 10 percent until he reaches age fifty-five will find that, if the tax rate is increased at that time (so that he pays the higher rate only ten years), the marginal return on the additional taxes is 30 percent. Both starting up and continuing the system are always attractive (in the relevant *marginal* sense) to older persons; thus, there is no reason to suppose that political support for the system will decrease over time.[12]

---

[12] For a more detailed discussion of how social security taxes and transfers are determined in a majority voting model, see Edgar K. Browning, "Why the Social Insurance Budget Is Too Large in a Democracy," *Economic Inquiry*, vol. 13 (September 1975), pp. 373–88.

For this reason, society may find itself politically locked into an unfunded social security system. Even if every young person today and all future generations would be better off providing for retirement in some other way, political support from the older members of the population may perpetuate the system.

The objection may be raised that this analysis assumes an unreasonable degree of knowledge on the part of the public. Certainly, many persons do not know that the current social security system is pay-as-you-go, nor do they make careful calculations of the marginal return that can be achieved by changing the scale of the system. Some persons may even make political judgments on grounds that have nothing to do with how the system affects them personally. The relatively elderly, however, are staunch supporters of the system—probably because they recognize, perhaps imprecisely, that such support is in their self-interest. After all, a retired person, or a person near retirement, does not need sophisticated understanding to realize that it is in his interest to have Congress vote higher social security benefits. That source of political pressure is a potent force shaping the development of the system.

Public Misunderstanding. Democratic government is, to at least some degree, responsive to the wishes of its citizens. But it cannot be presumed that the policies supported by the public are actually beneficial. People may support a policy that they believe is in their interest when in fact it is not. What counts in determining political support is people's perceptions of a policy's effects, not its true effects. If people generally underestimate the true costs of a policy, or overestimate its benefits, then political demands may lead politicians to enact policies that are harmful.

The fact that some people misunderstand the effects of a policy does not necessarily have any effect on the political outcome. Misconceptions may be mutually offsetting; some persons favor a policy that actually harms them, whereas others oppose the same policy not realizing that it benefits them. When this is so, political pressures emanating from a misinformed public may be the same as they would be if the public were fully informed. The relevant question is whether there is a systematic bias in the perceptions of the public in one direction or another. In the case of social security, I believe there is such a systematic bias that leads the public to favor a larger system than they would if they understood its true consequences. This is obviously a highly speculative issue; nevertheless, three important sources of public misunderstanding can be cited as the basis for this belief.

197

First, younger persons may overestimate the return they can expect on their taxes by basing their expectations on the experiences of early retirees. As pointed out earlier, people who are older when the system begins, or is expanded in scale, get a relatively good deal. And this start-up phenomenon extends over a long period of time. Because of the way the system has developed, with a gradually increasing effective rate of taxation, persons retiring today and perhaps even for the next twenty years can expect a rate of return greater than the rate of economic growth. For example, retirees in 1970 received annuities that represented an average return of 10.6 percent on the taxes they had paid.[13] Those retiring in earlier years did even better, while those retiring later will probably do worse. Eventually, the rate of return must fall until it equals the rate of economic growth.

The important point is that the favorable experiences of those retiring in the 1950s, 1960s, and 1970s greatly overstate what younger workers can expect to receive. But younger workers may base their views of social security partly on how well their parents and grandparents have fared under the system. If so, they will support the system more enthusiastically than the facts warrant.

This particular source of misunderstanding, in contrast to the two considered below, is a temporary phenomenon. Over time, the rate of return realized by retirees will continue to decline; thus, if expectations are based on the experience of actual retirees, they will eventually have a more realistic foundation.

Second, the public probably underestimates the tax burden it bears in financing social security benefits. The social security payroll tax comprises two equal rate levies on taxable earnings—one paid by the employee, the other by the employer. This splitting of the tax into two portions is irrelevant in terms of the true burden of the tax: the employee bears the entire tax, regardless of how it is nominally divided between him and his employer. It is not irrelevant, however, in terms of voters' perceptions of the tax cost they bear. The employee tax is visible; it shows up as an explicit deduction from a worker's earnings. The employer tax, by contrast, is a hidden tax. Workers may be entirely unaware of this tax. Even if they are aware of it, the fact that it is labeled an employer tax or "contribution" is likely to induce them to believe that "business" bears the burden of the tax. In either case,

---

[13] Alan Freiden, Dean R. Leimer, and Ronald Hoffman, "Internal Rates of Return to Retired Worker-Only Beneficiaries under Social Security, 1967–70," *Studies in Income Distribution No. 5*, Social Security Administration, Office of Research and Statistics (October 1976).

taxpayers will be aware of only half the true burden they bear. Consequently, taxpayers will consider social security less costly than it really is and will favor a larger system than they would if they were fully aware of the full cost.

Third, the public generally underestimates the opportunity cost of providing for their retirement through an unfunded system. The opportunity cost is the sacrificed return that would be available from investing social security taxes in real capital. Although the relevant return from the point of view of society is the before-tax yield, individuals are certain to consider only the much lower net return they can individually realize on their private saving. Because of the heavy taxation of capital income in the United States, the net yield most investors can realize is fully 60 percent below the gross yield. Individual savers are most unlikely to obtain a net real return above 3 or 4 percent, even though the before-tax return is in the neighborhood of 10 percent.

The rate of return from an unfunded social security system is far below the return available from real capital investment, but it is comparable to the after-tax return on private saving. Since the after-tax rate of return is what guides voters' decisions, they will be misled into viewing social security as a reasonably attractive way of providing for their retirement.

These three types of misinformation form the basis of my contention that the public generally believes that the consequences of the social security system are more beneficial than is actually the case. Little direct evidence can be offered showing that these factors play a role in influencing voters' opinions. The Social Security Administration, however, does little to dispel these sources of misunderstanding. On the contrary, the agency's publications perpetuate a view of social security that bears little resemblance to the facts.[14] This is fully in accord with public choice theory, which emphasizes that bureaucrats have incentive to inform the public and the Congress of the advantages of their programs but not the disadvantages.

Many other misconceptions about social security may distort the public's attitudes toward the system, and some of them may work to offset the three factors mentioned above. For example, recent articles in the popular press have emphasized the dwindling trust funds and warned of possible bankruptcy. It is doubtful that the uneasiness en-

---

[14] Milton Friedman has frequently criticized the misleading "advertising" of the Social Security Administration. See, for example, his "Second Lecture" in Wilbur J. Cohen and Milton Friedman, *Social Security: Universal or Selective?* (Washington, D.C.: American Enterprise Institute, 1972).

gendered by such treatments leads many people to believe that social security is worse than it really is, but the possibility must be acknowledged.[15]

Summary. Two sources of political bias have been considered. The first stems from the short-run, or start-up, effects of changing the scale of the system, and this bias would exist even if the public were fully informed. The second results from the public's misconceptions about the consequences of social security. Taken together, they provide an explanation of the political appeal of an unfunded social security system. Although the discussion has been in the context of the present system, the political forces identified can also be used to evaluate prospects for reform.

Major Reform Proposals

Most discussions of social security reform address the question of what *should* be done. Equally important is the question of what *can* be done through our political process. A proposed reform may seem quite attractive to a disinterested observer, but it may be unable to command the political support necessary for enactment. Politics does limit the reform that can realistically be expected. As an illustration, the political prospects of three rather far-reaching reform proposals will be considered: the Feldstein proposal, the Friedman proposal, and the Hsaio proposal.[16]

Feldstein proposes that the government build up a substantial fund and use the interest return to pay retirement benefits. The intention is to move from an unfunded system to a funded one in order to realize the higher real rate of return on the latter. Social security taxes would be increased now, but the additional revenues would not be used to increase retirement benefits; they would be used to build up a fund. Later, after a sizable fund is accumulated, taxes could be lowered.

Friedman proposes a gradual phasing-out of the social security system. Eventually, there would be no governmental program of retire-

---

[15] For an example of one treatment that appears to portray social security as worse than it is, see Abraham Ellis, *The Social Security Fraud* (New Rochelle, N.Y.: Arlington House, 1971).

[16] Martin S. Feldstein, "Toward a Reform of Social Security," *The Public Interest*, no. 40 (Summer 1975), pp. 75–95; Milton Friedman, "Second Lecture"; U.S. Congress, *Report of the Consultant Panel on Social Security to the Congressional Research Service, Prepared for the Use of the Committee on Finance of the U.S. Senate and the Committee on Ways and Means of the U.S. House of Representatives*, 94th Congress, 2nd session, August 1976.

ment benefits, and providing for retirement would again become a matter of individual responsibility. The transition to this ultimate outcome would be gradual because benefits already accumulated—based on taxes paid before the reform is adopted—would continue to be paid, but taxes paid after the program is adopted would not entitle one to any additional retirement benefits.

The proposal by William Hsaio recommends a gradual reduction in the replacement rates (the level of retirement benefits relative to the pre-retirement earnings of workers). This is quite similar to the Friedman proposal, but the reduction in average replacement rates would be slower. In addition, the social security system would never be phased out entirely; retirement benefits would simply become smaller and smaller relative to pre-retirement earnings.

Although it is seldom recognized, these three proposals are quite similar in terms of their general economic effects. All three produce a decreased reliance on unfunded social security and an increased reliance on a capital fund as a method of providing retirement income. Under Feldstein's proposal, the capital fund would be owned and administered by the government. Under the Friedman and Hsaio proposals, individuals would accumulate their own capital funds to substitute for the relative decrease in future social security benefits. Although the three proposals differ in many respects, this basic similarity raises the fundamental question of whether the political system will accept a movement away from the current unfunded approach. In view of the political support for an unfunded system, the prospects appear to be quite dim.

Consider the Feldstein proposal. An increase in social security taxes to finance a fund will clearly harm middle-aged and older workers. They will pay higher taxes for a period of years but will receive no increase in retirement benefits. Older workers and retirees would be better off if the higher taxes were used to pay greater current benefits on a pay-as-you-go basis: recall that even middle-aged persons can receive a marginal return of 10 percent from an unfunded expansion in the system, and older persons do even better. Even if the government began to build up a fund, however, the political pressures for converting it to a pay-as-you-go basis would be intense. (In its early years the social security system did begin to build up a fund, but it was quickly converted to an unfunded system.) The only opposition to this pressure is the interests of young workers and future generations, who do not vote. Moreover, it would be difficult to convince the public that the real yield (before-tax return) from a fund is high when the nominal yield (after-tax return) on the assets in the fund is so small. (The assets in the fund would yield only the after-tax rate of return, even though it is the before-tax return that is socially relevant.)

Exactly similar considerations hold true for the Friedman and Hsaio proposals. For example, under the Friedman proposal, middle-aged and older workers would continue to pay social security taxes for the remainder of their working lives at a rate almost as high as it would be if the unfunded system were to be continued. (Recall that already accumulated benefits must continue to be paid so the necessary tax rate would decline very slowly at first.) Yet these taxes are not linked to any retirement benefits: in effect, the rate of return on these taxes would be negative. By contrast, the marginal return on approximately the same tax payments would be very high if the unfunded system is continued. Undoubtedly, sacrificing the marginal return of an unfunded system would be strongly opposed by the retired and those approaching retirement. Only the young and future generations stand to gain, and the benefits will be hard for them to perceive because of the low net return they can receive on their saving.

These brief remarks cannot do justice to the complexity of the three proposals; they do, however, suggest some of the political difficulties the proposals must confront. The political support for an un-funded system is strongest among older members of the population, and it is precisely this group that is threatened by such proposals. Only if the political system undergoes a complete reversal, so that it caters to the interests of the young rather than the elderly, would these proposals appear likely to be enacted.

One other important factor in evaluating the need for, and the prospects of, reform is the expected demographic change in the population. Unless fertility rates make an unexpectedly sharp rise in the next few years, the retirement in the early twenty-first century of members of the postwar baby boom will produce a dramatic shift in the age distribution of the population. Today there are three workers for each retired person, but in the year 2030 there may possibly be only two workers per retiree. This means that, if tax rates remain unchanged, replacement rates for retirees will fall sharply. Alternatively, to keep average replacement rates at their current level, tax rates in the first part of the next century must be increased by more than 50 percent. Within the context of an unfunded system, either tax rates must rise sharply or relative levels of benefits will fall; there is no other option. Since both of these options appear unpleasant, some attention has focused on reform proposals that represent departures from an unfunded system.

The repercussions of the changing age distribution of the population can also be described in the context of the rate of growth of national income. The growth rate is the sum of the rates of growth in income per worker and in the number of workers. According to some projections, the absolute number of workers may fall by 20 percent between 2010 and 2040; hence, the growth rate of the economy is likely to be extremely low compared with the present, when a growing labor force makes a positive contribution to the growth rate. A lower growth rate means a lower rate of return under an unfunded social security system; thus, a constant tax rate will produce relatively lower levels of retirement benefits.

The projected change in the age distribution of the population has important implications for the political determination of social security policy, and hence for the type of reform likely to occur. An unfunded system is more attractive the older one is. Thus, the larger the fraction of the population that is relatively old, the more irresistible will be the political pressure for continuing or enlarging an unfunded system. To put this in perspective, 15 percent of the voting-age population is now over sixty-five, and the median age of potential voters is forty-one. (The actual political strength of older persons may be greater than suggested by their numbers because a larger percentage of older persons actually vote.) According to one pessimistic, but not totally unrealistic, projection (assuming a fertility rate of only 1.7), 26 percent of the adult population will be over sixty-five in 2040, and the median age will then be fifty.[17] By 2040, the older half of the population will be nearing retirement age or actually retired, and it will be in their interest to support a large unfunded system.[18]

In comparison to the future, the current U.S. population is relatively young. Restructuring the social security system in a fundamental way is politically more feasible now than it will be later. One argument for moving toward a funded system is based on the equity implications of the expected change in the age distribution. As Feldstein states:

> There is some glimmer of hope in the argument claiming it is
> unfair for us to expect the next generation to pay a 20 percent
> tax to support the same level of benefits we are supporting
> with a 10 percent tax. It [a fund] might be politically salable

---

[17] Calculated from data in U.S. Bureau of the Census, "Population Estimates and Projections," *Current Population Reports*, ser. P-25, no. 601, table 12. If the fertility rate rises to 2.1, 21 percent of the population will be over sixty-five and the median age will be forty-seven in 2040.

[18] One possible offset to the political pressure from the elderly is that there may be increased opposition from the young because of the slowdown in the rate of economic growth.

because people might think they were protecting their own or their children's future benefits with such a fund.[19]

It is unlikely that such an argument would affect voting behavior to any noticeable degree, even if the public could understand the issues well enough to appreciate it. In effect, it calls for present workers to bear a large sacrifice in the interest of an abstract and unfamiliar principle of equity. Not only would such action conflict with their self-interest, but even on grounds of equity it can be asked why present workers should sacrifice to help future workers who will be wealthier than they are—even if the future workers do pay higher tax rates.

Even in the unlikely event that the government does act to decrease reliance on an unfunded system in the near future, that policy will not be binding on the population in the twenty-first century. If a fund is accumulated in the near future, it would probably be dissipated and the system converted back to an unfunded basis on an even larger scale when the age distribution changes in the next century. Although the prospect is not appealing, government policy in the next century will reflect political pressures at that time, and little can be done now to change that fact.

Reform Proposals from a Public Choice Perspective

Public choice theory offers a completely different approach to policy reform. Instead of attempting to specify a detailed blueprint for reform and throwing it into the political arena, attention is concentrated on improving the institutions and procedures through which political decisions are made. With the public choice approach, for example, no attempt is made to identify the "ideal" level of benefits and taxes. What is sought is a method of political decision making and policy administration that will tend to produce acceptable results. Since what constitutes "acceptable" or "ideal" results presumably depends on the needs and values of the public, and we do not know those needs and values, what is required is a political mechanism that can be counted on to cater to the public's preferences, whatever they may be. Different political institutions may be appropriate for different types of policies, and there is no reason to suppose that the present method of determining social security policy is the best method.

This public choice approach can be applied to social security reform. Two general sources of political bias in present institutions have been identified: public misunderstanding and the incentive of the

---

[19] *Income Redistribution*, ed. Campbell, p. 119.

elderly to favor a large unfunded system. There are institutional changes that would diminish these sources of bias. Public misunderstanding might be reduced in three ways.

First, each individual's taxes could be more explicitly linked to his retirement benefits. Each year the Social Security Administration could send each taxpayer an annual statement reporting the implicit wealth he is accumulating. The statement would report current tax payments as well as accumulated wealth based on past taxes plus an interest rate equal to the average growth rate of the economy. Such a statement would closely parallel those provided by many private pension systems. Taxpayers would then be in a position to perceive more easily the actual return they are likely to receive from an ongoing system of pay-as-you-go social insurance. (The content of the annual statements should obviously not be left up to the discretion of the Social Security Administration.)

Second, the employer portion of the social security tax could be eliminated, with the employee required to pay the entire tax. This would not change the actual tax burden of taxpayers, but it would clarify how large the burden is. (To ensure no change in the total tax liabilities, it would be necessary to reduce income tax rates or to allow employees to deduct half of their social security tax from their income tax.)

Third, the taxation of income from capital could be greatly reduced or eliminated. This would increase the net return individuals could realize from providing for retirement privately, and it would thereby increase awareness of the true opportunity cost of an unfunded system.

If enacted, these proposals would not directly change the operation of the social security system.[20] Their purpose is not to prescribe how the system should be changed, but to create a framework in which the public can more easily grasp the benefits they receive and the costs they bear. If voters' perceptions are modified, then social security policy will be indirectly affected through a change in political pressures. Whatever the ultimate outcome, it should be welcomed as reflecting more fully the public's true interests.

None of these proposals would remove the second source of political bias in the present system. Even if the system is fully understood, older persons stand to gain from expanding the system, even though that may

---

[20] The first proposal would perhaps make it more difficult to use the system as a redistributive mechanism by giving the poor higher rates of return. Even this would not have to occur, but the redistribution would have to become more open than it now is.

not be in the long-run interests of the young and future generations. Political pressure from the elderly to expand the system cannot be avoided. The political procedures used to determine social security policy can, however, be modified so that greater weight is given to long-run considerations. Among those currently voting, only the relatively young have a strong personal stake in taking account of long-run effects; thus, the political decision process should reflect more strongly the lifetime interests of those who will pay taxes over a long period as well as receive benefits in retirement.

There are numerous procedures for making political decisions that would modify the system in this general direction. Two ways in which this could be done can be briefly mentioned. First, the level of social security taxes (and, hence, benefits in an unfunded system) could be decided by majority vote in an annual referendum in which only those below a certain age—say, forty or fifty—are permitted to vote. Alternatively, a voting procedure in which three-fourths of the entire voting population must approve of the level of taxes for the policy to be enacted could be used. Both of these procedures would have the effect of reducing the political impact of the desire of the elderly to expand the system.

Changes of this sort in the political decision-making process deserve more serious attention than they are likely to receive. The basic dilemma is that the existing, highly imperfect, political process must be relied on to reform this process. Although institutional changes that would provide a better framework for political decision making do exist, Congress is likely to feel little political pressure to enact them.

Conclusion

Economists are not known for the accuracy of their political predictions. It may be that the conclusions drawn from the present analysis will prove to be as erroneous as the widespread opinions of a few years ago holding that a volunteer army and flexible exchange rates were politically impossible. Unquestionably, the analytical model underlying this analysis is a simple one, and the political system is far more complex in its operations than suggested here. The important question is whether the factors that have been stressed do have an important impact in shaping the social security system. I strongly suspect that they do, but it is difficult to be completely certain.

If the analysis is basically correct, it supports the prediction that there will be no major changes in the social security system at least until the next century. Prospects for meaningful reform now are not very great, and they will be even poorer in the future. Since the population will probably become much older in the first half of the twenty-first century, political pressures at that time will generally favor a substantially larger system. Young workers at that time, however, faced with higher taxes and a lower expected rate of return, are likely to oppose the system more openly. A highly divisive political situation seems likely.

Commentaries

James M. Buchanan

My assignment is to discuss Edgar Browning's paper. Since I find little in the paper with which to disagree, I shall take one paragraph of the paper as the point of departure for extended remarks. Browning states:

> Society may find itself politically locked into an unfunded social security system. Even if every young person today and all future generations would be better off providing for retirement in some other way, political support from the older members of the population may perpetuate the system.

Such a statement pricks my Wicksellian proclivities and prompts me to search for ways to shift from the unfunded, pay-as-you-go system to a funded system (whether publicly or privately organized) in a way that will make everyone better off, as evidenced by their conceptual agreement on the change.

Browning does not say precisely that the unfunded system is Pareto-inferior to a funded system, but we can get that general impression from his paper, and certainly this assessment seems to be widely shared. If the existing system is Pareto-inferior, however, there must exist institutional ways and means of reforming the structure so as to secure general agreement on the changes. But does there exist a set of side payments or compensations that could be used to "buy off" or "bribe" the oldsters who are the net claimants on the current system and secure their agreement on the shift toward funding?

If such a Wicksellian reform is not possible, the existing pay-as-you-go system is Pareto-optimal, even in some intergenerational sense. If we classify the pay-as-you-go system as Pareto-optimal, we need not classify an alternative funded system as nonoptimal. A funded system may also be Pareto-optimal, but neither system may dominate the other in some Pareto sense.

After several runs at this comment, and after initial discussions with colleagues, I reached the somewhat pessimistic conclusion that we could not get there from here, that the existing system, warts and all,

I am indebted to my colleagues Lytton Stoddard, Robert Tollison, Gordon Tullock, and Richard Wagner for helpful comments at various stages.

s probably Pareto-optimal. But I had overlooked one central feature of a transfer system, a feature that allows me to conclude now that the system is nonoptimal. This implies that Pareto-superior changes can, at least conceptually, be suggested that would make everyone—both those in current and those in future time periods—better off under a funded system. As I shall demonstrate, however, the Pareto-superiority emerges in a manner that is not at all obvious, at least it was not to me.

Consider a simple numerical example. There is a stable population of three persons, of whom two are working and one is retired. Each person works for two successive time periods and retires for a third period. Suppose that a pay-as-you-go system is in effect, based on the presumption of a zero rate of return. The system is in a steady-state equilibrium as shown below:

	Worker, First Period	Worker, Second Period	Retiree
Earnings before tax and transfer	$100	$100	$ 0
Tax-transfer	25	25	50
Income available after tax and transfer	75	75	50

Each worker expects to get back during retirement exactly the number of dollars that he pays in taxes during his working periods. Let us further assume that the ratio of $75 to $50 is what is desired in terms of life-cycle optimizing by the persons in the model, all of whom are identical.

Assume that a 10 percent rate of return on real investment in the economy is available, and that an issue is raised about terminating the pay-as-you-go retirement system. The first step is to compute the net liability of the system. The person entering retirement holds a net claim of $50 against the system. The person entering the second of his two working periods has paid $25 during the first period. At a zero system rate of return, his net claim amounts to $25. Hence, the net liability of the system is $75. How can this liability be paid off?

We can consider the possible issue of consols (government bonds) in the amount of $75. These will require a service charge of $7.50. How can this service charge be financed? The second-period worker, to whom the $25 claim is paid, has $50 available for investment which represents his net claim's value plus the value of tax during the second period. He can, therefore, pay up to $5.00 in tax toward the debt service without being made worse off. The new entrant can pay a tax of up to $2.50, since he is relieved of a tax of $25. A total of $7.50 can be collected. No further resort to debt issue is necessary and the new regime settles down into a new steady state.

The set of changes suggested transforms the unfunded system into a funded system in such a way that no one is made worse off. But where are the gains? Those who must pay taxes to service the consols are no better off than they would have been by remaining under the unfunded scheme. Those who retire are equally well off under both systems. The shift is strictly Pareto-neutral.

This result should not be surprising. Once it is accepted that any pay-as-you-go system involves a net liability that is permanent, the opportunity cost of carrying this item in the economy's balance sheet should be recognized as the real rate of return on investment. The institutional changes only shift the form of the liability. It should be evident that no one is made better off, because there is no change in the net worth of persons in the economy intergenerationally. In order for members of the present generation to be made better off, the net liability of the system would have to be increased. In order for members of the future generations to be made better off, the net liability of the system would have to be reduced. As between generations, the game is zero-sum. There are no Pareto-superior changes that can be made.

There would be no argument for making a Pareto-neutral shift, as would be involved in a shift toward a funded system in the numerical example. But the steady-state equilibrium postulated is very important in this respect. If the existing system has not attained such an equilibrium and, furthermore, could not be expected to attain such an equilibrium, then the whole question of Pareto-optimality must be re-examined. The Pareto-neutrality results emerge only because it was assumed that the implicit rate of return on "retirement investment" under the pay-as-you-go system is zero. Under the assumptions of the example, if any positive rate is introduced, steady-state equilibrium can never be attained. The net liability of the transfer system must increase continually through time.

So long as the rate of return paid on retirement investment under the transfer system is below that on real capital investment in the economy, some scheme can be worked out that will make a shift to the funded system seem to be Pareto-neutral in the sense illustrated in the numerical example. That is to say, under a funded system, persons in every generation can be provided with a measured flow of payments, net of debt-service taxes and claims against the transfer system, that will be equivalent to those expected under the transfer system. The transfer system that incorporates some positive rate of return on retirement investment differs from the zero-rate system, however, in that the prospective entrants are pushed further and further from their optimal life-cycle financial plans as the system continues.

In the example above, it was assumed that the ratio of $75 to $50 is optimal. If a 10 percent rate of return is paid on retirement investment in a transfer system, using the same starting numbers as in the example, after only six time periods workers will have available net incomes of only $61 whereas retired persons will have available incomes of $78; clearly, there will be a substantial distortion from their optimal life-cycle plans. Faced with this increasing distortion through time, future period entrants would be willing to reduce measured income flows over their own lifetimes in exchange for movement toward their desired multiperiod plans. The precise arrangements that might be worked out here will, of course, depend on the form of the utility functions, the actual rate of return paid on investments in the transfer system, the length of time the system has been in operation, and other factors. But a set of changes can be worked out that will allow all persons to be made better off under the funded system than under the transfer system. This conclusion holds even if the rate of return paid on retirement investment is equal to or even exceeds the rate that is available on real capital investment.

In this analysis, I have ignored the possible effects of real growth in the economy, over and beyond what is attributable to real capital investment. To the extent that the size of the labor force increases through time or the productivity per man-hour increases, the distortion in life-cycle plans produced by the ever-increasing nominal liability of an unfunded retirement system is mitigated. So long as the real rate of return on investment exceeds such real growth, however, the essential conclusions of my argument seem to follow without change.

In a practical sense, the analysis suggests that refinancing the net liability of the existing transfer system by the issue of long-term debt may be Pareto-superior, even if equity demands that service charges on this debt be met by further issues of debt for an extended sequence of periods in the future. To make an attempt to issue debt in the amounts that would be required to refinance the whole of the net liability of the U.S. system in 1978 would, of course, disturb capital markets everywhere. But this difficulty is no argument against moving gradually toward the solution indicated. It should be possible to fund increasing portions of the system in ways that would secure the political support of all net claimants, while shifting tax costs far enough into the future so as to be reasonably well assured that those who must pay will in fact find themselves better off than they would be if the current system either continues on its present course or collapses completely.

The implication of my argument for short-run policy is that tax rates should not be increased and that emerging deficits in the system should be covered by explicit issue of social security debt, preferably consols. This policy has the effect of paying off net current claimants with tax charges levied on future-period workers; to the extent that tax increases on current-period workers are avoided, however, their subsequent claims against the system are reduced. In my scenario, future-period workers will have available a real rate of return on investment from which to pay off the explicit system debt. By contrast, an increase in current tax rates, with the correlate increase in future claims, will place obligations on future-period taxpayers without, at the same time, providing them with any real investment yields from which such obligations might be met.

J. W. Van Gorkom

I, too, found a lot to agree with in the papers that were presented. Since I am a businessman and not an economist, I am not able to criticize them from a technical point of view. Nevertheless, I do have some comments to make.

First, Edgar Browning states that there is really no need for a forced savings plan to make people save for their old age. Others have made the same point, and I think it is time to put that idea completely to rest; in my opinion, it has absolutely no validity. I do not even like to see the point presented to the public, because it is a concept that some people would embrace in order to do away with the system.

Browning estimates that only 10 percent of the people would not save enough money for their retirement, and of that 10 percent only 15 percent would be unable to work at age sixty-five. He therefore concludes that only 1.5 percent of the people would have to be supported by the state if we did not make them save by paying social security taxes. He cites no source for the 10 percent figure, which I think is very low when viewed in the light of the known data. In 1975, 12 percent of all families had annual incomes less than $5,000 and more than 20 percent had incomes less than $7,000. Families in these income brackets cannot be expected to save money voluntarily—not because they are wastrels, but because any saving would be at the expense of basic necessities. In addition, there are people with incomes greater than $7,000 who, because of illness or the size of their families or other factors, cannot be relied on to save for their later years. From my experience as a member of the board of directors of a bank, I have learned that there are people with incomes of $30,000 and more who do not save any money and are constantly in debt. Thus, I believe that at least 20 percent of the people would not save for their retirement if the social security system did not force them to do so, and the number is probably closer to 30 percent.

I object even more strongly to Browning's statement that, of those who would not save, only 15 percent would not be able to work after age sixty-five; that overlooks two basic facts. First, it is not merely a question of whether a person is able to work after sixty-five but whether he can obtain a job after that age, or even before it. Most employers are very wary of hiring older people, and they will be more so under the proposed law that prevents terminating employees before age seventy solely because of age. Second, even if some persons do find jobs after sixty-five, everyone eventually reaches a point at which he can no longer work. The problem may be deferred, but it must be faced eventually.

Browning does make a persuasive case that the social security system should be funded. Others have made the same point. They all seem to agree that the implicit rate of return on an unfunded system is less than the rate on real capital that society would earn if the money were not put into an unfunded system. No matter how valid these arguments may be, however, the general public will never understand them; the arguments are simply too technical to be understood by more than a handful of experts.

Even if it would be desirable to have the system funded, and I take no position on that, the opportunity to create a funded social security system was lost forty years ago when the system was first begun. Given the political system in the United States, we will never have another opportunity to fund the system. In fact, I strongly believe that, if we had stuck to the original concept of a funded system and had accumulated a substantial amount of money by the late 1940s or early 1950s, we would have found reasons to dip into it and eventually would have reduced it to its present inconsequential level.

I agree fully with June O'Neill that, if we do attempt to shift from an unfunded system to a funded one, some people are going to have to pay a double tax and, in view of the tax rates involved, such a proposal would be totally unacceptable to the majority of the people. Browning has pointed out why the elderly would resist any shift to a funded system, but I think that the young would be just as vigorous in their opposition because of the double tax burden required.

James Buchanan has an innovative idea, and I am not sure that I

213

completely understand it. It is based on the concept of selling consols. It assumes that the rate of return on the consols would be the same as the rate of return that would be earned on the fund. That certainly does not follow automatically, because a consol is a type of security that has never been sold in this country.

Browning refers to reform proposals by Martin Feldstein, Milton Friedman, and William Hsaio. He seems to equate the three proposals, but I find the Hsaio proposal considerably different in one important element. Hsaio would move from wage indexing to price indexing and I endorse that concept. Although I do not expect it to be adopted soon, I think it has an excellent chance of being adopted sometime within the next twenty years, if the general financial forecasts for the system prove to be accurate. The cost of the system may simply become higher than society wants to accept under the wage-indexing approach. Under the assumptions of the trustees of the trust funds, wage indexing constantly increases the real income of successive retirees. But that goes beyond the basic function of the system, which is to provide everyone with an acceptable minimum standard of living. I believe that Hsaio's price-indexing proposal can serve as a real and lasting solution to the finance problems of social security without changing the basic structure of the system.

O'Neill spoke briefly of the regressivity of the payroll tax. I am amazed that the public has been brainwashed into thinking that the social security system is completely regressive. This charge is constantly made in the media and is never refuted. The tax itself is regressive, but the benefits are very progressive. For example, the lowest-paid person receives roughly twice as much insurance for his tax dollar as does the highly paid individual. I cannot say whether the system is too progressive or not progressive enough. I would emphasize, however, that the system in total is definitely progressive, and this needs to be repeated again and again to counteract the myth that has been created about the regressivity of the system.

O'Neill also mentioned using general revenues to pay part of the cost of social security. In my opinion, this would destroy the system as we know it. Although the use of such funds might be modest to begin with, experience tells us that the temptation to use more of these funds would be overwhelming to a popularly elected Congress, and we would eventually reduce social security to another form of welfare.

A person's attitude toward financing from general revenues is a reflection of his basic philosophy on social security. Some people apparently believe that social security is supposed to do the entire job of income replacement after retirement or disability. But this was never the intention. It was always intended that the income replacement scheme would include three elements. The first would be private saving, including private pensions. The second would be social security, which is an enforced savings system. Since the underlying principle of the system is that the beneficiaries will pay for the benefits, social security could never do the entire job because there will always be some people who do not earn enough to cover an adequate level of benefits and who have no private saving. For these people, there must be the third element, which is a needs-tested program such as Supplemental Security Income (SSI). This last element is properly funded by general revenues. With the existence of such programs, however, there is no need to put general revenues in social security.

I would like to see the SSI program expanded to the point at which it could take over all of the social welfare aspects of the social security system, so that we could eliminate the tilted scale of benefits, the minimum benefit, and even the nonworking-wife's benefit. This last aspect of the system creates an apparent inequity for the working wife, who is treated unfairly only in relation to the nonworking wife who is treated so generously.

Alan N. Freiden

The papers at this session take very different yet complementary approaches to the two basic questions of long-run social security finance. These problems are, first, the magnitude of the share of real output that may be required to support the future elderly population and, second, the appropriate mechanisms for providing this support. June O'Neill deals with the positive economic analysis of the long-run burden of social security and alternative financing proposals. Edgar Browning is concerned with the extent to which the process for forming a political consensus is likely to impede both the attainment of maximum possible output and the satisfaction of normatively defined social security criteria.

Three elements in both analyses should be made explicit. First, the authors are concerned with the old-age part of the social security program. Although this is conventionally recognized as a pension component, the actual package of benefits is much broader. Second, any pension scheme that is not fully funded in real capital may be scrutinized within the framework presented here. State and local governments, for example, may be accumulating a significant total unfunded liability. Finally, neither author explicitly recognizes the importance of the redistributive character of the system. An analysis of the actual experience of recent retirees has shown that people with relatively low covered earnings receive better treatment.[1] Some of the workers with low covered earnings have had high incomes, which imply high rates of return. Apparent inequities of this sort are not a consequence of the income replacement motive and should be logically separated from problems arising in a quid pro quo system.

O'Neill begins with a description of the magnitude of the implicit burden of social security in the distant future. She correctly identifies the importance of demographic change in determining internal rates of return to future retirees. She also hints at the sensitivity of all long-run calculations to the specific assumptions used. We are dealing with growth rates in factors—for example, labor productivity—in which a quarter of a percentage point makes a big difference. We are also making guesses about linkages, such as the relation between declines in desired family size and desired human capital per child, with little empirical foundation. It is hoped that basic research of these questions will improve over time.

But the financing problem is surely real, and thus alternatives need to be considered. O'Neill considers three. First is the accumulation of a trust fund large enough to pay future benefits out of interest. This makes sense only if the fund represents real capital, and I think she is correct in pointing out the political difficulties implicit in such a system. Our experience with the highway trust fund indicates that no accumulation is immune to dynamic social preferences. Her analysis of proposals to increase the importance of private savings is somewhat flawed because she confounds redistributional motives with pension motives. If we could isolate the pension component, opposition to proposals for expanding the share of private saving in mandatory pension schemes would be difficult. Finally, there is one small problem with her analysis of using earmarked income taxes as a form of general revenue finance. Under this scheme, the income to private pension saving would in effect be taxed twice, lowering its rate of return. It should also be noted that at present the highest effective rates of social security taxation as a share of family income are borne by the middle class, increases in this burden have been most rapid for the middle class, and these same people appear to be the target of a precipitous increase in general tax liability if pending tax reform legislation is approved.

Kenneth Boulding has defined "economics imperialism" as an attempt on the part of economics to take over all the other social sciences.

---

[1] Alan Freiden, Dean R. Leimer, and Ronald Hoffman, "Internal Rates of Return to Retired Worker-Only Beneficiaries under Social Security, 1967–70," *Studies in Income Distribution, No. 5*, Social Security Administration, Office of Research and Statistics (October 1976).

Public choice theory looks like an attempt to move into political science, and Browning's paper indicates how fruitful this may be. Economists are also moving into other disciplines, however, and it may be that the most useful analysis of social security or the more broadly defined area called social insurance may be in the area Gary Becker calls "social interactions."

Browning alludes to the importance of looking at a motivation for redistribution that arises not from individual self-interest but from interdependence with the following double negative: "The least implausible reason why an unfunded system might not depress private saving is that it may substitute for voluntary intergenerational transfers among family members." This notion may be extended. Suppose people under age forty find it advantageous to impose taxes on all of society in order to make their own relatives better off. This is little different from the more direct self-interest underlying Browning's analysis, but it may lead to different conclusions. In particular, these people under forty may seek to support the elderly because they feel the elderly deserve it. They may also broaden the definition of the program to include survivors and disability insurance. Survivors insurance obviously benefits younger workers, and if the system as a whole constitutes an implicit political tie-in sale, younger workers and older workers have bargained to arrive at a mutually advantageous solution.

The scientific issue is that no one has found a consistent set of axiomatic preferences from which we can deduce a political construct resembling the current social security system. Since I am not up to this task, and since the role of discussant is to criticize, I will concentrate on a few points of Browning's paper.

First, I think it highly unlikely that his figure of 1.5 percent for the proportion of the elderly both unable to work and without resources is correct. That ill-health and diminished assets are correlated seems the rule rather than the exception. Therefore, I do not think it is productive to deny that there may be a substantial population who would be in genuine economic distress without some form of support.

Second, in attacking the pay-as-you-go nature of finance, Browning says that the arguments for pay-as-you-go strongly argue for government regulation of other aspects of our lives: "On exactly the same grounds, one could argue that government should choose the food people eat; force them to exercise; select their jobs." Only one lacking true faith in public choice theory would deny that the coercive power of the state, through Federal Drug Administration regulation and differential taxes and subsidies, does influence these other choices.

Third, Browning points out the implication of aging for the political process. In particular, he notes that, as the median voter grows older, strong pressures to expand social security are likely. Consider, however, another effect. As population growth slows, the implicit return to social security taxes should decline as well. Therefore, to reestablish balance in a portfolio of public and private assets, the *marginal* voter, who is just indifferent to expansion and contraction, should favor contraction. The comparative statistics are ambiguous.

Now, I will look at Browning's proposals for reform. First, he may get a report of his earnings and quarters of coverage at any social security office. He may then make his own calculation of accumulated wealth. Second, simply tell everyone they are really paying twice the taxes they see in their checks. Economists have been trying to get this across for thirty years, but we may have more success this time. Third, Browning would like to see an increase in the return to private saving. I am hard pressed to find an objection to that. Finally, we should hold a referendum on social security finance open to those under age forty. I support this—at least until I am forty.

As a final note, I wish to concur with Browning's conclusion that "a highly divisive political situation seems likely." Predicting the future is really the same as extending an explanation of the past, so this conclusion is certain. I hope, however, that in the future the problems of providing for an adequate productive capacity can be sorted out from those problems that result more from the convenient grafting of a redistributive mechanism onto a system better able to handle a different function.

Michael K. Taussig

The previous two discussants have stolen a lot of my points, so I can be fairly brief.

June O'Neill's paper continues the gloomy theme of the conference: there are no pleasant prospects ahead. As Barry Chiswick said, "It is just the chain letter coming home to roost."

I would like to present the neglected optimistic side. First, once the indexing problem is solved, the main financing problem for social security is the aging of the population. One nice thing about that is there is no real problem for another thirty years or so. If we are irresponsible, we can ignore the problem completely and let future generations worry about it. In any event, it is nice to have a problem that does not come due for thirty years.

Second, even with the highest taxes projected under wage indexing, workers in 2020 and 2030 will be a lot better off after they pay those higher taxes than workers are today. The relatively rich workers of the future will be paying the high taxes, not the poor people of today.

Third, all the long-range projections omit the possibility of changes in the U.S. immigration policy. If we do not like the implications of the aging of the population, we can obtain any age distribution we want by letting part of the excess supply of young immigrants enter the country. We can do this in a very Machiavellian way by bringing in people just for the short-run, perhaps for a time one day short of the qualifying period for social security benefits. Or we could be more humanitarian about it and let them stay. In any case, if the aging of the population in the future is the problem for social security financing, it is the kind of problem that has a solution, especially with thirty years or so to plan ahead.

Now, let me turn to Edgar Browning's paper. I found his paper stimulating, provocative, and a lot of fun. It reminds me that when I get tired of working, I sit around with my friends and discuss politics. As often happens in these political discussions, however, I find myself in complete disagreement.

Before I get to the political part of his paper, let me turn to the economics part. Browning attempts to refute the forced-saving argument for social security on the "empirical" grounds that only 1.5 percent of the population will both be unable to work and have insufficient savings for retirement in the absence of social security. His 1.5 percent figure is based on combining two estimates. From survey data, he estimates that only 15 percent of the elderly are physically unable to work. He further estimates, without giving any documentation, that only 10 percent will not save for retirement. He combines these two figures to get 1.5 percent who will be both unable to work and without savings. He concludes from this "quantitative" analysis that the forced-saving argument for social security is open to question.

I dispute this argument. The estimated 15 percent clearly is not relevant. For one thing, it applies to all people over age sixty and, as J. W. Van Gorkom said, most people will get to an age, eventually, when they will be unable to work. In any event, that is not an economically relevant number because it is just the individual's perception of his own disability. What is more important, from an economic standpoint, is the employer's estimate of the worker's productivity as he ages. If, in his employer's estimate, his productivity falls, he will be unable to hold his present or similar employment and will have to fall back on his savings. The widespread institution of compulsory retirement suggests that many employers do have low estimates of older workers' productivity. It is true, of course, that a nondisabled person can always find some employment if he is willing to lower his asking wage. An aged skilled worker whose eyesight fails him, for example, can still compete with teenagers for the job of mopping floors at a McDonald's or a Burger King, but I do not think that Browning would want to rest his case on this particular line of argument.

The 10 percent estimate of those who will not save for retirement seems completely absurd. The relevant economic issue is not how many will have good intentions to save, but how many will save successfully in sufficient amounts. Who among the audience has managed to save successfully in real terms in the last decade? Not I. Based on a casual sampling of my colleagues with Ph.D.s and high incomes, I suggest the more correct estimate of those unable to save on their own is in the range of 80 to 90 percent.

On the basis of this discussion, I put forward an alternative estimate to that of Browning. I estimate that at least 75 percent of the population will be unable to continue employment at some age well before their death, and that at least 80 percent of them will not be able to save enough to finance retirement when they can no longer continue to work. Combining these estimates, I come up with an estimate of 60 percent of the aged who must be provided for by society. I submit that my estimate is no more arbitrary than Browning's 1.5 percent, but I am not willing to go to the stake for it.

Browning places great stress on the difference between the 10 percent return on real capital and the 3 percent return that is available to savers. This wedge is mainly because of the effect of taxes on capital income. Browning argues that, because of this difference, it is irrational for people, collectively, to want to have a social security system. By the same token, however, it is irrational for them not to have their representatives abolish all taxes on capital. In this case, there would have to be a much higher tax rate on labor incomes and that might have some effects of its own on efficiency, but I will leave this point unexplored.

Let me turn to the political part of Browning's paper—his so-called public choice analysis of why social security has political support. He begins by noting that the social security program enjoys unusually wide and deep support among voters in this country and, I might add, in other developed countries as well. His problem is how to explain this fact from a public choice perspective. He could, of course, resort to my own simple-minded explanation that the social security program is a generally satisfactory response to the rational, informed preferences of the overwhelming majority of the population. Instead, he argues that a pay-as-you-go social security system appeals to the majority of voters largely because expansion of the system benefits the aged and, to a lesser extent, the middle-aged voters at the expense of the very young and future generations. In addition, Browning attributes support of the social security system to public misunderstanding of the program. I do not believe that Browning expects this part of his paper to be taken seriously, except perhaps for his point about the wedge between the social returns to capital and the private rates received by savers. There are some countervailing influences, among which, I might observe, are most of the papers at this conference. The public choice school is uncharacteristically modest when it fails to claim that its own arguments are effective in combating public misunderstanding.

Let me consider Browning's main argument that our political system is biased towards overexpansion of the social security system. His argument implies that the aged and middle-aged majority of the electorate always has an interest in expanding the system. That is true—at least, within broad limits. As the social security tax rate approaches 100 percent, such pressures to expand the system might begin to weaken a little bit. But based on comparisons with foreign countries, it seems that the United States is still pretty far from this kind of limit to expansion.

If we take this argument seriously, we should pursue it to its logical end. Specifically, I would ask why the aged and their middle-aged allies in the electorate are such "pikers" in voting themselves higher social security benefits. According to a recent *Social Security Bulletin*, the average monthly retirement benefit for retired workers is about $240. For a retired couple the average combined benefit is probably no more than $400. Those do not seem to be the kind of munificent benefits that Browning's analysis would suggest. Even after making all the possible adjustments to the income data from the Census Bureau, you cannot escape the conclusion that the aged, as a group, have a much lower level of per capita consumption that the rest of the population. It would be nice to convince ourselves that the aged do not need much income and that their relatively low incomes just reflect the fact that they like to live near subsistence levels because they cannot enjoy life as much as the young. But I do not really think that is true.

Browning observes that relatively high social security benefits have come about only since 1972. A problem for public choice theory is to explain the expansion of the social security system in the late 1960s and early 1970s after its many years of stability. It is hard for me to believe that this was because all of a sudden the aged gained a disproportionate influence on the political process. My impression is that the young gained a disproportionate influence on politics at about that time, because of the outcome of the war in Vietnam and the advent of

221

a lower voting age. Why did the young not lead a political struggle against the expansion of the social security system?

If Browning's view is correct, it seems to me that the aged and their middle-aged allies in the electorate could find other means of exploiting the young. They could pressure legislators to vote such policies as running larger budget deficits, selling off U.S. assets to foreigners, and generally running down the U.S. capital stock. If they were interested only in maximizing their lifetime consumption, why not do all of these things? And they could certainly do better than $240 a month from the government through the social security system. In fact, Browning should really apply his public choice perspective to answer precisely the opposite question to the one he poses; that is, why do not the middle-aged and aged—a majority of the electorate—put effective pressures on governments to maximize their own lifetime consumption at the expense of future generations? It is a difficult issue; fortunately, Robert Barro's comments covered most of the important points. Browning implicitly considers only the individual's own lifetime consumption as an argument in his utility function. The utility of future generations does not enter at all. If we postulate that the aged do care about their own children and grandchildren, and about future generations in general, then many of the problems that Browning has so much trouble explaining become a lot clearer. The majority of the electorate do not use the government to enrich themselves at the expense of the young and future generations. In fact, they care about future generations, they leave behind a larger capital stock than they received, they sacrifice to educate their own children, they vote subsidies to educate other people's children, and so forth.

In this view of the world, the social security system might be best looked at, as Alan Freiden said, as a mechanism to carry out systematic transfers from the young to the old—transfers that would occur, for the most part, in the absence of social security. The great advantage of the social security system is that it permits the social sharing of the total burden of supporting the aged and disabled. The fortunate young, the orphans, and others who do not have a retired or disabled person to support are made to share in financing the benefits to alleviate the burden of those less fortunate. The social security system is best seen as a social mechanism for effecting the transfer to the aged and disabled fairly. And the perceived fairness of the transfer is really the essence of explaining the political support for the system. If you look at the system in this way, it is the kind of system that the aged and the young can both support. This simple-minded conclusion stands in contrast to the much more complex arguments resorted to by Browning.

Discussion

DR. O'NEILL: Regarding the question about which groups benefit and which groups lose, the benefits of those already retired are price indexed under any of the decoupling schemes that have been proposed—whether price indexing or wage indexing; thus, this group is not explicitly affected by these discussions. Since most schemes would be phased in gradually, the people who would be most immediately affected by introducing one indexing scheme or another are those ten to twenty years away from retirement.

All of our projections assume that benefits after retirement are simply price indexed. As people start living longer, however, a price-indexed benefit will result in a reduced standard of living for retired persons living to advanced ages relative to the standards of the working population. As more people live into their eighties, it will be difficult to sustain price indexing after retirement; there will be pressure to change the system.

Another widely debated question is whether people will, on their own, save enough. I suspect that most of the discussants here from the academic world have social security plus the Teachers Insurance and Annuity Association and College Retirement Equities Fund (TIAA-CREF) plans. People with this combination would be saving roughly 20 to 25 percent of their earnings. They often do not save any more than that privately, because saving has been arranged for them institutionally. I think that, when people talk about having more private saving, they assume that arrangements for saving—such as private pensions, pooled investment plans, IRAs, and various similar banking plans—would be expanded. They do not assume that many individuals would suddenly develop sophisticated investment portfolios and start buying and selling stocks on their own. Instead, other private institutions performing the same function as social security would develop.

On another point, I did not mean to perpetuate the view that social security is highly regressive. The payroll tax is not as progressive as the income tax, but recently it has been found that the payroll tax as a percentage of family income is not highly regressive. When people evaluate the payroll tax, they usually look at it in terms of workers rather than families. This is misleading because low-wage earners are often members of high-income households. In terms of family income level, the proportion paid out in payroll taxes is progressive up to about the fourth quintile in the family income distribution (that is, about 80 percent of all families), and then it becomes slightly regressive. This occurs partly because many people in the bottom two quintiles (about 40 percent of all families) do not pay payroll taxes because they are transfer recipients or retirees and do not work. Also, families with multiple earners keep the payroll tax proportional for a good stretch beyond the point at which the maximum taxable wage is reached. Middle-income families often include several members who receive earnings below the taxable maximum. It is only when you get into high income levels that the payroll tax becomes regressive. Of course, if you take into consideration the implicit rate of return on benefits as well as the payroll tax, the social security system becomes quite progressive; the rate of return declines as income rises.

PROFESSOR BROWNING: I have puzzled about the same matter that Buchanan discussed, namely, how to convert the present pay-as-you-go system to a funded system so that some people are benefited and no one is harmed. In thinking about this issue, it is important to recognize the divergence between the rate of return on capital and the subjective rate at which people will sacrifice current consumption for future consumption. Because of taxes on capital income, the rate of return on capital is about 10 percent and the subjective rate is substantially lower, perhaps 4 percent.

I think that this divergence makes it possible to move in the direction of a funded system without harming anyone while benefiting some people, especially members of future generations. If the tax on young workers only is increased and the proceeds are invested in a fund, the return will be more than enough to compensate the young. The fund would yield, say, 10 percent, while only 4 percent would be required as compensation to keep from harming the more heavily taxed young workers. The difference, which is a net gain, is available to pay current retirees, thereby permitting a reduction in pay-as-you-go financing. Gradually phasing in a funded system in this way can accomplish a Pareto-optimal move. (I did not discuss this matter in my paper because my emphasis there was on why the political process would not convert the social security system to a funded system.) Note that this argument depends on the divergence in gross and net returns produced by taxation of capital income. Buchanan's comments seem to neglect the role of taxation, although he may well be correct in a world where such taxes are absent.

Van Gorkom, Freiden, and Taussig all criticized in similar terms my evaluation of the argument that people must be forced to save for retirement. I did not devote much attention to this issue in my paper because it was only tangentially related to the main theme. In view of the importance attached to the question by the discussants, some further remarks seem called for.

I questioned the argument that people who do not save must either be supported by the state when they reach retirement age or be allowed to starve. There is a third alternative: those who have not saved can continue working to support themselves. The relevant question then is how many people would both not save and be unable to work, since only this group would require support. I then conjectured that 10 percent of the population would not save and 15 percent of the elderly would be unable to work; accordingly, only 1.5 percent of the elderly would both have not saved and be unable to work, and they would require support from the state.

The discussants, especially Taussig, seem to believe that these numbers (10 and 15 percent) are unreasonable. Of course, the alternative numbers suggested by Taussig are ridiculous, as I am sure he realizes. Only thirty years ago, nearly half of all elderly men were working, and many more were physically able to work but chose not to. Today, about 45 percent participate in private pension plans, and other persons save in other ways. Many more would save in the absence of the disincentive created by social security. These facts do not demonstrate that my assumptions are exactly correct, but they do show that the truth must lie closer to my conjecture than to Taussig's.

Actually, my argument could have been strengthened, but I did not take the time and space in my paper. Now I will. What is really relevant is not the percentage of the elderly who are unable to work, but the percentage who belong to a family unit in which no one is able to work. If only one member of an elderly couple is able to work, the couple can be self-supporting. In principle, half the elderly could be unable to work and still require no governmental assistance if coincidentally they are married to the other half who can work. Thus, if 15 percent of the elderly are unable to work, fewer than 15 percent would require governmental assistance on that count. Overall, I think the thrust of my paper on this point is correct; certainly, no one has presented any reasons or evidence that make me think otherwise.

Turning to the public choice analysis, both Freiden and Taussig object that my analysis assumes people are motivated only by narrow

225

self-interest. I do believe that most people think of social security primarily in terms of how it affects them personally. It is possible that the young view it, to some extent, as a means of helping the old (possibly their parents), and the old may also care about the way the system affects the young (possibly their children). The question is whether, and how, such preferences would affect the political determination of social security taxes and benefits. Neither Freiden nor Taussig attempts to grapple with this issue. It is far from clear, however, that this matter would affect the analysis in any relevant respect. In fact, my earlier article, which develops the voting model more rigorously, does not contain the assumption that people cared only about how the system affects them; it simply posits that people have preferences concerning the size of the system.[1] As far as I know, it makes no difference to the substantive implications of the analysis whether people care about their parents or vice versa.

I suggested in my paper that, as the population becomes older in the next century, there will be stronger pressure to expand the system. Freiden mentioned an offsetting factor that I believe is correct; namely, the rate of growth of the economy will be lower at that time. This means that the marginal rate of return at every age level under social security will be lower. There will be more people over age forty-five in forty years, but the marginal return at that age then might be 8 percent instead of 10 percent as it is now. Although this is correct, I do not think it would be of any great quantitative importance. It clearly has no bearing on those who are already retired (who may constitute 25 percent of the voting population), and I doubt that it would be quantitatively significant for those nearing retirement age. Still, it is a factor to consider, and I am sorry that Freiden did not develop the point more fully.

I am surprised to learn from Freiden that I can easily find out what my accumulated wealth in social security is. What I suggested was that it would be desirable for people to know the present value of future benefits to which they are entitled or, alternatively, what rate of return they can expect on past taxes. It is not enough to know how much has been paid in taxes in previous years; yet I believe that is the only information one can obtain from the Social Security Administration. The point is that people do not know what kind of return they can expect from social security, and the Social Security Administration makes no attempt to inform them.

I believe Freiden misinterpreted another proposal I made near the

---

[1] Edgar K. Browning, "Why the Social Insurance Budget Is Too Large in a Democracy," *Economic Inquiry*, vol. 13 (September 1975), pp. 373–88.

end of the paper. He said that I favored an increase in the return to private saving, as if I was proposing that, in some magical way, society could increase the real return on capital. That was not what I suggested. I proposed a reduction in taxation on capital income so that the net return (not the real before-tax return, which is not directly affected) would be higher and people could more easily perceive the true opportunity cost of providing for retirement through an unfunded system.

At one point, Taussig said that he believes the public is well informed and supports social security. In general, the public is not well informed; one need only read a few public opinion polls to be convinced of this. The theory of rational voter ignorance, as developed by Anthony Downs and others, explains why this is to be expected. I think the existence of voter ignorance is well established; how importantly it affects the political process is the only real question. My concern is that the structure of the present system makes it unnecessarily more difficult for the public to perceive its true benefits and costs.

Taussig also misinterprets my model when he asks why the system will not expand indefinitely if I am correct. The system implied by this model has an equilibrium size—namely, the tax rate chosen by the median voter—and there is no reason to expect that rate to increase indefinitely over time. If the median voter is forty-five years old, next year's forty-five-year-old voter will face the same marginal rate of return of 10 percent as this year's forty-five-year-old voter. The equilibrium is determined by the amount of income the forty-five-year-old is willing to give up in return for a 10 percent marginal return. This equilibrium need not change over time, as I explain in detail in my article in *Economic Inquiry*.

In response to the question of why social security benefits increased sharply in 1972 rather than in earlier years, I have no definite answer. Actually, the real acceleration in the growth of social security was in 1965 when Medicare was enacted. The mid-1960s also marked the beginning of the rapid expansion in social welfare expenditures generally. Why the government's involvement in the whole social welfare area began expanding in the mid-1960s, rather than earlier or later, is the real puzzle. It would require a far more general model than the one I developed to analyze that issue.

PROFESSOR MYERS: As one who was fortunate enough to be associated with the social security program from its inception in 1934, and as an actuary and an amateur historian, it always grieves me deeply when people rewrite history. Let me give a few examples of this.

The O'Neill paper states that, before 1940, the original system was changed and shifted to a welfare orientation. I think the right word is not "welfare," but "social adequacy." Welfare implies needs tests and means tests. Adding dependents and survivors benefits did not destroy the contributory principal at all; it just moved away from individual equity a little toward social adequacy.

This shift in the 1939 act did not mean that funds were not accumulated any more, but that they were not accumulated so rapidly. Also, these amendments did not change the long-range average cost of the program; rather, they redistributed that cost. Furthermore, the same reserve financing principle was still used, but benefit outgo was higher in the early years than in the later years. The same type of partial-reserve funding was used, although not quite to the same degree.

Also, O'Neill states that, until the early 1970s, the increases in benefits were funded primarily by drawing down the surpluses in the trust funds and by raising taxes. This is not so. The trust funds were not drawn down. The benefits were funded chiefly by the actuarial gains to the system that resulted from the increasing earnings levels over the years. The higher payroll taxes resulted primarily from raises in the earnings base, not from raises in the tax rates.

It is often stated that the automatic indexing method in the 1972 amendments provided for double indexing or overindexing. This is not true. There are economic circumstances when the present automatic provisions, which I agree are faulty, could result in underindexing. Even when annual inflation is more than 2 percent, benefits could be underindexed—for instance, if inflation was 3 percent a year and wages went up 10 percent a year. What Congress provided in 1972 was merely what it had done on an ad hoc basis at every previous increase. Under previous conditions it had worked out beautifully, from the standpoint of both benefit structure and financing.

O'Neill mentions that the replacement ratio in 1975 was about 27 percent higher than the level that prevailed in the twenty years preceding 1972. That is correct, but it does not tell the whole story: the ad hoc adjustment that was made in 1973, combined with the first automatic adjustments that were made, resulted in a 5 percent decrease of that overexpansion. The planned decoupling in the 1977 amendments to the Social Security Act further offsets some of that overexpansion.

One point in Browning's paper seems to rewrite history. He states that the social security system was quickly converted to an unfunded system. I do not think that this is correct. Such conversion did not occur until the 1972 amendments. The same partial-reserve actuarial funding basis was in every bill before that. Also, it is not true that the system was on a full-reserve actuarial basis when it was developed in 1935 and that this was completely shifted in 1939.

Some participants have placed considerable emphasis on determining what are now referred to as "rates of return." To put that in layman's language, does the young man get his money's worth? I have worked on this problem for forty years, and I am convinced that it cannot be precisely solved. There are just too many variables involved. The difficulty with trying to measure rates of return is that, because the system is so complicated, the people who attempt to do this measuring usually oversimplify things. Another element involved is the use of consistent assumptions. Depending upon what interest rate is selected, you can get any answer you want. Another element that enters into calculating rates of return is whether the employer tax is assigned to the employee. I would agree that this should perhaps be done to employees in the aggregate. But I do not think that the tax should be assigned to employees individually. People who do this tend to think of pension plans like TIAA-CREF; they forget that, even if the employer's cost in the great majority of private pension plans in the country averages, say, 10 percent of payroll, this does not mean that the benefits for each person are worth 10 percent—it may be more and it may be less.

Finally, in measuring social security wealth, which Feldstein does, the answer obtained depends on the assumptions made, and these can be subject to such a wide range of variations that the results are rendered virtually meaningless. Freiden reported that people can get from the Social Security Administration a form that will enable them to determine their social security wealth. I challenge anyone to do this. You would have to get this form every four years because it does not give your wages each year in the past. It gives your wages for only the last few years and your accumulated wages. But, even assuming that you obtained a complete record of your earnings, you are still only one small step along the road to estimating benefits. With indexing under the 1977 amendments, the calculation will be even more difficult.

PROFESSOR JOHN GOODMAN, Southern Methodist University: I have a question about calculating social security wealth and implicit rates of return. Several persons have said that there seems to be some overall progressivity to the system based on assumptions about what is going to happen in the future. For example, Kaplan's calculations show some progressivity to the system. These calculations, however, have not taken into consideration several facts that we all know to be true, such as the fact that lower-income groups enter the labor force earlier and that their life expectancy is shorter. I do not see any reason to conclude that

229

the system is progressive overall until these factors are taken into account. I suspect that the social security system is probably not progressive.

DR. O'NEILL: My calculations did take those factors into account. I believe Dean Leimer's did, too. I used survival tables that adjusted for differences in education, race, and sex. Although it is difficult to estimate survivors benefits, I also attempted to estimate the additional survivors benefits for those who are married and who die young.

DR. FREIDEN: We looked at a sample of real people for whom longitudinal earnings data were available. It turned out that the highly educated people did not enter the labor force later than those with less education; they entered at the same time. During the period they were in college, the average taxable earnings of college students were about half those of high school graduates. There is also the strong possibility that highly educated people retire later.

PROFESSOR BARRO: Browning's comparison of social security rates of return with the before-tax rate of return on capital is interesting in a social context if, and only if, one believes that net social security wealth, as calculated, displaces private capital on a one-to-one basis. This is what I believe has now become popularly known as the Feldstein-Buchanan fallacy! I believe that neither economic theory nor empirical evidence supports the hypothesis that social security has materially reduced private capital formation.

On one other point, I think that there is a significant probability that workers underestimate the cost to them of the social security contributions paid by their employer. In fact, it is just about as high as the probability that workers overestimate that cost.

PROFESSOR BROWNING: My argument does not generally depend on whether social security reduces private saving. This is certainly true if the reason that saving does not fall is reduced voluntary transfers from children to parents or an induced retirement effect. If saving does not fall because the elderly increase their bequests, as Barro has argued, then I am not so sure my analysis would stand up without qualification. The argument that bequests will rise, however, is based on the assumption that the social security program is expected to be terminated sometime in the future; then the elderly have to increase bequests in the present to avoid harming the young in the future. If people do not expect the social security program to be terminated, as is surely true in general, then the elderly have no reason to increase their bequests. Consequently, I do not think that Barro's argument has much relevance here.

I do not understand Barro's statement that people are as likely to overestimate their burden from the employer portion of the tax as they are to underestimate it. Economists are virtually the only people I know who are even aware that employees bear any burden from this portion of the tax, much less the full burden.

MR. LANCASTER: O'Neill made a comment about the Social Security Administration's experience with disability insurance. The disability benefits in social security are flawed. If the earnings of a young worker up to about age thirty-five are as high as the taxable base, his disability benefit equals or exceeds his take-home pay when working. Private insurance companies would not underwrite a benefit like that. The unfavorable experience with social security's disability insurance seems to be affecting the private insurance system. It has induced private insurers to raise their premiums. The higher premiums are then passed on to employers who, in turn, pass the higher cost on to the economy through higher prices. In addition, the flawed disability benefit is a drag on the nation's economy because people who are out on disability and not working are not producing.

PROFESSOR PHILLIP CAGAN, Columbia University: I have two points to make. First, I am bothered by the use of the before-tax rate of return on capital. This assumes that taxes, which are a cost in the economy, will not rise as the amount of capital is increased. Then taxes are not a drain on the return that is going to be made on new capital.

If, in fact, the return on capital requires increased costs of government—for example, if a greater defense effort is needed because there is more to protect—then taxes are a net drain on the rate of return on capital, and we should use the after-tax return. If not all taxes are a true economic cost, we should use an in-between rate of return, but not the gross return before taxes.

My second point has to do with funding—that is, whether the social security system should be fully funded or completely pay-as-you-go. Although a fully funded system is attractive, everyone dismisses that as impossible. There is an in-between case that is being overlooked, however—partial funding in order to even out the tax rate over time. This has become an important issue because of demographic changes.

An alternative to the present absence of funding is to raise the tax rate now to a level at which it will remain constant in the future. A

231

fund would be built up in the short run, and it would then run down in the long run. Unlike full funding, which requires more than $2 trillion, this would be a more modest fund that could be handled by the economy. In the past, funding was dismissed because of the Keynesian assumption that the economy could not make use of additional loanable funds. Such ideas have now been swept aside. I think it is outrageous for us to take the attitude that, even though workers will have to pay through the nose thirty years from now, we can do nothing about it.

PROFESSOR MARSHALL COLBERG, Florida State University: Some references have been made to the implicit or internal rate of return on social security investments. This is a return with a catch. The catch is the retirement test under which recipients pay a 50 percent implicit tax on earned income over $3,000 a year. Although the retirement test may be changed by the present Congress, it has shown a lot of vitality over the years. Even during World War II when labor was scarce, persons with social security benefits could earn only $15 a month. If they did not report their earnings, they lost two months of social security benefits. This is quite a catch in the social security rate of return under the existing law.

PROFESSOR JAMES SCHULZ, Brandeis University: It may be unfair to bring up politics in a group of economists. Since the economists have not been adverse to bringing it up, however, I want to make a couple of comments on politics and social security and to disagree with some of the speakers.

I have detected in some of the comments an undertone that makes fun of the whole political process and describes it as irrational—particularly, with regard to social security. Browning states that political decisions are primarily a result of the numbers of people favoring and opposing certain policies. Toward the end of his paper, he talks about the political implications of rising numbers of elderly in the population and says that this indicates they are going to be politically more dominating and that this will probably result in some sort of social security policy that favors them.

This is not the point of view of a large body of political scientists. Many political scientists, such as Robert Dahl and Theodore Lowi, talk about political pluralism. They talk about the impact of organized political positions and the extent to which organizations with different power affect political outcomes. To them the political process is much more than a game of numbers.

Regarding the specific issue of how the aged behave as a voting bloc, and whether they can be characterized as a voting bloc, I think Browning ignores completely the findings of those political scientists who have studied the voting behavior of the aged. These persons have come to an entirely different conclusion. Robert Hudson and Robert Binstock have reviewed this literature succinctly in the *Handbook of Aging and the Social Sciences* and show the complexity of the issue.

In his discussion of the rationale for social security, Browning mentions the standard arguments of myopic behavior and the cost of decision making, and he then dismisses them. I disagree with his statement that no one has done a systematic study of myopic behavior in regard to saving. I think there is a large body of literature on this topic. Even if no one has done the kind of study that he would like, it is irresponsible to say that, because nobody has looked at the issue, it is not important with regard to the rationale for social security.

Finally, regarding the cost of decision making, Browning says in a footnote that it is not self-evident or necessarily true that decision making in connection with planning for retirement is complex. Again, I think that flies in the face of a lot of evidence about the behavior of people. Moreover, it is not necessarily irrational for people to be ignorant about social security. It may reflect a deliberate decision that social security is too complex for them to handle and should, therefore, be delegated to the political process, imperfect as that may be. Personally, I think there is some rationality in the political process.

PROFESSOR BROWNING: I did not intend to characterize the political process—either in general or as it applies to social security—as irrational. It is not a question of the process being rational or irrational. For example, we do not characterize the market system as irrational when people pollute, even though this may not be in the interest of society. Similarly, when the political process can be predicted to produce undesirable results because of the rational behavior of participants in that process, we should not refer to the process itself as irrational. Processes are neither rational nor irrational; people can be rational, however, and my model assumes that they are. This does not rule out the possibility that the political outcome will be undesirable.

I do not believe I stated that politics is based primarily on numbers, although numbers clearly are an important factor and one that my paper emphasizes. A politician who ignores the relative number of people harmed and benefited by the policies he advocates will undoubtedly be out of office before long. Relative numbers are not the only

233

force in the political process, but they are important, and no one has specified other factors that would tend to work in the opposite direction.

I did not look into the literature by political scientists on the voting behavior of the elderly because I felt it was irrelevant to my topic. I may be incorrect, but my impression is that this literature is concerned chiefly with how people have actually voted in elections. Since people have never had an opportunity to vote specifically on the social security program, a study of how the elderly have voted in elections would tell us little or nothing about their attitude toward social security. Nonetheless, their views affect the alternatives offered by the political process. It is no coincidence, I believe, that neither political party advocates eliminating social security or converting it to a funded system: they would lose more votes from the elderly and middle-aged than they could ever hope to gain from young voters.

If there is a large body of literature on myopic behavior concerning saving, as Schulz says, I am unaware of it. It is certainly not widely cited in the economics literature dealing with social security, even by those who use this argument, and judging from the present discussion, it is not widely known. I would have expected those who hold that people are myopic would have offered some evidence, if it existed, for this position, but they did not do so.

PART FOUR

INTERACTION OF
SOCIAL SECURITY AND
PRIVATE PENSIONS

The Future of the U.S. Pension System

Alicia H. Munnell

The development of the social security program and private pension system, in the wake of the Great Depression, reflected a shift in the nation's preference toward organized retirement saving. The two systems developed simultaneously since neither program alone provided adequate retirement income. In the 1970s, however, the climate for private pensions has changed dramatically. Social security benefits have grown rapidly as a result of ad hoc increases and automatic cost-of-living adjustments. For the average worker, the percentage of pre-retirement earnings replaced by social security benefits has increased from 30 percent to 45 percent and benefits are now awarded on earnings up to $17,700, as compared with an earnings base of $7,800 in 1970. As a result of the 1977 amendments to the Social Security Act, the benefit base will double again in a few years. The expansion of social security and the implications for the future of private pensions are the subject of this paper.

The first section briefly describes the evolution of the private pension system since the Depression, revealing that the inadequacy of social security benefits during the 1940s was an important factor in the drive of labor unions for private pension benefits. The second section presents an empirical analysis of the growth of social security and private pensions in the context of a model in which the expansion of the two programs is determined by the gap between desired and actual retirement assets. The results confirm that private pensions and social security are almost perfect substitutes for a large portion of the population. The third section explores the recent expansion of the social security program in light of the substitutability of the two types of retirement saving. The final section summarizes other factors such as the social security taxable wage base for employers, the rate of inflation, and the tax provisions, which will all determine the future of the U.S. pension system.

NOTE: The author would like to thank Sharon Spaight for excellent research assistance and Richard Kopcke for invaluable comments on the empirical work. Robert M. Ball, John A. Brittain, Janice Halpern, Stephen McNees, and Geoffrey Woglam also provided useful insights. Anna M. Estle expertly executed the secretarial tasks.

237

The conclusions are predictable. If the average social security replacement rate (the ratio of benefits to pre-retirement earnings) had been initially established at the current level of 45 percent, the private pension system as we know it today would not exist. In view of the recent expansion of social security to such levels, the role for private pensions has been limited. Because that role is more restricted, the favorable tax provisions, which accrue primarily to workers with above-average earnings, may receive renewed scrutiny. Finally, high rates of inflation will also limit the ability of private pensions to provide meaningful benefits and may lead to a further expansion of the social security program, which can provide automatic cost-of-living adjustments.

The Development of Private Pensions

The Great Depression seriously undermined American confidence in the historic tradition of self-reliance and in the virtue of individual thrift as a means of providing for income in old age. With 13 million people unemployed and the lifetime savings of many erased, the 1930s created a sympathetic environment for the passage of the Social Security Act of 1935 and the subsequent development of private pension plans. Although private pensions date officially from the establishing of the American Express plan in 1875, the present U.S. pension programs, both public and private, are rooted in the desperate desire for security that became part of the national psychology following the Great Depression.[1]

Although World War II diverted much of the nation's attention and resources that might have been directed toward improvements in provisions for old age, emergency wartime measures stimulated the interest of employers in pensions.[2] The wage stabilization program instituted during the war impeded employers' ability to attract and hold employees in the tight civilian labor market. In response to the legal limitations placed on cash wages, the War Labor Board attempted to relieve the pressure on management and labor by permitting employers to bid for workers by offering attractive fringe benefits.

The cost to the firms of establishing pension plans was minimal in light of the tax deductibility of contributions and the wartime excess profits tax on corporate income. The Revenue Act of 1942 clarified the

---

[1] For an excellent discussion of the historical evolution of private pension plans, see William C. Greenough and Francis P. King, *Pension Plans and Public Policy* (New York: Columbia University Press, 1976), chapter 4.

[2] Charles L. Dearing, *Industrial Pensions* (Washington, D.C.: The Brookings Institution, 1954), p. 41.

favorable tax provisions for pensions and instituted a procedure whereby companies could receive advance assurance from the Internal Revenue Service that employer contributions would be viewed as legitimate tax deductions before a plan was put into operation.[3] The deductibility of the contributions combined with the high corporate tax rates meant that the major share of pensions was financed by funds that otherwise would have been paid to the government in taxes.

Between 1945 and 1949, the rate of growth of new pension plans fell off markedly as employee interest focused upon increases in cash wages as they attempted to recover the lost ground suffered during the period of wage stabilization.[4] By 1949, however, pension benefits became a major issue in labor negotiation in the face of increased resistance to further wage increases and a weak economy. The situation was highlighted by the conclusions of a presidential fact-finding board that, although a cash wage increase in the steel industry was not justified, the industry did have a social obligation to provide workers with pensions.[5] This decision was based in part on the obvious inadequacy of social security benefits, which averaged $26 a month at the time. Labor's drive for pension benefits was aided further by a 1948 ruling of the National Labor Relations Board that employers had a legal obligation to bargain over the terms of pension plans.[6] Both the steelworkers and the United Auto Workers launched successful drives for pension benefits under the influence of the 1949 recession.

The Korean War provided another major stimulus to the growth of private pensions. The World War II experience was repeated, as employers competed for workers in the face of controls on wages and salaries and taxes on excess profits.

The mid-1950s marked the beginning of substantial collective bargaining gains in multi-employer pension plans. In contrast to the single-employer plans of the steel and automobile industries, which are characterized by a few relatively large employers, multi-employer plans were established in industries containing many small companies and involving frequent job changes of employees so that workers rarely remained with a single employer long enough to qualify for pensions. The multi-employer pension movement, encouraged by the success of

---

[3] Merton C. Bernstein, *The Future of Private Pensions* (London: The Free Press of Glencoe, 1964), p. 12.

[4] Joseph J. Melone, "Management and Labor Considerations in the Establishment of Private Pension Plans," in U.S. Congress, Joint Economic Committee, *Old-Age Income Assurance*, Part 4, 90th Congress, 1st session, 1967, p. 8.

[5] Inland Steel Co. v. National Labor Relations Board, 170 F.2d. 247, 251 (1949).

[6] Inland Steel Co. v. United Steelworkers of America, 77 NLRB 4 (1948).

the United Mine Workers, spread to such industries as construction, food, apparel, and transportation.

The growth of private pensions continued into the 1960s. Much of the increase in coverage during this decade, however, was attributable to an expansion of employment in firms that already had pension plans; this was in contrast to the growth during the 1950s, which resulted primarily from the introduction of new plans. Coverage under multi-employer plans grew more than twice as quickly as single-employer plans, in part because of the merger of single-employer plans into multi-employer ones.[7]

The growth of private pension plans since 1940 is summarized in Table 1. Currently, about 30 million wage earners and salaried employees are covered by private retirement plans financed by the employer alone or jointly with employees. Coverage under private plans more than doubled between 1950 and 1975, from 22 percent of the private labor force to 46 percent. Annual contributions to private pensions increased about fifteenfold, from $2 billion in 1950 to $30 billion in 1975. Contributions in 1975 amounted to more than half the $56 billion payroll tax payment to the OASI trust fund for the same year. On the benefit side, 7.1 million retirees and survivors were receiving payments from private pension plans in 1975. These beneficiaries were paid a total of $14.8 billion, which averaged slightly more than $2,100 a recipient.

The Interaction of Social Security and Private Pensions

The Great Depression created the psychological environment for institutionalizing saving for retirement, but the question of whether old-age income should be provided primarily through public or private mechanisms was not resolved at that time. The passage of the Social Security Act indicated that the federal government would be responsible for insuring at least a minimum floor of income, but social security failed to keep pace with the growth in wages, perhaps because of the diversion of resources for World War II. The average monthly benefit for a retired worker, which amounted to $22.71 in 1940, was only $29.03 in early 1950. Between 1940 and 1950, the average social security benefit actually declined from 27 percent of average earnings to 15 percent. Much of the pressure from unions for private pension plans was based on the inadequacy of social security benefits and on the belief that creation of such plans would provide an incentive for employers to

---

[7] Harry E. Davis and Arnold Strasser, "Private Pension Plans, 1960 to 1969—An Overview," *Monthly Labor Review*, vol. 33 (July 1970), p. 45.

TABLE 1

Growth of Private Pensions, Selected Years, 1940–1975

| Year | Contributions | | | | Benefits | | Reserves, End of Year (billions of dollars) |
| | Number of workers covered (thousands) | Amount of payments (millions of dollars) | | | Number of beneficiaries (thousands) | Amount of payments (millions of dollars) | |
		Total	Employer	Employee			
1940	4,100	310	180	130	160	140	2.4
1945	6,400	990	830	160	310	220	5.4
1950	9,800	2,080	1,750	330	450	370	12.1
1955	14,200	3,840	3,280	560	980	850	27.5
1960	18,700	5,490	4,710	780	1,780	1,720	52.0
1965	21,800	8,360	7,370	990	2,750	3,520	86.5
1970	26,100	14,000	12,580	1,420	4,740	7,360	137.1
1975	30,300	29,850	27,560	2,290	7,050	14,810	212.6

Sources: Alfred M. Skolnik, "Private Pension Plans, 1950–74," *Social Security Bulletin*, vol. 39 (June 1976), p. 4; Martha Remy Yohalem, "Employee-Benefit Plans, 1975," *Social Security Bulletin*, vol. 40 (November 1977), p. 27.

support increases of OASI benefit levels in order to reduce the burden on private industry for the provision of retirement income.[8]

Despite a major increase in social security benefits in 1950, private pension plans continued to grow rapidly. At first glance, the simultaneous expansion of both public and private programs during the last twenty-seven years seems to imply that social security has not infringed upon the development of private pensions. In fact, many argue that social security encouraged the growth of private pensions by establishing sixty-five as an accepted retirement age and by providing the basic retirement benefit which permitted workers to plan for an independent future. The simultaneous expansion of social security and private plans can also be explained, however, in terms of society's attempt to close the large gap between actual and desired retirement assets created by the Depression. The economic catastrophe of the 1930s resulted in a basic shift in taste from individual saving to organized saving for retirement; social security and private pensions were alternative vehicles to achieve a specific level of guaranteed retirement benefits. With a large gap between desired and actual retirement assets, the two programs could grow rapidly even if they were perfect substitutes.[9] As the gap narrowed, however, a major expansion of social security would lead to a relative decline in saving through private plans.

Stock Adjustment Model. This section presents an empirical analysis of the interaction of private pensions and social security in the provision of retirement income. The analysis is based on a stock adjustment model in which individuals are assumed to alter their accumulations in private pension plans and their other savings so that their combined retirement assets (including social security) will insure a desired level of retirement income. The model is designed to test the hypothesis that social security and private pensions have acted as almost perfect substitutes in the provision for retirement income.[10] Saving for retirement (RS) in any period is a function of the gap between the desired retirement assets ($RASS^*$) and the existing stock ($RASS_{t-1}$):

$$RS_t = f(RASS^* - RASS_{t-1}). \tag{1}$$

---

[8] Bernstein, *The Future of Private Pensions*, p. 13.

[9] Although social security and private pensions both provide retirement income, each has distinctive advantages. Social security is able to offer benefits indexed to inflation, universal coverage, and portability. Private pensions, in their various forms, can adapt to the specific characteristics of an industry.

[10] The analysis is based on aggregate economic variables and therefore ignores the differences in tax treatment and coverage between private pensions and social security.

The desired level of retirement assets $(RASS^*)$ is, in turn, a function of the target level of retirement income (RY^*) and the number of years the individual expects to live in retirement $(Years)$:

$$RASS^* = f(RY^*, Years). \qquad (2)$$

Desired retirement income is assumed to depend on permanent income, which is approximated by current and lagged disposable income $(YD_t$ and $YD_{t-1})$ and by the rate of unemployment (RU):

$$RY^* = f(YD_t, YD_{t-1}, RU). \qquad (3)$$

The existing stock of retirement assets includes the reserves in private pension funds $(PENASS)$,[11] accumulated social security benefits (SSW),[12] and the net nonpension wealth of consumers that will be allocated for retirement $[\lambda_1(W-PENASS)]$:

$$RASS_{t-1} = SSW_{t-1} + PENASS_{t-1} + \lambda_1(W-PENASS)_{t-1}. \qquad (4)$$

Retirement saving (RS) is composed of the net increase in the assets of private pension funds (PS), contributions to social security $(OASI)$,[13] and some fraction (λ_2) of other saving (SO):[14]

$$RS_t = PS_t + OASI_t + \lambda_2 SO. \qquad (5)$$

Therefore, combining equations (1) through (5), retirement saving can be expressed as follows:

$$RS_t = PS_t + OASI_t + \lambda_2 SO = f[YD_t, YD_{t-1},$$
$$RU, Years, (SSW+PENASS)_{t-1}, \lambda_1(W-PENASS)_{t-1}]. \qquad (6)$$

Expressing the relationship in terms of pension saving, the equation becomes:[15]

$$PS_t = f[YD_t, YD_{t-1}, RU, Years, (SSW+PENASS)_{t-1},$$
$$\lambda_1(W-PENASS)_{t-1}] - OASI_t - \lambda_2 SO_t. \qquad (7)$$

---

[11] To the extent that private pensions are not fully funded, pension reserves understate accumulated pension benefits.

[12] Since social security is financed on a pay-as-you-go basis, this value must be represented as the present discounted value of future benefits.

[13] Social security taxes are an imperfect measure of retirement saving because the system is financed on a pay-as-you-go basis and future benefits are not strictly related to current contributions.

[14] Retirement saving also occurs through other public pensions such as civil service, military, and state and local retirement systems. These systems have been excluded from the empirical analysis because they generally are either unfunded or only partially funded, and therefore no "wealth" data are available.

[15] Including other saving as an independent variable clearly introduces simultaneity bias since this value is determined by the same factors that influence total retirement saving. If appropriate instruments were available, equation (7) should be estimated by some limited information technique. The use of inadequate instruments, however, can introduce more bias than that resulting from the use of an ordinary least-squares (OLS) estimator. Therefore, the equation will be estimated directly by OLS, and the resulting coefficient will be biased. The equation is re-estimated excluding the SO_t variable.

243

TABLE 2

DATA FOR REGRESSIONS, 1929–1940 AND 1947–1974

(billions of 1972 dollars)

Year	YD	SSWG	SSWN	PENASS	W
Total					
1929	229.8	0.0	0.0	2.04	1,303.91
1930	210.6	0.0	0.0	2.29	1,269.43
1931	201.7	0.0	0.0	2.79	1,218.10
1932	174.3	0.0	0.0	3.48	1,144.80
1933	169.7	0.0	0.0	3.99	1,138.06
1934	179.7	0.0	0.0	4.07	1,118.28
1935	196.6	0.0	0.0	4.38	1,134.34
1936	220.7	0.0	0.0	4.90	1,209.67
1937	227.8	156.1	74.1	5.34	1,211.90
1938	212.8	139.6	65.7	6.14	1,167.32
1939	230.1	230.8	144.8	6.97	1,210.53
1940	244.3	256.9	158.0	7.79	1,288.96
1947	318.8	432.4	234.2	14.13	1,453.60
1948	335.5	452.5	239.8	15.67	1,511.63
1949	336.1	431.1	227.1	18.49	1,588.15
1950	361.9	477.4	246.1	21.30	1,642.96
1951	371.6	585.3	311.8	23.97	1,695.21
1952	382.1	612.9	325.2	27.95	1,701.13
1953	397.5	645.2	339.1	32.49	1,736.93
1954	402.1	639.1	336.9	37.42	1,775.16
1955	425.9	738.3	391.7	42.83	1,747.66
1956	444.9	793.5	419.8	47.94	2,036.64
1957	453.9	860.1	450.6	53.40	2,091.72
1958	459.0	876.7	468.1	59.19	2,115.77
1959	477.4	943.6	503.6	66.19	2,295.45
1960	487.3	979.0	527.0	72.52	2,414.23
1961	500.6	1,025.3	562.2	79.72	2,453.79
1962	521.6	1,134.9	643.6	86.28	2,602.99
1963	539.2	1,201.8	686.2	93.57	2,606.43
1964	577.3	1,334.2	771.4	102.64	2,797.89
1965	612.4	1,465.7	844.6	112.19	2,949.42
1966	643.6	1,611.5	927.7	120.43	3,080.71

OASI	SO	LF65+	RU	Deflator	Population (millions)
0.0		0.542	0.032	0.358	121.875
0.0	9.51	0.540	0.087	0.350	123.188
0.0	7.68	0.530	0.159	0.315	124.149
0.0	−2.47	0.520	0.236	0.279	124.949
0.0	4.10	0.511	0.249	0.268	125.690
0.0	−0.03	0.501	0.217	0.290	126.485
0.0	6.33	0.491	0.201	0.297	127.362
0.0	11.43	0.481	0.169	0.300	128.181
2.46	11.29	0.471	0.143	0.311	128.961
1.18	2.88	0.462	0.190	0.306	129.969
1.91	6.12	0.452	0.172	0.304	131.028
1.06	9.81	0.442	0.146	0.308	132.122
2.95	7.18	0.478	0.039	0.528	144.126
3.01	16.64	0.468	0.038	0.559	146.631
2.99	9.26	0.469	0.059	0.557	149.188
4.70	15.85	0.458	0.053	0.568	151.684
5.56	20.50	0.449	0.033	0.605	154.287
6.17	21.32	0.426	0.030	0.619	156.954
6.25	21.87	0.416	0.029	0.631	159.565
8.12	19.34	0.405	0.055	0.636	162.391
8.90	17.45	0.396	0.044	0.642	165.275
9.42	24.12	0.400	0.041	0.655	168.210
10.10	23.52	0.375	0.043	0.676	171.274
10.95	24.46	0.356	0.068	0.691	174.141
11.44	18.61	0.342	0.055	0.704	177.073
15.15	16.32	0.331	0.055	0.717	180.671
15.57	19.86	0.317	0.067	0.725	183.691
16.38	19.97	0.303	0.055	0.736	186.538
19.47	16.60	0.284	0.057	0.747	189.242
20.73	24.17	0.280	0.052	0.757	191.889
20.77	27.89	0.279	0.045	0.771	194.303
25.95	30.26	0.270	0.038	0.793	196.560

Table 2 continues next page.

Table 2 (continued)

Year	YD	SSWG	SSWN	PENASS	W
1967	669.8	1,728.7	1,001.2	130.50	3,007.38
1968	695.2	1,847.4	1,073.5	139.24	3,235.22
1969	712.3	1,951.5	1,132.1	144.41	3,440.68
1970	741.6	2,065.8	1,206.3	148.22	3,367.57
1971	769.0	2,163.8	1,276.6	156.73	3,425.47
1972	801.3	2,331.3	1,377.7	167.80	3,612.00
1973	854.7	2,590.2	1,532.8	170.81	3,810.43
1974	840.8	2,615.6	1,556.5	163.99	3,603.08
		Means (billions of 1972 dollars)			
1930–1974[a]	446.197	905.6	514.3	61.59	2,125.91
1947–1974	540.479	1,233.4	700.5	83.93	2,492.83
		Per capita means (thousands of 1972 dollars)			
1930–1974[a]	2.564	4.830	2.731	0.325	12.356
1947–1974	2.936	6.514	3.683	0.438	13.536

[a] Data for the war years, 1941–1946, were excluded.

SOURCES: Figures for disposable income, unemployment rate, deflator for personal consumption expenditures, and civilian population were obtained from the *Economic Report of the President, 1977*, tables B-22, p. 213, B-27, p. 218, B-26, p. 217, and B-3, p. 190. The labor force participation rate of males sixty-five years of age and older is from *Long Term Economic Growth*, series B-21, p. 194. Data for the years 1966–1974 are from *Manpower Report of the President*, 1972, table A-2, pp. 158–59, and the *Handbook of Labor Statistics*, 1976, table 4, p. 30. The

The Data. The dependent variable, pension saving (*PS*), is defined as the net increase in the book value of pension fund reserves during the calendar year. This figure is equivalent to the contributions of employers and employees plus investment earnings (excluding capital gains) minus payments to beneficiaries and administrative expenses.

Permanent income is represented by the current and lagged values of disposable income as defined in the national income accounts (NIA). The unemployment rate is the average percentage of the civilian labor

OASI	SO	LF65+	RU	Deflator	Population (millions)
28.46	37.27	0.271	0.038	0.813	198.712
28.04	31.21	0.273	0.036	0.846	200.706
31.58	28.36	0.272	0.035	0.885	202.677
32.71	44.65	0.268	0.049	0.925	204.878
34.91	44.51	0.255	0.059	0.966	207.053
37.78	33.00	0.244	0.056	1.000	208.846
43.58	54.88	0.228	0.049	1.055	210.410
44.55	51.92	0.224	0.056	1.169	211.901
13.15	20.20	0.383	0.085	0.623	165.410
18.08	25.75	0.341	0.048	0.749	180.317
0.068	0.113				
0.094	0.139				

annual net contributions to the OASI trust fund were found in Social Security Administration, *Social Security Bulletin, Annual Statistical Supplement, 1974.* Data for pension assets were obtained from Alfred M. Skolnik, "Private Pension Plans, 1950–74," *Social Security Bulletin,* vol. 39 (June 1976), table 1, p. 4. Pension saving was calculated as the net increase of book value in pension assets from one year to the next. Other saving was simply the differnce between personal saving from table B-8, p. 196, of the *Economic Report of the President, 1977* and pension saving. Martin Feldstein provided the series for net worth of consumers and social security wealth.

force that is unemployed. Data on the average number of years in retirement are unavailable; therefore, the labor force participation rate for men aged sixty-five and older was included as a proxy for the lengthening of the retirement period, reflecting the trend toward early retirement.[16] The variable is entered with disposable income because a

---

[16] Whether this trend will continue under the demographic characteristics of the next century is subject to debate.

multiplicative relationship is implied in the formulation of desired retirement assets.

The existing stock of retirement assets includes pension reserves, social security wealth, and an unknown fraction of other nonpension wealth of consumers. Pension assets include the reserves in private pension funds at book value as of the end of the year. The wealth series (W) is the net worth of consumers at market prices as originally presented by Albert Ando and Franco Modigliani,[17] and as updated from wealth data based on the same definitions from the MIT-Penn-SSRC econometric model. Pension assets are subtracted from the net worth data to calculate nonpension net worth of consumers $(W-PENASS)$. Social security wealth $(SSWG)$ is an estimate of the present discounted value of future benefits outstanding to current workers and retirees, taking into account the probabilities of living long enough to receive them. The value of social security wealth has increased rapidly and now is almost equivalent to the net worth of consumers. Since it is unclear whether individuals perceive their future payroll tax payments as an offset to future benefits or whether they view the social security tax as similar to any other government levy, a net social security variable was also constructed. Net social security wealth $(SSWN)$ is calculated by subtracting the present discounted value of future taxes from the gross wealth.[18]

The other forms of retirement saving included as independent variables are social security contributions and an unknown portion of other saving. Social security contributions represent the net total contributions to the Old Age Survivors Insurance $(OASI)$ Trust Fund. The other saving variable (SO) is simply NIA personal saving less pension saving (the net increase in pension reserves).

All variables were converted to constant 1972 dollars (deflated by the GNP deflator for consumption), and they have been divided by the total civilian population to obtain per capita values. The data are presented in Table 2. The final estimates were based on the following equation:

$$PS_t = \alpha_0 + \alpha_1 YD_t + \alpha_2 YD_{t-1} + \alpha_3 (LF65 + {}^{\cdot}YD)_t +$$
$$\alpha_4 (SSW + PENASS)_{t-1} + \alpha_5 (W - PENASS)_{t-1} + \alpha_6 OASI_t +$$
$$\alpha_7 SO_t + \alpha_8 RU_t . \qquad (8)$$

---

[17] Albert Ando and Franco Modigliani, "The 'Life Cycle' Hypothesis of Saving: Aggregate Implications and Tests," *American Economic Review*, vol. 53 (March 1963), pp. 55–84.

[18] Updated series for the net worth of consumers and social security wealth were provided by Martin Feldstein.

The stock adjustment model implies specific coefficients for each variable. Retirement assets, $(SSW+PENASS)_{t-1}$, should have a negative coefficient since an increase in the existing stock implies a reduction in the gap between desired and actual assets and thus less pension savings. Nonpension wealth should also have a negative effect on pension saving, although this coefficient should be significantly smaller than that of other retirement assets since only a fraction of consumer net worth is designated for retirement. Social security contributions $(OASI)$ should have a coefficient of -1 since the model implies that pension saving and social security payments are perfect substitutes. Other savings (SO) should have a negative coefficient, but it should be less than 1 because this form of saving is undertaken for purposes other than retirement. The coefficient of $(LF65+{}^{\cdot}YD)_t$—the labor force participation rate of males aged sixty-five and older, multiplied by current disposable income—should be negative since a decline in participation indicates an increase in the prevalence of retirement and thus an increase in the need for pension saving.

Results. Four variants of equation (8) were estimated for each of the time periods, 1930–1974 (excluding the war years) and 1947–1974. The results are presented in Table 3. The social security wealth variable entered the equations first as a gross value $(SSWG)$ then as a net value $(SSWN)$. The equations were also estimated with and without the other saving (SO) variable. This variable plays a legitimate role as a proxy for the decision about whether to consume or to save; it was deleted only to reveal that the results were not dependent on its inclusion.[19]

Since private pensions were relatively unimportant in the U.S. economy before World War II, the results for the 1947–1974 period probably deserve the most attention. The coefficients of the variables generally are consistent with the stock adjustment model. The major exception is the coefficient of nonpension wealth, which has a positive sign and is only a small fraction of its standard error. A likely explanation is that nonpension wealth is both a proxy for taste and a component in the stock adjustment process. As a taste variable, a positive coefficient implies that a higher level of nonpension wealth increases the desire to accumulate assets for retirement.

The main focus of the empirical analysis centers on the impact of the social security program on private pensions. The stock adjustment model assumes that social security contributions and private pension saving are perfect substitutes, implying a coefficient of -1 for

---

[19] All variants of the equations were corrected for autocorrelation and the results are presented in Table 4.

249

TABLE 3

THE EFFECT OF SOCIAL SECURITY ON PRIVATE PENSIONS, 1930–1974 (EXCLUDING 1941–1946) AND 1947–1974

Equation	YD_t	YD_{t-1}	RU_t	$(LF65+ \cdot YD)_t$	$(W-PENASS)_{t-1}$	$(SSWG+PENASS)_{t-}$
1930–1940 and 1947–1974						
1	0.18	−0.03	−0.03	−0.11	−0.0003	−0.013
	(0.04)	(0.03)	(0.09)	(0.05)	(0.0042)	(0.007)
2	0.19	−0.03	−0.02	−0.11	0.0012	
	(0.04)	(0.02)	(0.09)	(0.04)	(0.0038)	
3	0.13	−0.01	−0.09	−0.18	−0.0001	−0.006
	(0.05)	(0.03)	(0.12)	(0.05)	(0.0009)	(0.008)
4	0.15	−0.01	−0.05	−0.19	−0.0001	
	(0.05)	(0.03)	(0.12)	(0.05)	(0.0009)	
1947–1974						
5	0.37	0.01	−0.23	−0.22	0.0006	−0.050
	(0.08)	(0.05)	(0.21)	(0.06)	(0.0053)	(0.021)
6	0.32	−0.01	−0.20	−0.18	0.0019	
	(0.06)	(0.04)	(0.20)	(0.05)	(0.0052)	
7	0.37	0.01	−0.29	−0.29	0.0007	−0.055
	(0.10)	(0.06)	(0.28)	(0.08)	(0.0009)	(0.026)
8	0.27	−0.04	−0.18	−0.23	0.0004	
	(0.07)	(0.05)	(0.28)	(0.07)	(0.0009)	

NOTE: Numbers in parentheses are standard errors. All variables are expressed in per capita 1972 dollars. The dependent variable is pension saving, that is, the

OASI. The empirical results are consistent with this hypothesis, since the coefficients of −0.83 and −0.76 are not significantly different statistically from the hypothesized value of −1. Social security also enters the equation as the major portion of the stock of retirement assets ($SSW+PENASS$), and the results indicate that anticipated social security benefits have a large negative effect on pension saving. The social security wealth variable, which adjusts for future taxes, appear to provide a better explanation of savings behavior than the gross value

The other important explanatory variables are the labor force participation and other savings. The coefficient of other savings (SO) should be interpreted in terms of the original model as the value of λ_2

$(SSWN+ PENASS)_{t-1}$	$OASI_t$	SO_t	Constant	R^2	DW
1930–1940 and 1947–1974					
	−0.62 (0.36)	−0.28 (0.06)	−0.13 (0.08)	0.65	1.22
−0.025 (0.010)	−0.54 (0.34)	−0.28 (0.06)	−0.16 (0.08)	0.68	1.29
	−1.00 (0.41)		−0.02 (0.09)	0.41	1.07
−0.018 (0.013)	−0.09 (0.41)		−0.06 (0.09)	0.44	1.09
1947–1974					
	−0.83 (0.45)	−0.24 (0.07)	−0.40 (0.18)	0.64	1.50
−0.059 (0.021)	−0.76 (0.43)	−0.27 (0.07)	−0.35 (0.14)	0.67	1.86
	−0.83 (0.53)		−0.34 (0.19)	0.47	1.47
−0.045 (0.027)	−0.83 (0.55)		−0.16 (0.14)	0.44	1.54

net increase in pension fund reserves. Social security wealth is estimated as of January; therefore, current rather than lagged values were used to calculate the lagged stock of retirement assets.

the percentage of nonpension saving allocated for retirement. Since saving for retirement is only one of many motives for accumulating wealth and since other saving excludes increases in private pension reserves, a coefficient between 0.24 and 0.27 seems quite reasonable. Excluding *SO* from the equations does not significantly affect the results.

The labor force participation variable was introduced to reflect the trend since World War II toward early retirement; this trend results, in part, from the availability of social security and private pension benefits, the spread of compulsory retirement policies that accompanied the growth of these programs, and the social security earnings test. Earlier retirement implies a shorter working life and a longer period of de-

251

TABLE 4

Effect of Social Security on Private Pensions, Correcting for First Order Autocorrelation, 1930–1974 (Excluding 1941–1946) and 1947–1974

Equation	YD_t	YD_{t-1}	RU_t	$(LF65+ YD_t)$	$(W- PENASS)_{t-1}$	$(SSWG+ PENASS)_{t-1}$
1930–1940 and 1947–1974						
1	0.14	−0.04	−0.05	−0.08	0.0005	−0.009
	(0.04)	(0.02)	(0.10)	(0.06)	(0.0006)	(0.007)
2	0.16	−0.03	−0.03	−0.10	0.0005	
	(0.03)	(0.02)	(0.10)	(0.05)	(0.0005)	
3	0.07	−0.02	0.03	−0.08	0.0005	−0.004
	(0.04)	(0.02)	(0.13)	(0.09)	(0.0006)	(0.008)
4	0.09	−0.02	0.03	−0.09	0.0005	
	(0.04)	(0.02)	(0.13)	(0.09)	(0.0006)	
1947–1974						
5	0.34	—[b]	−0.23	−0.21	0.0005	−0.049
	(0.09)	(0.05)	(0.25)	(0.07)	(0.0006)	(0.021)
6	0.31	−0.01	−0.22	−0.18	0.0004	
	(0.06)	(0.04)	(0.22)	(0.05)	(0.0007)	
7	0.34	0.01	−0.26	−0.21	0.0006	−0.053
	(0.11)	(0.06)	(0.31)	(0.09)	(0.0001)	(0.027)
8	0.24	−0.02	−0.09	−0.22	0.0005	
	(0.08)	(0.05)	(0.30)	(0.08)	(0.0008)	

[a] Standard error of estimate.
[b] Less than 0.01.

NOTE: Numbers in parentheses are standard errors. All variables are expressed in per capita 1972 dollars. The dependent variable is pension saving, that is, the net increase in pension fund reserves. Social security wealth is estimated as of January; therefore, current rather than lagged values were used to calculate the lagged stock of retirement assets.

pendency upon retirement benefits, and thus it should be a major stimulant for retirement saving. The results are consistent with this view. To the extent that social security is responsible for either directly or indirectly lengthening the retirement period, this positive influence on the growth of pension plans must be considered as an offset to the negative impact of *OASI* benefits and social security wealth.

The importance of the empirical analysis for those interested in

$(SSWN+ PENASS)_{t-1}$	$OASI_t$	SO_t	Constant	SEE^a	DW
	−0.39 (0.28)	−0.25 (0.05)	−0.09 (0.07)	0.009	1.44
−0.022 (0.010)	−0.35 (0.28)	−0.26 (0.05)	−0.11 (0.07)	0.009	1.48
	−0.42 (0.32)		−0.05 (0.09)	0.009	1.17
−0.012 (0.014)	−0.39 (0.32)		−0.02 (0.09)	0.009	1.20
	−0.62 (0.41)	−0.23 (0.07)	−0.35 (0.16)	0.010	1.62
−0.059 (0.021)	−0.67 (0.42)	−0.27 (0.07)	−0.32 (0.12)	0.009	1.79
	−0.72 (0.50)		−0.30 (0.20)	0.010	1.56
−0.046 (0.031)	−0.70 (0.50)		−0.15 (0.17)	0.009	1.53

the future of private pensions is that the two systems are, for a large portion of the population, alternative mechanisms for accomplishing the same objective. For any level of income, wealth, and retirement patterns, an additional dollar of social security taxes implies about a dollar less in private pension fund reserves. Therefore, it is crucial to examine the recent changes in the social security program and their implications for private pensions.

Social Security in the 1970s

After three decades of relatively minor changes in the OASI program, the 1970s brought a significant expansion in retirement benefits.[20] Recent increases have been reflected in both higher replacement rates (the ratio of benefits to pre-retirement earnings) and a significant rise in the earnings included in the benefit calculation. As a result, social security alone now approaches a level of adequate retirement income for more than half of new retirees.

A succession of ad hoc benefit increases in the early 1970s, followed by automatic cost-of-living adjustments stemming from the 1972 amendments to the Social Security Act, have raised social security benefits by 105 percent (see Table 5).[21] The doubling of benefits in the 1970s is especially striking when compared with the 59 percent increase between 1950 and 1969. The benefit increases have resulted in a major adjustment in replacement rates from 30 percent of pre-retirement earnings in 1969 to 45 percent in 1977 (see Table 6).

At the same time, the taxable wage base has also increased dramatically. In 1969, benefits were calculated on earnings up to a maximum of $7,800; by 1978, the maximum had increased to $17,700. According to recent data, only 15 percent of workers have earnings that exceed the social security tax base (see Table 7).

The net result of the increase in replacement rates and the expansion of the earnings base is that social security now represents a substantial source of retirement income for a large portion of the population. A worker retiring at age sixty-five in January 1977 with a history of median earnings received a monthly benefit of $329, or 45 percent of earnings in the year before retirement. For a married worker, the monthly benefit increased to $493, or 67 percent of pre-retirement earnings. Table 8 summarizes benefits and replacement rates for other types of beneficiaries and earnings histories.

The adequacy of social security benefits can be assessed against two alternative measures: an absolute standard of living or the mainte-

---

[20] The social security program as a whole did expand during the three decades through broader coverage, the introduction of disability and health insurance, and provisions for early retirement. During this period, OASI benefits generally kept pace with wages, yielding a replacement rate that hovered around 30 percent. In addition, ad hoc adjustments generally insured that retirees' benefits kept pace with price increases after retirement.

[21] The ad hoc increases amounted to 15 percent effective in January 1970, 10 percent in January 1971, and 20 percent in September 1972. The automatic cost-of-living adjustments were 11 percent in June 1974, 8 percent in June 1975, 6.4 percent in June 1976, and 5.9 percent in June 1977.

TABLE 5

CUMULATIVE EFFECT OF STATUTORY AND AUTOMATIC INCREASES IN PRIMARY INSURANCE BENEFITS UNDER OASDHI PROGRAM, 1950–1977

(percent)

Effective Date of Increase

Base Date	January 1959	January 1965	February 1968	January 1970	January 1971	September 1972	June 1974	June 1975	June 1976	June 1977
September 1950	31	41	59	83	101	142	168	190	202	214
January 1959	—	7	21	39	53	84	104	120	134	148
January 1965	—	—	13	30	43	72	91	106	119	130
February 1968	—	—	—	15	27	52	69	82	94	105
January 1970	—	—	—	—	10	32	47	58	68	78
January 1971	—	—	—	—	—	20	33	44	53	62
September 1972	—	—	—	—	—	—	11	20	28	35
June 1974	—	—	—	—	—	—	—	8	15	21
June 1975	—	—	—	—	—	—	—	—	6.4	13
June 1976	—	—	—	—	—	—	—	—	—	5.9

SOURCES: Social Security Administration, *Social Security Bulletin*, *Annual Statistical Supplement 1974*; Office of Actuary for updated data.

TABLE 6

SOCIAL SECURITY REPLACEMENT RATE FOR A SIXTY-FIVE-YEAR-OLD
MALE RETIREE EARNING THE MEDIAN WAGE,
SELECTED YEARS 1940–1977

Year of Retirement	Replacement Rate[a]
1940	0.292[b]
1945	0.222[b]
1950	0.192[b]
1955	0.344
1960	0.330
1965	0.314
1966	0.302
1967	0.289
1968	0.310
1969	0.296
1970	0.311
1971	0.349
1972	0.342
1973	0.381
1974	0.388
1975	0.404
1976	0.433
1977	0.447

[a] The replacement rate is the value of the benefit in the year of retirement divided by the median wage in the year before retirement. The benefit is for a hypothetical male earning the median wage for each year in the averaging period.

[b] Replacement rates for 1940–1950 were approximated by the ratio of average benefit award to average taxable wages. For later years, this ratio is very similar to the actual replacement rate. The figure for 1950 pertains to January through August; a legislated benefit increase became effective in September.

SOURCES: Social Security Administration, *Social Security Bulletin, Annual Statistical Supplement 1974*, table 59, p. 89; Congressional Budget Office, *Financing Social Security: Issues for the Short and Long Term* (July 1977), table 4, p. 16.

nance of pre-retirement living standards. Social security benefits for a retired couple with median earnings approximate the intermediate budget calculated by the Bureau of Labor Statistics for retired couples (see Table 9). The benefits for low-income workers are roughly equivalent to the lower budget. The expansion of social security has also been reflected in the poverty statistics. In 1969, the aged accounted for 26

TABLE 7

PERCENT OF WORKERS WITH TOTAL ANNUAL EARNINGS BELOW THE
ANNUAL MAXIMUM TAXABLE, BY SEX, SELECTED YEARS, 1940–1978

Year	Maximum Taxable Earnings (dollars)	Percent of Workers with Earnings below Maximum		
		Total	Men	Women
1940	3,000	96.6	95.4	99.7
1945	3,000	86.3	78.6	98.9
1950	3,000	71.1	59.9	94.6
1955	4,200	74.4	63.3	93.9
1960	4,800	72.0	60.8	93.4
1965	4,800	63.9	51.0	87.3
1966	6,600	75.8	64.4	95.6
1967	6,600	73.6	61.5	94.2
1968	7,800	78.6	68.0	96.3
1969	7,800	75.5	62.8	96.0
1970	7,800	74.0	61.8	93.5
1971	7,800	71.7	59.1	91.7
1972	9,000	75.0	62.9	93.9
1973	10,800	79.7	68.9	96.2
1974	13,200	84.9	76.2	97.8
1975	14,100	85.0	76.2	97.5
1976	15,300	85.0	76.2	97.5
1977	16,500	85.0	76.2	97.5
1978	17,700	85.0	76.2	97.5

SOURCES: Social Security Administration, *Social Security Bulletin, Annual Statistical Supplement 1975*, table 40, p. 73; Office of Research and Statistics for revised and updated data.

percent of families below the poverty line; in 1975, this percentage had dropped to 9 percent.[22]

Alternatively, if social security benefits are to be measured against pre-retirement living standards rather than against a monetary standard, then replacement rates are the relevant measure rather than benefit levels. The replacement rates reported earlier, however, understate the extent to which social security benefits permit retirees to maintain their previous standard of living. Because of reduced work expenses, Medicare, and lower taxes, retirees generally require only 65 to 80 percent

[22] U.S. Bureau of the Census, *Current Population Reports*, ser. P-60, no. 10, "Characteristics of Population below Poverty Level, 1975" (June 1977), table 20, p. 86.

TABLE 8
MONTHLY BENEFITS, REPLACEMENT RATES, AND FAMILY BENEFIT AS A PERCENT OF PRIMARY INSURANCE AMOUNT (PIA), BY TYPE OF BENEFICIARY, JANUARY 1977

Type of Beneficiary	Family Benefit as Percent of PIA	Monthly Benefit (dollars)			Replacement Rate[d]		
		Low[a] ($4,416 in 1976)	Median[b] ($8,832 in 1976)	Maximum[c] ($15,300 in 1976)	Low[a]	Median[b]	Maximum[c]
Worker							
Aged 65	100.0	214	329	413	0.582	0.447	0.324
Aged 62	80.0	171	263	330	0.466	0.358	0.259
Worker aged 65 with wife							
Aged 65	150.0	320	493	619	0.873	0.671	0.486
Aged 62	137.5	294	452	567	0.800	0.615	0.445
Worker aged 62 with wife							
Aged 65	130.0	278	427	537	0.756	0.582	0.421
Aged 62	117.5	251	386	485	0.684	0.526	0.380
Widow aged 65, spouse retired at							
Aged 65	100.0	214	329	413	0.582	0.447	0.324
Aged 62	82.5	176	271	340	0.480	0.369	0.267

[a] Assumes annual income equal to half the median for males.

[b] Assumes annual income equal to the median for all male workers covered under social security. Median income figure for 1975 is preliminary from the Social Security Administration. Median earnings for 1976 estimated by increasing the 1975 figure by 7.3 percent, which is the factor of increase in average weekly earnings for 1976. See *Economic Report of the President, 1977*, p. 227.

[c] Assumes income equal to the maximum taxable amount each year.

[d] The ratio of the PIA at award to monthly taxable earnings in the year just before retirement.

SOURCE: Social Security Administration, Office of the Actuary.

TABLE 9

JANUARY 1977 SOCIAL SECURITY BENEFITS FOR A RETIRED COUPLE AS A
PERCENTAGE OF BUREAU OF LABOR STATISTICS (BLS) BUDGETS,
AUTUMN 1976

	Social Security Benefits as a Percentage of BLS Annual Budget for a Retired Couple		
Earnings Level for Retired Worker and Spouse Aged 65	Lower budget ($4,695)	Inter-mediate budget ($6,738)	Higher budget ($10,048)
Low earnings ($4,416)	0.82	0.57	0.38
Median earnings ($8,832)	1.26	0.88	0.59
Maximum earnings ($15,300)	1.58	1.10	0.74

SOURCES: U.S. Bureau of Labor Statistics, *Three Budgets for a Retired Couple, Autumn 1976* (August 4, 1977); and Table 5 above.

of pre-retirement earnings (see Table 10). For retired couples with earnings up to the median, social security provides virtually all the required income. Social security benefits do constitute less than 65 percent of pre-retirement income for workers whose wage history exceeds the median; most of these families, however, have other sources of retirement income.

According to the 1968 Survey of the Aged, 59 percent of those aged sixty-five to seventy-two owned homes with a median equity of $12,000 ($21,882 in 1977 dollars); of these homes, more than 80 percent were mortgage free.[23] Nearly three-quarters of retirees aged sixty-five to seventy-two also had some type of financial assets, although the median value was only $750 ($1,368 in 1977 dollars). An updated survey would probably reveal a significant increase in the number owning homes and holding other assets.

The fact that social security benefits are now approaching an adequate level for most workers was highlighted in a recent statement by Bert Seidman of the AFL-CIO: "In the past, the labor movement generally felt that the most important steps to improve the social security system were to effect across-the-board increases in benefits plus even

[23] Social Security Administration, Office of Research and Statistics, *Demographic and Economic Characteristics of the Aged*, Research Report no. 45 (1975), tables 6.1, 6.2, 6.7, and 6.9, pp. 106, 108, 113, and 115.

TABLE 10

RETIREMENT INCOME EQUIVALENT TO PRE-RETIREMENT INCOME FOR MARRIED COUPLES RETIRING JANUARY 1976, SELECTED INCOME LEVELS

(dollars)

	Pre-retirement Tax Payment			Reduction in Expenses at Retire-ment[b]	Equivalent Retirement Income[c]	
Pre-retirement Income	Federal income	OASDHI	State and local income[a]		Dollars	Percent of pre-retirement income
4,000	28	234	4	544	3,190	80
6,000	330	351	43	816	4,460	74
8,000	679	468	89	1,088	5,676	71
10,000	1,059	585	139	1,360	6,857	69
15,000	2,002	824	262	2,040	9,872	66

[a] In 1974, state and local income tax receipts were 13.1 percent of federal income tax receipts. This percentage probably rose in 1975 because federal taxes were decreased while state taxes increased. Therefore, the percentage of pre-retirement income needed to maintain living standards is probably slightly overstated.

[b] Consumption requirements for a two-person husband-wife family after retirement are 86.4 percent of those for a similar family before retirement (aged fifty-five to sixty-four). Savings are therefore estimated at 13.6 percent of pre-retirement income.

[c] Assumes that retirement income is not subject to tax. If retirement income is subject to taxation, a larger pre-retirement disposable income would be needed to yield the equivalent retirement income.

SOURCES: Commerce Clearing House, *1976 U.S. Master Tax Guide* (Chicago: Commerce Clearing House, 1975); U.S. Bureau of Labor Statistics, *Revised Equivalence Scale for Estimating Equivalent Incomes or Budget Costs by Family Type*, Bulletin 1570-2 (1968), p. 4; estimates of state and local income tax receipts as a percentage of federal income tax from Bureau of Economic Analysis.

more sizable boosts in the minimum benefit. Overall benefit increases may be needed again at some time in the future, but that is not where we place our priority today."[24]

In short, social security now meets most of the retirement needs for workers, particularly those who are married, with earnings up to the median. Additional retirement resources will still be required for

[24] Bert Seidman, "Concepts of Balance Between Social Security (OASDI) and Private Pension Benefits," in *Social Security and Private Pension Plans: Competitive or Complementary?* ed. Dan M. McGill (Homewood, Ill.: Richard D. Irwin, 1977), p. 86.

the 35 percent of workers with earnings between the median and the maximum taxable amount and for the 15 percent who earn above the maximum. The future role of private pensions in the provision of this required supplementary income, however, hinges on the future of social security.

The 1977 amendments corrected the overindexing of the benefit formula which had contributed to the upward drift in replacement rates during the 1970s.[25] The new procedure for computing benefits will yield replacement rates slightly lower than current levels, but generally it insures that the average worker will continue to receive benefits equal to at least 40 percent of pre-retirement earnings.

Although the 1977 legislation stabilized replacement rates, it significantly increased the tax and benefit base. The 1978 base of $17,700 was scheduled to increase automatically each year in line with the growth of average wages (a provision introduced in the 1972 amendments). Congress suspended the automatic adjustments, however, and instead prescribed three years of ad hoc increases—namely to $22,900 in 1979, to $25,000 in 1980, and to $29,700 in 1981—after which the automatic provisions once again take over. The prescribed base for 1981 of $29,700 represents a 36 percent increase over the projected level of $21,900 that would have resulted from automatic increases. By 1981, only 6 percent of all workers will have earnings that exceed the social security earnings limit. The significant increases in the earnings base will greatly increase the tax burden of highly paid workers, but they will also result in higher benefits to these individuals. Although the increase in eventual benefit amounts will not be proportional to contributions because the benefit formula is weighted in favor of low-income workers, the extension of benefits up the income scale will certainly have a profound effect on the private pension system.

Indirect Effects of Social Security on Private Pensions

In addition to the direct impact of social security benefits, the future of private pensions will also depend on employers' contributions to

---

25 The 1972 amendments introduced a mechanism by which benefits are adjusted to reflect changes in the cost of living. The provision insured that the purchasing power of benefits remained unchanged during retirement; unfortunately, a technical flaw overcompensated current workers for the effect of inflation since the same benefit formula applied to both retirees and those still in the labor force. For retirees, inflation had no effect on determining average monthly earnings, upon which benefits were calculated. For those still working, however, wage increases over the long run should compensate them for inflation. Their average monthly earnings would reflect these increases, resulting in higher social security benefits. Subsequent adjustments in the benefit formula would compensate them again for inflation.

social security, the rate of inflation, and any changes in the tax treatment of private pensions as a result of their more limited role since the expansion of social security. Developments in each of these areas suggest that private pensions will become relatively less important over time in the provision of retirement income.

Increasing the maximum on earnings subject to the social security tax, as occurs under the 1977 amendments, significantly increases the cost to employers of high-wage workers—precisely the group for whom private pensions are important. Since the increase in payroll taxes will have no effect on the productivity of labor, employers who wish to maximize their profits will continue to pay the same total compensation for that unit of labor, reducing wages or fringe benefits by the amount necessary to pay the additional tax. Thus, it is likely that the higher social security levy will result in lower private pension benefits for high-wage workers even if they receive no benefits from the additional employer contributions.

The proportion of retirement income derived from private pensions will probably decline if the United States continues to experience high rates of inflation. With an inflation rate of 6 percent, a private pension benefit of $2,101 (the average in 1975) is reduced to $1,173 in ten years. The cost to firms of providing automatic cost-of-living adjustments is extremely high (see Table 11). Only the federal government would be able to guarantee benefits that keep pace with prices in the face of high rates of inflation. In this environment, social security would probably expand beyond current projections with a corresponding increase in costs, and private pensions would become relatively unimportant.

With the role of private pensions narrowed by the expansion of social security, the favorable tax provisions, which accrue primarily to workers with above-average earnings, may receive renewed scrutiny. Currently, pension contributions made by an employer are a deductible business expense. At the same time, they are not regarded as taxable income to employees until the benefits are paid out. The earnings in pension funds are also allowed to accumulate without payment of any income tax. These provisions result in a significant tax savings to individuals for two reasons: first, the employee's marginal tax rate is generally lower during his retirement years than during his working life because of lower income and special tax provisions for the aged (such as the retirement income credit); second, current aggregate pension contributions and investment income which are not taxed exceed aggregate amounts paid out as taxable benefits. These favorable provisions were introduced to stimulate development of private pensions by em-

TABLE 11

COST IMPACT ON HYPOTHETICAL PRIVATE PENSION PLAN OF
INSTITUTING COST-OF-LIVING ADJUSTMENTS

Rate of Inflation (percent)	Percentage Increase in Plan Cost
2	18.9
3	29.4
4	41.3
5	53.6
6	68.2

NOTE: The calculations are based on the following assumptions: (1) interest rate: 6 percent; (2) retirement age: sixty-five; (3) proportion of participants who are male: 75 percent; (4) proportion of annual contributions allocated to normal cost: 60 percent; (5) proportion of past service liability already funded: 50 percent. An 8 percent rate of interest would reduce the costs by about 10 percent. A higher percentage of past service liability already funded (assuming the same percentage of contribution allocated to normal cost) would increase the costs significantly since prior funding would not have anticipated the higher level of post-retirement benefit and future deposits would include funding increments to make up for the past. On the other hand, if a greater proportion of contributions were allocated to normal cost (assuming the same proportion of past service liability already funded), the increased cost to the pension plan would be less than the figures shown in the table.

SOURCE: Edward H. Friend and Company, *Quarterly Newsletter*, 3rd quarter 1976, vol. 1, no. 4, tables 2 and 3.

ployers. This was a rational policy when the gap between desired and actual retirement assets was large and private pensions were needed for all workers to supplement "the floor of protection" offered by social security. In fiscal year 1977, however, 75 percent of the $6.5 billion estimated revenue loss from these provisions accrued to individuals with annual incomes higher than $15,000 (17 percent to those with incomes of $50,000 and over).[26] If this tax break for high-income workers were eliminated, pension plan growth would be affected severely.[27]

[26] U.S. Congress, Senate, Committee on the Budget, *Tax Expenditures: Compendium of Background Material on Individual Provisions*, 94th Congress, 2nd session, 1976, pp. 115–16.

[27] On the other hand, if private pensions were financed through after-tax contributions by the employee, many of the problems of vesting and portability would disappear. Furthermore, low-income workers with adequate social security benefits would be excluded, thereby avoiding the inequity of denying benefits through offset formulas to workers who have sacrificed some wages to become eligible for their firm's pension plan.

Conclusion

The simultaneous expansion of social security and private pensions since 1940 reflected the nation's desire to accumulate a large stock of retirement assets to insure adequate income in old age. Since social security and private pensions are substitutes, however, the recent increase in social security benefits, to levels that insure adequate income for most new retirees, will reduce the need for supplementary benefits from private pensions. In addition, private pensions would be affected adversely by an increase in the maximum social security tax base for employers, continued high rates of inflation, or the elimination of the favorable tax provisions.

A shift from private pensions toward social security implies a reduction in saving and capital accumulation. The reduction occurs because, while the decline in individual saving because of anticipated retirement benefits is offset by an increase in assets of private pension funds, no such offset occurs in social security, which is financed on a pay-as-you-go basis. A dramatic decline in the proportion of saving through private pension has already occurred: in the 1960s pension saving averaged 30 percent of total personal saving; in the 1970s this percentage has dropped to 22 percent during a period when social security benefits have increased substantially.

The importance of the relative decline in pension saving should not be exaggerated, however, because alternative mechanisms are available to stimulate capital formation. Furthermore, the $20.9 billion increase in the assets of pension funds in 1975 was offset by a $5.2 billion revenue loss to the federal government because of the favorable tax provisions.[28]

The important implication of recent developments is that the perpetual debate over the appropriate role for private pensions and social security appears to have been resolved de facto in favor of social security. The role of private pensions will be limited to providing supplementary benefits to individuals with earnings above the median. Even this more limited role may be in jeopardy if inflation persists or the favorable tax provisions are eliminated.

---

[28] For the increase in assets of pension funds, see Martha Remy Yohalem, "Employee-Benefit Plans, 1975," *Social Security Bulletin*, vol. 40 (November 1977), p. 27. For the loss to the federal government, see Senate, Committee on the Budget, *Tax Expenditures*, p. 114.

How Social Security May Undermine the Private Industrial Pension System

Dennis E. Logue

In 1950, retired employees with private industrial pension benefits received on the average $1,350 a year in 1970 dollars. By 1975, the amount received had risen to only $1,575 in 1970 dollars (see Figure 1). Over the same period, average real social security benefits rose from roughly $800 to more than $1,700 (see Figure 2). In 1950, the average retiree who was a recipient of both private and social security retirement benefits derived the bulk of his pension income from private sources. This is no longer the case. Moreover, social security retirement benefits together with other public assistance programs for the aged have become sufficient, or very nearly so, to support most individuals in retirement.

As the need to rely on private pensions diminishes, the value to employers of offering private pensions is reduced. The perceived value of a pension of a given magnitude in fostering employee loyalty and initiative declines. Moreover, the costs of maintaining private pension systems have increased because of regulations imposed by the Employee Retirement Income Security Act of 1974 (ERISA). As a result, the number of private pension plans and the percentage of the work force covered will probably be reduced dramatically.

An objective of this paper is to show how and why social security retirement benefits have damaged the private pension system. First, the theory of private pensions is briefly described. The discussion focuses principally upon why such plans exist. Next, the mechanics of the interaction between social security and private plans is taken up. How does social security affect private pensions under present institutional arrangements? What is the extent of integration? This is followed by a discussion of some of the prospective problems and broad issues related to the relationship between social security and private pension plans.

One reason why ERISA was enacted is the belief that "strengthening" the private pension system will decrease the demands on the social security system—that it will reduce the political pressure for larger social security benefits. Offsetting this effect is the possibility that ERISA will lead to a cutback in private pension plans by employers. If so, the effect of ERISA would be to increase the demand for more

FIGURE 1
AVERAGE ANNUAL PRIVATE PENSION BENEFIT, 1950–1974
(constant 1970 dollars)

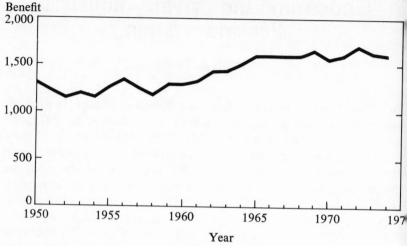

SOURCE: Alfred M. Skolnik, "Private Pension Plans, 1950–74," *Social Security Bulletin*, vol. 39 (June 1976).

FIGURE 2
AVERAGE ANNUAL SOCIAL SECURITY
RETIREMENT BENEFIT, 1950–1974
(constant 1970 dollars)

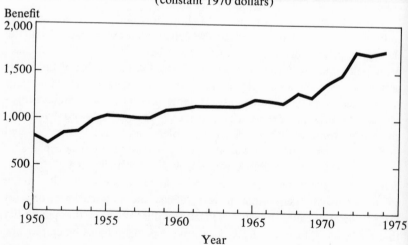

SOURCE: *Social Security Bulletin*, various issues.

generous social security benefits. In addition to the effects of ERISA, recent and prospective changes in the social security system have weakened the private pension system and will increase further the demands on social security. In particular, the indexing of social security benefits reduces the need for the equity-type investments typically made by pension funds as a "hedge" against inflation; similarly, the comparatively high benefit levels and the supplemental programs such as Medicare reduce the need for private pension benefits. Finally, the increased social security tax rates that were recently enacted reduce the funds available for private pension savings, other things being equal.

A Theory of Private Pensions

Private pensions are commonly viewed in two ways: first, that they are altruistic rewards given to employees for long years of faithful service; and, second, that they are deferred wages, savings that are forced on employees by their employers.[1] Neither of these theories has much support. Most plans are *defined benefit plans*; that is, pension payments represent a fraction of the retired employee's average salary multiplied by the number of years worked. An employee's salary may be averaged over his entire career or computed over a shorter period before retirement. Some plans are *defined contribution plans*; that is, a percentage of a worker's salary is set aside annually and retirement benefits depend upon the performance of the pension fund. In defined benefit plans, the firm protects employees against the risk of a decline in the value of the assets held by the pension fund.

Two other features characterize most corporate pension plans. First, pension benefits do not vest immediately. Employees must typically work for the firm a certain number of years before property rights to pension benefits are acquired. Second, pension benefits are currently viewed by management and by labor as rights to be bargained for. Pension benefits are typically no longer granted solely at the discretion of the employer.

The latter characteristic of private pensions is in sharp contrast to the altruistic theory that in the early 1900s was thought to be the primary reason why pension plans were being set up by the geographically spread-out railroads and other decentralized firms.[2] Moreover, from the

---

[1] In the interest of brevity, only the basic description of the theory of pensions is presented here; the full details and verification are found in Dennis E. Logue, *Legislative Influences on Corporation Pension Programs* (forthcoming).

[2] See, for example, Lee W. Squires, *Old Age Dependency in the United States* (New York: Macmillan, 1912), p. 272.

267

point of view of competitive theory, the position that charitable inten
tions alone motivated the granting of pensions is difficult to support
Instead, employers probably offered pension benefits because they wer
able to gain some benefit during the period of employment. By holding
out the promise that an employee may receive financial support from
the firm in his old age, the firm was probably able to derive a greate
contribution from the employee than it otherwise could have.

The deferred-wage theory was popular in the 1940s and was rec
ognized by the courts in the famous Inland Steel decision.[3] Both the
practice of defining benefits and the requirement of vesting raise ques
tions about the validity of this concept. In the deferred-wage theory, the
firm's pension contribution must be viewed as part of the employee's
direct compensation. Conceptually, the marginal product is split into a
least two components—the wage paid and the pension contribution. I
the pension contribution forms part of the employee's current marginal
product, why would an employee risk losing this by accepting any vesting requirement other than immediate vesting? In addition, under this
theory it is difficult to explain why firms would bear the downside risk
of pension fund performance, as many do under defined benefit plans.

Private pensions usually require employees to fulfill certain requirements before gaining full entitlement to pension benefits. Because there
is a risk of not meeting these requirements, one would expect that employees would insist that the firm add some amount to the deferred
wages to gain the tax advantage associated with such forms of compensation.[4] By accepting conditions regarding the receipt of pension
benefits, employees enter a contingent claim contract with employers.
Once they do so, employees must be compensated. But what advantages
accrue to employers?

Vesting provisions (as well as other requirements for eligibility)
in a pension contract probably reduce labor turnover. Also, such contracts induce employees to avoid getting fired before vesting and cause
workers to work harder with less supervision. As a result, the employer
benefits.

Low turnover in the labor force reduces expenditures for hiring
and training new employees. Because employees work harder to avoid
being fired, the firm may spend less on monitoring and supervising

---

[3] Inland Steel Co. v. National Labor Relations Board, 170 F.2d. 247 (1949).

[4] A tax advantage arises because pension fund contributions are tax deductible
for an employer and are not taxed for the employee. When taxable pension benefits start flowing to the retired employee, the employee is normally in a lower
income tax bracket than when he was working. Income has been shifted from a
relatively high tax period to a relatively low tax period.

employees. These "savings" by the firm can then be passed along to employees as compensation for bearing the risks of taking compensation in the form of an option.

This hypothesis implies that the higher the hiring and training costs of a particular type of employment, the more stringent should be the vesting requirement and the more generous the pension benefit schedule. There should also be a trade-off between vesting requirements and benefit levels, assuming other conditions are the same. Although data on hiring, training, and other similar costs for individual firms are not available, casual observation indicates that the most generous private programs are in those industries in which the degree of skill and the relative independence of employees is greatest.

Private pensions are not deferred wages, nor are they altruistic. Rather, it seems that they represent a contingent claim contract. The "sweetener" offered by the firm to the employee for bearing the risk of not fulfilling the conditions of the contract is a portion of the firm's savings on the hiring, training, and monitoring costs that would otherwise be incurred. Thus, private pension plans embody incentives for employees to avoid being fired and to minimize the amount of direct supervision required. This would be in addition to the income tax advantages of deferred wages.

Integration of Social Security and Private Pension Plans

Why and How. The integration of private pension with social security benefits means that, in terms of replacement rates (the ratio of retirement income to final pay), the benefits from the private pension and from social security are negatively related. When social security benefits are increased, private pension benefits are adjusted downward. Low-income earners obtain comparatively high replacement ratios from their social security benefits but relatively smaller replacement ratios from their private plans. High-income earners, on the other hand, receive relatively low replacement ratios from social security because of its truncated taxable wage base and relatively high replacement from private plans. The intent of integration, therefore, is the maintenance of roughly constant replacement ratios across employee income groups.

The concept is capably described by Raymond Schmitt:

> The Internal Revenue Code permits private pension plans to integrate their benefit formulas with benefits provided under Social Security. . . . Social Security laws set a ceiling on the amount of wages subject to payroll tax. Since Social Security benefits are related to covered earnings they also have a built

269

in ceiling. Thus, Social Security income replacement rates decrease as preretirement income increases. It was considered logical, therefore, to permit the private pension system to pick up where the Social Security system left off by providing supplemental benefits based upon earnings above the Social Security wage base.

Congress recognized this in 1942, when it first wrote into the law the proviso that although a tax qualified plan could not discriminate in favor of the higher paid workers its benefit structure could not favor those with earnings above the Social Security ceiling provided that when the public and private benefits were considered together, their combined benefits did not give preference to the higher paid. So long as the ratio of combined benefits to earnings is no higher for employees whose wages exceed the taxable wage base than for those whose wages are fully taxed by Social Security, Congress said a plan would be held to be nondiscriminatory.

A ruling by the Internal Revenue Service implements this nondiscrimination requirement by specifying certain limits to benefits (or contributions) that a private pension plan must observe in order for the plan to receive special tax treatment. These limits govern the extent to which retirement benefits based on earnings above the Social Security taxable wage base can exceed benefits basic on earnings below it.[5]

The integration of defined contribution plans with social security is typically done through the reduction in the contribution made by the employer to the private plan. Suppose that an employer contributes 10 percent of an employee's salary to retirement plans—social security plus private pensions. If the employer's share of the social security contribution is less than 10 percent, the difference goes to the private pension plan.

In defined benefit plans, there are two types of integration—the offset approach and the excess approach. Under the offset approach, the defined benefit pension including social security is computed according to the established formula (a percentage of years of service times compensation base). From that is subtracted a percentage (from 50 percent up to 83⅓ percent) of the social security benefit. The amount of the private pension benefit is equal to the remainder; if the remainder is zero or negative, there is no private benefit unless the firm has established a minimum pension.

---

[5] Raymond Schmitt, "Integration of Private Pension Plans with Social Security," in U.S. Congress, Joint Economic Committee, Subcommittee on Fiscal Policy, *Studies in Public Welfare,* Paper no. 18, *Issues in Financing Retirement Income,* 93rd Congress, 2nd session, 1974, p. 175.

TABLE 1

ILLUSTRATION OF OFFSET METHOD FOR INTEGRATING SOCIAL SECURITY
AND DEFINED BENEFIT PENSION PLAN
(dollars)

Average Monthly Earnings over Last Three Years	Monthly Benefits		Total	Total Replacement Ratio
	Social security	Private pension	Total	
500	260	0	260	0.52
1,000	360	270	630	0.63
2,000	387	706.5	1,093.5	0.55

SOURCE: Author's calculations.

Table 1 shows the monthly benefits under the offset method of integration for three different employees retiring in 1975, each with thirty years of service. The formula is:

1.5 percent multiplied by the number of years worked multiplied by average monthly salary for last three years minus 50 percent of social security benefit.

Although the offset approach discriminates strongly against the low-wage worker with respect to private pension benefits, his total replacement rate is not much different than that for the high-wage earner because of the social security integration. The middle-wage earner fares best because of the comparatively higher replacement from social security.

The excess method of social security integration allows for different private pension benefits on different levels of income. An excess plan typically would pay private benefits on earnings above some stipulated level, and no benefits or benefits at some lower rate on earnings below that stipulated level. When the benefits paid on earnings below the stipulated level are greater than zero, the plan is usually referred to as a "step-rate" excess plan.[6]

Table 2 shows what the monthly benefits for three different employees, each with thirty years of service, under the excess plan and the step-rate excess plan might be. The formula for the excess plan is:

---

[6] For elaboration of these and several other methods that have common features to the excess approach described, see ibid.

TABLE 2

ILLUSTRATION OF EXCESS METHODS FOR INTEGRATING SOCIAL
SECURITY AND DEFINED BENEFIT PENSION PLAN

Compensation Base (dollars)	Excess		Step-Rate Excess	
	Private pension benefits (dollars)	Private replacement rate	Private pension benefits (dollars)	Private replacement rate
500	30	0.06	126	0.252
1,000	180	0.18	276	0.276
2,000	460	0.23	576	0.288

SOURCE: Author's calculations.

1.0 percent times years of service multiplied by (monthly compensation base minus $400).

The formula for the step-rate excess plan is:

1.0 percent multiplied by years of service multiplied by (monthly compensation base minus $400) plus 0.8 percent multiplied by years of service multiplied by $400.

The social security replacement rates at the three wage levels, using data from Table 1, are 0.52, 0.36, and 0.19, respectively; these social security payments reduce private pension benefits. The data in Table 2 are contrived. In practice, firms can choose an excess break-point up to the average maximum social security wage base. The larger the wage base chosen, the less the private plan must pay, other things being equal.

The Internal Revenue Service (IRS) has set limits on the degree of integration—that is, on the percentage offset and on the allowable step-rate wage base and percentage differentials. These limits, in effect, prevent firms from discriminating against nonmanagerial employees. Without such limits, it would be possible, in principle, to trade private pension benefits on a dollar-for-dollar basis with social security benefits. The limits tend to insure that private pension benefits will be reduced by less than one dollar for every dollar in social security benefits. The limits set by the IRS appear to reflect the agency's beliefs about the portion of the firm's social security payments on behalf of employees that is actually borne by the firm and is not reflected in a lower pay heck. These limits are changed from time to time, but the methodology used by the IRS in setting the limits seems arbitrary.

The notion of integration does not support the deferred-wage theory on pensions. If pension contributions were deferred wages, the pension wealth held for the employee would belong to the employee once he achieved vested status. Such pension wealth would not fluctuate in amount as a result of a change in the social security law. Under an integrated plan, however, an employee's share in the pension fund varies every time there is a change in social security benefits. On the other hand, if pensions are an incentive-type arrangement, the employee's rights would not be violated by integration. The firm has promised to provide retirement income to its employees in old age, irrespective of the source of the income. The firm treats the contingent claim of the employee as one against income—with the individual bearing the risk of unanticipated changes in social security benefits—rather than as a right to accumulated wealth (a share of the pension fund asset) or a deferred wage. It does not follow, however, that integration of private and social security benefits must occur in the contingent claim view; there may still exist a rationale for additional incentives through additive private pensions.

The Extent of Integration. In this section, three studies of the extent of integration are examined; the studies are by Raymond Schmitt, the Bankers Trust, and the Wyatt Company. Schmitt's study, which is the most comprehensive survey available, is based on a sample of 369 large plans (more than twenty-six employees) and 425 small plans (fewer than twenty-six employees); it is believed to be representative of approximately 412,300 active corporate pension, profit-sharing, and stock bonus plans.[7] His principal findings are:

- Some integration with social security is found in 60 percent of the plans.
- Only 25 to 30 percent of the workers covered by private pension plans are in integrated plans; the incidence of integration is higher in plans covering fewer than twenty-six members.
- Integrated plans typically affect salaried employees rather than hourly employees.

Schmitt's findings concerning the greater incidence of integration for salaried than for hourly employees conforms quite closely to data reported in various issues of Bankers Trust's *Study of Corporate Pen-*

---

[7] Ibid., p. 174.

TABLE 3
INTEGRATION OF CONVENTIONAL PLANS WITH SOCIAL SECURITY, 1970 AND 1975
(percent)

Formula	1970	1975
Final Pay Formulas		
Offset	50	52
Step-rate	38	34
Excess	1	1
Nonintegrated	11	13
Career Average Formulas		
Offset	3	3
Step-rate	85	81
Excess	3	3
Nonintegrated	9	13

SOURCE: Bankers Trust Co., *Study of Corporate Pension Plans*, various issues.

sion Plans. But his findings concerning incidence in small and large pension plans, and thus his findings concerning the portion of covered workers, may be misleading.

Table 3 shows the percentage of firms out of a total of 190 surveyed by Bankers Trust that use various types of integration techniques and those that do not integrate their pension plans with social security. The table is divided according to plans based on final pay formulas and those based on conventional career average formulas. Final pay plans use several years (typically five) of salary history just prior to retirement to determine pension benefits. Career average plans use the average salary over the entire employment period to determine benefits; conventional career average plans involve a single employer. Among final pay plans, offset formulas appear to be most popular; among career average conventional plans, most use the step-rate excess approach. For both types of plans, integration seems to be becoming less popular. In 1975, 13 percent of final pay plans did not integrate, as compared with 11 percent that did not integrate in 1970; for career average plans, the increase in nonintegrated plans was from 9 percent to 13 percent over the period.

In addition to the decline in the percentage of firms integrating their plans, the magnitude of integration also declined over the period 1970–1975.[8] With respect to offset plans, 12 percent of the sample

[8] Bankers Trust Co., *1975 Study of Corporate Pension Plans*, p. 28.

irms reduced the private benefit by more than 50 percent of the primary ocial security benefit in 1975, whereas 43 percent of the sample firms ised offset percentages of more than 50 percent in 1970. In 1975, 65 ercent used offsets of 50 percent, as compared with 45 percent that hose 50 percent offsets in 1970. Similarly, in 1975, two out of three irms using an offset approach graduated the offset by length of service. For an employee reaching retirement age before the maximum period or offset, the offset percentage will be lower. With a maximum service of forty years and a 50 percent social security offset, a worker retiring after only thirty years of service may face an offset of only 40 percent. In 1970, only one out of every three firms using the offset method of ntegration used a graduated approach.

With respect to the breaking point used in excess and step-rate excess methods, firms are tending to "index" to the social security taxable wage base, rather than specifying dollar amounts. In 1970, four out of five excess plans indicated specific dollar amounts; in 1975, less than three out of five did so, while the remaining two out of five set the breakpoint as a fraction of the social security taxable wage base.

In general, there has been a mild reduction in the incidence and stringency of social security integration over the past several years. This would have had the effect of pushing private benefits up if there had been no other changes in the computation formulas. But there apparently have been enough changes to keep private benefits from rising by more than final salary, so total replacement ratios have not changed by any appreciable amount.

The Wyatt Company's *Survey of Retirement, Thrift and Profit Sharing Plans Covering Salaried Employees of the 50 Largest U.S. Industrial Companies as of July 1, 1975* provides information on the incidence and magnitude of social security integration for a small sample of very large firms. Of the fifty largest U.S. industrial firms (utilities excluded), forty-eight offered pension plans; the other two (Proctor and Gamble and Xerox) have profit-sharing plans. Of the forty-eight plans, forty-three integrate some portion of their benefits (including the minimum pension) in some way with social security benefits. Twenty-six plans use an offset approach in some instances, and for twenty-one the maximum offset is 50 percent of the primary social security benefit. Twenty-three, including some using an offset formula for other purposes, use an excess approach in some fashion. Some of them use both methods in various aspects of their plans, such as in alternative computations of benefits, in arriving at a minimum pension benefit, or in determining the employee's contribution to the plan. This broad finding of incidence of social security integration conflicts with Schmitt's find-

275

TABLE 4

Social Security Integration for the Forty-Eight Largest U.S. Industrial Corporations with Pension Plans as of July 1, 1975

Firm	Offset	Excess	Minimum Pension	Employee Contribution
Amerada Hess	50%, G	n.a.	n.a.	n.a.
Armco Steel	65%	n.a.	n.a.	n.a.
Ashland Oil	n.a.	career average 1.5% of $1,000 2.25% of excess final pay 1% of $750 1.5% of excess	n.a.	3% excess over $1,000
Atlantic Richfield	n.a.	1.15% of social security tax base 1.5% of excess	n.a.	n.a.
Beatrice Foods	50%, G	n.a.	n.a.	n.a.
Bethlehem Steel	50%	n.a.	n.a.	n.a.
Boeing	50%	n.a.	n.a.	n.a.
Borden	n.a.	noncontributory 1.5% of excess over social security tax base contributory 1% of excess over social security tax base	n.a.	5% of excess over social security tax base
Caterpillar Tractor	n.a.	n.a.	n.a.	n.a.
Chrysler	n.a.	n.a.	offset 60% of social security tax base	2.5% of excess over ⅔ social security tax base

Continental Oil	50%, G	n.a.	n.a.	n.a.
Dow Chemical	50%, G	n.a.	n.a.	n.a.
DuPont	50%	n.a.	n.a.	n.a.
Eastman Kodak	n.a.	1.2% of average social security tax base 1.4% of excess	n.a.	n.a.
Esmark	50%	n.a.	n.a.	
Exxon	50%, G	n.a.	n.a.	n.a.
Firestone Tire and Rubber	50%, G (final pay)	1.3% of $900	n.a.	n.a.
Ford	n.a.	2% of excess (career average) 2% of excess above ⅔ social security tax base	n.a.	3.5% of excess over $900 3.5% of excess above ⅔ social security tax base (subject to maximum)
General Electric	n.a.	1% of $550 2.1% of excess	n.a.	3% of excess over $550
General Motors	n.a.	1.5% of excess above $500 1.0% of excess above $1,150	n.a.	3% of excess over $500
Goodyear Tire and Rubber	n.a.	1.75% of earning in excess of monthly base amount (unspecified) (final 5 yrs.)	n.a.	3.5% of excess over $1,050 until age 55 then 4% of excess over $1,050
W.R. Grace	50%	n.a.	n.a.	n.a.
Greyhound	n.a.	n.a.	n.a.	n.a.
Gulf Oil	50%, G	n.a.	n.a.	n.a.
IBM	n.a.	1% of $400 1.5% of excess over $400	n.a.	n.a.
International Harvester	n.a.	2% of excess over social security tax base	55% of highest year less social security benefit	6% of excess over social security tax base

Table 4 continues next page.

Table 4 (continued)

Firm	Offset	Excess	Minimum Pension	Employee Contribution
International Telephone and Telegraph	50%, G	n.a.	n.a.	n.a.
Kraftco	n.a.	1% of $300 to $600 2% of excess 0.667% of average earnings over $400 (final ten years)	50% of social security benefit	3% of $300 to $600 6% of excess
Lockheed Aircraft	n.a.	1.5% of excess over $350	n.a.	n.a.
LTV Corp.	50%, G	n.a.	n.a.	n.a.
Mobil Oil	50%, G	n.a.	n.a.	n.a.
Monsanto	n.a.	1.5% of excess over social security tax base 1.1% of social security tax base 0.75% of excess over social security tax base (final 5 yrs.)	n.a.	4.5% of excess over social security tax base
Occidental Petroleum	n.a.	n.a.	n.a.	n.a.
Phillips Petroleum	50%, G (final pay)	1.3% of social security tax base 1.75% of excess (career average)	benefit reduced by social security benefit	n.a.
RCA Corp.	n.a.	1.125% of $550 2% of excess	n.a.	3% of excess over $550

R.J. Reynolds Industries	n.a.	1.25% of $650; 1.5% of excess	n.a.	n.a.
Rockwell International	n.a.	1.5% of excess over $566.67	n.a.	n.a.
Shell Oil	50%, G	n.a.	n.a.	n.a.
Standard Oil of California	37.5%, G	n.a.	n.a.	n.a.
Standard Oil of Indiana	50%, (final pay)	1.5% of social security tax base; 2% of excess (career average)	1.5% of social security tax base; 2% of excess (career average)	n.a.
Sun Oil	50%, G	n.a.	n.a.	n.a.
Tenneco	n.a.	1.375% of $350; 2.25% of excess	n.a.	n.a.
Texaco	45%, G (final pay)	1.31% of $650; 2% of excess (career average)	1.31% of $650; 2% of excess (career average)	0.655% to $650; 1% of excess
Union Carbide	n.a.	n.a.	n.a.	n.a.
Union Oil of California	50%, G	n.a.	n.a.	n.a.
U.S. Steel	n.a.	n.a.	n.a.	n.a.
United Technologies	n.a.	1.5% of $1,175; 2.25% of excess	50% of social security benefit	2% of excess over $1,175
Westinghouse Electric	n.a.	2.1% of excess over $550	n.a.	2.5% of excess over $550

n.a.: Not applicable.

G indicates that the social security offset is graduated by years of service.

NOTE: For an explanation of the column labels, see the text.

SOURCE: The Wyatt Company, *Survey of Retirement, Thrift and Profit Sharing Plans Covering Salaried Employees of the 50 Largest U.S. Industrial Companies* (Washington, D.C., July 1, 1975).

ings, but it is consistent with the study by the Bankers Trust. Although the firms sampled by Bankers Trust and Wyatt may be unrepresentative because of their size and sophistication, these firms are trend-setters. Table 4 shows some of the important features of each of the forty-eight pension plans. In the column labeled "offset," the table shows the maximum social security offset percent and indicates whether it is graduated by years of service with the symbol "G." In the column labeled "excess," the excess amounts and percentages appear. Some plans have entries in both columns because of alternative computations that may be used to determine benefits. In the column labeled "minimum pension," the offset percentage or excess percentage and amounts are shown. Finally, in the column labeled "employee contribution," the excess amounts and percentage contributions are shown, if applicable. Some of these firms may have altered their plans since the completion of the survey, and these plans cover only salaried employees. Nevertheless, this survey provides valuable information on the scope and nature of integration in big business.

For the ten firms that do integrate with social security—either through the offset method or through excess methods in which the breakpoint meshes with social security tax bases—increases in social security benefits and wage bases result in the lowering of private pension benefits. None of these firms' plans are currently set up (nor can they be) so that private benefits would be likely to cease for employees at all income levels in the event of a surge in real social security benefits. But if social security benefits and the social security tax base rise faster than wages, an increasing number of employees of these firms will receive very small private benefits. As a result, the phenomenon of integration, coupled with rising real social security benefits, could undermine private pension plans. As expected benefits from private plans decline, the incentive effects of private plans decline as well. This, in fact, could be the reason for the mild trend toward liberalized integration rules suggested by the Bankers Trust survey.

The Effect of Integration. In his study of integration, Schmitt asks how much it would cost firms to substitute private benefits for the private benefits displaced by social security. He surveyed life insurance companies that manage the pension plans of small firms. Despite some admitted methodological difficulties and data problems, he estimates that the average increase in pensions costs for integrated plans would be 58 percent.[9]

---

[9] Schmitt, "Integration of Private Pension Plans with Social Security," p. 185.

If integrated plans were not allowed to integrate their pension benefits with social security, private benefits would be reduced, so the 58 percent increase in cost is undoubtedly too high. In addition, this reduction would apply only to new workers and to the remaining portion of the careers of older workers. If legislation prohibiting integration were passed, however, and if it did not "grandfather," or exempt, past pension benefit contracts, the increase in costs could put many firms in severe financial difficulty. Even if past arrangements were grandfathered, many firms might simply drop their pension plans. The perceived benefit levels might be so low that they would not provide the incentive effects necessary to justify the pension. This is especially true in view of recent tax legislation allowing employees in firms that do not offer pension plans to establish their own tax-deferred savings plans through Individual Retirement Accounts.

Perhaps more revealing than an examination of the costs to firms of eliminating social security integration is an examination of how existing social security integration methods may alter firms' private pension obligations in the future. In particular, we seek to determine how the replacement ratios of private pension benefits may change in response to two different possible future courses in social security.

Column 1 of Table 5 shows the private pension replacement ratio for a worker retiring in 1975 at age sixty-five after thirty-five years of participation in the pension plan of forty-eight of the fifty largest U.S. industrial firms. The assumed starting salary is $5,271.04 a year, and it is assumed that the salary rose by 4 percent a year, yielding a final monthly salary of $1,667.65, or an annual salary of $20,012.04. The monthly social security benefit used in all offset formulas is $341.60, and excess methods vary according to specifications.

Column 2 of Table 5 shows the private pension replacement ratio for a worker retiring in 2010 at the age of sixty-five without automatic social security increases. The starting salary is assumed to be $15,000, and the salary is assumed to grow by 4 percent a year. The final salary is $57,514.80 a year, or $4,742.90 a month. The monthly social security benefit is fixed at $522.80 and the taxable social security wage base is also fixed.

Column 3 shows private pension replacement ratios with automatic social security increases for a worker retiring in 2010 at age sixty-five with thirty-five years of service. Salary assumptions are the same as for column 2. The monthly primary social security benefit at the time of retirement is allowed to grow to $2,003.40, or by 3 percent a year, in line with the cost of living. The resultant figures are used in offset formulas. The social security tax base is assumed to grow at 4 percent

281

TABLE 5

EFFECTS OF SOCIAL SECURITY GROWTH ON INTEGRATED PRIVATE
PENSION BENEFITS AS MEASURED BY PRIVATE REPLACEMENT RATIOS
(percent)

Firm	Retire 1975 (1)	Retire 2010 with No Automatic Social Security Increases (2)	Retire 2010 with Automatic Social Security Increases (3)
Amerada Hess	38.4	43.1	27.5
Armco Steel	35.3	41.4	32.9
Ashland Oil	42.6	47.4	47.7
Atlantic Richfield	47.4	47.5	44.2
Beatrice Foods	35.1	39.9	32.4
Bethlehem Steel	38.4	43.1	29.5
Boeing	33.5	25.0	10.9
Borden	47.2	51.5	28.0
Caterpillar Tractor*	48.6	48.6	48.6
Chrysler	40.6	39.7	21.0
Continental Oil	43.6	48.4	32.8
Dow Chemical	39.0	39.9	24.3
DuPont	38.9	43.1	38.9
Eastman Kodak	45.4	45.4	40.9
Esmark	38.4	43.1	27.5
Exxon	43.6	48.4	32.8
Firestone Tire and Rubber	37.2	41.9	26.8
Ford	57.7	56.9	55.2
General Electric	37.7	36.3	36.3
General Motors	53.5	56.0	56.0
Goodyear Tire and Rubber	35.7	30.7	10.9
W.R. Grace	39.6	43.8	30.1
Greyhound*	48.1	48.1	48.1
Gulf Oil	43.6	48.4	32.8
IBM	38.7	27.6	27.6
International Harvester	45.4	44.0	12.8
International Telephone and Telegraph	39.6	43.8	30.1
Kraftco	44.3	44.2	44.2
Lockheed Aircraft	41.8	46.2	46.2
LTV Corp.	38.4	43.1	27.5
Mobil Oil	43.6	48.4	32.8
Monsanto	48.4	43.5	37.7
Occidental Petroleum*	39.7	39.7	39.7
Phillips Petroleum	43.6	48.4	32.8
RCA Corp.	36.6	39.1	39.1
R.J. Reynolds	45.2	47.4	47.4

282

Table 5 (continued)

Firm	Retire 1975 (1)	Retire 2010 with No Automatic Social Security Increases (2)	Retire 2010 with Automatic Social Security Increases (3)
Rockwell International	36.9	46.6	46.6
Shell Oil	36.9	41.6	26.0
Standard Oil of California	44.5	48.1	39.7
Standard Oil of Indiana	45.9	50.6	35.0
Sun Oil	41.5	46.2	30.6
Tenneco	37.2	41.4	41.4
Texaco	48.0	52.3	38.2
Union Carbide[a]	38.9	38.9	38.9
Union Oil of California	43.6	48.4	32.8
U.S. Steel[a]	51.8	56.2	56.2
United Technologies	38.4	46.4	37.2
Westinghouse Electric	41.4	40.4	40.4

[a] Nonintegrated plan.
NOTE: For an explanation of the column labels, see the text.
SOURCE: The Wyatt Company, *Survey of Retirement*, Exhibits II a, b, and c.

a year. This growing wage base forms the basis of the excess method computation, in which excess is a function of the taxable wage base. Without automatic social security increases, the social security replacement ratio is 21 percent; with automatic social security increases, the social security replacement ratio is 42.2 percent.

The differences between column 2 and column 3 demonstrate the power of social security integration. As social security benefits rise over the period to 2010, the private pension replacement ratios in the plans of these large corporations decline. The average private pension replacement ratio for a worker retiring in 1975 is 42.1 percent, and the average private pension replacement ratio for a worker retiring in 2010, assuming no automatic social security benefit increases, is approximately the same, 44.4 percent. For employees retiring in 2010, assuming automatic social security increases, the average private pension replacement ratio is 35.3 percent.

For the five nonintegrated plans shown in Table 5, the average private pension replacement ratio is 46.3 percent. Social security payments will provide, assuming automatic increases, a replacement ratio of 42.2 percent. Employees retiring with these plans would have a total replacement ratio of 88.5 percent.

Given the lower income taxes at age sixty-five, the exclusion of social security benefits from income taxation, and the reduction in work-related expenses at retirement, employees belonging to nonintegrated plans may enjoy higher after-tax income in retirement than they had while working. Superficially, this should not trouble firms offering nonintegrated plans, because they specified the contracts and they wrote the rules for their own reasons. In fact, such high total replacement ratios may pose a problem for some firms if the ratios induce employees to retire before age sixty-five even though the firm would prefer them to keep working.

In integrated plans, private benefit payments decline as social security benefits rise. The reduction in private payments in integrated plans raises a question of equity. Is it fair to withhold private benefits just because public benefits have risen? This also raises questions concerning the magnitude of the incentive effects of private pensions that remain after adjustments are made for social security.

Only 13 percent of the 190 firms in the Bankers Trust sample were not integrated. Among the fifty largest U.S. industrial firms, forty-eight have pension plans; of these forty-eight firms, only five do not integrate private pension benefits with social security.

Two Prospective Problems

Firms that integrate benefits must prepare for two possible problems. The first problem is the possible elimination by the Congress of the integration arrangement. This would affect salaried workers primarily and, according to Schmitt, would affect only about 30 percent of the workers covered. The second problem is the magnitude of social security benefits and the declining need for private pensions in providing retirement income. This problem affects both integrated and nonintegrated plans.

Regarding the prospect of changing integration rules, the House Ways and Means Committee report on H.R. 12855 in 1974 stated:

> On the one hand, the objective of the Congress in increasing Social Security benefits might be considered to be frustrated to the extent that individuals with low and moderate incomes have their private retirement benefits reduced as a result of integration procedures. On the other hand, your committee is very much aware that many present plans are fully or partly integrated and that elimination of the integration pro-

cedures could substantially increase the cost of financing private plans. Employees, as a whole, might be injured rather than aided if such cost increases resulted in slowing down the rate of growth of private pension plans.[10]

Though the committee proposed no precipitous action, it did ratify the administrative procedures of the Internal Revenue Service that prohibited integrated pension plans from using increases in social security benefits as a reason for reducing the pension benefits of retired employees or of employees separated from the plan before retirement but already vested. The committee also tried to freeze integration at 1974 levels until 1976, but it was unsuccessful in this attempt.

The view implied by the committee is that, if integration is ended, a company's pension benefit formulas would be changed by removing the offset or by applying excess percentages to total compensation—that is, setting a breakpoint of zero. Most firms would probably not respond in this way, however; instead, they would probably rewrite their pension arrangements so that the total funds paid out by the pension fund would remain roughly unchanged. Not rewriting the arrangements would imply that firms wanted to pay more in pension benefits; if they did rewrite the arrangements, the firms could eliminate the integration procedure, or they could retain the procedure but boost benefits by changes in other components of their formulas. Accordingly, it is not clear that eliminating the integration procedure would really raise pension costs or benefits.

If integration were eliminated and if firms maintained their pre-elimination level of pension benefits by altering benefit formulas, employees would not really gain. If, however, gain to employees is the objective of legislation intended to eliminate integration, it is possible that this would also be legislated by prohibiting all but the most modest changes in pension formulas, thus insuring growth in private pension costs. Given existing integration formulas, the increase in costs to firms would be approximately half the amount of the social security benefits that the firms' retired employees will receive. This could be very costly.

The second problem is that the growth of social security as a complete pension program may undermine the efficacy of private pension plans and lead to a reduced role for private pensions. Table 6 shows social security benefits as a percentage of pre-retirement earnings for five male workers retiring at age sixty-five with different salary histories from 1952 to 1976. For each category of worker, social security benefits have risen relative to final salary. Since each category experienced gains

---

10 Reported in ibid., p. 173.

TABLE 6

SOCIAL SECURITY BENEFITS AS A PERCENTAGE OF EARNINGS IN THE
YEAR BEFORE RETIREMENT FOR FIVE SINGLE MALE WORKERS
AT DIFFERING WAGE LEVELS AT THE AGE OF SIXTY-FIVE,
SELECTED YEARS, 1952–1976
(percent)

Retire-ment Date	Minimum Wage	Retail Trade	Service Industry	Manufac-turing	Construc-tion Industry
1952	38	30	29	22	19
1955	44	39	36	32	26
1960	41	37	35	31	25
1965	38	36	32	29	23
1970	43	40	34	32	24
1971	46	43	36	35	25
1972	45	42	34	34	23
1973	53	48	39	38	27
1974	51	47	38	37	26
1975	55	49	40	39	29
1976	58	51	41	40	31

SOURCE: Alicia Munnell, *The Future of Social Security* (Washington, D.C.: The Brookings Institution, 1977), p. 64.

in productivity, constant real dollar social security benefits would result in declining replacement ratios. Yet, not only did social security benefits keep up with productivity and inflation, they also rose relative to final salary.

Table 7 shows replacement ratios for three income levels for men retiring at age sixty-two and age sixty-five on January 1, 1976. Low- and medium-income workers do comparatively better than high-income workers. The differences in replacement ratios for early and normal retirement are not particularly large.

High and rising social security benefits should be a matter of extreme interest to firms with private plans—and not only because of the rising tax rates these benefits might imply. Regardless of whether private plans are integrated with social security, the past and prospective increases in social security benefits have enormous implications for private pension plans.

First and most obviously, the trend is increasingly toward retire-

TABLE 7

REPLACEMENT RATES FOR THREE INCOME LEVELS ON JANUARY 1, 1976

Income Levels	Male, Sixty-two Years of Age	Male, Sixty-two Years of Age, with Wife	Male, Sixty-five Years of Age	Male, Sixty-five Years of Age, with Wife
Low ($3,439 in 1975)[a]	0.53	0.911	0.663	0.994
Medium ($8,255 in 1975)[b]	0.369	0.635	0.462	0.693
High ($14,100 in 1975)[c]	0.264	0.453	0.330	0.495

[a] Income in the years before 1975 figured to be at the minimum wage level in each year.
[b] Taxable earnings in the years before 1975 figured to be equal to median taxable earnings in each year.
[c] Income calculated to be at the maximum social security wage base in each year.
SOURCE: Munnell, *The Future of Social Security*, p. 26.

ment before age sixty-five.[11] This means that many valuable, skilled employees may leave the firm before the firm would prefer them to leave. This has been made possible by the firm's own early retirement provisions and by the dramatic general increase in social security benefits, particularly those applicable to early retirement. To reduce this effect of the interaction of private pensions and social security, firms need only tighten their own retirement requirements. This may be difficult to do, however, if contractual arrangements have already been made.

James Schulz has estimated that, to maintain pre-retirement living standards in retirement, income replacement should be approximately 60 to 65 percent.[12] As Table 7 shows, social security retirement benefits alone come close to providing these income needs for lower- and median-income workers. Together with transfers in kind, such as health

---

[11] Alicia Munnell, *The Future of Social Security* (Washington, D.C.: The Brookings Institution, 1977), chapter 4; and Michael J. Boskin, "Social Security and Retirement Decisions," *Economic Inquiry*, vol. 15 (January 1977), pp. 1–25.

[12] James H. Schulz, *The Economics of Aging* (Belmont, Calif.: Wadsworth Press, 1976), p. 72.

care benefits and food stamps, total pecuniary and nonpecuniary benefits may provide these retirees with sufficient income. In fact, even for high-income workers, the shortfall between need and social security benefit is not way beyond the lifetime capacity of the individual for private saving. Even for high-earning retirees (those who earned considerably more than the social security maximum wage base), the absolute size of the social security benefit ($6,041 in 1974) automatically adjusted for inflation exceeds the minimum income standards needed by elderly couples to enjoy an intermediate standard of living.[13]

In short, the "need" for a private pension has diminished. Its role of helping retired employees achieve satisfactory living standards during retirement years has, to a measurable degree, been displaced by the social security benefit system.

To view this issue from a more theoretical perspective, consider the form of the typical employee's utility-for-income function. Several researchers have found that the utility-for-income function for individuals is one that exhibits diminishing marginal utility for income.[14] There is likely to be a decreasing rate of marginal substitution of current income for leisure. That is, a $1 increment to a $500 income is more highly valued that a $1 increment to a $1,000 income. This finding can now be applied to private pensions.

The utility an employee expects to derive from a pension claim (or replacement ratio) of a known size is a function of the magnitude of that claim and other income expected to be received over the period during which the pension claim is to be paid off. Thus, the utility to the employee of a pension claim of a specified size, given the fact of diminishing marginal utility of income, declines as other expected income (for example, income to which the right is certain and guaranteed by government) rises. An employee's claim to a private replacement ratio of, say, 30 percent in the early 1960s, when social security replacement ratios were little more than half the current level, provided the worker with more utility than a private pension claim of the same magnitude now.

One of the prime motivations of pension plans is to provide the employee with incentives to remain on the job, to perform the job satisfactorily, and to do so with reduced monitoring by the firm. It is

[13] William C. Greenough and Francis P. King, *Pension Plans and Public Policy* (New York: Columbia University Press, 1976), p. 212. The reported figure is based on a study prepared by the U.S. Bureau of Labor Statistics.
[14] Irwin Friend and Marshall Blume, "The Asset Structure of Individual Portfolios and Some Implications for Utility Functions," *Journal of Finance*, May 1975, pp. 585–604, and references cited there.

highly probable that the degree of the incentive effect of the private pension plan is directly and positively correlated to the expected utility of the pension benefit. In this light, the private replacement ratios that prevailed when social security benefits were comparatively low, now not only provide less expected utility to the employee, but also provide less of an incentive to the employee to perform in ways appropriate to achieving vested status.

For firms to achieve once again the same degree of utility and incentive for employees, private pension benefits (replacement ratios) must rise. In light of diminishing marginal utility, however, they must rise by more than the increase in social security benefits. Pension benefits, in fact, may have to rise by so much that the benefits to the firm fall short of the costs. Alternatively, firms may simply accept the reduction in the incentive effect of their private pension plans and decide either that they should continue the plans because their value still matches or exceeds the costs, or that they should abandon the plan.

Two Broad Issues

This section treats two broad issues connected with social security that have implications for private pensions. The first issue is the magnitude of the deficit in the social security program; the second is the effect of social security on private saving.

In recent years, much has been written about the problem of the deficit in the social security program.[15] The deficit has implications for corporate pension plans.

J. W. Van Gorkom has shown that, even if the current flaw in the social security system is corrected, the deficit may approximate 1.63 percent of taxable wages in the years 1976–2000, 3 to 5 percent of taxable wages in the years 2000–2025, and 6.92 percent of taxable wages in the years 2026–2050.[16] These estimates were made by the Social Security Administration, which has not had a particularly good

---

[15] For illustrative estimates of deficits and prescriptions for their cure, see, for example, Munnell, *The Future of Social Security*; and J. W. Van Gorkom, *Social Security: The Long-Term Deficit* (Washington, D.C.: American Enterprise Institute, 1976).

[16] Van Gorkom, *Social Security: The Long-Term Deficit*, p. 17. Essentially, the flaw arises because the current method of adjusting for inflation raises the percentage benefit (relative to covered earnings) by the inflation rate. Individuals already retired keep up with inflation this way, but the wages of those still working rise with inflation, too. Those soon to retire benefit from higher (inflation-adjusted) benefit percentages and higher wages against which the higher percentage will be applied. Proposals to eliminate this flaw are known as "decoupling" proposals.

289

forecasting record. Estimates for 1971 made by the administration in 1967 underestimated outgo of the system by 46.9 percent, underestimated income by 10.4 percent, and overestimated the balance in the trust fund by 25.9 percent.[17] In view of the direction of error in these forecasts, the estimated future deficit may be understated.

To cover the deficit, payroll taxes rates must rise and so must the social security wage base. In 1977, the payroll tax rate was 5.85 percent levied equally on employer and employee on wages up to $16,500. Although the 1977 amendments to the Social Security Act raised payroll tax rates and the taxable wage base sharply, the increases in the tax rate and the tax base may not eliminate the projected deficit. Some additional payroll tax revenues or movement to financing from general revenues will be needed to maintain the current level of benefits.

For the most part, past increases in social security taxes and wage bases have been announced far enough in advance so that a firm could begin to make appropriate adjustments in its pay policies and in its private pension plans. Thus, in the long run at least, the incidence of the social security tax burden has fallen almost exclusively on the firm's employees, rather than on its shareholders or its customers.[18] But if the social security deficit is as large or larger than forecast and if the financing of that deficit results in a firm's receiving little warning that tax rates, wage bases, or both will rise, then a greater portion of the burden may fall on shareholders and consumers of the firm's products, at least until the firm can make the necessary long-run wage adjustments.

Firms might respond to the higher uncertainty implied by unexpected increases in payroll taxes by altering their financing mix of debt and equity. The higher the degree of uncertainty, the fewer fixed contractual financial obligations firms may want to have. Private pension plans are a type of fixed financial obligation. Such obligations may be reduced along with other fixed financial obligations. Unanticipated increases in social security taxes could lead to the termination or cutback of private pension plans.

A second issue is the effect of social security on private saving. Recent studies by Martin Feldstein and Alicia Munnell have pointed out that prospective social security benefits reduce net incentives to save,

---

[17] F.J. Crowley, "Financing the Social Security System—Then and Now," in Subcommittee on Fiscal Policy of the Joint Economic Committee, *Studies in Public Welfare*, Paper no. 18, *Issues in Financing Retirement Income*, Appendix II, p. 101.

[18] See John A. Brittain, *The Payroll Tax for Social Security* (Washington, D.C.: The Brookings Institution, 1972).

though the magnitudes implied by each study differ.[19] Similarly, private pension plans reduce individual saving, though on balance the results suggest slightly higher total personal saving.[20] That is, a $1 increase in expected private pension benefits reduces individual saving by something less than $1. As institutionalized saving (prospective social security benefits and private pension benefits) grows, individual saving declines.

With respect to private pension plans that integrate their benefits with social security benefits, as social security benefits rise relative to final wages, the private benefit falls relative to final wages. As the contractual benefits of integrated private plans fall, the firm has less need to accumulate pension fund assets because the pension benefits that must be paid decline. Other things being equal, integration could thus lead to less private saving. If social security leads to reduced individual saving and, through integration, to lower private pension fund accumulation, there may be lower total saving.

Concerning nonintegrated plans, and integrated plans as well (though perhaps to a lesser extent), it has already been noted that rising social security benefits undermine or reduce the perceived value or utility of the benefits they provide; thus, it would not be surprising to find some firms reducing or eliminating pension plans and other firms not undertaking new pension plans. If Feldstein's and Munnell's general findings hold, rising real social security benefits may further reduce private saving by reducing private pension saving.

Rising social security benefits may reduce aggregate pension plan saving and personal saving, as well. This would have deleterious consequences for capital formation in the United States. The decline in private savings—hence, the decline in the demand for financial claims on real assets or, alternatively, the decline in the supply of real asset financing—may cause the cost of capital to firms to rise to such an extent that investment activity will not keep pace with the level of activity desired to allow the rate of real economic growth in the future to match expectations. This is a serious problem for firms and for the country at large,

---

[19] See Munnell, *The Future of Social Security*, chapter 6; and Martin S. Feldstein, "Social Security, Induced Retirement, and Aggregate Capital Formation," *Journal of Political Economy*, vol. 82 (September-October 1974), pp. 902–26. Their finding is not universally accepted, however. Conflicting results are analyzed in Robert J. Barro, *The Impact of Social Security on Private Saving: Evidence from the U.S. Time Series* (Washington, D.C.: American Enterprise Institute, 1978); and Michael R. Darby, *The Effects of Social Security on Income and the Capital Stock* (Washington, D.C.: American Enterprise Institute, forthcoming).

[20] Alicia H. Munnell, "Private Pensions and Saving: New Evidence," *Journal of Political Economy*, vol. 84 (October 1976), pp. 1013–32.

for without real growth the promised social security benefits may be undeliverable.

Summary

Many firms integrate private pension plans with social security benefits. Integration is more common in pension plans for salaried workers than in plans for hourly wage earners. In a sample of 190 plans made by Bankers Trust, only 13 percent of the private pension plans were not integrated with social security benefits. In another sample of the fifty largest industrial firms in the United States, of the forty-eight firms offering pension plans, forty-three were integrated, using either an offset approach or an excess approach. As real social security benefits rise, the amount relative to final salary contributed by firms to employees' retirement incomes falls.

The social security system's interaction with the private pension system suggests several issues that deserve further study. The first issue is what will happen if the Congress eliminates the procedure for integrating social security benefits with private benefits. Will plans simply terminate or drastically reduce benefit formulas to keep pension payments equal to what they were before the elimination of the integration procedure? Will they be allowed to? The answer to the first question is likely yes; the reply to the second seems to be "who knows."

A second issue derives from considering private pension benefits as additive to social security benefits. In recent years, real social security benefits have risen rapidly relative to final salaries, and prospects for continued increases (or at least no substantial reductions) are good. If individuals' utility functions show declining marginal utility of income, then the employee's perceived value of a private pension benefit declines as social security benefits rise. For firms to maintain the same perceived value of pension benefits, the same degree of incentive effects, private pension benefits will have to rise by more than the rise in social security benefits. Because firms will not find this attractive, they may reconsider the value to them of existing pension arrangements. Many firms may find the attractiveness of existing plans to be far less now than when these plans were originally implemented.

A third issue is that, to salvage the social security system with its large and possibly growing deficit, large tax increases of unanticipated timing and magnitude may be necessary. This may cause higher uncertainty for the firm, which will be manifested through greater volatility of its return on investment, and it could lead to the contraction of fixed financial obligations, pensions among them.

A fourth issue is that increasing expected social security benefits may undermine private incentives to save. This may result in a decreased ability of the nation to support its social security system. Such an occurrence would be fraught with difficulties, not the least of which might be the recontracting of the social security claim structure: if the promised level of benefits cannot be afforded, they will be reduced.

All considerations of the interaction of the private pension system with the social security system point to a decline in the importance of the private pension system. As a result, future pressures on the social security system to provide even greater benefits to make up for the loss of the private system may be far more intense than they were in the past. It is probably too late to make the policy adjustments necessary to undo the damage to the nation's welfare caused by the decline of the private pension system and its replacement with a public one.

Commentaries

Edwin F. Boynton

I am a pension consultant and thus I began to get a little concerned about my future when I read the papers by Alicia Munnell and Dennis Logue. Then I stopped and did a little arithmetic. I think Wyatt Company actuaries are administering about 10,000 plans. If it took, on the average, a couple of man-weeks of actuaries' time to terminate all these plans, it would come out to 20,000 man-weeks, or about 400 man-years. I am number three in seniority in the Wyatt Company; the two people ahead of me have a total of about ten years to go before retirement. So, think I have a chance of lasting out before the whole thing falls apart.

The paper by Munnell includes economic analysis that is somewhat beyond my area of expertise. I might comment, though, on the point she made that it is enormously expensive for private pension plans to provide for cost-of-living increases. That is true, but it is also enormously expensive for the federal government to do so. One of the problems with the present funding of social security is that the federal government has never recognized cost-of-living increases in advance, whereas a private plan has to.

Let me comment on a point made in Logue's paper. He states:

> The view implied by the committee [the House Ways and Means Committee] is that, if integration is ended, a company's pension benefit formulas would be changed by removing the offset or by applying excess percentages to total compensation—that is, setting a breakpoint of zero. Most firms would probably not respond in this way, however; instead, they would probably rewrite their pension arrangements so that the total funds paid out by the pension fund would remain roughly unchanged.

I want to give some examples showing the serious consequences of taking such action. The problem is not quite as simple as removing the social security offset or devising new nonintegrated formulas of approximately the same cost levels.

Examples of this are illustrated in Tables 1 and 2. Table 1 is basic cost table for three types of private pension plans. The basic

TABLE 1

ILLUSTRATIVE ANNUAL CONTRIBUTIONS TO VARIOUS INTEGRATED
AND NONINTEGRATED PENSION PLANS
(in dollars, except for "Number of active employees")

	Plan I, Integrated[a]	Plan II, Non-integrated[b]	Plan III, Non-integrated[c]
Basic data summary			
Number of active employees	563	563	563
Average annual compensation	15,677	15,677	15,677
Average projected final average pay	40,003	40,003	40,003
Average projected pension	14,187	21,351	14,234
Basic valuation results (in thousands)			
Gross accrued actuarial liability			
Active employees	6,429	8,539	5,693
Retired and vested employees	2,865	2,865	2,865
Total	9,294	11,404	8,558
Valuation assets	5,454	5,454	5,454
Net accrued actuarial liability	3,840	5,950	3,104
Annual normal cost	316	452	301
Illustrative annual contribution (in thousands)			
Annual normal cost	316	452	301
Amortization of net actuarial liability over 30 years	289	448	234
Total annual contribution	605	900	535

Plan I = (1.5 percent of final five-year average pay minus 1.25 percent of social security primary insurance amount) × (years of service).

Plan II = (1.5 percent of final five-year average pay) × (years of service).

Plan III = (1 percent of final five-year average pay) × (years of service).

NOTE: Economic assumptions: interest = 7 percent a year; salary increases = 5.5 percent a year; wage base increase = 4 percent a year; and consumer price index (CPI) increase = 3 percent a year.

SOURCE: Author's calculations.

economic assumptions made are shown in the note at the bottom of the table. In the first column is Plan I, which is a typical integrated plan providing a reasonably generous level of benefits—1.5 percent of final average pay per year of service less 1.25 percent of the social security benefit. For long-service employees, it provides 60 percent of final average pay minus 50 percent of social security. Turning it around and looking at total retirement income, it would produce a total retirement income of 60 percent of final average pay plus 50 percent of social security. Or, if the person had a spouse at age sixty-five, it would amount to 60 percent of final average pay plus 100 percent of social security.

There are only a couple of key numbers in this table to focus on. This is an actual case covering 563 employees that we worked out using these illustrative benefits. Note that if current pay is projected out with a salary scale factor, the final average pay is $40,000 (even though the current average is $15,600), and the projected pension is $14,187. As shown in the bottom line, this plan requires a total annual contribution by the firm of $605,000.

Suppose a law is passed which says that you cannot have integrated plans. Obviously, this is not going to happen overnight; the phase-out would probably be gradual. The tables are designed to show the situation before and after the phase-out. Assume first that the social security offset is eliminated. This is shown in Plan II, which is the same as Plan I except that the offset is eliminated. Note that the average projected pension rises to about $21,000, approximately 50 percent higher than in Plan I. Not surprisingly, the total annual contribution required for Plan II increases to $900,000, also about 50 percent more than in Plan I.

When a plan sponsor looks at this situation, he has to reconsider and decide what he is going to do. He may not be able to afford the additional costs, and the benefits appear to be too high. A possible solution, which is expressed in Logue's paper, is to redesign the plan so that the benefits will be lowered enough to keep the costs at about the same level.

Plan III comes reasonably close to doing that. It is not integrated because integrated plans are not allowed, and the formula is lowered from 1.5 to 1 percent of final average pay. The average projected pension is now $14,200. By coincidence, it is almost identical to the original plan. The total annual contribution is $535,000, which is slightly lower than in Plan I. That is helpful. Maybe the firm can pay some additional social security taxes with that!

The key point is that, although Plans I and III cost about the

296

same and produce the same average pension, the average may be misleading.

Table 2 illustrates what happens to individual employees. There are fourteen examples—six for employees who enter the plan at age twenty-five and eight for employees who enter the plan at age thirty-five. The economic assumptions are slightly different than in Table 1, but the principle is the same.

There are four types of employees in Table 2. The first is Mr. Plodder, who goes along and has pay increases at a rate of 4 percent a year, slightly below the assumed rate of 5 percent a year for the wage base. The second, Mr. Mediocre, goes along with pay increases of about 5 percent a year, staying even with the increase in the wage base. The third, Mr. Smart Guy, has pay increases at about 7 percent a year, well ahead of the wage base increases. Then, fourth, there is Mr. Hotshot who has average pay increases of 10 percent a year. He winds up somewhere at the top of the heap in the company.

I have omitted the dollar amounts of the benefits because the compounding effects of annualized rates of increase in relation to today's dollar become mind boggling. I have given the 1977 salary at entry and, as a point of reference, have shown in footnotes the estimated wage base in the year of retirement based on the 1977 social security maximum wage base of $16,500. Then, the final year's pay is expressed as a percentage of the final wage base.

The first person in the table, Mr. Plodder, winds up with final pay equal to one-third of the final social security wage base, which by today's standards would be only $5,500. On the other hand, Mr. Hotshot who entered at age twenty-five winds up at 577 percent of the final wage base, which would amount to almost $100,000 by today's standards.

Note what happens to persons with different rates of increase in their annual income. Skip the first case because it is really not typical of someone covered by an integrated plan. The second person, earning $8,000 with an annual rate of increase in income of 5 percent, stays up with the increases in the wage base. His final pay is about half the wage base at the time he retires. Social security will provide him with 78 percent of his final pay. Plan I would give him another 16 percent. Column 4 shows that he receives a total retirement income equal to 94 percent of pay, which is pretty generous but necessary for someone at that earnings level. If integration is removed (column 5), his replacement ratio balloons out to 133 percent. If the gross benefit formula is reduced from 1.5 percent to 1 percent, he still winds up in good shape with 115 percent of pay.

Consider now Mr. Hotshot, whose starting salary is $15,000 and

TABLE 2

ILLUSTRATIVE RETIREMENT INCOME BENEFITS FROM SOCIAL SECURITY AND PRIVATE PENSION PLAN COMBINED, UNDER INTEGRATED AND NONINTEGRATED PLANS

(percent)

Entry Age and Salary at Entry	Rate of Increase in Annual Pay (1)	Final Pay as Percentage of Final Social Security Wage Base (2)	Income from Private Pension plus Social Security Primary Insurance Amount as Percentage of Salary at Age 64			
			Social security only (3)	Social security plus Plan I[a] (4)	Social security plus Plan II[b] (5)	Social security plus Plan III[c] (6)
Entry age 25[d]						
$ 8,000	4	33	104	108	159	141
8,000	5	48	78	94	133	115
8,000	7	102	45	75	97	80
15,000	5	90	53	81	107	89
15,000	7	191	26	65	78	61
15,000	10	577	8	54	59	42

Entry age 35[e]

$10,000	4	45	78	90	119	105
10,000	5	60	62	80	103	89
10,000	7	106	40	65	80	66
18,000	5	108	42	67	83	69
18,000	7	190	24	54	63	50
30,000	5	180	25	57	66	52
30,000	7	317	14	48	54	41
30,000	10	727	6	41	44	31

NOTE: Social security assumptions: wage base increase = 5 percent a year; consumer price index (CPI) increase = 4 percent a year.

a. Plan I = (1.5 percent of final five-year average pay minus 1.25 percent of social security primary insurance amount) × (years of service).

b. Plan II = (1.5 percent of final five-year average pay) × (years of service).

c. Plan III = (1 percent of final five-year average pay) × (years of service).

d. Forty years of service at retirement; wage base in years of retirement = $117,600.

e. Thirty years of service at retirement; wage base in year of retirement = $72,000.

SOURCE: Author's calculations.

whose annual income increases at 10 percent. He is the fellow who winds up in upper-management levels of the company. He winds up with a social security benefit of only about 8 percent of his final pay, and the present integrated plan, including social security, would provide him with 54 percent of his final pay. Although this is considerably below the 94 percent of Mr. Mediocre, almost all retirement plans taper the percentage down with increasing pay. If integration is dropped, as shown in Column 5, Mr. Hotshot's benefit will go up an additional 5 percent, much less than the 39 percent in the case of Mr. Mediocre. When you shift to the 1 percent formula (column 6), Mr. Hotshot winds up with a replacement ratio of only 42 percent.

Thus, if you change to a nonintegrated plan that costs about the same as an integrated plan, the replacement ratio at the low end of the spectrum rises from 94 to 115 percent. The replacement ratio of an executive, however, falls from 54 percent to 42 percent. You have had a big difference. And the same difference is found for persons with thirty years of service. Even though the average benefit looks the same, the reallocation of the contributions in the long-run favors the lower-paid employee.

I believe that changing to a nonintegrated formula will not work. It makes it impossible to provide a reasonable pension for middle- and upper-income employees without providing excessive benefits to lower-paid employees.

I agree with the analysis and the conclusion in both papers that, if present trends continue, the outlook for private pension plans is not favorable. The die seems to be cast. It appears that social security will take over a much greater part of the retirement income system in the United States, thereby diminishing the significance of private plans. It is indeed unfortunate that this shift of retirement income financing to the federal government is taking place in view of how well private plans have met their financial obligations and how poorly the federal government has handled the financing of the social security system and the plans for its own employees in the military system and the federal civil service system.

The expansion of the role of social security will probably be gradual and will diminish the role of private pensions over a period of time. I am alarmed, however, by the rumor that the Carter administration will make an effort either to reduce integration or to phase it out entirely. It is difficult to find out exactly what is being proposed, but there is at least one rumor that the administration proposes to phase out integration by 1990.

Logue referred to the diminishing utility of private plans. It is a term that I have not heard used before in this context. Many recent changes have been leading to this diminished utility: for example, imposition of expanded disclosure in reporting requirements for plan sponsors; establishment of mandatory minimum funding requirements; imposition of frightening fiduciary responsibility on the plan sponsors; requirements for liberalized vesting; imposition on plan sponsors of liabilities for the Pension Benefit Guaranty Corporation; and the possibility of getting involved with yet another government agency, the Securities and Exchange Commission. Other changes being proposed are the imposition of maximum benefit limits and the elimination of cost-of-living adjustments. In the face of all these restrictions and the distribution of benefits that would emerge if integration is phased out, plan sponsors would probably look to alternative means of providing retirement benefits for middle- and upper-income employees.

Where this leads is anyone's guess. It may well result in placing greater emphasis on savings plan arrangements, assuming that the government does not impose restrictions on them. Undoubtedly, there will be greater emphasis on deferred-compensation contracts and pay-as-you-go arrangements.

Firms have set up pay-as-you-go arrangements, which are tax deductible when paid to the employee by the employer, as the only workable solution left if integration is phased out. This approach has not yet come under serious attack and the government has not yet decided to establish maximum amounts of direct compensation. With present trends, however, who knows what might next come out of the administration?

Norman B. Ture

In considering the interaction of social security and the private pension system, Alicia Munnell and Dennis Logue have provided us with some useful analytical insights and observations, which was their intent, and a couple of Orwellian horror tales, which they may not have intended. If their forecasts prove to be correct, we are likely to see in the relatively near future the virtually complete socialization of provision for retirement income. Indeed, the thrust of both Munnell's and Logue's analysis does not confine the displacement effects of a galloping social security system to private saving for retirement. In her empirical examination of the determinants of private pension plan saving, Munnell might have specified total personal saving, not merely pension plan saving, as her dependent variable; I strongly suspect that she would

301

find, with at least equal statistical reliability and conceptual elegance, that social security has substantially the same displacement effect in the case of total personal saving as in the case of pension saving. Similarly, Logue's brief analytical use of the utility function with respect to income to show the displacement effect of social security has no logical limit at future income provided through private pension plans; it applies with equal force to any and all provisions individuals might make for obtaining future income streams. Hence, the expected expansion of social security benefits should materially displace all private personal saving—not only private pension plan saving—in Logue's approach, just as in Munnell's.

Regrettably, neither Munnell's nor Logue's analysis specifies the basic functions that determine how much people want to save and in what forms. Although their conclusions are not necessarily ruled out by an analysis that does rely on such specifications, neither are they unique outcomes of that analysis.

Both Munnell and Logue trade heavily on the notion of a targeted amount of retirement income—and, by extension, a targeted replacement ratio—as the principal determinant of personal saving for retirement. Given this notion, it follows quite simply that an increase in social security retirement income benefits relative to pre-retirement income displaces other forms of saving for retirement. (Logue adds an interesting, often neglected twist to the argument by pointing to the integration features in some private pension plans that automatically reduce the benefit obligations of private plans for many covered workers as social security benefits increase.) The validity of their conclusions clearly hinges on the validity of the target retirement income and replacement ratio.

Neither Munnell nor Logue addresses the questions: Where do target retirement income levels come from, and are these likely to be stable? Superficially, the notion of a stable ratio between desired retirement income and pre-retirement permanent income is unappealing. Somewhat more acceptable is the idea of some minimum amount of income for retirement that is not likely to be closely correlated with permanent income before retirement. If one were to ask a person in the labor force how much income he or she wants after retiring, the sensible answer one should expect is that this depends on the costs of obtaining various amounts of such income. Clearly, these costs are the amount of foregone current consumption. The lower the cost, the greater the amount of retirement income one will want to buy. Then, unless the cost of retirement income is invariant, one should not expect to find a stable relationship between targeted retirement income and working-period permanent income. And if this relationship is not stable, an unusually rapid growth of projected social security benefits does not necessarily imply that the displacement of private personal saving for retirement will be unusually severe.

What is needed to assess the impact of growth in projected social security benefits on private saving, including pension plan saving, is an estimate of the relative costs, perceived by the employee, of the alternative future income streams. In short, any change in the amount of privately supplied future income that the employee demands depends on his perception of the substitutability of social security retirement annuities for privately provided future income streams and the relative costs to him of social security and privately provided future income.

Suppose, in the first instance, the social security annuities the employee is required to buy are perceived to be perfect substitutes for private annuities. This means, among other things, that the price the employee is required to pay for the social security annuities is the same as the prevailing market price he is paying per dollar of privately supplied future income.

On these assumptions, the employee would feel the same about the amount of social security annuities he is required to have and an equal amount of privately supplied future income. His initial response would be to reduce the amount of the privately supplied future income streams that he currently owns dollar for dollar with the social security annuity stream he is required to have. To be sure, taken by themselves the payroll taxes he is required to pay for the purchase of social security annuities reduce his aggregate permanent income by reducing the income flow available to him from his work. It is assumed, however, that this loss is precisely offset by the proceeds from his sale of the capital providing the future income streams for which social security annuities are deemed to be a perfect substitute. Initially, therefore, upon the substitution of social security for private future income, the employee has the same aggregate future income and the same rate of current consumption as in the equilibrium condition without social security.

The dollar-for-dollar substitution of social security for privately supplied future income, however, reduces the employee's demand for the latter; at any given market price, either the amount of such future income streams he wishes to have is smaller now than in the past, or the price he will be willing to pay for any given amount of them is less. At their previous market price, the quantity of such income streams demanded decreases. With the given supply of these future income streams, however, their market price cannot remain unchanged. It will, instead, decline. In the new equilibrium, the price of privately supplied

303

future income will be less than in the absence of social security, and the amount of such future income the employee will own, while less than if there were no social security, will not have decreased by the full amount of the social security annuities.

The adjustment to the new equilibrium clearly involves dissaving and disinvestment. The extent of this dissaving and disinvestment is less than if the price of privately supplied future income were fixed at its initial level; given the magnitude of the shift in the demand for privately supplied future income, it depends on the respective elasticities of the demand and supply functions.

In the new equilibrium the stock of sources of private permanent income streams is less than in the absence of social security. If government were to use the payroll tax collections to produce perfect substitutes for these privately supplied stocks, total income and wealth would be unchanged. In reality, however, the tax collections are transferred as benefit payments to social security annuitants. Hence, with given initial amounts of human capital and other productive services, total production capacity and the total flow of income is reduced.

In a dynamic context, the introduction of social security annuities as perfect substitutes for private future income streams reduces the growth path of the equilibrium stock of the sources of these income streams. When these stocks are not fully replaced by government-provided perfect substitutes, the growth path of total income is also reduced. While positive saving and investment continue, the amount of such saving and investing at any point in time is less than it would have been in the absence of social security.

Since the price of privately supplied future income is lower in the new equilibrium than if there were no social security, and since this price is the amount of foregone consumption per dollar of future income, it is less relative to the price of consumption than in the absence of social security. The fraction of the reduced flow of disposable income which is saved—that is, used to purchase additional amounts of privately supplied future income—will thus be larger than in the absence of social security, even though the total amount of such saving will be less than in the absence of social security.

Now assume that the social security annuities the employee is required to purchase are not perfect substitutes for private future income streams—that is, the price he is required to pay for social security annuities exceeds the prevailing market price for private future income. In this case, since the price of social security annuities is by assumption greater than that of private future income, the substitution of the former for the latter is not as great as in the case of perfect substitution. The demand for private future income streams, therefore, will decrease less than in the case in which social security annuities are a perfect substitute for private future income.

As in the previous case, social security results in dissaving and disinvestment in the static equilibrium context, and reduces flows of saving and investment through time in the dynamic context. But the decrease in the equilibrium stock of sources of private future income is less than in the case of perfect substitutibility; in the dynamic context, the reduction in the flow of saving and investment, compared with these flows in the absence of social security, is less than if social security annuities were perfect substitutes. By the same token, the fraction of the reduced flow of disposable income that is saved will be greater than in the absence of social security and greater than if social security annuities were perfect substitutes for private future income. Finally, although the amount of total private saving and investment will be less than in the absence of social security, it will be greater than if social security annuities were perfect substitutes for private future income, since the decrease in the flow of income will be less than in the first case.

The third case is that in which the "price" of social security annuities is set below the prevailing market price for private future income. In this event, the initial effect is a greater inclination by the employee to substitute social security annuities for the more expensive private future income streams than in the first instance in which the price of social security annuities is set equal to the prevailing market price of private future income. The demand for private future income streams will decrease more than in the first case of social security annuities as perfect substitutes for private future income.

In this case, social security results in greater dissaving and disinvestment in the static equilibrium context and in greater reduction in the flows of saving and investment in the dynamic context than in the previous cases. Similarly, the decrease in the flow of income in the new equilibrium will be greater and both the fraction of that income saved and the amount of saving will be less than in the former cases.

The displacement of different private saving outlets by social security depends on the respective elasticities of supply of the alternative sources. The more elastic the supply of any such source, the greater the reduction in the flow of saving into additions to the stock of such sources. Expansion of the social security system might result in an increase in provision for retirement through private pension plans relative to other private retirement income saving. In all likelihood, the elasticity of supply of sources provided by pension funds is substantially less than that of other private sources, since there are substantial limitations, imposed by statute and regulation, on the adjustment of pension plan provisions. Private provisions for retirement income through private pension plans should, therefore, be expected to increase as a fraction of total private provisions.

This type of analysis urges that accelerating expansion of social security may, indeed, accentuate the displacement of aggregate private saving (not merely that achieved through pension plans). The magnitude of this effect, however, cannot be estimated merely by reference to estimates of prospective replacement rates. It will depend very largely on covered employees' perceptions of the changes in relative costs per dollar of retirement income from alternative sources that is entailed by a quickening rate of expansion of the social security system. Moreover, these changes in relative costs differ among covered employees, depending on a number of differentiating characteristics, a major one of which is age. Since the distribution of employees by these characteristics is not fixed, neither is the prospective change in relative costs. By the same token, the severity of the effects on aggregate private saving are likely to vary over time. So, too, will the impact of social security expansion on private pension plan provisions for retirement income.

This is by no means to suggest that there is no occasion for concern over the prospective social security boom. If it is not largely forfended, it may well have seriously adverse effects, not only on private pension plans, but on all private saving, hence on the pace of the economy's progress. While their analyses call for substantial modification and elaboration, Munnell and Logue have done well to focus this conference's attention on the threat that the likely future development of social security poses to the economic well-being of us all.

Thomas C. Edwards

Alicia Munnell and Dennis Logue have each depicted a growing, glowing future for social security, to be fed in no small part by fuel syphoned from a dwindling private pension sector.

Munnell, through empirical analyses based on models and medians, reaches several conclusions:

1. That private pensions and social security are alternative mechanisms for accomplishing the same objective and "are almost perfect substitutes" for each other.
2. That social security alone now provides adequate retirement income for more than half of new retirees. For retired couples

with earnings up to the median, social security provides virtually all the income required to maintain their previous standard of living—65 to 80 percent of pre-retirement earnings. ("Adequacy" is in the eyes of the beholder, and I wonder how many of these newly retired couples could agree that an income of $6,000 from social security provides for them adequately.)

3. That, in the face of high rates of inflation, only the federal government can guarantee benefits that keep pace with prices because doing so would be very expensive for private pensions. (Keeping up with prices will be very expensive no matter who does it, and it will have to be paid for out of the gross national product no matter who pays it.)

4. That, as social security expands and as private pensions narrow, the tax treatment of pension contributions becomes increasingly a tax advantage accruing primarily to high-salaried workers, a result that will place in jeopardy the deductibility of employer pension costs as a business expense. (I question her characterization of the deductibility of employer pension costs as a "revenue loss," but not her prediction of greater federal scrutiny of such deductibility.)

5. That a shift from private pensions toward social security implies a reduction in saving and capital accumulation. She says we should not worry, however, because alternative mechanisms are available to stimulate capital formation.

6. In summary, she states in her closing paragraph that: "the perpetual debate over the appropriate role for private pensions and social security appears to have been resolved de facto in favor of social security. The role of private pensions will be limited to providing supplementary benefits to individuals with earnings above the median. Even this more limited role may be in jeopardy if inflation persists or the favorable tax provisions are eliminated."

Logue offers not only an excellent description of how pension plans are integrated with social security, but also examples of why, if private pension plans follow their present course, most of them appear doomed to atrophy at best, or to extinction at worst. For example, he concludes:

1. That social security is emerging as a regular pension plan of sorts rather than as a pure social insurance scheme.

2. That, in absolute terms, social security retirement benefits in conjunction with other government programs to assist the aged are sufficient, or very nearly so, to support an individual in retirement.

This fact, together with some of the less desirable features of private pension plans, will put the latter up against the wall, he says, with a dramatic reduction in the number and the percentage of the work force covered by private plans.

3. That one major weakness of private pensions is that, although their benefits are often characterized as deferred wages, they clearly are not deferred wages before they vest in the employee who has worked to earn them. And even when vested, pension benefits earned under the typical defined benefit plan cannot truly be considered deferred wages for two reasons: because the employer bears the downside risk of pension fund performance, and because the employee's vested pension wealth can be bled white by social security integration.

4. That integration of accrued benefit levels with social security flies in the face of the deferred-wage concept because accrued pension wealth, already earned, is reduced every time there is a change in the social security law. And, he adds that, if accumulated pension wealth is the compound value of deferred wages, an exogenous event should not reduce it.

5. If future legislation outlaws integration, many private plans will be terminated, and there will be a widespread reduction in the benefit levels of surviving plans, unless such reductions are prohibited by the same legislation. And without such legislation, integrated defined benefit plans as we know them today will be made superfluous in the future by rising real social security benefits.

6. That one way out of this dilemma, short of terminating plans, is for private plan benefit levels to rise by more than the rise in social security benefits, but this appears unlikely because of the costs.

7. Finally, that social security replacement of private pension benefits "may cause the cost of capital to firms to rise to such an extent that investment activity will not keep pace with the level of activity desired to allow the rate of real economic growth in the future to match expectations." This, he says, "is a serious problem for firms and for the country at large, for without real growth the promised social security benefits may be undeliverable."

At the risk of having missed their meanings, I question Munnell's assumption that private pensions and social security "are almost perfect substitutes" and Logue's conclusion that social security is emerging as a regular pension plan of sorts rather than as a pure social insurance scheme.

Social security is a social, pay-as-you-go program for transferring earned income from the currently working members of society to former workers and dependents on a "presumed needs" basis. The payments from the younger generations to the older ones are made by converting current wage taxes from the former into current benefit checks for the latter, with Congress making the social judgments about the transfer amounts and the levels of presumed need. The tax on today's workers not only pays the benefits to today's retirees, it also entitles today's worker to an open-ended "IOU," to be redeemed out of the wages of future workers.

Social security was never intended to be, nor has it become, a competitive annuity, insurance, or investment scheme, no matter what esoteric measures are used to measure its rate of return or its actuarial present value for selected cohorts. The fact that social security has been an actuarial bargain for the early generations covered, as well as for anyone close to the cutting-edge of benefit increases, results from the start-up method required for such a broad social program and from the attractive marginal returns for older people whenever benefits are increased. But the actuarial bargains of the past should not be—indeed, cannot be—extrapolated into the hereafter, as some models seem to do.

Private pension plans provide benefits funded by and directly related to individual earnings, years of service, and investment results. Pension plans do not incorporate broad social or congressional decisions about presumed need, nor do they transfer savings from high-income to low-income workers, from single to married, or from one generation to another. Pension plans are based on individual equity; social security is based on social equity. Neither is a "perfect substitute" for the other, nor are they intended to be interchangeable.

We need both systems, and I do not believe either system standing alone could serve the country well. Social security has proved its worth as a national, compulsory (for most), portable, and contributory means of providing a basic level of retirement income through intergenerational transfers. There are some basic flaws in the system that need corrective measures. In general, though, the social security system has succeeded remarkably well in providing social equity with dignity and as a matter of right.

But social security's current financial problems, its vulnerability to recessions, and the demographic shift toward the older ages that are expected in the decades ahead all help to illustrate the need for continuing a strong private pension system as well. As the nonworking group receiving social security benefits grows larger and the working group smaller, the burden on the latter to pay current social security benefits out of current wages becomes heavier, even without social security benefit increases. With continuing benefit increases and more takeover of pension plans by social security, future workers may well come to perceive the increasingly heavier tax burden as confiscatory, especially when compared with what they could be doing on their own through private saving, insurance, and annuities.

Thus, we need a strong private pension system to help social security survive the financial impacts of recessions, demographic shifts, and high rates of inflation. Private pension funds augment the supply of capital, which in turn helps to increase national income in the future. Through private pension funding, the capital accumulation of one generation helps to produce the retirement benefits for that same generation. The cost is not passed ahead to one's children and grandchildren. A strong private pension system can help to reduce the pressures for ad hoc liberalizations of social security benefits; such pressures are bound to come regardless of what the Congress does now to shore up the system. Together then, the two systems—social security and private pensions—can provide attractive retirement benefits without confiscatory social security taxes.

I agree with Logue about the role of private pensions in capital formation and the growth of the economy. He foresees real dangers in the substitution of social security taxes for aggregate pension plan savings, including the $30 to $40 billion of new pension funds that flow in for investment each year. But I will leave this discussion to him and Munnell, who apparently sees adequate, if not perfect, substitutes for the capital formation now provided by private pensions.

Logue's warning for private pensions is clear: social security is moving in for the takeover through doors left open in the structuring of most pension plans. But while the warning comes through clearly alternatives do not. One logical alternative would be for the Congress to consider the long-term financial viability of the social security system, and its cost to future generations, as equal in importance to political pressures for more and larger benefits today. I am not convinced that the current actions to amend the system are proof that the Congress has moved up to the level of fiduciary responsibility they expect—indeed demand through the Employee Retirement Income Security Act (ERISA) —from the private sector. But so much for logic.

I do not agree with the speakers that the infirmities of private pensions are terminal. Certain restorative measures, well known to the pension community and to employers, could be prescribed. For one thing, much broader private pension coverage of workers seems essential. But this will take some turn-around effort from employers and some encouragement from the government. In recent years, ERISA's red tape and the existence of Individual Retirement Accounts have given smaller firms an excuse to drop existing pension plans or to postpone setting up new ones. And Senator Jacob Javits (R-N.Y.) has suggested to the Congress that the federal government establish two federally sponsored and administered pension plans—one a defined contribution plan and the other a defined benefit plan—to which employers with twenty-five or fewer employees could make tax deductible contributions with minimal reporting and disclosure requirements, and with no need to apply to the Internal Revenue Service for qualification. Once again we see the government imploding into a vacuum left by the private sector. Why is it that the private sector is not encouraged to do the job instead of being discouraged or threatened with government red tape and takeover?

Private pensions need to improve their image as a true part of compensation. The more earned pension wealth is perceived as deferred wages, the greater the stake each participant—each voter—will have in the well-being of his or her pension plan, and the greater the potential for public resistance to government takeover of this earned pension wealth. Logue's timely warnings hint at how this could be done. Much quicker vesting is one example. Delaying vesting for "only" ten years— the new norm in industry—is a great improvement over the situation that prevailed not so long ago. But ten years is still about one-third of a person's career, and it leaves too much room for pension forfeiture. How can people feel protective about a system from which they will receive no benefits if they are fired, quit, or die before qualifying for vesting? My friends in the pension community would say that plan participants who are fired, quit, or die have not lost a thing because they knew the rules of the game when they started playing. Okay, but those rules may be making private pensions the real loser.

Full and immediate vesting has been widespread throughout the college world for more than half a century. It is affordable, it works, and—in the broad sense of total employment costs, career development and mobility, job satisfaction, and efficiency—it is probably much less expensive than the hidden costs of forfeiture plans, especially if forfeiture plans are helping to bring on the slow death of private pensions. Early full vesting, then, is essential to the concept that pension benefits are deferred wages.

Both speakers pointed out that defined benefit plans have locked themselves and their participants into an automatic wasting-away process through social security integration. When referring to this erosion of accrued private pension wealth, however, neither speaker pointed to a countervailing force at work for the employee. When employers with

311

plans based on final pay increase an individual's salary, they retroactively increase his private pension wealth for accrued service. Although social security may subsequently replace such increases through integration, this fact should have been mentioned.

On the subject of integration, it is one thing to adjust a pension plan for social security changes, because they affect the pension contributions and benefits that will be earned with future service. It is quite another thing to allow congressional action or increases in the consumer price index to reduce employee pension wealth that has already been earned, even though that process has been agreed to in collective bargaining. I doubt if any bargainers of the late sixties could possibly have realized how much of the private pension system they were bargaining away—in reduced employee benefits and reduced employer pension liabilities—through integration.

This automatic replacement of private pensions by social security can be prevented if integration is not retroactive, so that accrued pension wealth, once earned, remains intact. Such protection of employee benefits occurs automatically under defined contribution plans, target benefit plans, and those defined benefit plans that have frozen the step-rate point at which they integrate.

Logue points out, however, that more and more firms are tending to "index" their integration to the social security wage base. That builds into the plan the automatic substitution of social security for accrued pension wealth before a person retires; the exception to this is terminated employees who leave the plan with vested benefits. If the erosion of accrued pension wealth can be halted for terminated employees, there must be some way to prevent the erosion for employees who remain covered by the plan.

In closing, I would be remiss in not pointing out that, knowingly or unknowingly, Logue has presented a strong case for the defined contribution plan, or at least for some elements of such a plan. He spoke about pension wealth being placed irretrievably in the hands of plan participants as it is earned—and that is what defined contribution plans are all about. With early or immediate vesting, defined contribution benefits meet the test of deferred wages. Any integration with social security occurs only at the point of the contribution. Thus, all benefits are fully and irrevocably funded as they are earned, and they cannot be reduced by subsequent changes in the social security law or by price-indexed increases in the level of social security benefits. Any changes in the plan's integration formula can affect only those contributions and benefits related to service after the change. The employer's trade-off for this is that each year's pension funding is completed each year;

here are no financial time bombs down the road because of benefits
ied to unknown future salaries or because of poor pension fund per-
ormance.

Any changes in the provisions of a pension plan that improve the
ntegrity of the individual's accrued private pension wealth will cost
something. It costs more to pay pension benefits than not to pay them.
But the alternative, as set forth so emphatically and clearly by Munnell
and Logue, is likely to cost employers, employees, and the economy a
great deal more. The cost will appear not only in heavy tax drains on
present and future generations, but also in lost opportunity as funds
now being set aside, through capital investment, for future consumption
are shifted into current consumption and into the government over-
head required to administer the doling out of all the nation's retirement
income.

Discussion

Mr. LANCASTER: I am going to exercise the chairman's prerogative and ask Mr. Boynton two questions. One of the key aspects of the original ERISA legislation was that it legislated certain "funding standards" for private defined benefit plans. My first question is: Based on your experience with private pension plans, has funding increased, decreased or remained about the same since the enactment of ERISA?

MR. BOYNTON: The aggregate effect of the minimum funding standard has not been very great, except to introduce more confusion and more government forms. The legislation has had an impact in a few situations that have become nationally known—the horror stories. In some cases the trustees, who had been put under fiduciary responsibility, discontinued in that role. They had generally been operating without competent actuarial advice and, after the legislation, they had to hire fiduciaries and get competent advice. By and large, however, the legislation has done very little. Most private plans were funded on standards that were more stringent than those prescribed by ERISA.

The language in ERISA, which calls for the actuary to give a realistic appraisal of future costs when he makes a certification, required all pension plans to reexamine their assumptions. In many cases the actuaries were probably being too conservative, and their plans were overfunded; consequently, they reduced the funding level. Thus, because of the requirement in the law that an actuary has to certify future costs, overall the level of funding may have actually gone down slightly.

MR. LANCASTER: My second question has to do with the integrating of private pension plans. Would you comment on that?

MR. BOYNTON: I cringed a few times when some of the other panel members made comments about how disgraceful it was that anyone's pension should be reduced because social security benefits went up. We have to bear in mind that the employer is paying 50 percent of the social security taxes. The total pension provided by an employer is a combination of a private plan plus social security. When social security axes go up, 50 percent of that increase is being financed by the employer.

Dr. Ture: I think that the complaints about integration that surfaced in the papers and comments relate to unanticipated changes in the social security benefit formula. In general, however, both employees and employers regard pension benefits as part of the overall compensation package. The employee may perceive some risks attached to the realization of the benefits, and the employer may perceive some risks with respect to what it will cost to provide pension benefits as opposed to cash—wage or salary. But, presumably, the final bargain that is made between employer and employee represents some adequate weighting of those risks in calculating their present value.

Now, the greater the amount of a pension benefit that will be provided—with no surprises, thus allowing perfect foresight and planning—by some system other than the private pension plan, the lower will be the cost to the employer of providing any given amount of private pension benefits for any given estimated number of employees. And employees will perceive this reduced cost of getting some risk-weighted future private pension benefit as allowing them to have more income in an alternative form—current cash, wage or salary.

I do not see how anybody with this foresight is abused. The only thing that could possibly mistreat some randomly selected employee is surprise. That is where the focus of attention ought to be. Integration, itself, is not evil. It is in no way a device for doing harm to employees. The only way that it may turn out to harm or bilk them is if some surprise development occurs in the social security system. Let's stop those surprises; they cost us dearly.

Professor Schulz: I think there are some important qualifications to Munnell's findings. First, she bases her discussion on the worker with the average wage in the economy. The more relevant base to look at concerning the replacement rate is the average wage for the cohort of workers that is close to retirement. In some of her tables, she uses an earnings base of $7,800 with a 45 percent replacement ratio, but $7,800 is not the right number. The earnings base for the cohort approaching retirement now is much closer to $14,000. If you use $14,000, however, the replacement rate is not as large as 45 percent.

Second, her analysis is biased because it looks at one-worker couples. More than half of the couples now have two workers. The couple's social security benefit does not necessarily go up as a result of the second worker. If you look at the total benefit in relationship to

315

the couple's pre-retirement earnings, you get a lower replacement rate.

Third, and less important, is the fact that early retirement lowers the replacement rate. Some early retirement is involuntary because of poor health or inability to find a job. The benefits of those who retire early are also reduced.

I have one comment on Logue's paper. I think that the extent of integration is far more limited than he characterizes it. The data he uses are not a representative sample of the total pension population. I have been examining a more representative sample, and I get different results. For example, I found workers covered by plans with offsets in fewer than 20 percent of the plans. Offsets are concentrated in very small plans and in certain large plans, as Logue points out. This is largely an historical phenomenon related to a particular set of plans with offsets that were introduced in the 1940s and early 1950s.

More important, the step-rate plans that Logue mentions are not updated. According to my investigations, the wage base at which integration usually occurs has not been updated. Only a minority of such plans automatically adjusts the level of integration with the social security wage base. I found that only about one-third of the plans did so.

For these and other reasons, I do not agree with the two authors that private pension plans are on their way out.

PROFESSOR LOGUE: I would like to pick up on the subject of integration. I used it as an illustration of the mechanical way in which social security may displace private pensions. I am not saying that there is going to be a general decline in thrift in the United States, but that private pension plans, as an institutional form, may be at least partially displaced. There are alternative ways of saving—Individual Retirement Accounts, Keogh plans, and so on.

If a private pension plan with a vesting arrangement is seen as a call option that the employee has against the employer, the longer the period before that call option can be exercised—that is, the longer the vesting period—the more that call option is worth to the employer. If the period of vesting is shortened, as ERISA has done, the call option is worth less from the point of view of the employer. The result will be a reduction in the pension that is offered to the employee. Because of the combination of ERISA and the encroachment of social security, other institutional forms of private saving may become superior to many of the pension plans.

MR. BOYNTON: I want to comment on the 20 percent factor that was used in discussing integrated plans. Wrong conclusions can be drawn

om that number. It is similar to the case illustrated by my Table 1,
'hich shows that the two average benefits are the same, even though
ıe distribution of benefits is radically different. A relatively high pro-
ortion of the plans covering salaried employees in all companies are
ıtegrated. Hourly employees covered under Taft-Hartley arrangements
enerally have flat benefits. In short, you have to look at the different
/pes of employees, not at the average for all employees.

PROFESSOR DARBY: Since Munnell never got a chance to defend her-
elf, I will do it. The first point is that disposable income is not decreased
ı a consumption function by any increase in social security taxes be-
ause benefits equal taxes in the national income accounts. One is sub-
·acted, the other is added; there is no change in disposable income.

The second point is about the change in the marginal costs of
ınnuities. In effect, Munnell examined the demand for annuities. When
ıe compulsory amount of social security you buy is changed, this does
ot change the marginal costs of private retirement annuities you can
uy. The only margin for choice is with respect to pension funds and
ıe various other private annuities. The cost of social security is purely
·relevant to that decision.

The third point is that, if you had an equal offsetting decrease in
ension funds and private savings, as Ture suggested, then the whole
ecrease would be in the pension funds; there would be no decrease in
ıe other components of saving.

Now, I will make two quibbles. The first is about the conception
f 'revenue loss with respect to pension funds and deferred saving. I
/ould argue that there are many good arguments for consumption
ıxation. Basically, pension funds and IRAs are a step in the direction
f consumption taxation. It is not a matter of revenue loss; it is a dif-
:rent type of tax system.

The other quibble is that social security plus total pension fund
ontributions amount to 25 percent of salaries and wages, and that is
ır in excess of the historic saving ratio of 10 percent. It is advan-
ıgeous to "oversave" in this tax-sheltered form and then borrow to
educe total saving to a more normal rate. I am doing the same thing,
ıyself, by investing as much as I can in Teachers Insurance and An-
uity Association (TIAA) and borrowing to finance consumption.

PROFESSOR MYERS: Munnell says that the cost to firms of providing
ıutomatic cost-of-living adjustments is extremely high. In my opinion,
ıis is not so—it just appears to be so. Many firms have set up pension
lans in which the pension amount does not change once benefit pay-

317

ments have begun. The firms have costed this out using an artificial high interest rate equal to what they are earning—for example, 8 pe cent. What they should do is to value pension plans at something lik 3 percent interest and to consider any excess interest earnings as bein available to index the pensions. I think that private pension plans w run themselves out of business if they do not do this, because soci security will make automatic adjustments. As Boynton said, the cost fc automatic adjustment of pensions is high no matter who does it. Th social security system has no magic means to do this, and the only mag means in private pension plans is to use excess interest earnings.

Another point is that Munnell quotes a figure of $6.5 billion a the estimated loss in income tax revenues that occurs because the en ployer's contribution to pension plans is exempt from tax. If this ta exemption were eliminated, employers might pay all the money to th employees in wages. As far as the employers are concerned, they woul be in the same position. They would not pay any more taxes. But the the employees would have to pay income taxes on the additional wages which would generally be at a lower rate than the roughly 50 percen corporation rate. Or, if the employees put the money into IRAs (that i workers would move from group plans to individual plans), there woul be the same so-called tax loss.

DR. MUNNELL: You are right, if employees moved from pension plan to IRAs. But, if you made the employee's contribution to the pensio fund from the employee's after-tax earnings, would you not recou that tax loss?

PROFESSOR MYERS: Part of it, anyhow.

DR. MUNNELL: Yes. I like that idea because it offers a kind of imme diate vesting. It also provides portability because the employee put the money in the fund. The money is his and he can keep it from th beginning.

PROFESSOR NICOLAUS TIDEMAN, Virginia Polytechnic Institute an State University: I would like to elaborate on the point that Myers wa just making with respect to inflation. First, there is a way in whic inflation makes private pension plans more viable than individual sav ing, and that arises through the substitutability of private pension plan for individual saving. If you are considering saving for your retiremen and then inflation raises nominal interest rates on individual saving, th effective tax that you have to pay goes up because the tax is paid on th

flationary increase in interest rates as well as on the real interest rate.
n the other hand, if you put your money into a private pension plan,
is tax exempt, so there is no tax loss from the inflation. From this
erspective, inflation should make private pension plans more viable.

I agree that people are fooling themselves when they use these
igh interest rates in calculating the cost of pensions and then do not
orry about the cost-of-living increases. If you could compare two
tuations that differed only in the rate of inflation, but had the same
al interest rate, it should cost the same in both cases to fund the same
al benefits to pensioners.

There is another way in which inflation undermines private pen-
on plans. Times of high inflation tend to be times of high uncertainty
bout the rate of inflation. Because we do not have indexed securities
which private pension plans can invest, the amount that they ought
set aside for these imponderable cost-of-living increases becomes
ery uncertain. If pension plans could guarantee that they would get a
ormal 2 or 3 percent real rate of interest plus whatever the rate of
flation is, they could absorb cost-of-living increases, if they were
roperly funded. But, if pension plans have to invest in assets on which
ey will lose if there is an excessive rate of inflation, they cannot afford
provide the same kind of cost-of-living guarantee that perhaps the
cial security system can.

ABRIEL RUDNEY, U.S. Deparment of Treasury: My comments are ad-
ressed to Boynton's paper. First, he showed that excessive replacement
tios result from nonintegration. That result is based on his assumption
at we would move completely to nonintegration. But lower ratios will
e obtained if the benefit formula is changed to accommodate another
rm of integration. Of course, the nondiscrimination rules of the tax
de impose restrictions. But, if the nondiscrimination rules were changed
accommodate a different integration approach, the ratios need not be
high as Boynton shows.

Second, I would like to ask Boynton a question: If the rationale for
tegrating social security taxes is the cost to the employer, is that ra-
onale consistent with the findings of the study by the Brookings Insti-
tion which found that employer payroll taxes were shifted to the
mployee? How do those empirical findings mesh with your reasoning
at integration is justified because employer payroll taxes are employer
sts?

R. BOYNTON: On the first point, I am not sure I follow you. I agree
at the social security replacement ratios can vary widely depending

upon the assumptions that are made about future increases in the wag
base and in the consumer price index. I am using the present soci
security law.

MR. RUDNEY: I meant the assumption of complete nonintegration tha
you used in the 1 percent plan in your tables. You could enact rule
and have formulas that would maintain integration and still be accep
able from a policy standpoint.

MR. BOYNTON: My point is that, if you cut the formula back to 0.
percent of pay so that benefits to lower-paid employees do not excee
100 percent of pay, the highly paid person at the end of the line end
up with a replacement ratio of only 25 percent.

MR. RUDNEY: But could you weight the formula more heavily towar
the later earnings years—have a formula that depends not on all years

MR. BOYNTON: That is illegal. You cannot weight a formula towar
the later years. You can use the final average pay, which is what is don
in my calculations, but you cannot weight the percentage formula towar
later years. According to ERISA, you are then not being fair to peopl
who terminate early because you have deterred their vested benefit
According to current law, if you reduce the percentages applicable t
lower-paid employees to make them more reasonable, the reductio
must be applied all the way down the line.

PROFESSOR CAGAN: I would like to reiterate what Tideman said abou
inflation. The papers have not adequately dealt with the problems o
inflation, although I am sure the authors are aware of them. I onc
thought that our social security system allowed plenty of room for pri
vate pensions, at least for people in the upper-income scale. These peopl
are not adequately covered by social security and would want the sam
replacement ratios as those with average incomes.

But inflation may kill private pensions. Inflation will probabl
continue and, as Tideman suggested, not at a stable rate but at a fluc
tuating rate. Private pension plans will not be able to index their pay
ments, as social security does, because they will not be in a position t
guarantee the wide range of possibilities that might develop. At th
same time, what people want is a pension that they can count on in rea
terms thirty years down the line.

Indeed, our financial markets are going to be tremendously affecte
by the fact that we are not sure that we have a private financial instru

ient that will protect against inflation. Bonds are not an effective
edge. You can build a fixed rate of inflation into an interest rate, but
ou cannot handle fluctuations in interest rates. As soon as the rate of
iflation becomes higher than anticipated, bonds go down in value. And
ommon stocks have so far turned out to be a fiasco. I am not sure
iow stock prices will be affected by inflation over the next forty years,
iut there is considerable concern whether common stocks will be a
iatisfactory hedge against inflation. Moreover, private pension plans
vould probably not be in a position to put all of their assets into com-
non stocks, even if that were the best thing to do.

Private individuals are searching for types of saving in addition to
iocial security that are effective hedges against inflation, but none has
iroved to be effective. People may turn to real or residential property.
They will not be interested in private pension plans because such plans
vill not be able to give an effective inflation hedge.

DR. TURE: If one takes Cagan's first premise literally, he is saying that
:here are no financial claims into which individuals would be willing to
iut their saving. He is forecasting a system in which private accumula-
:ions of wealth will be a near impossibility, except in real estate. Inci-
dentally, if real property—land and structures—is the only real saving
iutlet, what about the mortgage market under the circumstances of
erratic and unanticipated inflation? I think what he is saying is that we
will be dealing with an economy that is not organized along the lines
of a private market system. In that case, our discussion becomes academic.

PROFESSOR KAPLAN: There is nothing unique about the indexing of
social security benefits. In the situation Cagan described, the public
would demand indexed bonds. Even though it would be risky for private firms to issue indexed bonds, the government could issue them and
this could be done independently of the social security system. It is an
idea whose time may have come. Other governments issue indexed
bonds.

PART
FIVE

THE FUTURE OF THE
SOCIAL SECURITY SYSTEM

*this session of the conference, a panel discussed various proposals for
eeting the rising costs of social security. This discussion was video-
ped for educational and commercial TV, and the edited transcript pre-
nted here was published separately as an AEI Round Table.*

ROUND TABLE

ᴏʜɴ Cʜᴀʀʟᴇs Dᴀʟʏ, former ABC News chief and forum moderator: This
ᵘblic Policy Forum, part of a series presented by the American Enterprise
ɴstitute, is concerned with the future of the social security system.

For some time now, the social security system has shared an unhappy
ꜱtate with the weather; everybody is talking about it, but nobody is doing much
ꜱbout it. The basic problem is financial, and it is very familiar to all of us; it is
ᴀlled an excess of outgo over income.

One can read in the press that with no change in the present law the
ɪsability trust fund will be "depleted" by 1978 or 1979, and the old age trust
ᴜnd will be depleted early in the 1980s. So at this eleventh hour in 1977, both
ᴧe U.S. Senate and the House are driving hard to pass a new social security
ᴧancing bill before the end of this session.

Some persons propose a sharp increase in social security taxes and maxi-
ᴜum taxable wages, scheduled perhaps over the next twenty years. Others
ʀopose mandatory coverage of federal, state, and local government work-
ʀs—a universal coverage concept phasing out the now separate pension sys-
ᴇms in these areas.

Still others, concerned that general treasury revenues will be used to bail
ᴜt the social security system, propose termination of the system's authority to
ᴏrrow money from the treasury income-tax revenues. They seem to worry
ᴏout the "foot in the door" that could lead to "a great treasury raid."
ʀgument swirls around indexing, double-dipping, unequal status for women,
ᴇgressive taxation, and so forth. It is clear that something has to be done; the
ᴜestion is, what?

To establish a broad base for the dialogue, gentlemen, will you briefly
ᴅdress that question?

First, Mr. Congressman?

ʟ Uʟʟᴍᴀɴ, United States representative (Democrat, Oregon): The social
ᴄcurity system is such an important American institution that there is no way
ᴇ Congress will allow it to get into a "defunct" status, where it will not be
ᴅle to pay benefits.

325

It is not easy to manage a fund of that size and to raise taxes, but there ar many ways the problem can be approached. We in the Congress are in the throe of doing that. There is one thing we can be sure of—we will keep it solvent, an the benefits will be there.

I am opposed to using general revenues to keep social security solvent, an I think the rest of Congress is, too. We must maintain the integrity of th trust-fund concept: when we increase benefits, we must also increase taxes. O course, that puts a heavy strain on the payroll tax system, and at some point i the future we may look for alternative revenue sources. But as far as I ar concerned, the source will not be general revenues. If we look to other source of revenue, they must be special taxes designed to keep the fund solvent.

BARBER B. CONABLE, JR., United States representative (Republican, Nev York): I agree with Congressman Ullman that the social security system is very central, important, and visible part of our security in this country. It is a important and growing part of the government, and, with the rest of th government, it shares this problem: it is difficult for politicians to restrain the enthusiasm for making it all things to all people.

We must restrain that enthusiasm. It has started encroaching on the priva pension system to a substantial degree. The private pension system is a important source of capital formation in this country; it adds to the flexibility c our retirement plans and social security. If we are not careful, we could destro that.

We have to keep the social security system financially sound, as Co gressman Ullman has said. The kind of publicity it has had lately is vei destructive; it causes people to lose confidence in the future of the system. Th fact that it is a mandatory system is particularly irksome to Americans who hav to participate in it. Therefore, I think we must move toward universal coverag for political, if not for economic, reasons.

The members of Congress themselves must participate in the social sec rity system, or the public may become increasingly cynical about our nonpa ticipation and our manipulation of it for political reasons.

We must stay away from the welfare relationship. Because there are po people on social security, there is a tendency to make it into a welfare system but we already have a good welfare system—particularly the Supplementai Security Income program* for elderly people. It is paid for by all the taxpayer not just by those who pay through payroll taxes.

We must always keep in mind the means of financing social security. Th payroll tax, since it is a tax on labor, can become very destructive in econom

---

*This term is defined on p. 350.

326

erms, if we let it get out of control. Whatever we do, we must restrain our
nthusiasm for letting the system expand to the point where it gets in bad shape
r destroys other valuable aspects of our government and private programs.

V. ALLEN WALLIS, chancellor, University of Rochester, and adjunct scholar,
American Enterprise Institute: I thought Mr. Daly was taking a chance in asking
what should be done about social security. If we were to tell him, that would end
the program right now, but I can see that will not happen.

That is what makes this issue so discouraging. As we think about what
ught to be done, we can think of many comparatively small things, but nobody
as really come up with a satisfactory answer for the long run. There have been
number of studies on the issue; advisory councils meet to discuss it every four
ears; and Congress studies it continuously.

One important step that can be taken is to correct a technical error made
ive years ago involving the automatic cost-of-living adjustment. The level of
enefits is now out of control. The benefits are blown around in the wind of a
ariety of forces, such as demographic changes, price levels, and changes in
roductivity. And they are not controlled by Congress anymore.

It would be fairly simple to correct this, and Congress is beginning to do it
ght now. It would eat up over half of the long-run deficit that is anticipated,
nd that is not at all inconsequential.

Then there are many comparatively smaller things that need to be done,
uch as making coverage universal and revising the retirement test so that a
erson past sixty-five can earn and keep his earnings. Now if he earns more than
certain amount, he loses some of his social security. While there are good
easons for that, it is impossible to sell them to the public. The public sees that a
erson getting a million dollars a year clipping coupons off of bonds gets his full
ocial security, but a person working and earning $5,000 a year loses his social
ecurity. No amount of explanation seems to convince anyone that that is
quitable.

There is an enormous amount of complexity in the system. A simplified
anual was put out when I served on the advisory council, and I kept it on a
ielf to entertain people in my office. I would tell a person to open it at random
d read a paragraph. He might discover, first, that he had to find out which of
ve categories he was in. If he was in Category 3, some provision would apply
cept if he was a chicken farmer; if he was a chicken farmer and also hatched
ickens, then he would not be in that section, but a different one. That example
not literally true, but it gives an idea of the complexity.

The system is impossible to understand. I guarantee that none of the
irteen people who served with me on the advisory council understood it, and
e each confined ourselves to only parts of it.

It is important to try to simplify the system so that the public will have
me understanding. It undermines their confidence to go to a social security

327

office and find they cannot get an answer to a question, or that they can get two answers in different offices. That is unavoidable with the present system.

Finally, it is important to make some basic studies. The system has never really been studied thoroughly, and only in the last three or four years have any economists taken it seriously. Only labor economists and welfare economist have really studied it, as if it were part of social service. At last there are some studies under way, many of them sponsored by the American Enterprise Institute, which will lay the groundwork for much more careful study of issue such as the effect on investment and the long-run effect on the income of the country.

JAMES B. CARDWELL, commissioner, Social Security Administration: The firs part of my answer to the basic question of what should be done I will direct t the two principal members of the House Ways and Means Committee who are on our panel.

The first step is to pass some legislation during this session of Congres that will provide some near-term refinancing of the basic system. I am quite confident that the Congress will do just that.

Next, I have to agree with the panel members who have said that we need to improve public confidence in the system. But before we can improve the public's understanding, we ourselves need to understand better what the prob lems now facing the system are, and we need to put before ourselves some choices.

It is no longer possible to look into the future of social security without looking at many other interrelated factors. In the years ahead, we will have fewer workers and more older people drawing retirement benefits, and w probably will also have fewer children and young people as a burden to or society and our economy. We need to understand how these factors wi interrelate. We must examine the interrelationship between the welfare pro gram, social services, and social security. In short, we must realize that we a deciding the future of a very important American institution.

Like all important institutions, we cannot take social security for grante There comes a time when we should reassess it and perhaps make some new an even different choices about what we want it to be.

MR. DALY: Let's go back to the beginning of social security, the 1930s. birth, social security was considered an actuarially sound retirement insuran program.

Congressman Ullman, has its basic character changed to, for instance, guaranteed annuity, perhaps with no sound actuarial funding basis?

CONGRESSMAN ULLMAN: Social security has changed significantly over t years. It is more than a retirement program now. It is a disability program,

328

survivors program, and a health Medicare program. All of these are part of social security. So, when people talk about investing some money in a private pension plan and being able to do as well as they would with social security, they generally forget about disability, survivors, and the other benefits.

The program has changed in other ways. It was never intended as a full retirement program. It was intended as a base layer of retirement; therefore, investment-type incomes are not taxed. Everyone within our system is expected to do whatever he can to develop other kinds of benefits for his old age, from rentals, from stocks, or from private pension programs.

That is one of our problems now in trying to include federal workers. I think that ultimately we will need to have universal coverage. But the problem is in integrating the two systems so that no real hardship is rendered on those involved. It can be done. An integrated system can be developed where social security is interwoven with retirement. Participants will get approximately the same benefits but will be contributing to the social security system.

It is intended that every American participate in the social security program. Over the years, we have added farmers, small-business people, doctors, lawyers, and others. Almost all American workers are now included, except for the federal workers. About 75 percent of the state and local employees are now covered. So, the system has been changing. And as it changes further, we must look at its actuarial basis and funding.

Another significant change is the amount of outside earnings participants can make and still draw social security. If we eliminate any restriction on outside earnings, then it becomes an annuity program: participants can continue on the job and still draw social security. Many people want to do that, but it changes the nature of the program. It is an evolving system that is still basically sound; it is the basic layer of retirement income, disability, and survivors insurance for all Americans, and that is what it should be.

CONGRESSMAN CONABLE: Congressman Ullman has described a number of changes within the program, and it clearly is an evolving program. In some ways, it has evolved too much. It is interesting, also, to note that the society in which this is a central institution has changed dramatically. For instance, in 1935, when the social security program was enacted, there were virtually no women in the work force. As a matter of fact, there weren't many men either at that time. [Laughter.]

MR. DALY: An unhappy memory.

CONGRESSMAN CONABLE: Certainly, there were no women. The great concern was taking care of housewives, who were not in the work force, through their husbands. Today, the situation has changed dramatically. The work force is approaching 50 percent women. Working women are not really taken care o adequately by this institution because it was not designed to do that.

Fortunately, demographic changes and changes in the work force are determinable. For instance, we can determine what demographic forces wil bear on this program through the next twenty or thirty years by looking at the birth rate and other statistics.

Even though government does such things badly, this is one institution fo which we can plan, knowing what the facts will be. So we ought to conside issues like how to take care of a third of our population in the year 2010, wit only two-thirds of the population working. We will clearly have to face suc issues. And for that reason, we should plan ahead. We do not have to operate a we do on so many other political issues, doing whatever we feel like doing. W have access to the facts about what forces will bear on this system in a changin world.

CHANCELLOR WALLIS: It is depressing to take a long-run view of the system; am not as disturbed by the short-run view. When problems become acute Congress will act just in the nick of time, as it appears to be about to do.

I don't think Congress or the government in general has the capacity t plan ahead. Some members know what will happen, and some committee know. Some committees see the need for universal coverage, but the whol Congress doesn't see it.

CONGRESSMAN CONABLE: If you are depressed about that, Allen, try being congressman. [Laughter.]

CHANCELLOR WALLIS: Congressmen feel the political pressures that prever taking action.

If we take the long-run view, it is clear that the people born in the "bab boom," from 1945 to the late 1960s, will begin to retire around 2010 and wi keep retiring for twenty or thirty years after that. They won't disappear the yea after they enter retirement either. Longevity is increasing.

They will be supported by the people who were born in the "birth dearth of recent years. It is estimated that for every person now being supported o social security, there are three workers sharing the burden; by that time, ther will only be two.

Try to imagine the consequences of that. If present benefits are mai tained, the taxes will have to be raised. And raising taxes will have a substanti disincentive effect that will show up in a variety of ways.

For instance, people will not be as willing to move to jobs where they a more productive. They will want to move away from the northeast to th southwest or the sunbelt—areas where they can lie around in the sun or g

330

shing and get income in kind. The government cannot lay its hands on that
come.

There will be a tendency to avoid money income, and that will make it
ecessary to raise the tax even higher than it would have been. It will be a
umulative effect. Some people may think that will control the benefits. But
ook at the politics. Politicians today turn handsprings, do cartwheels, get their
aces lifted, and dye their hair to appeal to the young. [Laughter.]

In the future, they will be having wrinkles implanted and their hair
leached white, and affecting canes and crutches to appeal to the predominantly
ged public. [Laughter.]

They will not cut the benefits; they will raise them. If they have to raise the
enefits but cannot raise the taxes, what will they do? They will have to print
ore money.

We can see the effects of that in many other countries. That has been the
istory of social security systems almost everywhere.

It takes 60 to 100 years for the problems to culminate. The social fabric is
orn asunder in all kinds of ways; the middle class is wiped out; and everyone
ets the idea that the way to look after themselves is to get control of the
overnment. Everybody is at each other's throats.

Happily, there are some offsetting factors. Commissioner Cardwell said
nat with fewer children we will not have to put as many resources into
ducation in the future. I worry about the political angle, though; the education
obby is the most effective lobby in the country.

COMMISSIONER CARDWELL: That is true, but those in it will not expect us to
pend a disproportionate amount on education in the future.

CHANCELLOR WALLIS: They already do. Even as the enrollment goes down,
ney do. But let's be optimistic. To my knowledge, all social forecasts of the
ort I just made have proved worthless. [Laughter.]

MR. DALY: Commissioner Cardwell, would you give us your view of the social
orecast we have just heard?

COMMISSIONER CARDWELL: Chancellor Wallis has laid out some of the vital
tatistics. It is true that the ratio of workers paying into the system, compared
ith retirees going out of the system, will change in the future. The statistics of
aree to one and two to one are correct.

There is also a sad fact of life that we must face. We must realize that the
resent benefit formula fails to provide adequate benefits for many people,
articularly those living in large urban areas, who have no other means of
etirement support. And when we look at the demographics, we see that the
roblem will grow worse in the long term.

331

If we take a fairly moderate view of the long-term American economy, w must conclude that the system is seriously underfinanced. If the present formul with the fault in the consumer-price-index benefit device is not changed, th cost seventy-five years from now will be more than double today's cost.

Today slightly less than 12 percent of the total payroll is taxable under th Social Security Act. By the years 2025 to 2050, that figure could go as high a 27 percent. We can bring it down to around 19 percent by changing the way w apply the consumer price index to benefits, and I hope the Congress will do tha in this session. But even when we have brought it down through that device, w still have a serious long-range problem facing us. We have to recognize th problem and make some choices about our willingness to pay more, or w might have to decide to change the kinds and classes of benefits that we offer.

I think the congressmen on the panel will agree with me that the disability portion of the program is clearly costing more than its originators anticipated. I the facts were laid out to the American public, my guess is that it costs mor than they are probably willing to pay. We have to look at that aspect of th benefit structure with a view to reducing the benefit costs. But some of th public are mounting drives to increase benefit costs. I have already mentionec that many people now served by the program do not have adequate income fo old age.

Another force that would tend to drive benefits up is the interest that th women's movement has in equal treatment for women. I think that will carry a significant price tag. I don't mean to say that the price tag is not justified, but i does represent a trade-off that we will have to face.

CONGRESSMAN CONABLE: Making choices is the business of government, and refuse to succumb to pessimism when we know what choices we have to make.

I acknowledge that Congress and the government have not been good at planning ahead, but they frequently have to deal with options that occur in a much shorter time frame than the options we are talking about here. I see nc reason why we cannot plan ahead; we know what the facts will be.

One thing that may very well happen to the social security system is tha we may separate from the system those elements that are not actuarially based Take Medicare, for instance: total coverage is available to everyone who ha basic social security coverage. There is no relation between what a person takes out of the system and what he pays in. Disability presents a similar situation.

These may eventually be passed along to all the taxpayers, not just the payroll taxpayers. I would hate to see us do that with the actuarially based par of the system—the insurance part that deals with old age and survivorship.

CHANCELLOR WALLIS: The advisory council did recommend that Medicare be taken off the payroll tax, since the benefits have no relation to average earnings.

CONGRESSMAN CONABLE: We cannot load up the system with many parts that are actuarially unrelated. If we do, it is pretty clear that the entire system will flounder.

CONGRESSMAN ULLMAN: There has been too much pessimism about the long-range and short-range future of the social security fund.

We have had a drain on the system in recent years, due partly to the recession, partly to inflation, and partly to the build-up in disability, for reasons we do not fully comprehend. But it is not a difficult task to set the short-term problem right. In fact, about 60 percent of the long-range problems can be taken care of by making the proper adjustments in the cost-of-living allowances, and I think Congress is ready to do that.

It is not fair to characterize Congress as irresponsible. Certainly we have a propensity to vote the easy issues and avoid the hard issues. That's human nature; that's not Congress. [Laughter.]

But when it comes to keeping this social security system solvent, for the short run and the long run, the Congress will do it. As Congressman Conable said, our business is looking at alternatives and making decisions. I have great confidence that this Congress will face up to not just the short-range problem, but probably 85 percent of the long-range problems. It will not take a lot of adjustments to solve the short-range problem, and I am confident that we will.

We have an ongoing committee and an ongoing responsibility. There are study commissions, including advisory commissions, coming in with recommendations. In two, three, or four years, we will have to look at additional areas, for instance, universal coverage. All these things will happen, but not until a system is laid out, and that will take some study and some work.

But the determination is there. The system does work, and we will keep this fund solvent.

CHANCELLOR WALLIS: When I said Congress lacked the capacity to plan ahead, I did not attribute that lack to the irresponsibility of Congress or congressmen. I attribute it to the influence of pressure groups in the electoral process.

COMMISSIONER CARDWELL: I want to defend the Congress for a moment. I think that our basic political system, the executive branch as well as the Congress, has an inherent difficulty in developing long-range plans.

It is a price I'm willing to pay, though. The other aspects of our system make it worthwhile. We are not the most efficient long-range planners in the world, but who is?

MR. DALY: Before we get away from it altogether, let us identify, specifically, the problem of indexing, which we read about in the newspapers. I am very impressed with the conviction expressed here that the indexing problem can be

333

straightened out in the near term and that over half of the deficit will disappear with it overnight.

Which of you will define indexing for us, telling us what we have been doing and what the actual change will be?

CHANCELLOR WALLIS: "Indexing" simply means adjusting something according to an index number. Indexed benefits are benefits that are automatically adjusted to changes in the cost-of-living index.

The proposal for correcting the error amounts to indexing a person's recorded wages. Instead of carrying on the books what someone earned twenty years ago, that amount will be adjusted for the change that has occurred in average earnings between twenty years ago and today. The number carried on the books will be an indexed wage, reflecting the changes in wage levels that have occurred since the wages were actually earned. And the error of the present system is that when the cost-of-living adjustment was put in, it was right only for people who had just retired or were already retired. It raised these people's benefits as the cost of living rose.

But we forgot that someone who had not yet retired would find his benefits going up too, because his wages would be inflated along with the price level. And if he were to work for his whole career under the new level, he would not need a raise in the benefit schedule because his higher wages would have brought him higher benefits anyway. So, in effect, he gets greater benefits than he should—the phrases "double-dipping" and "double-indexing" are used to describe it.

CONGRESSMAN CONABLE: There is no mystery about how much money it amounts to. Through 1977, the system has been 8.2 percent out of balance over a seventy-five-year period.

If we decouple benefits and index according to wages, the correction will be 4.5 percent of the 8.2 percent, so more than half of the imbalance can be taken care of in that way. I know of no one who resists changing that and correcting the error.

CHANCELLOR WALLIS: There is one point to keep in mind, though. We have said that an error made in 1972 has caused the benefits to go up about twice as fast as the cost of living. If we look at the preceding history of the system, we see that the benefits were raised by Congress about twice as much as the cost of living over the entire period.

CONGRESSMAN CONABLE: But that was because Congress was indexing it regularly, not because of a formula that automatically indexed it.

CHANCELLOR WALLIS: I just wonder if they'll do some more of that now. Laughter.]

MR. DALY: Again I have heard the phrase "double-dipping," which is a concept that has support from some quarters. It is evidently not acceptable to a majority of the Congress at this time, and there is a request for further study on the matter.

Congressman Ullman, is the double-dipping issue still a lively one?

CONGRESSMAN ULLMAN: Let me briefly explain what double-dipping is. The ordinary person who works and pays social security pays it on the first dollar he makes and on every dollar thereafter up to the wage base limit, until he retires. So those people who are not in the system, such as federal employees, can go through most of their working lives without paying anything into the system. They can move into it by moonlighting or working again after retirement—and about half of them do. Therefore, they can pick up social security benefits the cheap and easy way, by paying only a short period of time during their working lives, whereas the normal citizen pays during all of his working life.

That is what we call double-dipping. It is a very serious problem and is one reason why universal coverage has to come about eventually. But we cannot correct the problem until we get an integrated program in which federal employees can participate with the understanding that they will not be hurt, from the standpoint either of deductions or of benefits.

CONGRESSMAN CONABLE: Double-dipping would not be a serious problem if it were not for the fact that we have weighted the benefits at the low end of the scale, on the theory that those who have borne scant relation to the work force are poor people. In fact, many of them are not poor, but have been working under a system not covered by social security. So they get a windfall as a result of having just the minimum social security coverage and then being paid on the assumption that they are poor.

CHANCELLOR WALLIS: Commissioner Cardwell, wasn't it estimated that at least a third of the funds allocated to take care of the very poor at the bottom of the scale goes to people who are very well off?

COMMISSIONER CARDWELL: Easily a third, probably more.

CHANCELLOR WALLIS: And because they worked only a short time under social security, the social security books indicate they didn't make much during their careers.

335

COMMISSIONER CARDWELL: Yes. The system shows the record of ten years of post-retirement work by a federal employee, who has a very generous retirement to begin with, as if he were a poor person. It gives him an extra benefit, assuming that he is poor when in fact he is not.

MR. DALY: I have read that if we could terminate double-dipping, it would save about a billion paid-out dollars a year. Is this figure in the ballpark?

CONGRESSMAN CONABLE: That's small in social security terms. [Laughter.]

CHANCELLOR WALLIS: That's only five days outgo. [Laughter.]

CONGRESSMAN CONABLE: This is why we must not try to make social security into a welfare system. People are entitled to social security as a matter of right, but if we give them an especially large return on their investment, on the theory that they are poor, then we are loading down what should be an insurance system with what should be borne by all the taxpayers, not just those who work within a certain wage level.

CHANCELLOR WALLIS: Let us come back to the point about equalization of treatment of men and women. The ironic fact is that most of the discrimination against women consists in not allowing their male relatives to get certain benefits that the female relatives of men get.

For example, if a man dies, his widow automatically qualifies for a widow's benefit. If a woman dies, the widower would have to prove that he had received more than half of his support from her in order to collect benefits. If we equalize those provisions, we will have to eliminate benefits to widows (which is not likely to happen) or else give widowers exactly the same benefits we give widows. The right the woman lacks is not to get money for herself, but to have her male dependents get the funds.

There are some other aspects to the matter of equal treatment of men and women. A lot of women who pay social security taxes all their working lives will never get a penny more than they would have gotten without paying.

CONGRESSMAN CONABLE: That is the problem women see and object to. As working wives, they say that they are subsidizing the system and getting nothing back in return. Since they work intermittently in many cases, having families and so forth, they never will draw enough to reach the level of the benefits they derive through their husbands. Therefore, everything they pay into social security adds nothing to their pension, and that is something that should be corrected, regardless of the cost, as a matter of fairness.

CHANCELLOR WALLIS: The advisory council did recommend doing something about that.

COMMISSIONER CARDWELL: Another problem that the working wife has is seeing the nonworking wife automatically obtain 50 percent of her husband's benefit by reason of having been married to someone covered by the system, even though she did not pay directly into it herself.

MR. DALY: Let's come at this from another angle. Last week, in the *New York Times*, there was a letter to the editor from a man who described himself as an individual taxpayer and the owner of a small business with seventeen employees. He objected strongly to substantial increases in social security taxes, saying that they directly confront two of the nation's most urgent priorities, reducing inflation and reducing unemployment. In the face of substantial increases, he said, he would have to lay off two or three of his workers.

He believes that the proposed increase is of such magnitude that it will decrease actual disposable income for Americans earning over $15,000, which includes a great number of workers. And he said that the only way companies could afford to pay the increased costs of social security would be to increase prices, thus creating new inflation.

I want to ask the congressmen on the panel if this is, indeed, a concern. What impact will raising social security taxes have on inflation and unemployment?

CONGRESSMAN CONABLE: It has to be a concern. If we tax something, we discourage it. There is an old saying that the power to tax is the power to destroy.

In this case, we are taxing labor, and it is bad to raise taxes when there is a high unemployment rate. As a matter of fact, it is bad to raise taxes generally, but this is a particularly onerous tax, in an economic sense.

We are raising the cost of labor without increasing its productivity, and doing that reduces the demand for labor. For that reason, we ought to try to find other ways of taxing and keep the burden on the payroll from becoming too great.

CONGRESSMAN ULLMAN: There have been proposals to put the whole burden on employers, which we have resisted very strongly. I think the Ways and Means Committee feels that the traditional fifty-fifty split between employer and employee is fair and should be continued.

There is a problem with regard to the self-employed, and I think we have arrived at a sensible formula for it. We figure 75 percent of the tax as a good criterion of what the self-employed should pay. This is a fairly heavy burden on the self-employed; there is no question about that. Yet, we must realize that the

337

self-employed person gets the full benefits out of the fund, with a 75 percent contribution, that another employer would get by paying 100 percent.

We must balance out these problems in an equitable way. There is no tax that is not onerous and no tax that is not, in a sense, inflationary, because the consumers ultimately pay all taxes. It is our job to determine what is most equitable.

We have a very difficult problem in deciding between base and rate increases. Most members of Congress think it is easier to go the base route because it affects fewer people.

Our base next year will be $17,700. Between 85 and 86 percent of the work force earns less than that base, so increasing the base affects only about 14 percent of the people of the country. Therefore, that is the way the Congress in general feels it should go. But we must try to maintain a proper mix between rate and base increases, and, in general, we have done pretty well at it so far.

CONGRESSMAN CONABLE: There are some problems, though, with raising the base, even though it is less painful. As we raise the base, we also raise the potential pension, and there will be a much bigger spread in pensions eventually. Congress will be strongly tempted to tax benefits, which we should not do because the employees have paid in with after-tax money. Therefore, as a matter of strict tax principle, they should not be taxed on their social security benefits.

Yet, if those pensions go way up after raising the base, there will be a temptation to do that. Also, under the existing law, we have been financing cost-of-living increases by raising the wage base. As we continue to raise the wage base, we reduce our capacity to finance cost-of-living increases because there are fewer and fewer people above that base.

There are many difficulties with raising the wage base, including the fact that the increase cuts into the private pension plan system more than a rate increase does. But the rate increase is objected to primarily because it affects everybody, including people at very low wages.

COMMISSIONER CARDWELL: If we elect to use the tax rate in lieu of the wage base as a revenue-development device, we increase the tax burden on the lowest-paid worker. Many people feel that the lowest-paid workers are already bearing a disproportionate share of this tax, and I agree that it is wrong to add to that.

CONGRESSMAN CONABLE: But a rate increase helps to make the system actuarially sound, while a wage base increase ultimately involves a higher payout down the road and does not help the actuarial status of the system at all.

CONGRESSMAN ULLMAN: As we move up the base scale, of course, fewer and fewer people are involved. We could achieve a lot with a few hundred dollars base increase at the lower levels, but as we approach $30,000 we have to raise the base several thousand dollars to get the same amount of revenue.

The problem will solve itself. We will run out of base one of these days and will have to go to rates. [Laughter.]

COMMISSIONER CARDWELL: Let me make one last point about the wage base versus the rate increase. I think that as we increase the wage base, we are adding to the tax burden on the middle wage earner, and over time this tends to undermine his support of the system. He is the wage earner who has felt, rightly or wrongly, that he has had to carry the high share. We have to consider that in the equation.

CONGRESSMAN ULLMAN: But he does get a retirement program, a disability program, and increased benefits. He is buying a retirement program, and a very good one, in the process of paying more as the base goes up.

That is one of the things people criticize. One of these days, the highest-salaried people will be receiving social security benefits of $1,000 or $1,500 per month, while somebody else might get only the minimum, though he has paid in all his life. That kind of disparity in the system will create some problems.

CONGRESSMAN CONABLE: The high-salaried person does not get any more disability benefits or Medicare benefits than the person at the very low wage, and that is another reason why his confidence is undermined. If the base is raised a great deal, it affects only his retirement pension. It does not affect any of the other elements of coverage, which now amount to over 30 percent of the total payout of the social security system.

CHANCELLOR WALLIS: Congressman Conable raised a point in passing that is worth discussing further, and that is the possibility of reporting social security benefits on the personal income tax statement. I don't see why that should not be done. It would clear up a lot of problems. The argument that social security benefits are bought with after-tax income does not really carry much weight.

CONGRESSMAN ULLMAN: I could give you some good political reasons why you can't sell it. [Laughter.]

CHANCELLOR WALLIS: That I can believe, but at least it would have some alleviating, compensating effect on all this double- and triple-dipping.

339

CONGRESSMAN CONABLE: I disagree, because that is another step toward making it a needs-related system, which we should not do.

CHANCELLOR WALLIS: No, it is not needs-related.

CONGRESSMAN CONABLE: If we start taxing people above a certain level—

CHANCELLOR WALLIS: Oh, no, everybody should add it in for tax purposes.

CONGRESSMAN CONABLE: Now I am beginning to agree with Congressman Ullman all the way. That is political dynamite. [Laughter.]

CHANCELLOR WALLIS: Certainly, but you implied there was something wrong with it in principle, in the fact that it comes out of after-tax income—

CONGRESSMAN CONABLE: Political principle.

CHANCELLOR WALLIS: There is no such thing. [Laughter.]

MR. DALY: There is one last area that we should cover. In view of the Pepper bill, which proposes to extend the age for compulsory retirement from sixty-five to seventy, what would happen to social security? If the retirement age were changed, would it be beneficial to the problems social security now faces, or would it be a further burden?

COMMISSIONER CARDWELL: As with most of the choices that must be made, there are two edges to the sword. It would reduce the total long-term cost of the program. Having people retire later reduces the size of the benefit rolls. On the other hand, if the retirement age is raised to sixty-eight, as has been discussed recently, and the optional retirement age remains sixty-two, we are inviting more people to retire early. It tends to create a work disincentive. The question needs to be examined very carefully before we make a choice.

MR. DALY: All right, gentlemen, let us continue our discussion of the future of social security as we turn to members of our audience for the question-and-answer session. May I have the first question, please?

SAMUEL H. PHILLIPS, coordinator of graduate economics, George Mason University: My question is addressed to the two congressmen from the House Ways and Means Committee.

A week or two ago, the *Wall Street Journal* reported that the Ways and Means Committee voted to provide standby authority for the social security trust fund to borrow from the treasury's general revenue fund whenever the

ssets of one of the trust funds drops below 25 percent of the fund's annual
utflow. What will be the repercussions of this? Will the social security system
nen pay the treasury interest, or will the treasury's general fund ultimately
inance all of social security?

CONGRESSMAN ULLMAN: The system only provides for borrowing if the reserve
ets down to a 25 percent level. It does provide for interest payments. The
ocial security system has been lending money to the federal government for
orty years, and there is no reason why it should not now borrow.

Also, a tax increase is triggered automatically if the funds dwindle to that
xtent, so that there will be a payback, not from general revenues.

· Mr. Conable will probably have a different opinion on this. I am strongly
pposed to the use of general revenues, but a borrowing authority is not dipping
nto general revenues, particularly with the strong payback provision that we
re talking about.

CONGRESSMAN CONABLE: It is only the first step down a primrose path.
[Laughter and applause.]

CONGRESSMAN ULLMAN: That is what I expected you to say.

ROBERT J. MYERS, professor of actuarial science, Temple University: I was
hief actuary of the Social Security Administration from 1947 to 1970.

I want to address my question to Commissioner Cardwell. In view of the
act that until now every administration proposal to change the social security
ystem has been financially balanced, providing adequate long-range financing
or the system, why did the current administration proposal leave a very serious
ong-range deficiency amounting to almost 2 percent of taxable payroll, espe-
ially when this could have been remedied by recommending increased tax
ates in the future?

COMMISSIONER CARDWELL: The answer is a fairly direct and simple one. The
dministration did not feel that it would be appropriate to call for tax increases
fter the turn of the century without having some better idea of what the benefit
tructure and other structural arrangements will be at that time.

The administration's view was that many of the choices that need to be
made about the long-term future of social security will have to be made later. It
vas reasoned that reducing the deficit from 8.2 percent to 2 percent over
eventy-five years would be a reasonable and quite significant accomplish-
ment.

CONGRESSMAN CONABLE: Are we to assume, then, that they are going to less
nan a seventy-five-year actuarial period?

341

COMMISSIONER CARDWELL: No. Mr. Myers is asking why the entire deficit will not be financed at this time. The Senate Finance Committee in its current deliberations does have a plan that would do that, but we are forecasting that the tax rates would be very high after the turn of the century. The House does not seem so inclined. They will reduce the deficit but keep it in the 1.5 to 2 percent range.

WILLIAM C. HSIAO, professor of economics, Harvard University: In the past, Congress has maintained the financial integrity of the social security program by providing adequate financing for a seventy-five-year period. In correcting the double-indexing problem, Congress has adopted a benefit formula that is indexed by the increases in the average wages in the economy. The cost of such a benefit program at the turn of the century would require the payroll tax to rise as high as 18 or 19 percent.

At present, the House has chosen not to provide adequate financing for the next seventy-five-year period; instead, it will only provide adequate financing for the next twenty-five to thirty years.

There is an alternative to indexing the benefit. We could use the consumer price index, which would give Congress the option to provide adequate financing for the whole seventy-five-year period. Why did Congress decide that would not be a desirable option?

CONGRESSMAN CONABLE: At the present time, our system is providing roughly a 45 percent replacement rate.

MR. DALY: And what is a replacement rate, sir?

CONGRESSMAN CONABLE: It is 45 percent of final pay, and that is considered by many people to be inadequate.

Indexing to the consumer price index would reduce the replacement rate still further. It is true that it would help correct the actuarial imbalance, but there was a political decision not to go below a 40 percent replacement rate.

We are likely to wind up with between 40 and 45 percent, which historically has been the level of replacement. Isn't that correct, Congressman?

CONGRESSMAN ULLMAN: Yes, that is my understanding.

COMMISSIONER CARDWELL: Let me add an observation on that. In a way, this is a choice between future benefit rights that would keep pace with future prices versus benefit rights that would assure today's workers that upon retirement they will enjoy the improvement in the standard of living that occurs between now and then. That is another way to describe dropping below the 40 percent area.

342

The last two administrations examined these two choices very carefully, and both a Republican administration and a Democratic administration came to the same conclusion. The House and Senate have examined the two choices and have also come out at the same point. This is one area in which a difficult choice will have been made with a very strong bipartisan consensus.

CHANCELLOR WALLIS: The advisory council was part of that consensus.

COMMISSIONER CARDWELL: Correct.

CHANCELLOR WALLIS: Mr. Hsiao left an important fact out of his question, which is that wages generally rise about 2 percent more per year than prices do; therefore, it does make quite a difference which we index by.

MR. DALY: Chancellor Wallis, as the one educator on the panel, will you elaborate further on the replacement rate, so that everyone will understand it?

CHANCELLOR WALLIS: The replacement rate is the ratio of a person's social security benefit to his final pay while he was working. If the rate is 43 percent, as it is for a husband and wife at the highest level under social security, it means that their social security benefit is 43 percent of the part of their final pay that was subject to social security tax. That is, if a man was making $100,000 a year, his and his wife's benefits are 43 percent of the wage base, which has now gone up to $16,500. So it is simply the percentage of a person's final social security payment that he is now getting in benefits.

The rate is higher than 43 percent for people in lower income brackets.

STEPHEN CALKINS, attorney, Washington, D.C.: Congressmen Ullman and Conable have both said that it is difficult for politicians to vote to tax social security benefits. I would like to ask whether they are opposed to taxing social security benefits as a matter of principle, even if the benefits are earned by people making tens of thousands of dollars.

CONGRESSMAN ULLMAN: We have been talking to the treasury about this possibility in connection with tax reform. And the treasury came out with a plan that will probably not be recommended. The plan would start taxing, not at the first dollar, but at $15,000 and above, or something like that.

We do the same thing with veterans' benefits and unemployment compensation. And it does seem to me that we should be moving in this direction. We would begin to tax all income.

It is very difficult politically, but, as a matter of principle, we should move that direction. It will be a while before we get there. And, certainly, we would start in the higher brackets, rather than in the lower brackets.

CONGRESSMAN CONABLE: I am in favor of taxing all income in some way, bu certainly not twice. That is what we will be doing if we tax pensions resultin from after-tax contributions.

CHANCELLOR WALLIS: But that is done all the time, Congressman.

CONGRESSMAN CONABLE: It is done all the time, but I don't approve of it. As matter of principle, I do not want us to treat people differently under the socia security system because some people do not need the money that is paid back t them as a result of their contributions. We already have too much of that sort c thing in our system.

CHANCELLOR WALLIS: Are you suggesting that, if I take $100 out of m after-tax income and put it in a savings bank, the interest I get should b tax-exempt? [Laughter.]

CONGRESSMAN CONABLE: If you want to advocate that, my friend, I will dea with it when you do. We are talking about social security here tonight. We hav a contract with the American people on social security which I am reluctant t change. One important aspect of the contract is that the receiving of benefits not to be need-related.

If we start taxing benefits, it will be a big step toward need-relation instead of contribution-relation.

RICHARD V. BURKHAUSER, project associate with the Institute for Research c Poverty, University of Wisconsin, Madison: I want to ask the congressmen ho the House can almost unanimously approve an end to mandatory retireme rules, thereby encouraging older people to work, and yet do nothing about wh amounts to a 70 percent tax rate on these people (because of loss of soci security benefits and payment of federal income taxes) if they continue to work

CONGRESSMAN ULLMAN: The Congress is moving toward increasing the incen tives to remain in the work force. Social security benefits now increase by percent for each year retirement is postponed, and the Congress is talking abo raising it to at least 3 percent. That would certainly be some compensation.

CONGRESSMAN CONABLE: But we never have been afflicted by the hobgoblin little minds. [Laughter.]

It is remarkable to me that the Congress has taken the fast track on raisi the retirement age but has been reluctant to increase the full retirement age f social security twenty-five years in the future, when the demographic facts w be very different from those at present.

344

So, if you are looking for consistency, you are looking in the wrong body.
‿aughter.]

‿ONALD J. SENESE, senior research associate, House Republican Study Com-
‿ittee: There is a possibility that next year Congress will consider a national
‿alth insurance program. If such a proposal is considered, will it be tied to
‿cial security? What would be the administrative and financial effect on the
‿cial security system?

‿ONGRESSMAN ULLMAN: I approach it from the viewpoint of a sponsor of one
‿alth proposal in the Congress. As we get into an overall health program that is
‿t just for the elderly and the poor, but one that will fill in the cracks, so that
‿surance is available in a standardized program to everyone, we will probably
‿ve to develop a separate financing mechanism.

In the process of doing that, it may be possible to withdraw from social
‿curity and thus give some general relief to the social security system.

‿ONGRESSMAN CONABLE: I do not favor putting national health insurance, by
‿hatever name or form, on a payroll-tax financing basis. As I said at the outset,
‿e payroll tax can be very destructive.

We have already passed the level that Secretary Ribicoff, during the
‿ennedy administration, described as the maximum that should be loaded on
‿e payroll in terms of taxation. We have gone way past it.

We have to restrain our enthusiasm for using this type of financing
‿echanism if we are not to disrupt the economy further.

‿R. DALY: Commissioner Cardwell, would you like to comment on this one?

‿OMMISSIONER CARDWELL: No, except to say that the administration is looking
‿ a series of alternatives, and the choice has not yet been made.

‿ERT SEIDMAN, director, department of social security of the AFL-CIO: I am
‿re we would all agree that the social security program is a social insurance
‿stem, and, while the benefits are related to wages, they are not exactly related
‿ wages. As some members of the panel have said this evening, those in the
‿wer wage brackets receive proportionately higher benefits.

In addition to that, in the early years of the program there were people who
‿ceived benefits far out of proportion to any taxes that had been imposed on
‿em.

Since the social insurance program *is* a social program and, therefore,
‿fferent from a private program, should its entire revenue source come from
‿yroll taxes? Or aren't there some costs which ought to be borne by the whole
‿untry and ought to come from sources other than the payroll tax? I think the

345

funding of social security ought to come from a more broadly based source such as general revenue. What are the congressmen's opinions on that question?

CONGRESSMAN ULLMAN: We have about come to the end of the road on payroll taxes. As a matter of fact, we may have exceeded the proper level on payroll taxes, but that doesn't necessarily mean that we should dip into general revenues. I am strongly opposed to doing that.

I believe in the trust fund concept. Imposing general revenues, even in part, would lead to a feeling of social security as welfare rather than a matter of payment and right. As we think about this long-range problem, we should think of a new tax component, so that we can back off a little on payroll taxes. But should be a separate tax and one that is related, as much as possible, to payroll. Certain transaction tax systems would do that and would not have to come out of general revenue.

CONGRESSMAN CONABLE: I do not support the idea that the general revenue should be a source of funds, even borrowed funds. I regret that Congress and the administration seem intent on taking that step.

I don't deny that because it is mandatory the program does affect many people who otherwise would save nothing, and that there is a social advantage in keeping them off the welfare rolls. But we got in trouble when we assume the people at the bottom of the scale are poor, without knowing whether they are or not. For that reason, we have tended constantly to pump up the system putting an additional $6 billion into benefit increases in order to get a billion of to the people at the bottom of the scale who are assumed to be poor.

Several years ago, we initiated SSI, a general treasury welfare program that was automatic, administered by the Social Security Administration. That involved all the dignity and sense of right that people have with social security and yet it was kept administratively separate and was paid for by all the taxpayers, not just those who are paying a payroll tax.

Welfare should be paid for by everybody through the general treasury and through the graduated income tax. But I want to restrain the enthusiasm for turning social security into a welfare system. We cannot tell an American worker who has been paying into that system for thirty or forty years that it just another tax, not an investment in his retirement, and that the guy across the street who hasn't worked in twenty years will take out in the same proportion because he needs it more. That would be the likely result of going to general treasury funds; it would violate the insurance character of the system.

Once we do that, we will be sitting on a time bomb. What will be the response from all those investing workers who thought they were contributing to their retirement rather than just paying another tax?

MR. DALY: Chancellor Wallis, as quadrennial advisory council chairman, would you comment on this subject?

CHANCELLOR WALLIS: I don't really have anything to add. The council considered this and came out with the same view as both congressmen—against general revenue financing.

LI M. SPARK, emeritus professor of law, Catholic University: I would like to address this question to whoever among the panel considers himself the least political. [Laughter.]

There must be some social security systems, somewhere in the world, that attempt to be actuarially based. I assume that is true because a good friend of mine, a retired justice of the state supreme court in Brazil, gets a pension which only buys himself and his wife one dinner per month.

If there are such systems, I wonder how we got so far away from the concept of actuarial provision. The amount of contributions can be calculated, and the actuaries can figure out how much can be spent without running a deficit.

Beyond that, whatever an individual beneficiary gets in the way of returns—whether in the form of new things added, like Medicare, or in the form of the original payment, or disability benefits—must always come out of public largesse, paid for by taxes on people other than the recipient and by man-made inflation.

MR. DALY: In my judgment, Chancellor Wallis, you are probably the least political. Would you go ahead? [Laughter.]

CHANCELLOR WALLIS: I'm tempted to ask him to repeat the question. [Laughter.]

CONGRESSMAN CONABLE: I think he overstates the lack of actuarial relation.

CHANCELLOR WALLIS: I object to the use of any term like "actuarial," which just does not seem relevant to social security. The system is not operated that way. If it were, it would not be a social system. The whole purpose is to have some redistribution from the higher income people to the lower. Maybe it should not, as Congressman Conable says, be just another tax, but it is an earmarked tax, like many other earmarked taxes.

Many people are completely misled about this. They think money is being put aside in an account for them, the way a private insurance company would do. If it earns enough and the government tends it well, they will get the yield on when they retire. They are very alarmed to read all the stories in the papers about how the system is bankrupt, or something of the sort. That just is not pertinent.

347

What they will get when they retire depends on whether or not Congress will appropriate money to pay it. Congress can get the money either by taxing people who are then working or by some other method. And as Congressman Ullman said early in the program, there isn't a chance in the world that Congress will fail to appropriate the funds, no matter where they come from.

COMMISSIONER CARDWELL: Since my bosses do not think I understand politics, I will assume I am not very political. Mr. Spark is wrong to assume that other countries have what he described as an actuarial system. Let me define the term as I think he means it.

He is talking about a system that pays back only what a person put in invested at interest. There are no systems like that elsewhere in the world. Most systems in the industrialized nations are very similar to ours. They all have social weighting as one of their features, and most of them draw more heavily on general taxes than our system does. This has always been a fundamental part of the social security movement throughout the world.

CONGRESSMAN CONABLE: We should define the term *actuarial* in the social security sense, because, once again, Chancellor Wallis has overstated the nonactuarial character of the system.

It has been our goal to balance income and outgo over a period of time, and the system is actuarial in that sense. It is not actuarial in the sense that private insurance is, because the insurance company is required to pay into a fund that will be sufficient to cover all claims against it. We simply cannot maintain a fund that big, full of investments in government bonds, which are IOUs, in effect.

The system is actuarially balanced so that income and outgo will match each other over a seventy-five-year period, and the fund exists only as a cushion to cover possible additional outflow due to a period of high unemployment or some other temporary condition.

Again, it is not actuarial in the voluntary insurance sense, because it will presumably continue to be a mandatory program. Therefore, we can calculate how much will be paid in; that is something a voluntary insurance program cannot do.

CONGRESSMAN ULLMAN: Chancellor Wallis indicated that the payments depended on congressional appropriations, but that might be misleading to a lot of people.

We have a trust fund that has always been and will continue to be solvent, and we have automatic appropriations into that trust fund. The payments do not depend upon any specific appropriations bill. Our job is to apply the taxes that will keep that trust fund solvent. The level of taxes and of the fund is a matter of judgment that varies from time to time. We started out with one year's payout as n adequate trust fund and then went to 50 percent of a year's payout. Now the ayout is about 40 percent and is going down. That is the nature of the emergency in the system, and that is why Congress will pass a bill that will ring the payout back up above 30, 40, 50, 60 percent.

No one should think that benefits will be dependent upon any particular ppropriation. They are dependent upon keeping that trust fund solvent and solated from the general revenues, so that the funds will always be there for eneficiaries.

CHANCELLOR WALLIS: I certainly accept that clarification. When I mentioned n appropriation by Congress, I meant merely that if the trust fund were to run ut, Congress would certainly put some money in somewhere. But the trust und is not the crux of the matter; it is just a petty cash fund.

CONGRESSMAN CONABLE: It is the cushion.

CHANCELLOR WALLIS: The income and the outgo do not match exactly, but what is paid out is basically what was taken in this morning from people who are paying taxes.

COMMISSIONER CARDWELL: At the risk of giving more of an answer to the question than was wanted, let me try to add another dimension.

It is very important that this system be recognized as an income transfer arrangement. The system knowingly, deliberately, and willingly takes some income from the current work force and transfers it to older people who are retired. It does take some income from the "haves" and transfers it to the "have nots." This is a deliberate part of the program and always has been.

ROBERT E. FULTON, senior analyst for income security, Senate Budget Committee: I would like the panel's comments on the possibility of dealing with some of the problems of the "have nots" through the Supplemental Security Income program or a reformed welfare system, instead of social security. Rather than use social security revenues, why not shift the skewed benefit burdens over to one of the programs that is funded by general revenue?

CONGRESSMAN CONABLE: I think it should be done.

CONGRESSMAN ULLMAN: As we begin to reform the welfare system, some of that can be done, but the SSI program has already accomplished a great deal in unifying benefits for the elderly. It is part of the social security system.

MR. DALY: Would you define the SSI? We have mentioned it several times, and the public may need a better explanation.

CONGRESSMAN ULLMAN: It is the special old-age program that was put into effect a few years ago. It established a uniform set of benefits for the elderly in the country. Perhaps Commissioner Cardwell, who administers the program, would like to explain further.

COMMISSIONER CARDWELL: SSI stands for Supplementary Security Income program. It is a means-tested program, financed entirely from general revenues. People over age sixty-five who are without resources or income are eligible for a benefit. Today there are about 4.3 million elderly and disabled persons on those benefit rolls.

It is a means-tested program, very similar to the welfare program as it applies to families.

ALICIA H. MUNNELL, assistant vice-president, Federal Reserve Bank of Boston: I wonder why there has been so little support for the 1974 advisory council recommendation that all or part of the health insurance funds be transferred to old age, survivors, and disability insurance. It seems reasonable to finance these benefits from the payroll tax because they are related in some way to earnings.

It does not seem reasonable to finance health insurance benefits or Medicare from the payroll tax, because everyone does not suffer grave sickness. This would be an obvious way to relieve part of the payroll tax burden and to use general revenues without mucking up the OASDI portion of the program.

CONGRESSMAN ULLMAN: The main reason this isn't done is that we have a $60 or $70 billion deficit in the general revenues now. [Laughter.]

We just don't have sufficient funds in general revenues. Most people who ask the question assume that general revenues are unlimited. At some point, when we do get into overall health insurance, we should change the present type of financing. But it is foolish to assume that the general revenues will be there for that purpose. We may well have to institute a special tax to accommodate the problem, in or out of general revenues. General revenues are not unlimited, and we have had problems balancing the budget lately.

BARRY CHISWICK, senior fellow, Hoover Institution: My question relates to the issue of replacement rates. Congressman Conable mentioned that the replacement rates are now about 44 percent, but historically they were closer to 31 percent. From 1950 to 1969 they averaged 31 percent, according to a recent Congressional Budget Office report.

Much of the deficit that would remain after going to a wage-indexing system could be eliminated if we take the further step of gradually lowering the replacement rate from the current 44 percent back to 31 percent. Would the members of the panel consider this as one means of gradually eliminating the long-term financing problem of the system?

CONGRESSMAN CONABLE: Yes, it is one means of doing so. But I think it is unlikely that the Congress will go back to a replacement rate as low as that. It is one aspect of the system that is likely to be decided politically.

But once we decide what level of replacement rate to aim for, we should remember that we will have to finance it.

JUNE A. O'NEILL, chief, Human Resources Cost Estimates Unit, Congressional Budget Office: When Congress decides on a higher level of benefits, which is really what it is doing when it decides on a higher replacement rate, it is saying, in effect, that taxes must rise because they will have to be paid. The benefits do have to be paid for, even if the money comes from general revenues; essentially the same workers that pay the income taxes pay the payroll taxes.

People will then have to put aside a larger proportion of their income for social security. To what extent is this considered? We are not necessarily doing workers a favor by voting higher benefits down the pike.

CONGRESSMAN CONABLE: The Ways and Means Committee is more inclined to look at the price tag than are many of the other committees in Congress simply because we are accustomed to having to finance the excesses of Congress through the tax rate. Many of us consider the burden along with the benefit and are thereby criticized for being too conservative.

CONGRESSMAN ULLMAN: Certainly, we have to consider the price tag. But the minute we talk about reducing benefits, millions of people become greatly alarmed. It is a difficult political stand to take.

I hope that the overall study commission that will probably be set up will have some recommendations. If we did have a long-range program, we might find that we could gradually shift to a somewhat lower replacement rate. But it is a difficult political problem.

CONGRESSMAN CONABLE: If we go to a lower replacement rate, I hope we will adjust some other government policies to encourage thrift. Then it may be possible for people to live on the results of that thrift, as well as on social security.

For years, the government has been stimulating aggregate demand as an economic panacea and has been penalizing thrift. It is small wonder that we now have to pay a higher proportion of the higher replacement rate than we did when people had shorter lives and had been encouraged by government policies to look out for themselves more.

JAMES M. BUCHANAN, professor of economics, Virginia Polytechnic Institute and adjunct scholar, American Enterprise Institute: I realize the political popularity of playing on illusions about the employer portion of the social security tax. But the economists here should not let Congressman Ullman get away with suggesting, as he did, that the employer portion of the tax is not paid by the employee in some way. Surely, Congressman Ullman, you don't believe that nonsense. [Laughter.]

CONGRESSMAN ULLMAN: Of course not. [Laughter and applause.]

MR. DALY: This concludes another Public Policy Forum presented by the American Enterprise Institute for Public Policy Research. On behalf of AEI our heartfelt thanks to the distinguished panelists, Chancellor Wallis, Congressmen Ullman and Conable, and Commissioner Cardwell, and to the guests and experts in the audience for their participation.